Buddhist Psychotherapy

Buddhist Psychotherapy

Connecting Early Buddhism
to Mindfulness and
Western Psychotherapy

Liang Tien,
Debra M. Kawahara, and
Venerable Dhammadinna

AMERICAN PSYCHOLOGICAL ASSOCIATION

Published by
American Psychological Association
750 First Street, NE
Washington, DC 20002
https://www.apa.org

Order Department
https://www.apa.org/pubs/books
order@apa.org

Typeset in Charter and Interstate by Circle Graphics, Inc., Reisterstown, MD

Printer: Gasch Printing, Odenton, MD
Cover Designer: Gwen J. Grafft, Minneapolis, MN

Library of Congress Cataloging-in-Publication Data

Names: Tian, Liang, author. | Kawahara, Debra M., author. | Dhammadinna, Venerable, author.
Title: Buddhist psychotherapy : connecting early Buddhism to mindfulness and Western psychotherapy / by Liang Tien, Debra M. Kawahara, and Venerable Dhammadinna.
Description: Washington, DC : American Psychological Association, [2025] | Includes bibliographical references and index.
Identifiers: LCCN 2024055857 (print) | LCCN 2024055858 (ebook) | ISBN 9781433841637 (paperback) | ISBN 9781433841644 (ebook)
Subjects: LCSH: Psychotherapy--Religious aspects--Buddhism. | Buddhism--Psychology.
Classification: LCC BQ4570.P76 T53 2025 (print) | LCC BQ4570.P76 (ebook) | DDC 294.3/36150195--dc23/eng/20250211
LC record available at https://lccn.loc.gov/2024055857
LC ebook record available at https://lccn.loc.gov/2024055858

ISBN 9781433841637 (paperback)
ISBN 9781433841644 (epub)
ISBN 9781433849305 (pdf)

https://doi.org/10.1037/0000453-000

Printed in the United States of America

10 9 8 7 6 5 4 3 2 1

Contents

Prologue

*Our Background and Interest in Linking Buddhism
With Psychotherapy*

Buddhist Psychotherapy examines the early Buddhist philosophical roots of mindfulness and provides a model for modern psychotherapy, showing how mindfulness can help clients alleviate suffering. This book is a collaboration between two practicing psychologists, Liang Tien and Debra M. Kawahara, and an ordained Buddhist nun, Venerable Dhammadinna. Here, the authors share their background and describe their interest in linking Buddhism with psychotherapy.

LIANG TIEN

The idea for using Buddhism as a theory of psychotherapy started when I was doing some fieldwork in the United Nations High Commission on Refugees (UNHCR) Beldangi Bhutanese refugee camp on the outskirts of Damak, Jhapa, Nepal. This refugee camp had been struggling to deal with a high suicide rate among the refugees. Significant resources had been devoted to train Nepalese mental health paraprofessionals to work with the refugees. The Transcultural Psychosocial Organization Nepal (TPO Nepal) had an intensive 6-month training series that very much resembled master's degree first-year coursework in mental health counseling. In addition to this base-level training, the paraprofessionals had continuous training with psychiatrists for psychoanalytic psychotherapy and with experts in cognitive behavior therapy (CBT). Despite their efforts in the provision of mental health services, the high suicide rate persisted. After much consultation, the UNHCR partnered with the Hindu American Foundation to fund a clinical psychologist to study this problem. Their design was to have a clinical psychologist be in residence, to form impressions and make recommendations to the UNHCR, TPO Nepal, and the Hindu American Foundation. I received a travel grant with the directive to live there for a month or so and share my opinion in terms of how to approach the mental health situation in the refugee camp.

The obvious stumbling block came during my very first encounter with a Bhutanese refugee in a treatment session. I was in attendance with a Nepalese mental health paraprofessional who had been trained in CBT. In a very professional and clinically appropriate manner, the paraprofessional asked the refugee, "What were your thoughts about the situation?" The refugee then asked, "What is a thought?" At that point, the Nepalese paraprofessional turned to me expectantly, as if I had an answer to this client's question.

I had never been asked that question in all my years of doing clinical work in the United States. It seemed that in the United States, no client or clinician would have asked the question, "What is a thought?" because the answer was so obvious. The Nepalese mental health paraprofessional later confirmed that it was an often-asked question, which was a stumbling point when they tried to use CBT. I then talked to several Nepalese paraprofessionals, asking: "If you were not here to help these people with their mental health problems, who would these people go to for help and what would they do?" Their answers pointed me to their spiritual healer and their use of meditation and Buddhism to address their mental health problems. This started my approximately 15-year study of Buddhism; along the way, I earned a master's degree and a doctorate in Buddhist studies, attended many meditation retreats, and took on a meditation practice under the guidance of Venerable Dhammadinna at the Bodhiheart Sangha in Seattle—all in the effort to answer the question, "What is a thought?" *Buddhist Psychotherapy* is the product of my combined knowledge and experience in clinical psychology and Buddhist studies.

DEBRA M. KAWAHARA

It was fortuitous that my path crossed Tien's when she was the program director of the PsyD in Clinical Psychology Program at the California School of Professional Psychology (CSPP), Alliant International University, Hong Kong. I had the great fortune of being able to work with Tien as an administrator and adjunct faculty for the program. As faculty, I would travel to Hong Kong to teach an intensive family systems course over a 2-week period, while staying at the university apartment where Tien lived. This allowed Tien and me the opportunity to get to know each other and share our work as well as our professional and personal lives.

During our late-night conversations while I was in Hong Kong, Tien spoke about integrating her experience and expertise in clinical psychology with her ongoing studies in early Buddhism. Her vision was to integrate clinical psychology with early Buddhism as theoretical bases to therapeutic cases. This vision was also to connect early Buddhism texts and concepts to psychological interventions of mindfulness and meditation-based interventions that were becoming so prolific in the United States. Tien strongly believed that these interventions would be even more effective if the conceptualization were tied to the cultural origins in which these interventions were created.

Our conversations led to my excitement of Tien's vision becoming another theoretical orientation, and because I truly believed that the U.S. practice of separating mindfulness and meditation interventions from their Buddhist roots was a form of cultural imperialism. Tien and I continued to discuss and work on the idea of Buddhist psychotherapy as a theoretical orientation. I also began my own studies of early Buddhism. What I realized is that I brought the lens of a U.S. therapist and how to present early Buddhism in an understandable manner for therapists who would have a very limited knowledge of early Buddhism. (Tien's two-cents worth: If it were not for Debra's ability to transform Tien's ideas for therapists, this book would never have seen the light of day.)

Our first step was to offer a graduate clinical psychology course in Buddhist psychotherapy at CSPP, Alliant International University. This course has been offered since 2020. We then followed with the development of an experience area, including a theory and practice course in Buddhist psychotherapy and two consultation courses, for graduate clinical psychology programs; an institute within Alliant International University; and a continuing education seminar for licensed practitioners. We also have been presenting nationally, and the response from audiences has been very positive. We now embark on this book as a culmination of our lived experiences, knowledge, and connection.

VENERABLE DHAMMADINNA

I met Tien in January 2008, when she began a personal journey delving into Buddhist practice at the Dharma Center in Seattle, where I teach. At that point, I had only been back in the United States for a year and a half after spending 21 years in Myanmar, Thailand, and India, studying, practicing, and teaching Buddhism in monastic settings.

Tien and I struck up a friendship and enjoyed learning from each other. I took the support of Tien's guidance and recommended reading when I needed to deepen my sensitivity to issues of race. And she showed herself to be a diligent student of meditation. When she started studying early Buddhist theory and texts in Hong Kong, we would meet on Zoom time and again to discuss her meditation and her courses. When Tien came back to Seattle for visits, we would meet for lively, leisurely conversations. As time went on, her master's degree led to a doctorate and to her moving back to Seattle.

At that point, Tien convened a handful of professional friends to discuss the themes she was developing in the clinical application of Buddhist theory, and she invited me to join as the Buddhist among the psychologists. Then came the task of shaping the material she had developed into a university course and webinar. I asked to see the webinar to learn what I could from her work. We ended up spending long afternoons together, with me offering challenges and edits to the material, and asking many questions of my own about the practice of clinical psychology. When the webinar was finished, Tien said she was writing a book. Naturally, I was curious to see what more may be revealed in the book. I worked my way through it chapter by chapter, offering feedback and learning more about the art and science of psychology and how Buddhist theory may be applied therein. I am thrilled to see this well-considered and insightful work come to fruition.

Buddhist Psychotherapy

INTRODUCTION

Linking Western Mindfulness to Early Buddhism

Mindfulness and mindfulness meditation were first introduced to U.S. psycho-therapy by Jon Kabat-Zinn (1984) with a mindfulness meditation program for the treatment of patients experiencing chronic pain. Kabat-Zinn said, "Mindfulness meditation has roots in Theravāda Buddhism where it is known as sattipatana [*sic*] vipassanā or Insight Meditation" (1984, p. 34). The *APA Dictionary of Psychology* defines *mindfulness* as "awareness of one's internal states and surroundings . . . to help people avoid destructive or automatic habits and responses by learning to observe their thoughts, emotions, and other present-moment experiences without judging or reacting to them" (American Psychological Association, n.d.). In the APA secular definition, mindfulness is mere awareness without judging or reacting. The secular mind-fulness meditation method has often been used for relaxation with the goal of inducing a state of calm. Mindfulness approaches have been manualized and promulgated for application in school classroom exercises with children, executive coaching, and yoga in exercise gymnasiums, to name just a few, and as part of treatment approaches for illnesses ranging from stress and chronic pain to cancer. Additionally, there has been a proliferation of web-based or

https://doi.org/10.1037/0000453-001
Buddhist Psychotherapy: Connecting Early Buddhism to Mindfulness and Western Psychotherapy, by L. Tien, D. M. Kawahara, and V. Dhammadinna

smartphone applications that can be downloaded to any mobile device and guide the user through meditative breathing, relaxation exercise, or both.

In the arena of psychotherapy, there have been three major mindfulness-based treatment approaches for the treatment of psychological distress and mental illness: mindfulness-based stress reduction, mindfulness-based cognitive therapy, and dialectical behavior therapy. Acceptance and commitment therapy uses mindfulness and meditation techniques that are integrated into its own theoretical approach to psychotherapy. Studies regarding the use of these intervention programs report their efficacy and effectiveness for the intended client population (see Britton et al., 2012; Eeles & Walker, 2022; Goldberg et al., 2018; Kriakous et al., 2021; Linardon et al., 2024; Querstret et al., 2020).

As Kabat-Zinn (1984) noted, mindfulness meditation has roots in Buddhism, but the meditation practices used in mindfulness-based psychotherapy are taught independent of the religious and cultural beliefs associated with them from their countries and traditions of origin. This is because in the United States, "mindfulness meditation is intellectually and experientially unfamiliar in our culture" (p. 34). Kabat-Zinn reasoned that because Western culture does not share the same religious and cultural beliefs as traditional Buddhist cultures in Asia, Americans would reject Eastern religious practices if mindfulness meditation were closely linked to Buddhism. This deletion of the context within which mindfulness meditation was developed has contributed to the adoption of mindfulness meditation technique without theory. Although there is evidence that meditation and mindfulness-based interventions work, there is no explanation as to why they work. Explication of why a technique is efficacious necessitates a theory. Indeed, mindfulness-based interventions within the field of mental health intervention have been limited to the level of technique, without a theoretical basis. Without a theoretical foundation, further development and research on this approach is limited (Davidson & Kaszniak, 2015).

This book seeks to remedy the situation by providing the theory for mindfulness meditation and thus linking modern mindfulness-based psychotherapy with its early Buddhist roots. We will present the teachings of the Siddhartha Gotama Shakyamuni—the founder of Buddhism, also referred to as simply the Buddha Gotama—as cited in the early Buddhist texts of the *Nikāya*, which is the documentation of the more than 10,000 talks given by the Buddha during his 45 years of teaching. We present the Buddha's theory on the human experience of existence, which is the theoretical basis of mindfulness meditation and one of the mechanisms the Buddha Gotama used to relieve suffering or unsatisfactoriness (*dukkha*, which is discussed extensively in this book) and increase joy and satisfaction in life (*sukha*). Furthermore, other intervention techniques taught by the Buddha Gotama, in addition to mindfulness meditation, will be introduced, discussed, and examined for clinical use in mental health treatment. Our hope is that by providing the theory for mindfulness, meditation, and mindfulness-based psychotherapies, we will enable researchers, practitioners, and theorists to expand their understanding of mindfulness and ultimately develop new interventions for psychotherapy. Theory allows us to hypothesize what techniques will work, so researchers can develop and test new techniques. Examining the place of insight, mindfulness meditation, and other interventions from early Buddhism provides a much fuller understanding of why mindfulness meditation offers efficacious techniques for mental health interventions.

To highlight the promise of theory, if we examine the literature in early Buddhism, it is evident that U.S. mindfulness interventions are extremely limited. One of the primary texts in which the Buddha taught meditation is the Satipaṭṭhāna Sutta (*Majjhima Nikāya* [MN], 1995, 10: The Foundations of Mindfulness). The text outlines four large categories for objects of meditation. The first category is the body. Contemplation of the body starts with the breath, with four further subcategories for meditations on the body. After the body, the text then specifies three more categories, each of which contains numerous subcategories, for meditation. The present-day mindfulness interventions build on only one part of the first of four objects of contemplation explicated in this text. With an expanded understanding of how mindfulness works that includes all four categories of contemplation, psychotherapists can offer new treatment options to alleviate clients' suffering.

A NOTE ABOUT THE SCOPE OF THIS BOOK

Those who are Buddhist and have their own extensive practice may notice that the approach taken in this book is extremely narrow. It does not fully encompass the overall approach that the Buddha took in addressing the experience of and liberation from suffering. Rather, the book maintains a narrow focus because it is written for psychotherapists who may or may not be Buddhist. We limit the scope of this book to the material that we see as applicable to the process of psychotherapy.

The intent of this book is to translate the lexicon used in early Buddhist texts to the lexicon used in the mental health field so that ideas from early Buddhism are more accessible to psychology. The approach taken and the subjects selected in this book assume that the reader holds the necessary foundational knowledge and skills to enter into the study of a theoretical orientation for psychotherapy. The terminology used in this book is intended for mental health practitioners looking to respecialize in a different theoretical orientation, researchers and developers of mental health intervention programs, and graduate students in mental health fields such as psychology, clinical social work, counseling, and other mental health professions.

There is a long Buddhist tradition of commentaries on the mind, because a large portion of Buddhist practice concerns itself with the mind. The Buddha said,

> I don't envision a single thing that—when untamed, unguarded, unprotected, unrestrained—leads to such great harm as the mind. . . . I don't envision a single thing that—when tamed, guarded, protected, restrained—leads to such great benefit as the mind. (Ekadhamma Suttas; *Aṅguttara Nikāya* [AN], 2012, 1:39: The Mind: A Single Thing)

There are abundant current publications on Buddhism and psychology or counseling (e.g., by Padmasiri De Silva, Mark Epstein, Beth Jacobs, and George Lee) as well as on Buddhism and the mind (e.g., by David Kalupahana, Y. K. Karunadasa, Geshe Lhundub Sopa, Tenzin Gyatso the 14th Dalai Lama, and Thich Nhat Hanh). There is also a tradition for Buddhist practitioners and scholars to first approach the teachings of the Buddha with fresh eyes prior to engaging with the commentaries and the published literature. This book takes the second approach, with fresh eyes from the authors. As such, there is an absence of what social science would normally consider a necessary review of the scholarly literature in this book. However, this book's take on the meaning of early Buddhist texts does not significantly deviate from the commentarial Theravāda Buddhist interpretation of these texts.

HOW THIS BOOK IS ORGANIZED

The content of this book provides a more thorough examination into Buddhism as it relates to a theoretical orientation for psychotherapy. This book is organized around a key tenet of Buddhism, which is the *three marks of existence*. According to the Buddha, there are three universal truths, or marks, of existence; these can be thought of as laws of reality. They are laws in the same sense as used by Thorndike (1911) in his Laws of Behavior in General (p. 241). The three marks of existence (with Pali terms in parentheses), as stated in the *Khuddaka Nikāya Dhammapada* (Dhp; 1996, 277–279: The Path), are as follows:

- All conditioned things are impermanent (*aniccā*).
- All things are not-self (*anattā*).
- All conditioned things are unsatisfactory (*dukkha*).

In other words, suffering occurs when people fail to understand, acknowledge, and recognize these three marks of existence, instead craving for reality to be different than it is. We will explore each of these three marks in depth, along with the Buddha's remedy for suffering and how this applies to modern psychotherapy. Along the way, we will discuss the Buddhist framework of the Four Noble Truths and the Noble Eightfold Path.

Part I (Chapters 1 and 2) provides an overview of the philosophical and cultural context of Buddhism, as well as how Buddhist psychotherapy differs from the Buddhism religion and Buddhist practices. Part II (Chapter 3) covers one mark of existence, which is impermanence (aniccā). Part III (Chapters 4–6) covers another mark, which is the not-self (anattā). Part IV (Chapters 7–12) covers a third mark, which is dukkha. Finally, Part V (Chapters 13–18) covers the use of Buddhist interventions for psychotherapy in the format of the Noble Eightfold Path.

PART I

FOUNDATIONS OF
BUDDHISM AND
BUDDHIST
PSYCHOTHERAPY

1 BACKGROUND ON THE BUDDHA AND EARLY BUDDHIST TEXTS

In this chapter, we provide some context for understanding Buddhist psychotherapy. We begin with a basic introduction to the historical Buddha, who he was, and why he mattered. We then discuss which texts will be drawn on in this book to illustrate the Buddha's teachings; this includes a brief explanation of how his teachings were first assembled and transmitted orally and then eventually written hundreds of years later. We will explain the basic citation format used in this book when referring to early Buddhist texts. We conclude with advice from the Buddha about how readers might approach Buddhist psychotherapy.

WHO WAS THE BUDDHA?

At the time the Buddha lived, the Indian subcontinent had already established a long and esteemed tradition of wandering ascetics. These were individuals following a variety of doctrines (e.g., Jain) who had given up life at home and had chosen to go forth into homelessness. By convention, they gave up

https://doi.org/10.1037/0000453-002
Buddhist Psychotherapy: Connecting Early Buddhism to Mindfulness and Western Psychotherapy, by L. Tien, D. M. Kawahara, and V. Dhammadinna

all their material possessions, put on saffron robes, and wandered the land, surviving off the generosity of others offered in alms of food. This type of saffron-robed wanderer undertook a spiritual quest to realize the nature of the self, the world, and the universe.

Siddhartha Gotama Shakyamuni—who would later be known as the Buddha Gotama, or simply *the Buddha*—was such a wanderer who also undertook the same spiritual quest. Countless tales, books, and movies recount his origins as a prince who grew up in luxury and lived a life of privilege. At the age of 29, he left his life of luxury for the life of an ascetic (Ñāṇamoli, 2015). Six years after leaving the life of a householder (i.e., someone who lives in a house), he gained enlightenment under a Bodhi tree. It is at this point that he became a buddha. The word *buddha* is Pali, which is the dialect spoken by the Buddha, and is translated as "having attained enlightenment" (Pali Text Society, n.d.).

After gaining Buddhahood, the Buddha taught for 45 years. The Buddha was clear about what he sought for himself and his followers. Of all the talks the Buddha gave in his 45 years of teaching, he claimed that "what I teach is suffering and the cessation of suffering" (Alagaddūpama Sutta [*Majjhima Nikāya* (MN), 1995, 22.86]: Simile of the Snake). The Buddha Gotama was not concerned with speculation; rather, he was concerned with the human lived experience. He found that for most people, the human lived experience of existence is characterized by suffering (*dukkha*).

The teachings of the Buddha Gotama were in the service of ending dukkha, the pains and sorrows that are found in the human experience of existence. Along the way to the ending of dukkha, Buddhism aims to increase the experience of joy and satisfaction in life (*sukha*). Taking dukkha and sukha as its subject matter, the teachings of the Buddha Gotama align with the purpose of psychotherapy. Both endeavors have a clear objective: that is, to reduce suffering and to increase joy and satisfaction in the experience of existence.

HISTORICAL BACKGROUND OF EARLY BUDDHIST TEXTS

Because Buddhist psychotherapy is primarily aligned with early ideas as taught by the Buddha himself, rather than the beliefs espoused by subsequent philosophers and cultures that embraced Buddhism, this book will rely primarily on early Buddhist texts that most closely resemble what the Buddha probably taught. A brief history of early Buddhist texts is helpful.

The accounts of what occurred when the Buddha Gotama passed away at the age of 80 vary among the orthodoxy, religious beliefs, and scholarly studies. No account disputes that a large contingent of monks traveled to the site of the Buddha's demise (Reat, 1994). However, what occurred at this gathering is of some dispute. Buddhist orthodoxy asserts that the teachings of the Buddha and the monastic rules laid down by the Buddha were recited by those present at this gathering (Warder, 2015). Scholars of early Buddhism debate the viability of this claim. Nevertheless, for the purposes of Buddhist psychotherapy, it may be more interesting to consider the narrative from the Buddhist orthodoxy.

When the monks heard that the Buddha was dying, they journeyed to gather at the site. Among them was a monk named Subhadda, who said,

> Enough, friends, do not sorrow, do not lament. We are well rid of the Great monk [the Buddha Gotama]. We have been frustrated by his saying "This is allowed to you; this is not allowed to you." But now we shall do as we like and we shall not do as we do not like. (*Dīgha Nikāya* [DN], 1987/1995; Ñāṇamoli, 2015, p. 330).

Subhadda's sentiment alarmed some of the monks. Knowing that this kind of drift would be inevitable, the senior monks decided to document what they remembered of the Buddha's teaching. The renowned elder monk, Mahākassapa, called a meeting of 500 arahants. An *arahant* is "one who has attained the Summum Bonum of religious aspiration (Nibbāna)" (Pali Text Society, n.d.). More specifically for this meeting, the arahants were the disciples of the Buddha who had reached liberation following the teachings of the Buddha. This meeting is now referred to as the *First Buddhist Council*. The task of the First Buddhist Council at Rajagaha was to establish the authoritative collection of the Buddha Gotama's teachings (Morgan, 1956). There is some dispute as to how the information was collected (Bapat, 1971). Regardless of the method used, what emerged were the *Vinaya Piṭaka*, the monastic rules given by the Buddha, and the *Sutta Piṭaka*.

The *Sutta Piṭaka* is the collection of the Buddha's teachings. In Pali, *sutta* means "a thread" (Pali Text Society, n.d.). Think of a sutta as a thread of ideas in a lecture. *Piṭaka* is the Pali word for "baskets" (Pali Text Society, n.d.), which refers to how these writings were stored. People in countries of the Asian subcontinent, such as India and Sri Lanka, wrote on palm leaves, which formed the pages of a book. These palm leaves were rolled, tied up, and stored in baskets. The *Piṭaka* thus evokes the image of a shelf lined with baskets, and baskets could be catalogued according to the topics of the books contained in them. The sutta basket contained suttas, holding the recollections of the Buddha's teachings. The collection of suttas, not the *Vinaya*, forms the basis for Buddhist psychotherapy.

Pali, the written language used in the *Piṭaka*, originated from vernacular dialect used by the Buddha. So, the remembered teachings and events were documented in the oral tradition, employing repetitions and rhyme. These suttas have been retained by group recitation over these 2,500 years. The suttas chanted in the 21st century are the same ones that were developed at the First Buddhist Council. When the suttas were eventually written down, several hundred years after the First Buddhist Council, they retained the repetitions that are a characteristic of the oral tradition. Although we have tried to limit repetition in this book for modern readers, we quote suttas to illustrate key tenets of Buddhist philosophy. Some repetition is inevitable.

The *Sutta Piṭaka* is, by tradition, arranged in five different collections. Each is called a *Nikāya*, which means "collection, class, group, assemblage, or volume" (Pali Text Society, n.d.). By convention, the five collections are the *Aṅguttara Nikāya* (AN), the *Dīgha Nikāya* (DN), the *Majjhima Nikāya* (MN), the *Saṃyutta Nikāya* (SN), and the *Khuddaka Nikāya* (KN). The KN is subdivided into the *Khuddakapatha* (Khp), *Dhammapada* (Dhp), *Udana* (Ud), *Itivuttaka* (Iti), *Sutta Nipata* (Sn), *Theragatha* (Thag), and *Therigatha* (Thig). The reasoning for where a sutta is found in the collection is specified in the name of the *Nikāya*. The AN is *The Numerical Discourses of the Buddha* (2012) and contains suttas that speak of things that are countable. The DN is the *Long Discourses of the Buddha* (1987/1995) and contains long suttas. The MN is the *Middle-Length Discourses of the Buddha* (1995) and contains suttas that are shorter than those in the DN. The SN is the *Connected Discourses of the Buddha* (2000) and contains suttas that have the same or similar subjects. The KN is the collection of short miscellaneous suttas.

There are more than 10,000 suttas retained in the five *Nikāyas*, spanning the 45 years of the Buddha Gotama's teachings. The topics of his teachings were wide ranging and were not delivered in any particular order. Some were lectures given to monks who were well advanced in meditation, whereas others were answers offered to lay people who came with random questions. It would be reasonable to organize the suttas by something that is more internally coherent. Over several hundreds of years of teaching new monks and lay followers, various groups undertook the task of analyzing and condensing the material from the *Sutta Piṭaka* into some semblance of coherence that could be more easily taught. These various groups of Buddhist practitioners then documented their own organization and understanding of the suttas. These expositions of the suttas are referred to as the *Abhidhamma* and there are two related usages and translations of the term, which can be broken down into two parts: When used as a modifier, *abhi* means "over above, in addition, par excellence, super" (Pali Text Society, n.d.); *dhamma*, in this context, means teachings. In direct translation, the term Abhidhamma means "in addition to the teachings"; when used as a single word, it means "theory of the doctrine, the doctrine pure and simple (without any admixture of literary grace or of personalities, or of anecdotes, or of arguments ad personam)" (Pali Text Society, n.d.). In function, "an *Abhidhamma* analyses the materials it collects from the sutta, poses questions and answers them, works out a systematic treatise. In a sense then it explains the sutta" (Warder, 2015, p. 13).

The more engaging story for the origin of the Abhidhamma is that the Buddha Gotama taught us earthlings with lots of embellishments, examples, analogies, and different ways of saying the same thing to explain the ideas, given the proclivities of the listener. The Abhidhamma, unadorned, was taught by the Buddha in one sitting to his mother who was residing in the heavenly realm of the 33 gods, of which Sakkha, also known as Indra, was reckoned as the chief (Sīlānanda, 2012, p. 18). Sāriputta, one of the Buddha's disciples, was present at this teaching. Alternatively, according to lore, when the Buddha came to earth every day for the alms round, he related to Venerable Sāriputta the content of the lectures given in the heavenly realm. Sāriputta later transmitted this teaching through the Abhidhamma. Thus, the term Abhidhamma is the Buddha's teaching in its most analytical form without any kind of embellishments (Sīlānanda, 2012).

The geographic area where Buddha wandered is contained mostly in present-day Bihar, a state in India. As the teachings of the Buddha expanded eastward and westward, it seems that the various groups developed their own Abhidhamma. There may have been any number of Abhidhammas, but only two survived to date: the Theravāda Abhidhamma and the Sarvāstivāda Abhidhamma. The group that developed the Theravāda Abhidhamma was in Eastern India. From there, the Theravāda system of Buddhism spread south of the Himalayan mountains to southeastern countries such as Myanmar (formerly Burma), Thailand, and Sri Lanka.

The Sarvāstivāda Abhidhamma developed in the Western region and was written in Sanskrit, the religious, scriptural language of Brahmanic India, not the vernacular dialect of Pali. The Sarvāstivāda Abhidhamma traveled around the Gobi Desert, along the Silk Route into Tibet, China, Mongolia, Korea, and Japan. Present-day Tibetan Buddhism was derived primarily from the Sarvāstivāda Abhidhamma. The present-day Mahayana school of Buddhism in China, Mongolia, Korea, and Japan is derived mainly from the Āgama, the Chinese translation of the *Nikāya* and the Sarvāstivāda Abhidhamma.

From there, variations of Buddhism evolved, such as Chan Buddhism in China and Zen Buddhism in Japan.

All of these Buddhist sects are growing in the United States, including those derived from the Sarvāstivāda Abhidhamma as well as those of the Theravāda Abhidhamma. The Theravāda Abhidhamma is of interest to Buddhist psychotherapy. The ideas used in Buddhist psychotherapy are from the *Nikāya*, with some ideas taken from the Theravāda Abhidhamma.

CRITERIA FOR SELECTION OF SUTTAS FOR PSYCHOTHERAPY

The concepts in early Buddhism, as recorded in the suttas of the *Nikāya*, are the result of the Buddha Gotama's exploration of the experience of human existence. More than 10,000 suttas were recollected at the First Buddhist Council, accounting for the Buddha's 45 years of teaching. His talks ranged from politics to family relationships. Not all of the topics are relevant to psychotherapy. For the purposes of this book, only those suttas with relevant use for a theory of psychotherapy have been extracted. The information used in Buddhist psychotherapy is limited to, and the selection is based on, the following criteria, in order of priority:

1. The passage accurately presents the relevant ideas found in the *Sutta Piṭaka*. The authenticity of the ideas is evidenced by direct quotes from the suttas found in the *Nikāya*. Sometimes quotes from the Theravāda Abhidhamma will be used if the ideas are unchanged but better stated. Ideas from the Sarvāstivāda Abhidhamma and Mahayana Buddhism are not included in this volume.

2. The passage represents central, or core, ideas in Buddha's exploration of the experience of human existence.

3. Finally, the passage represents Buddha's ideas that are applicable to psychotherapy, based on the first two authors' (this volume) combined experience of providing more than 60 years of clinical psychotherapy, their more than 50 years of experience teaching clinical psychology at the postgraduate master's and doctoral levels, and their cumulated professional knowledge of theory construction. Additionally, Buddha's ideas that are applicable to the practice of insight meditation are based on the third author's (this volume) experiences in teaching meditation for more than 30 years.

The definition and explanation of selected ideas found in the *Sutta Piṭaka* and the Theravāda Abhidhamma are presented in the most basic and most simplistic form. In its simplicity, what is written may appear reductionist. This simplicity is to be in keeping with the idea expressed by Wampold (2019) that "a theory of psychotherapy ought to be simple enough for the average therapist to understand but comprehensive enough to account for a wide range of eventualities" (pp. 1–2). Too much complexity can hinder the ability to grasp the essential meaning. Too much specificity in the details may get in the way of the necessary flexibility needed for application in the psychotherapeutic treatment room. Treatment interventions by a psycho-therapist are often not unlike the many different responses and interventions Buddha Gotama gave to questions posed by individuals from various walks of life. Each person comes into psychotherapy with their own unique cir-cumstances and personality. Psychotherapists need to have the flexibility to tailor interventions that address their clients' characteristics and specific situations. This type of flexibility can be derived from a simplistic presen-tation of the fundamentals found in the *Sutta Piṭaka* and the Theravāda Abhidhamma.

In Part V of this volume, the discussion of each parallel track of the Noble Eightfold Path will be based on the guidance given in the suttas. The Sāleyyaka Sutta (MN, 1995, 41: The Brahmins of Sālā) will be used to address the track of conduct (*sīla*). The Abhiṇhapaccavekkhitabbaṭhāna Sutta (AN, 2012, 5.57: Themes) will be used to address the cause and effect of a deed (*kamma*). The Satipaṭṭhāna Sutta (MN, 1995, 10: The Four Foundations of Mindfulness) will focus on discussion of the types of objects for the training of concentration (*samādhi*). Finally, the Sabbāsava Sutta (MN, 1995, 2: Discourse on All the Taints) is examined to addresses the track of wisdom (*paññā*).

SUTTA CITATION FORMAT

For each quote from a sutta, this book will follow an examination and dis-cussion format to introduce the Buddhist concept, to cite its early Buddhist texts from the *Nikāya* or Theravāda Abhidhamma, to give the Buddha's expla-nations of the idea, and then to translate the concept into the lexicon of psychology and therapeutic work. Clinical case material will be interwoven into the explanation to render these ideas more usable in psychotherapy. The convention for referencing each sutta consists of the following at its first mention in each chapter: (a) its name in Pali, (b) which of the five *Nikāyas* it is in, (c) the corresponding year in the reference list for this volume, (d) the numerical location of the sutta in that *Nikāya*, and (e) the English trans-lation of the Pali name. The text of the sutta is given in quotation form.

For example, the Buddha's claim that "what I teach is suffering and the cessation of suffering" is cited as follows: Alagaddūpama Sutta (MN, 1995, 22.86: Simile of the Snake). Alagaddūpama Sutta is the Pali name for the sutta. MN is the abbreviation for the *Majjhima Nikāya*, the middle-length collection of suttas. 1995 is the year the translation of the *Nikāya* we refer to was published. The number 22 refers to the numerical location of the sutta in the *Majjhima Nikāya*, with 1 being the first sutta in the collection. The number 86 refers to the 86th paragraph of the 22nd sutta in the *Majjhima Nikāya*. The phrase "Simile of the Snake" is the English translation of the Pali name for the sutta, Alagaddūpama.

Suttas in the *Nikāya* have a set structure. The structure is similar to APA-style in-text citation guidelines for citing information from traditional knowledge or oral traditions. The suttas start with "thus I have heard," followed by the location, the time, the persons involved in the conversations, and, lastly, what was said. For example, the sutta of the Buddha's conversation with Potaliya (Potaliya Sutta [MN, 1995, 54]: To Potaliya) starts with the following:

> Thus I have heard.

This is followed by the location:

> On one occasion the Blessed One was living in the country of the Anguttarāpans where there was a town of theirs named Āpaṇa.

Next is the time:

> When it was morning, . . . he went to a certain grove for the day's abiding.

The description of to whom was the Buddha talking is given next:

> Potaliya the householder, while walking and wandering for exercise, wearing full dress with parasol and sandals, also went to the grove.

The following is what was said:

> Which is the list of behaviors the followers of the Buddha practices to give them the status of not being a householder.

The selection of suttas was not done with a soteriological goal of practice for liberation (*nibbāna*). In the Buddhist application, the term nibbāna means "extinguishing of fire" (Pali Text Society, n.d.). When the fire of craving for existence is extinguished, then one obtains liberation from the trials and tribulations—the suffering—in life. Nibbāna is the goal of Buddhist religious practice. However, Buddhist psychotherapy is not equivalent to Buddhist religion. The texts from early Buddhism were selected with the goal of formulating a theory that can be used in psychotherapy and, hopefully, will reduce clients' suffering and increase functioning in their life as a householder—that is, in everyday life, regardless of spiritual practices.

ATTITUDE FOR APPROACHING BUDDHIST TEACHINGS AND BUDDHIST PSYCHOTHERAPY

It might be useful to consider the viewpoint that the Buddha suggests for any-one who approaches his teachings (*dhamma* in Pali; *dharma* in Sanskrit). In original usage of the term, dhammas are laws, as in the declarations engraved on the Aśokan pillars described in Chapter 2 (this volume). Dhammas are thus the laws of the empire and have been translated as laws. This trans-lation is deceptive, however. The term dhamma has been translated variously to mean "laws of nature," "principles," "teachings," and "instructions." The Pali Text Society (n.d.) defines dhamma as a "doctrine, right, or righteous-ness, condition, phenomenon." For the purposes of Buddhist psychotherapy, dhamma can be considered the teachings of the Buddha as documented in the *Nikāya*.

Two types of approaches to the sayings of the Buddha are often made. One is in regard to the authenticity of the claim that something was said by Buddha Gotama. Many sayings are attributed to Buddha Gotama, and verification of their authenticity is easily made by noting the reference to the *Nikāya*. The other approach is to ask, even if verified through the *Nikāya*, how is one to judge the usefulness of what the Buddha Gotama said. In its application to Buddhist psychotherapy, the question would be whether what the Buddha Gotama taught is efficacious in psychotherapeutic treatment.

This same question was put to the Buddha in the Kesamutti Sutta (AN, 2012, 3.65: With the Kālāmas of Kesamutta). This sutta takes place in Kesamutta, a market town at a trade crossroads. Many travelers, merchants, and wandering ascetics traveled through Kesamutta, and its residents were called *Kālāmas*. The Kālāmas had been exposed to the beliefs and teachings of many different wandering ascetics; so when the Buddha came into town, he was just one of many spiritual leaders claiming to know the Truth, with a capital T. The Kālāmas, having been exposed to so many different claims, asked the Buddha Gotama to help them sort through these teachings from different wandering ascetics. To be more specific, they said,

> Bhante [a polite salutation, similar to Sir], there are some ascetics and brahmins who come to Kesaputta. They explain and elucidate their own doctrines, but disparage, denigrate, deride and denounce the doctrines of others. But then

some other ascetics and brahmins come to Kesaputta, and they too explain and elucidate their own doctrines, but disparage, denigrate, deride, and denounce the doctrines of others. We are perplexed and in doubt, Bhante, as to which of these good ascetics speak truth and which speak falsehood. (AN, 2012, 3.65)

The Kālāmas asked for the Buddha's help with how to discern truth and value. Buddha laid out how one should go about deciding what to adopt for one's own use. The Buddha's response contains three ideas. One is when to doubt, the second is what not to use when resolving doubt, and the third is what to use. The Buddha first stated an assessment, then listed situations that are not to be relied upon, followed by a list of metrics that can be used for the means to discern what to adopt. His response started with "it is fitting for you to be perplexed . . . fitting for you to be in doubt. Doubt has arisen in you about a perplexing matter" (AN, 2012, 3.65). Saying that the matter in question is perplexing affirmed the lived experience of the Kālāmas. In its application to psychotherapy, when a client starts debating with themselves and doubt their capacity, their situation, their decision, and so on, the psychotherapist can first examine whether doubt has arisen about a perplexing matter. Often, doubt is used as a way to obscure the actuality of an experience in a situation that is not perplexing.

Consider the following example: A client reported that she remembered an incident in which her mother told her to slap herself 100 times for some unrecalled transgression. The client doubted whether it was a real memory or, even if the memory was real, whether she was inappropriate in her reaction to being angry and feeling abused. In this situation, doubt has arisen about a matter that is not perplexing. This client's mental status was normal and stable; therefore, there is no reason to question the actuality of the remembered incident. Having a child slap herself 100 times, regardless of the offense, is abuse. The client's doubt about whether her mother loved her based on the experience of abuse is a perplexing matter, but whether the mother made the client slap herself 100 times is not. Thus, in psychotherapy, the first step in resolving doubt is to question whether the doubt is appropriate—that is, whether it is a perplexing matter. Indeed, considering whether to use early Buddhist ideas as a psychotherapeutic approach is a perplexing matter; thus, doubt is appropriate. In matters that are perplexing, it is good to question, it is good to doubt, and it is good to examine—be critical.

Going beyond affirming the Kālāmas' experience of getting the message from so many ascetics, the Buddha gave the following list of criteria for what not to use when resolving doubt:

Come, Kālāmas, do not go by oral tradition, by lineage of teaching, by hearsay, by a collection of scriptures, by logical reasoning, for inferential reasoning, by reasoned cogitation, by the acceptance of a view after pondering it, by seeming competence of a speaker, or because you think: The ascetic is our guru. But when, Kālāmas, you know for yourselves: These things are unwholesome; these things are blameworthy; these things are censured by the wise; these things, if accepted and undertaken, lead to harm and suffering, then you should abandon them. (AN, 2012, 3.65)

The Buddha lists situations that are not sufficient in and of themselves to be relied upon for the means to discern what to adopt. These situations are as follows:

1. *Do not go by oral tradition.* For instance, do not just believe everything your professor or supervisor said back in graduate school. Oral tradition is not sufficient in and of itself as a basis for adoption. For instance, in years past, clinical programs were teaching that the best practice for suicide prevention was a suicide contract. If practitioners of that generation continued to provide treatment interventions based on the lineage of teachings, suicide contracts would still be used, disregarding later studies that developed much more efficacious approaches to suicide prevention.

2. *[Do not go] by lineage of teaching.* Here is an example, "My teacher said this, and their teacher taught it to them, and their teacher's teacher taught it," and on it goes. In short, the Buddha says do not accept something based simply on transmission from a teacher. Lineage of teaching is not sufficient in and of itself. Do not accept the idea that something should be done a certain way just because it has always been done that way. A clinical example would be the tradition of weekly hour-long psychotherapy treatment sessions. The Buddha would say, take a critical look at the reasons why one should schedule weekly outpatient psychotherapy sessions, or why those sessions should be 1 hour, 50 minutes, or 45 minutes.

3. *[Do not go] by hearsay.* Think of the common claim of teenagers trying to convince their parents to allow them to attend some social event: "Everyone is going, so why can't I?" Or maybe you tried mindfulness meditation in your treatment sessions because you heard that it was efficacious. Buddha is saying, do not do something based on hearsay. Positive or negative reports from others, while meaningful, are not sufficient in and of themselves for adoption.

4. *[Do not go] by a collection of scriptures.* If we substitute the word "text" for "scriptures," the Buddha is saying do not do something just because

it is written in text. Most professions require their members to know what has and is being published. The practice of reading evidence-based studies probably falls under the Buddha's category of not doing something based on a collection of texts, hearsay, and or lineage of teaching. In this regard, examine any research study and its conclusions from an extremely critical stance. What is published is not sufficient in and of itself for adoption.

5. [Do not go] by logical reasoning. Logic used for statistical analyses in social science research is based on assumptions. In social science research, one can lie with numbers as easily as they can with words. Logic and analysis are not sufficient in and of themselves for adoption.

6. [Do not go] for inferential reasoning. Examine published studies carefully, question the methodology used, and take care not to infer applicability of conclusions drawn from one population to a diverse or different population. Do not infer clinical significance from statistical significance.

7. [Do not go] by reasoned cogitation. The saying "it stands to reason" does not always hold up in actuality.

8. [Do not go] by the acceptance of a view after pondering it. After thinking something over, one can talk oneself into all sorts of justifications for doing something that may be harmful to either oneself or to others.

9. [Do not go] by seeming competence of a speaker. A good political speaker is in the business of persuading the public to their point of view by crafting arguments for why their position is the right stance. The more polished a speaker is, the more competent they appear and the more persuasive their argument. It is best to look past the surface appearance of things.

10. [Do not do something just] because you think, "The ascetic is our guru." Not believing something just because the Buddha said so means do not go by faith. The Buddha does not ask the Kālāmas to accept his teaching on faith. Faith in the sense that is usually thought of in the religious and spiritual term is not something that the Buddha supports. Faith, in the Buddhist sense, is inevitably trusting something will occur based on repeated past experiences. For example, one of the scariest things to start doing in downhill skiing is to lean the whole body down the slope, but that is what is needed to master parallel skiing. Those who have mastered parallel skiing have the experience of control when using the edge of the ski. They would have absolute faith in the edge of the ski to navigate any kind of slope. In this example, the neophyte

skier would hold a provisional trust in the ski instructor and faith in their instructions. In the same way, one might place provisional trusting confidence in the guidance of the Buddha until, following the Buddha's guidance, the practitioner gains their own experiential knowledge. In Buddhism, faith is based on this personal experiential knowledge. (AN, 2012, 3.65)

After providing the long list of what not to do, the Buddha then went on to give some criteria for what one should use for settling doubts:

> But when you know for yourselves: These things are wholesome; these things are blameless; these things are praised by the wise; these things, if accepted and undertaken, lead to welfare and happiness, then you should live in accordance with them. (AN, 2012, 3.65)

The Buddha provided the following five criteria for consideration before adopting beliefs and actions for one's own use:

1. *But when you know for yourselves.* The Buddha directs the Kālāmas, and by extension all of us, to use one's own experience as the first bases for determining what is good to adopt. This means honor your own experience and, in psychotherapy, honor the client's experience. Things that are learned by cognition also need to be learned by experience for an embodied experiential knowledge.

2. *These things are wholesome.* The Pali term *kusalā* is translated here as "wholesome." The Pali Text Society (n.d.) defines kusalā as "clever, skillful, expert, good, right, meritorious." The Buddha then explains that kusalā (skillful, wholesome) refers to acts that are not generated by greed, hate, and delusion. If someone tells you something, investigate the motivation for what the person is saying. If you decide that it is not motivated by greed, hatred, or delusion, then it is probably okay to follow. The Buddha's reasoning is that acts motivated by greed, hate, or delusion are conducive to harm and suffering for oneself and others.

3. *These things are blameless.* The Pali word *sāvajjā* is translated here as "blamelessness" and "blameworthiness." The term sāvajjā has also been translated as "censurable" and "sin" (Pali Text Society, n.d.). What the Buddha probably means by blameless can be thought of as censurable. The Buddha is saying, if someone tells you to do what common sense tells you or you know from experience will get you in trouble, then do not do it.

4. *These things are praised by the wise.* Bhikkhu Bodhi translated the Pali word *viññupasattha* as "wise." Bhikkhu Sujato translated the word as

"sensible people." The root is *viññu*, which is defined as "intelligent learned wise" (Pali Text Society, n.d.). In the *Pali Text Society's Pali–English Dictionary*, the term viññupasattha is defined as "un-attacked, not deficient, unmolested, undisturbed . . . extolled by the wise" (Pali Text Society, n.d.), which could entail thinking of someone who is considered wise by many in society. Most likely, a wise person would not be motivated by selfishness if they recommended a course of action. If one is reluctant to tell such a person what one has done, one should probably not do it.

5. *These things, if accepted and undertaken, lead to welfare and happiness* if undertaken as points to experiential knowledge. The Buddha tells the Kālāmas, and by extension all of us, to first apply the three criteria listed earlier, and then by experience via turning cognitive knowing into embodied knowledge. If believing or doing what the Buddha taught increases a client's welfare and happiness, then one should adopt it.

In its application to Buddhist psychotherapy, the Kesamutti Sutta (AN, 2012, 3.65) suggests that one comes to this theory with curiosity and a critical mind. And if, in the Buddha's words, it increases one's welfare and happiness, then you are invited to try using the ideas from Buddhist psychotherapy.

CONCLUDING THOUGHTS

Having set the direction (using ideas from early Buddhism for psychotherapy), having set one's comportment (which is orienting toward the dhamma, or the teachings of the Buddha, and documented in the collection of suttas, or the *Nikāyas*), and having donned our mental attitude (one of critical curiosity blended with experiential knowledge), it is time to examine the suttas for the purpose of a theory of psychotherapy.

2 BUDDHIST PSYCHOTHERAPY VERSUS BUDDHISM THE RELIGION

In this chapter, we present the most foundational structure of Buddhism and describe how Buddhist psychotherapy uses these foundational theses for a theory of psychotherapy. This chapter starts with an overview of the three marks of existence and then discusses their links to the Four Noble Truths, and the Noble Eightfold Path. We end this chapter with clarification of the differences between Buddhism and Buddhist psychotherapy.

FOUNDATIONS OF BUDDHISM

In the lexicon of social science research, the Buddha Gotama undertook a study using the phenomenological approach, single-case design, to answer his research question: "What is the human experience of existence?" He stated his research findings in terms of the three marks of existence, the Four Noble Truths, and the Noble Eightfold Path. Subsequent chapters will elaborate on each of the categories within each mark of existence.

The Buddha's the three marks of existence are the most succinct statement of his research results. These marks are stated in the form of laws, and they are

https://doi.org/10.1037/0000453-003
Buddhist Psychotherapy: Connecting Early Buddhism to Mindfulness and Western Psychotherapy, by L. Tien, D. M. Kawahara, and V. Dhammadinna

laws in the same sense as used by Thorndike (1911) in his Laws of Behavior in General (p. 241). Think of the Four Noble Truths as the discussion section of a research study, in which the Buddha addresses the implication for the three marks of existence and answers his research question: "What is the human experience of existence?" In Buddhism, the Four Noble Truths guide people toward the realization of the three marks of existence. The Noble Eightfold Path is akin to the Buddha's intervention strategies; think of the path as treatment interventions in psychotherapy. The Four Noble Truths and the Noble Eightfold Path are aimed at helping people realize, or achieve the embodied knowledge of, the three marks of existence. The benefit of the embodied knowledge of the three marks of existence is the reduction and elimination of suffering (*dukkha*). In Buddhist practice, the goal is for the complete liberation from dukkha. In Buddhist psychotherapy, the goal is for sufficient reduction of dukkha to enable increased daily functioning.

The organization of this book is based on the format of a research study. The remainder of this chapter briefly outlines the Buddha's research project. We start with the Buddha's journey in search of his research question. We then provide an overview of his results with the three marks of existence, and we provide a discussion of the Four Noble Truths and the Noble Eightfold Path. Along the way, we list the most essential principles of Buddhism to provide the foundational ideas of Buddhism and Buddhist psychotherapy. The overall structure of this book follows the format of the Buddha's results, which are the three marks of existence, the Four Noble Truths, and the Noble Eightfold Path.

Buddha's Research Question: The Noble Search

In the Ariyapariyesanā Sutta (*Majjhima Nikāya* [MN], 1995, 26: The Noble Search), the Buddha recounted his questioning of the purpose of his life engaging in earthly pursuits. He then reported that he understood the danger [of such activities involved in earthly pursuits, so] "I shaved off my hair and beard, put on the yellow robe and went forth from the home life into homelessness" (MN, 1995, 26.14). At the time, the questions that shaped most spiritual seekers' quest were essentially as follows: "Is the self eternal or finite? Is the self universal or individual? What is the permanent basis for the self?" (Pande, 2015). Another way to think about the Buddha's research question is this: "What was my self before I was born, and what will become of my self when this body of mine dies?"

It was a common practice for wanders on a spiritual quest to study under various renowned ascetics of the time, embarking on the practice of meditation for enlightenment. Think of it as similar to enrolling in a graduate program. The Buddha Gotama's quest took him to study under two well-known ascetics at that time, Āḷāra Kālāma and Uddaka Rāmaputta. The Buddha undertook his teachers' practices that were thought to cut through the superficial appearance of things to realize the ultimate nature of the self and reality, and thus bring about liberation. However, having practiced to the point of starvation, the Buddha observed, "but by this racking practice of austerities I have not attained any superhuman states, any distinction in knowledge and vision worthy of the noble ones. Could there be another path to enlightenment?" (MN, 1995, 36.30). Thus, the Buddha set out on his own path of practice with silent meditation and self-reflection. Buddha Gotama's study of the question of the nature of the self is summed up in the Brahmajāla Sutta (*Dīgha Nikāya* [DN], 1987/1995, 1: The All-Embracing Net).

The Buddha realized that the quest for the ultimate nature of the self and the world was, in the lexicon of social science research, unfalsifiable. No matter which positions one holds regarding the ultimate nature of the self, those positions are all based on speculation. During the Buddha's time, and even now, there is no known verifiable and repeatable method to travel to the beginning of time to answer the question: "What was my self before I was born?" Similarly, there is no known verifiable and repeatable method to answer the question: "What will become of my self when this body of mine dies?" Speculations about the origins of the self before birth and the fate of the self after the death of the body are just that—speculations; thus, they are not valid or fruitful research questions.

With this realization, the Buddha turned away from the quest for the nature of the self and turned toward a question that could be reliably verified: "What is the nature of the human experience of existence?" This question can be said to be the Buddha's research question. His result is, in the lexicon of Buddhism, the three marks of existence. The First Noble Truth answers that question ("What is the nature of the human experience of existence?"). The Second and Third Noble Truths are logical follow-ups to the First Noble Truth. The Fourth Noble Truth spells out the interventions in the form of the Noble Eightfold Path, which expands on with implications by providing intervention strategies. The Noble Eightfold Path can be thought of as the treatment methods.

The Three Marks of Existence

Based on his research, the Buddha concluded that there are three universal laws of existence, known as the three marks of existence (or, in the Pali dialect spoken by the Buddha, *tilakkhaṇa*). Again, these marks are like Thorndike's (1911) Laws of Behavior in General (p. 241). According to the Buddha, as stated in the *Dhammapada*: The Path (*Dhammapada* [Dhp], 1996, 277–279) of the *Khuddaka Nikāya*, these three marks or "laws" are as follows: all conditioned things are impermanent (*anicca*), all things are not-self (*anattā*), and all conditioned things are unsatisfactory (*dukkha*).

Aniccā is usually translated as "impermanence." The *Pali Text Society Pali–English Dictionary* offers the following definition of aniccā:

> unstable, impermanent, inconstant; evanescence, inconstancy, impermanence.—
> The emphatic assertion of impermanence (continuous change of condition) is a
> prominent axiom of the dhamma, & the realization of the evanescent character
> of all things mental or material is one of the primary conditions of attaining
> right knowledge. . . . In this import aniccā occurs in many combinations of
> similar terms, all characterizing change, its consequences & its meaning, esp.
> in the famous triad "aniccaŋ dukkhaŋ anattā." (Pali Text Society, n.d.)

Anattā is usually translated as "not-self" or "non-self." The *Pali Text Society Pali–English Dictionary* translates anattā as "not a soul, without a soul" (Pali Text Society, n.d.). Extensive exploration of this mark of existence will be discussed in Part III this book.

Dukkha is usually translated as "suffering" or "unsatisfactoriness." However, its full meaning is a bit more nuanced. The *Pali Text Society Pali–English Dictionary* defines dukkha as follows:

> (adj.) unpleasant, painful, causing misery (opp. sukha pleasant). . . . There is no
> word in English covering the same ground as Dukkha does in Pali. Our modern
> words are too specialized, too limited, and usually too strong. Sukha & dukkha
> are ease and dis-ease (but we use disease in another sense); or wealth and ilth?
> from well & ill (but we have now lost ilth); or wellbeing and ill-ness (but illness
> means something else in English). We are forced, therefore, in translation to use
> half synonyms, no one of which is exact. Dukkha is equally mental & physical.
> Pain is too predominantly physical, sorrow too exclusively mental, but in
> some connections they have to be used in default of any more exact rendering.
> Discomfort, suffering, ill, and trouble can occasionally be used in certain con-
> nections. Misery, distress, agony, affliction and woe are never right. They are all
> much too strong & are only mental. (Pali Text Society, n.d.)

For psychotherapy purposes, dukkha can be thought of as anything that a client complains about that is just not okay with the client, regardless of what that complaint may be.

The Four Noble Truths

Through not realizing the three marks of existence, we human beings come to experience the First Noble Truth. We long to experience the world as different than it is—so much so that we fail to see the three marks of existence. We perceive as permanent that which is impermanent, we perceive as satisfactory that which is unsatisfactory, and/or we perceive as self that which is not the self; as a result, we fail to perceive the reality as stated in the three marks of existence. This failure to perceive the truth of reality characterizes the human experience of existence, which is the First Noble Truth. Once the First Noble Truth is acknowledged, the other three Noble Truths follow logically. Subsequent chapters will elaborate on the categories within the Four Noble Truths as they fit with the findings of the three marks of existence. For now, we will briefly state the Noble Truths. Table 2.1 quotes Buddhist writings (*suttas*) from the *Nikāyas* relating to the Four Noble Truths.

- The First Noble Truth states that an untaught human's experience of existence has the characteristics of dukkha (Saccavibhaṅga Sutta; MN, 1995, 141: The Exposition of the Truths). In other words, someone who does not know the baetyl teachings of the Buddha Gotama (*dhamma*) will experience life as suffering. Someone who knows and practices the

TABLE 2.1. The Four Noble Truths

Truth	Excerpt from Buddhist writings
1. The human experience of existence primarily contains characteristics of suffering.	"And what, friends, is the noble truth of suffering? Birth is suffering; aging is suffering; death is suffering; sorrow, lamentation, pain, grief, and despair are suffering; not to obtain what one wants is suffering; in short, the five aggregates affected by clinging are suffering" (MN, 1995, 141.10).
2. The pursuit to satisfy one's craving leads to suffering.	"Now this, bhikkhus, is the noble truth of the origin of suffering: it is this craving which leads to renewed existence, accompanied by delight and lust, seeking delight here and there; that is, craving for sensual pleasures, craving for existence, craving for extermination" (SN, 2000, 56.11).
	"In this way too, headman, it can be understood: Whatever suffering arises, all that arises rooted in desire, with desire as its source; for desire is the root of suffering" (SN, 2000, 42.11).
3. Nonpursuit to satisfy one's craving lessens or eliminates suffering.	"Now this, bhikkhus, is the noble truth of the cessation of suffering: it is the remainderless fading away and cessation of that same craving, the giving up and relinquishing of it, freedom from it, nonreliance on it" (SN, 2000, 56.11).
4. The way to lessen or eliminate craving is to follow the Noble Eightfold Path.	"Now this, bhikkhus, is the noble truth of the way leading to the cessation of suffering: it is this Noble Eightfold Path" (SN, 2000, 56.11).

dhamma will likely experience happiness. This Noble Truth points to the emotional suffering people experience due to being in conflict with the three marks of existence.

- The Second Noble Truth states that the cause of suffering is craving (*taṇhā*; Dhammacakkappavattana Sutta, *Saṃyutta Nikāya* [SN], 2000, 56.11: Setting in Motion the Wheel of the Dhamma; Bhadraka Sutta, SN, 2000, 42.11). We crave pleasant experiences to be permanent and under our control as well as to be persistently enjoyable. Sadly, habituation to the pleasant leads to decreased enjoyableness of the pleasant. The loss of the enjoyableness of the pleasant pushes us to take action in pursuit of that lost enjoyableness. We desire for impermanent things, like relationships, to be permanent. We want our body to be as we think it should be, and we suffer when that body ages, becomes ill, looks different, or is a different gender or otherwise differs from our constructed view of ourselves. And we desire for there to be no unsatisfactory things, only satisfactory things. We crave for only pleasant things to experience; we crave to never experience unpleasant things; and we crave for our delusions of how the universe should be to be reality. We crave for the three marks of existence to be not true. In the Buddhist lexicon, we perceive as permanent that which is impermanent, we perceive as satisfactory that which is unsatisfactory, and/or we perceive as self that which is not the self. As a result, we fail to perceive the reality as stated in the three marks of existence.

- The Third Noble Truth states that there is a way to ameliorate, and for some to eliminate, the experience of dukkha, and that way is to lessen or eliminate craving (SN, 2000, 56.11). This is akin to telling a friend that they could escape their unhappiness by seeking the services of a psychotherapist for depression, anxiety, or other mental distress or issues.

- The Fourth Noble Truth states that the way to ameliorate suffering is through the Noble Eightfold Path (SN, 2000, 56.11), which aims at recognizing the truth of the three marks of existence. The methods are explicated as the Noble Eightfold Path, which includes the following: right concentration, right view, right intention, right speech, right action, right livelihood, right effort, and right mindfulness. Modern readers may interpret the term "right" in a moralistic way, so that right action and right speech, for instance, are the actions and speech that are morally correct. However, in Buddhism, the term right refers more to accuracy. Right action and right speech are consistent with and help us realize the truth of the three marks of existence. Table 2.2 quotes suttas relating to the

TABLE 2.2. The Noble Eightfold Path

Component	Excerpt from Buddhist writings
Right concentration	"Bhikkhus, there are these four developments of concentration. What four? (1) There is development of concentration that leads to dwelling happily in this very life. (2) There is a development of concentration that leads to obtaining knowledge and vision. (3) There is a development of concentration that leads to mindfulness and clear comprehension. (4) There is a development of concentration that leads to the destruction of the taints" (Samādhibhāvanā Sutta; *Aṅguttara Nikāya* [AN], 2012, 4.41).
Right view	"And what, friends, is right view? Knowledge of suffering, knowledge of the origin of suffering, knowledge of the cessation of suffering, and knowledge of the way leading to the cessation of suffering—this is called right view" (Saccavibhaṅga Sutta; MN, 1995, 141.24: The Exposition of the Truths).
Right intention	"And what, friends, is right intention? Intention of renunciation, intention of non-ill will, and intention of non-cruelty—this is called right intention" (MN, 1995, 141.25).
Right speech	"And what, friends, is right speech? Abstaining from false speech, abstaining from malicious speech, abstaining from harsh speech, and abstaining from idle chatter—this is called right speech" (MN, 1995, 141.26).
Right action	"And what, friends, is right action? Abstaining from killing living beings, abstaining from taking what is not given, and abstaining from misconduct in sensual pleasures—this is called right action" (MN, 1995, 141.27).
Right livelihood	"And what, friends, is right livelihood? Here a noble disciple, having abandoned wrong livelihood, earns his living by right livelihood—this is called right livelihood" (MN, 1995, 141.28).
Right effort	"And what, friends, is right effort? Here a bhikkhu awakens zeal for the non-arising of unarisen evil unwholesome states, and he makes effort, arouses energy, exerts his mind, and strives. He awakens zeal for the abandoning of arisen evil unwholesome states, and he makes effort, arouses energy, exerts his mind, and strives. He awakens zeal for the arising of unarisen wholesome states, and he makes effort, arouses energy, exerts his mind, and strives. He awakens zeal for the continuance, non-disappearance, strengthening, increase, and fulfillment by development of arisen wholesome states, and he makes effort, arouses energy, exerts his mind, and strives. This is called right effort" (MN, 1995, 141.29).
Right mindfulness	"And what, friends, is right mindfulness? Here a bhikkhu abides contemplating the body as a body, ardent, fully aware, and mindful, having put away covetousness and grief for the world. He abides contemplating feelings as feelings, ardent, fully aware, and mindful, having put away covetousness and grief for the world. He abides contemplating mind as mind, ardent, fully aware, and mindful, having put away covetousness and grief for the world. He abides contemplating mind-objects as mind-objects, ardent, fully aware, and mindful, having put away covetousness and grief for the world. This is called right mindfulness" (MN, 1995, 141.30).

Noble Eightfold Path. In the lexicon of psychology, the Noble Eightfold Path can be thought of as akin to treatment intervention. In the future, the mental health profession might consider using elements of the Noble Eightfold Path for the development of treatment programs, like using mindfulness for mindfulness-based stress reduction.

Interventions: The Noble Eightfold Path

The components of what the Buddha called the Noble Eightfold Path are designed for the realization of the three marks of existence. His interventions are aimed at helping us achieve embodied knowledge of the three marks of existence.

The eight paths can be divided into three broad categories, as shown in Figure 2.1. These categories are as follows:

- conduct (*sīla*)
- concentration, mind-training, or meditation (*samādhi*)
- wisdom (*paññā*)

The Pali word sīla is translated as "nature character habit behavior usually as [in] . . . 'being of such a nature' like having the character of . . . stingy" (Pali Text Society, n.d.). In the context of the Noble Eightfold Path, sīla refers to adopting the habit of engaging in ethical conduct in actions and behavior of the body, speech, and mind. Samādhi is translated as "concentration; a concentrated, self-collected, intent state of mind and meditation" (Pali Text Society, n.d.). Samādhi refers to the practice of meditation for training the mind to develop concentration. Secular mindfulness meditation is one type of concentration taught in Buddhism. The term paññā is translated as "wisdom endowed with knowledge or insight possessed of the highest cognition" (Pali Text Society, n.d.). Paññā refers to the insight and then the embodied knowledge one experiences from applying the teachings of Buddha; this is akin to the psychoeducation we use in psychotherapy. Conduct (sīla), concentration (samādhi), and wisdom (paññā) training are parallel tracks for engagement.

In the context of psychotherapy, think of conduct (sīla) as what we psychotherapists recommend to our clients. Concentration (samādhi) is what we do in our own practice in order to effectively use Buddhism-based interventions or (only if deemed appropriate) mindfulness meditation for the client. Finally, wisdom (paññā) is psychotherapists' reframing of clients' difficulties in the structure of Buddhist conceptualization of reality.

FIGURE 2.1. The Noble Eightfold Path

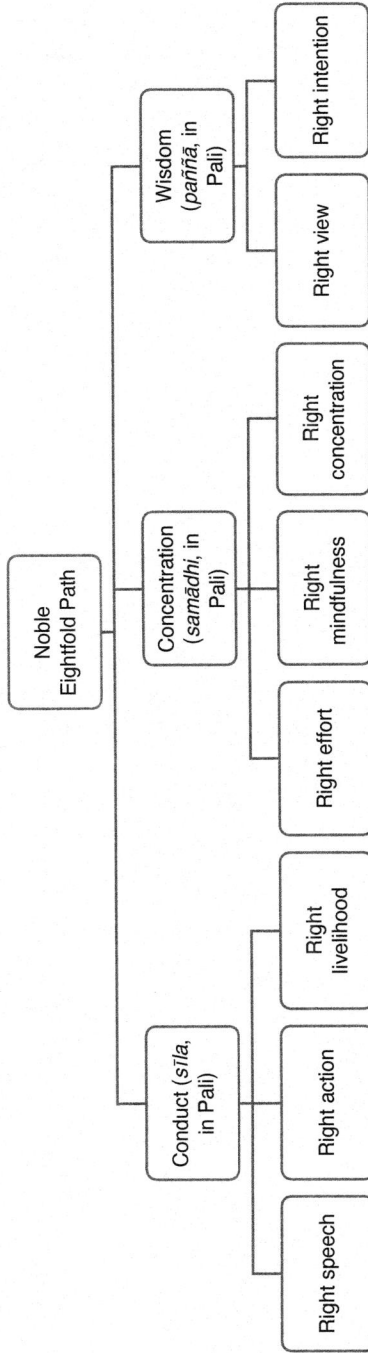

The First Noble Truth answers the question, "What is the experience of existence?" with "Dukkha." The Second Noble Truth gives the cause of dukkha (suffering, unsatisfactoriness) and explains how dukkha is constructed. The Third Noble Truth assures us that there is a remedy for dukkha. The Fourth Noble Truth gives the method for the elimination of dukkha. Think of an automobile mechanic who has a manual that provides exact details of how a car is constructed; when something goes wrong with the car's functioning, the mechanic can fix it by knowing how to deconstruct and then reconstruct the relevant dysfunctional part. The three marks of existence are akin to describing a fully functioning car, and the Fourth Noble Truth is like the manual of how the car is constructed. Within the Fourth Noble Truth is the Noble Eightfold Path. In Buddhist psychotherapy, the Noble Eightfold Path can be thought of as the Buddha's treatment program to intervene in the human experience of dukkha.

WHAT IS BUDDHIST PSYCHOTHERAPY?

Just as this book is intended for any psychotherapist, Buddhist psychotherapy can be used for any client—whether Buddhist or non-Buddhist. When we use the term *Buddhist psychotherapy*, we are referring to a theoretical orientation, which is an approach for understanding and addressing a client's difficulties from a Buddhist framework.

Buddhism, as well as Buddhist psychotherapy, seeks to help individuals see the three marks of existence. In Buddhist psychotherapy, the psychotherapist (a) listens to the client discuss their concerns; (b) identifies the nature of the client's difficulties; (c) reflects their understanding of the client's situation back to the client (ideally using the client's words and terminology, either with or without any reference to Buddhist teachings); and (d) helps the client use early Buddhist conceptualization, with or without reference to mindfulness or to Buddhism, to address the source of their difficulties. Importantly, the Buddhist framework for understanding a client's situation and their suffering is compatible with other religions and cultures. It does not rely on any specific belief about a deity, the creation of life, or an afterlife.

In general, the process for engaging clients in psychotherapy treatment is not unlike that for any other theory for psychotherapy. The three common arenas for health interventions are assessment, diagnosis, and treatment. For our purposes, the difference here is in the approach that Buddhist psychotherapy takes in each of the arenas of assessment, diagnoses, and treatment

FIGURE 2.2. Three Arenas of Buddhist Psychotherapy

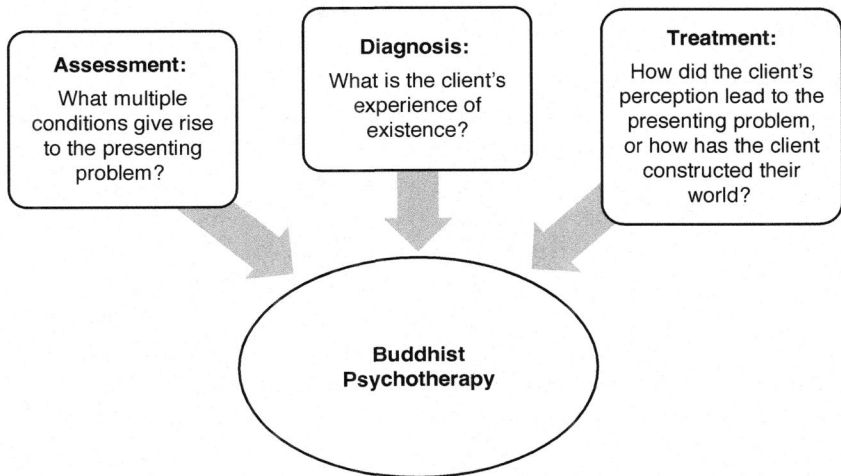

Assessment:

What multiple conditions give rise to the presenting problem?

Diagnosis:

What is the client's experience of existence?

Treatment:

How did the client's perception lead to the presenting problem, or how has the client constructed their world?

Buddhist Psychotherapy

(Figure 2.2). We will explore each arena in depth in later chapters. For now, we present the arenas briefly:

- **Assessment:** In this arena, we operationalize "all conditioned things are impermanent" (aniccā), one of the marks of existence. We ask and seek to answer this question: "What multiple conditions give rise to the presenting problem?" Buddhism teaches that multiple *conditions* contribute to our experience of reality. The Buddha Gotama refers to this as *dependent arising of phenomena in consciousness*. If a client is suffering, Buddhist psychotherapy seeks to determine the multiple internal and external conditions that led to the problematic situation. Which internal or external factors can be modified to result in less suffering? Think of assessment as an enactment of aniccā (all conditioned things are impermanent), the first mark of existence.

- **Diagnoses:** In this arena, we observe and note that "all conditioned things are unsatisfactory" (dukkha). We ask and seek to answer this question: "What is the client's experience of existence?" Buddhism teaches that a person's notion of self is constructed. We build our notion of ourselves from the functioning of the five aggregates plus the addition of clinging or craving (or *five aggregates subject to clinging*). If a client is suffering, Buddhist psychotherapy seeks to determine how the client has experienced a stimulus through their constructed notion of a self. How might an alternative notion of themselves, built from a different interpretation of their experience, result in less suffering? This involves listening for dukkha (all conditioned things are unsatisfactory) and then reframing the client's experience within the reality of the three marks of existence.

- **Treatment:** In this arena, "all things are not-self" (anattā). We ask and answer this question: "How did the client's perception lead to the presenting problem, or how has the client constructed their world?" Treatment interventions are aimed at deconstructing that notion of the self and then, for Buddhist psychotherapy, reconstructing to a more functional notion of the self. Buddhism teaches that our experience of existence is based on our construction of reality. There is an external stimulus (something we see, hear, touch, taste, or smell; or a thought), but our attention is what makes us aware of the stimulus, and our understanding of the stimulus through the constructed notion of a self is what we experience. The Buddha Gotama taught that there are five components, or five aggregates (*skandhas* in Pali), that together make up how a person experiences life. These five aggregates work together to construct a person's notion of a self through which they experience existence. If a client is suffering, Buddhist psychotherapy seeks to determine the functioning of the five aggregates at the moment that gave rise to the client's complaint. Buddhist psychotherapy sidesteps the constructed notion of the self through which the client experiences their painful or unpleasant reality. This is the enactment of anattā (all things are not-self).

Recall the three parallel tracks of the Noble Eightfold Path shown in Figure 2.1. We psychotherapists are engaged in all three parallel tracks with our clients. In terms of conduct (sīla), psychotherapists do make recommendations for what a client might do. The Buddha's recommendations for actions of body, speech, or mind (or all three) are so basic to civilized behavior that no major system of religion, philosophy, or ethics contradicts these recommendations, including those that are used for interventions in most major schools of psychotherapy. Almost all psychotherapy interventions are congruent with the prescribed ethical conduct in Buddhism.

If meditation or mindfulness techniques are used in psychotherapy, we are assisting our clients in the path of concentration or mind-training (samādhi). Additionally, when psychotherapists make in-session observations of a client's state of mind as the client engages in reports of their concerns, we are performing the same function as mindfulness. *Mindfulness* in the Buddhist lexicon is the awareness of what is occurring in the mind at that moment and in each and every moment of one's life; in Buddhist psychotherapy, the psychotherapist serves this function of mindfulness by stating that awareness to the client and facilitating the client's development of this awareness on their own. Think of Buddhist psychotherapy as essentially an enactment of mindfulness, with the psychotherapist taking on the same functions as mindfulness in their in-session dialogues with the client.

The paraphrasing and reframing done within psychotherapy imparts knowledge and falls within the realm of what Buddhism would consider wisdom (paññā). Wisdom, in the lexicon of Buddhism, is what psychotherapists do when clients' concerns are reframed within a worldview of a theoretical orientation.

HOW BUDDHIST PSYCHOTHERAPY DIFFERS FROM BUDDHISM THE RELIGION

Buddhist psychotherapy is not a religious practice or a branch of religious studies. Neither were the practices developed by the Buddha Gotama a religious practice. The Buddha Gotama developed the following early practices for an ascetic monastic community, as opposed to a religion. He proclaimed, in the Potaliya Sutta (MN, 1995, 54: With Potaliya the Householder), that in order to practice as he does, one is to engage in the following:

1. No killing of living beings
2. Taking only what is given
3. Truthful speech
4. Unmalicious speech
5. No rapacity and greed
6. No spite and scolding
7. No anger and irritation
8. No arrogance

Buddhism as a religion began to appear about 400 years after the Buddha's death. The transition (Warder, 2015) commenced with Emperor Aśoka. Aśoka was said to be a great warrior who conquered and united most of the Indian subcontinent. After the particularly bloody conquest of Kaliṇga, he was overwhelmed by the carnage before him. It was at this point that he met a Buddhist ascetic, gave up conquest by arms, and began his own Buddhist practice. Emperor Aśoka's laws of the land were proclaimed throughout his empire on stone pillars, called *Aśokan pillars*. Engraved on them were his laws. Many of these laws were Buddhist ideas, such as the message of nonharming.

Emperor Aśoka also dismantled the original burial mound that contained the remains of the Buddha. He then took "the relics of the Buddha . . .

divided into 84,000 parts and built as many pagodas as possible in order to distribute them all over his empire" (Warder, 2015, p. 257), to be enshrined in burial mounds (*stupas*). He employed people for upkeep of these stupas. Buddhist scholars think that over time, the interactions between the keepers of the stupas and the lay people who visited them developed traditions that ultimately evolved into the Buddhist religion. Emperor Aśoka also instituted a practice of conquest by ideas, instead of arms, by sending out Buddhist emissaries to bordering countries. Thus, the practice and the religion of Buddhism spread.

Buddhist psychotherapy does not contain those items of religious worship developed during and after the reign of Emperor Aśoka. A psychotherapist who uses Buddhist psychotherapy as their theoretical orientation may or may not identify as a member of the Buddhist religion. A psychotherapist can practice Buddhist psychotherapy without being a Buddhist, or they also could be a Buddhist. Essentially, there is a boundary between the practices of Buddhism as a religion and the therapeutic use of Buddhist psychotherapy as a theory of psychotherapy.

Similarly, Buddhist psychotherapy does not ask or expect the reader or anyone who chooses to use the ideas of the Buddha Gotama in psychotherapy to adopt or follow the ascetic practices listed earlier. Nor does it require anyone to practice meditation as described in the religion of Buddhism. However, we strongly recommend that mental health practitioners have their own meditation practice to enable an elementary level of embodied knowledge for the meditation approach explicated in the Satipaṭṭhāna Sutta (MN, 1995, 10: The Foundations of Mindfulness). Instead, Buddhist psychotherapy uses the framework and techniques from early Buddhism in the service of providing psychotherapy.

Buddhist psychotherapy provides a theory, which, in part, provides a broader rationale behind mindfulness meditation, as used in today's secular mindfulness movement and various mindfulness-based treatment programs. The expectation is that having been introduced to the theory underlying mindfulness meditation, the mental health practitioner will be much more sophisticated and nuanced in the therapeutic use of mindfulness meditation. Ultimately, the ideas from early Buddhism will deepen the practitioner's therapy skills. Additionally, unlike Buddhism, Buddhist psychotherapy does not aim for total liberation from dukkha. Buddhist psychotherapy aims for a sufficient reduction in the client's level of dysfunction to enable them to engage in a fruitful life; it is hoped that alongside the reduction of suffering is the increase in joy and satisfaction.

HOW SUBSEQUENT CHAPTERS WILL ADDRESS THE THREE MARKS OF EXISTENCE, THE FOUR NOBLE TRUTHS, AND THE NOBLE EIGHTFOLD PATH

The Introduction provided a brief overview of how subsequent parts of this book cover the three marks of existence. Here, we look at how specific chapters relate to different aspects of Buddhism, as laid out in this chapter, including the Four Noble Truths and the Noble Eightfold Path.

Part I (Chapters 1 and 2) consists of background chapters to offer further context on the historical Buddha and early Buddhist texts, as well as explanations of some fundamental differences between Buddhism and the Western scientific method.

Part II (Chapter 3) covers impermanence (anicca). This chapter discusses the Buddhist concept of impermanence, how it is structured, and how it most likely manifests in psychotherapy. We will offer a system for operationalization of how to assess and use this concept in psychotherapy.

Part III (Chapters 4–6) covers the not-self (anattā). The chapters start with a presentation of the Buddhist explanations of how human interpretation of stimuli (āyatana in Pali) work and interact with the universe. The parts of a human that are involved in interactions with the environment (i.e., the five aggregates) will be listed and then defined. From there, we address how craving constructs a notion of a self (the five aggregates subject to clinging) and leads to misperceiving reality. It is the experiencing through the notion of a self, the misperceiving of anicca and anatta, that sets the stage for dukkha.

Part IV (Chapters 7–12) covers dukkha. Part IV is an extensive exploration of the First Noble Truth and links two of the three marks of existence, not-self (anattā) and suffering or unsatisfactoriness (dukkha), because they are inextricably bound together. We cover the four types of suffering, what they may look like in psychotherapy, and how they manifest in the mind culture, all of which only prevent people from seeing reality clearly. These chapters explore how suffering manifests as a result of the misperceptions born out of experiencing stimuli through the notion of a self, which is the Second Noble Truth. Included in these chapters are instructions on the development of concentration and mindfulness as methods for handling dukkha, as well as how psychotherapists might use Buddhist teachings to address each type of suffering with clients.

Finally, Part V (Chapters 13–18) addresses the Fourth Noble Truth and the Noble Eightfold Noble Path, the Buddha's treatment interventions and treatment manual for dukkha, respectively. These chapters focus on clinical implications, including how to assess for the cause of clients' suffering as well as how to employ the three parallel tracks of the Noble Eightfold Path (conduct, concentration or mindfulness, and wisdom) in therapy. This section also revisits the model of three arenas for intervention in Buddhist psychotherapy and provides case studies. Finally, we conclude with an Afterword with a brief summary that includes a simile for psychotherapy and considers future directions for Buddhist psychotherapy.

PART **II** IMPERMANENCE

3 IMPERMANENCE

Having introduced the Buddha Gotama and set the context for his teachings, we now direct our attention to the essentials of his teachings that are of relevance to psychotherapy. As mentioned previously, the Buddha, in the lexicon of psychology, undertook a research study that asked this question: "What is the human experience of existence?" The most concise statement of his results, in the lexicon of Buddhism, is the three marks of existence. They are stated in the form of laws in the same sense as used by Thorndike (1911) in his Laws of Behavior in General (p. 241). The three marks of existence, as described in the *Dhammapada* (Dpn; 1996, 277–279: The Path) of the *Khuddaka Nikāya*, are as follows:

- All conditioned things are impermanent (*aniccā*).
- All conditioned things are unsatisfactory (*dukkha*).
- All things are not-self (*anattā*).

In this chapter, we engage in a more detailed examination of aniccā.

https://doi.org/10.1037/0000453-004
Buddhist Psychotherapy: Connecting Early Buddhism to Mindfulness and Western Psychotherapy, by L. Tien, D. M. Kawahara, and V. Dhammadinna

OBJECTIVITY AND SUBJECTIVITY VERSUS INTERNALITY AND EXTERNALITY

To prepare for examination of Buddhist ideas, it is worthwhile to discuss one concept mentioned in the Buddha's teachings but not expounded on by him. At times, some items within a culture are of such common understanding, there is seemingly no need for exposition. However, as is the nature of translating ideas across cultures, some ideas may lead to confusion and erroneous conclusions if taken without some explanation. The concepts of objectivity and subjectivity versus internality and externality are one such example: Objectivity and subjectivity are basic ideas in the Western scientific method. Internality and externality are basic ideas in Buddhism but are not the same as objectivity and subjectivity.

Within the Western scientific method, one fundamental bifurcation is subjective versus objective information. The term *objective* is defined as "dealing with facts or conditions as perceived without distortion of personal feelings, prejudices or interpretations . . . independent of individual thought and perceptible by all observers . . . having reality independent of the mind" (Merriam-Webster, n.d.). The term *subjective* is defined as "characteristic of or belonging to reality as perceived rather than as independent of mind . . . arising from conditions within the brain or sense organs and not directly caused by external stimuli . . . lacking in reality or substance" (Merriam-Webster, n.d.). Objective things can be measured independently of how the observer thinks or feels about them; subjective things depend on how the observer thinks or feels about them, thus lacking in reality. The scientific method considers observable objective information as a legitimate source of evidence. However, many serious philosophical strands of inquiry have argued about the standard of objectivity as evidence of truth, fact, or reality. Some question whether there is such a thing as objective facts, while others question whether subjective claims can be considered as facts.

In Buddhism, the bifurcation is not subjective versus objective, but internal versus external. The term *internal* refers to the sense bases, which are six elements within the human body that are involved in the experience of existence. The term *external* refers to the sense objects, which are those items existing in the universe that are detectable by the six internal sense bases. Items considered internal and external in Buddhism do not correspond to what would be considered subjective and objective in the scientific method. The distinction between subjective and objective is somewhat meaningless in Buddhism because all objects in themselves (*noumena*) are first contacted by one of the six sense bases and then processed through the mind; thus, nothing in the realm of human experience is objective as defined by the Western scientific method. The nature of human experience is "a process of interaction between the internal sense-faculties and the external sense-objects" (Karunadasa, 2015a, p. 59). The stimulus for an experience can be internal (e.g., a thought) or external (e.g., the sound of someone speaking). Human experiences are not objective or subjective—rather, they are only stimulated internally or externally, both of which are then processed internally. Everything experienced is a representation; thus, there is no human experience that can be considered objective as defined in the Western scientific method.

To consider the universe and objects in the universe in terms of objectivity or subjectivity does not reflect the actuality of psychotherapy. Psychotherapy is an interactive activity between people, most often carried on in the medium of spoken words. It is understood that these interactions are based on the verbal representation of the phenomena within each person and occurring between the psychotherapist and the client. This distinction between internality and externality—and how internal sense bases interact with external sense objects—is often referred to in Buddhism and will be used extensively in the concepts discussed in Buddhism.

Having clarified that Buddhism considers all human experience as subjective in the Western scientific method, the distinction is between internal or external stimulation. Regardless of where the stimuli originates, all items are processed internally and thus a representation of noumena. With that distinction in mind, we now return to an examination of anicca (impermanence) its meaning, and its possible use in psychotherapy.

IMPERMANENCE (*ANICCĀ*)

The mark of existence that all conditioned things are impermanent is summed up in one word: *aniccā*. There are two ideas in that one phrase: "conditioned things" and "impermanent." We will define and describe the concepts of conditioned things and impermanence, provide the Buddha's analysis of aniccā, and then conclude with a discussion of its application to Western psychology and how it may be used in psychotherapeutic intervention.

The first concept, *conditioned things*, essentially says that things exist in dependence on something else. The human experience of existence is, at a minimum, dependent on the functioning of the body's sense bases. At the most basic level, we do not interact with the universe without the medium of the six internal sense bases (*āyatana* in Pali), the processing functions of the mind (the concept of *citta*), and a stimulus. At a complex society level, we are influenced by and are an influence on our social environment. At the level of survival, humans live in dependence on goods and services provided by other humans and the natural environment. Occurrences in the mind— thinking, noting, a train of thought, emotions, and so on—take place in conjunction with and dependent on one's environmental and social contexts. For example, seasonal affective disorder is dependent on the condition of the seasons and manifests in a person's psychological state; generalized anxiety disorder is usually dependent on one's social condition and manifests in the soma with a combination of headaches, stomachaches, and aches and pains in various parts of the body. That is, humans' lived experience is conditioned. What we experience is an amalgamation of many events internally and externally; that is, humans are embodied beings living a conditioned existence.

In regard to the second concept, anicca̅ is defined as "unstable, impermanent, inconstant; evanescence, inconstancy, impermanence" (Pali Text Society, n.d.) and is usually simply translated as *impermanence*. A more colloquial English term that is equivalent in concept to impermanence is *change*. The Buddha observed that a characteristic of our lived experience is that of change. Our bodies change, maturing from infancy through adulthood to old age and death. The situations of our lives change from the dependency of childhood to independent living in adulthood, from study to work, from childhood to child-rearing, and from employment to retirement. Not only do our environmental situations change, but the environment of the mind changes even faster. We go from restfulness after a full night of sleep to preoccupation with our ever-present to-do list. Our environment of the mind changes even more quickly and constantly. The Buddha observed that these changes do not occur without rhyme or reason. He saw a pattern in the changes. This pattern is articulated in his formulation of dependent origination, as described next. Sections of this formulation are used in Buddhist psychotherapy.

DEPENDENT ORIGINATION (*PAṬICCASAMUPPĀDA*) AND DEPENDENT ARISING

The Buddha observed that a characteristic of our lived experience is that of continuous change. The Buddha observed and articulated the pattern of this change as follows:

When this exists, that comes to be;
with the arising of this, that arises.
When this does not exist, that does not come to be,
with the cessation of this, that ceases to be. (*Saṃyutta Nikāya* [SN], 2000,
12.21.1)

This formulation of the way that change occurs and the specific pattern and
the sequencing of the change are usually referred to as *dependent origination*
(*paṭiccasamuppāda* in Pali), also sometimes referred to synonymously as
dependent arising. Sections of dependent origination give us a formulation
of the change in such a manner that can be used in psychotherapy. To distinguish the section that is relevant for psychotherapy, the term dependent
arising will be used in this book.

Dependent arising predicts the inevitability of circumstances changing as
situations evolve. Implicit in dependent arising is impermanence (anicca).
The formulation has two parts: One addresses the conditions for the emergence of a situation, whereas the other addresses the conditions for the dis-
appearances of that situation. For the purposes of psychotherapy, for "when
this exists, that comes to be," think of beginnings; for "with the cessation
of this, that ceases to be," think of endings (SN, 2000, 12.21.1). There is no
ending without a beginning, and there is no beginning without an ending.
Some examples are the dysregulation from divorce (e.g., the ending of a
marriage and the subsequent divorce are dependent on getting married, for
no one who is unmarried goes through a divorce) or the despondency of losing
a wage-earning job (e.g., the ending of a job depends on applying for that
job in the first place).

The sutta's formulation is further analyzed and elaborated on in the
Theravāda Abhidhamma's principle of *paṭṭhānanaya*, which is the Pali term
for "conditional relations or causal relationships":

- Nothing arises without the conditions necessary for its arising.
- Nothing arises from a single cause.
- Nothing arises as a single effect, as a solitary phenomenon.
- From a plurality of conditions arises a plurality of effects. (Karunadasa,
  2015b, p. 276)

This further elaboration is a more detailed delineation of the pattern of
change. This conceptualization of the pattern in how situations emerge and
change is familiar in the mental health field. For example, multiple factors have
been proposed to cause depression, including "genetic, biological, environmental, and psychological factors" (National Institute of Mental Health, n.d.,

What is depression?). There is not a 1:1 correlation between one causal factor and depression. Instead, multiple factors contribute to the arising of depression in a person. In other words, "nothing arises from a single cause" (Karunadasa, 2015b, p. 276). Buddhist psychotherapy guides us to look for the multiple conditions that necessarily must be functioning for the client's situation to exist. It also guides us to look across all of those conditions to choose, in collaboration with the client, some conditions to eliminate, because dependent arising tells us that "with the cessation of this, that ceases to be" (SN, 2000, 12.21.1). This concept means that disrupting those conditions will weaken the structure and allow for the difficult condition to cease to be.

Additionally, the Theravāda Abhidhamma further describes the principle of paṭṭhānanaya, or conditional relations or causal relationships. It states, "Nothing arises as a single effect, as a solitary phenomenon" (Karunadasa, 2015b, p. 276). This principle, too, is familiar to mental health practitioners. With depression, individuals may experience the following:

> persistent sad, anxious, or "empty" mood; feelings of hopelessness, or pessimism; feelings of irritability, frustration, or restlessness; feelings of guilt, worthlessness, or helplessness; loss of interest or pleasure in hobbies and activities; decreased energy, fatigue, or feeling "slowed down"; difficulty concentrating, remembering, or making decisions; difficulty sleeping, early morning awakening, or oversleeping; changes in appetite or unplanned weight changes; thoughts of death or suicide, or suicide attempts; aches or pains, headaches, cramps, or digestive problems without a clear physical cause that do not ease even with treatment; suicide attempts or thoughts of death or suicide. (National Institute of Mental Health, n.d.)

In other words, "Nothing arises as a single effect, as a solitary phenomenon. From a plurality of conditions arises a plurality of effects" (Karunadasa, 2015b, p. 276).

Dependent arising also tells us that the confluence of all these conditions is unstable, and that situations will change. Situations are like building castles out of sand: When we build those castles and expect them to last forever, regardless of whether the castle is pleasant and appealing or unpleasant and ugly, we are bound to be disappointed. Implicit, and embedded within dependent arising, is anicca (impermanence, transitory). For good and for bad, things do change. When an unpleasant situation stops, the change is welcomed and experienced as a happy occurrence. When situations change from pleasant to unpleasant, we are unsettled, disoriented, and suffer. This reaction to the change is dukkha (unpleasant, painful, causing misery, unsatisfactoriness). People do not usually seek out psychotherapy to address pleasant changes. Therefore, the Buddhist theory for psychotherapy may cursorily mention, but will not focus on, those pleasant changes that are also experienced in the human lived experience of existence.

OPERATIONALIZATION OF CONDITIONS

Many psychotherapy clients come to treatment attributing their problem to a single cause (e.g., "I am depressed because my spouse asked for a divorce"). Not everyone whose spouse asks for a divorce experiences depression—there must be a plurality of conditions specific to this person at this specific point in time that conditions this person to experience depression. The request for a divorce is but one of the conditions. The Theravāda Abhidhamma formulation indicates that many conditions need to be in place for a situation to occur. Beyond the idea that many conditions need to occur for an experience to arise, Buddhism does not go further. Although Buddhism is exquisitely attentive to the internal mental culture, it is not as focused on the contextual situation of human existence. To operationalize the conditions referred to in the idea of dependent arising, we borrow from other areas of social science. One framework is Bronfenbrenner's ecological systems theory, and another is the concept of social positionality. These two models contextualize the idea of conditions in the social and cultural settings within which the individual lives. These two models provide further context (or in the Buddhist lexicon, *conditions*) to the understanding of the client's world. They enhance the psychotherapist's conceptualization of the multifaceted universe that conditions the client's lived experience. It is beyond the scope of this volume to present these models in detail, and the authors assume that readers are familiar with these frameworks. Please refer to Bolton and Gillett (2019) for more on the biopsychosocial model; to Gabel (2023) for more on social identities, positionality, and intersectionality; and to Bronfenbrenner and Ceci (1994), Bronfenbrenner and Evans (2000), and Bronfenbrenner and Morris (2006) for a review of Bronfenbrenner's ecological systems theory and proximal processes.

OPERATIONALIZATION OF IMPERMANENCE

The Theravāda Abhidhamma theory of momentariness is a more detailed analysis of aniccā (impermanence). *Momentariness* posits that a phenomenon in consciousness arises and passes away from moment-to-moment dependence on conditions. The culture of a client's mind that gave rise to their discomfort, pain, or presenting complaint (or all three) is a dependently arising phenomenon in consciousness that is subject to impermanence (anicca). This application of impermanence directs the psychotherapist to conduct an analysis of momentary conditions.

The goal of the aforementioned analysis is to fully understand the conditions occurring at any given moment. For the practice of Buddhism, it is immaterial which moment is examined because all elements are at play in every moment of the human experience. However, for psychotherapy, not all moments of a person's life are equivalent. Clients seek assistance regarding a specific problem, which is usually identified in their presenting complaint. It is thus appropriate to engage in an analysis of the pivotal moment in the critical incident that gave rise to the client's awareness of their presenting complaint and to conduct a more detailed exploration of the moment when the client's presenting problem last occurred. This approach differs from searching for the first remembered moment, usually in childhood, when the client felt the uncomfortable emotion. Seeking the first moment when the client remembers experiencing their presenting problem is akin to seeking the origin or genesis of their presenting problem. Seeking origins will most likely take the in-session conversation to the client's remembered childhood experiences.

In Buddhist psychotherapy, the psychotherapist would inquire for the most recent moment, and specifically for the last time the client became aware of their presenting complaint. This awareness may be a thought, a painful feeling, a physical pain, or any other form of discomfort. Seeking the last time (not the first time) the client's presenting problem occurred will hopefully take the conversation to the present moment in the treatment room or to a relatively recent situation. Based on the identified most recent moment, the psychotherapist would then inquire for the sense contact that precipitated the discomfort. The psychotherapist's sentence prompt may sound something like this: "When was the last time you noticed this problem?" or "When was the last time you noticed the absence of this problem?" For example, for clients presenting with anxiety, the psychotherapist might ask: "When was the last time you felt anxious? What was the situation?" If the client cannot answer these questions, the psychotherapist could follow with: "Did you wake up feeling anxious, or did the anxious feeling appear sometime after you first woke up this morning?" From the sense contact of that moment, then the psychotherapist and the client would coconstruct a full understanding of the conditions that were present at the moment of that sense contact.

CLINICAL APPLICATION

Many clients come to treatment dealing with either the beginnings of something bad or unpleasant or the ending of something good or pleasant. With every ending, there is embedded in the person's way of coping with that ending the seed of a beginning for the next phase in their life. This small beginning often goes unnoticed by the client; look for it, notice it, and point it out to the client. Doing so is not the same as trying to intentionally figure out what to do to cope with an ending. Rather, it involves paying careful attention to how the client is shifting and shifting in such a way that they are slowly, almost imperceptibly, shifting into something new.

In the mechanics of this change, if we, as psychotherapists, look for ways to destabilize the conditions, then we hasten and possibly influence the direction of the change. While the client lives in their experience of permanence, we can consider and approach the situation with a mindset of impermanence—looking for ways to disrupt the conditions that allow for the arising of the client's problem. We can work with our psychotherapy clients to choose the most easily removed element or condition in their life, which in turn would disrupt the confluence of conditions that give rise to their difficulties because so many elements cannot stay static for any length of time. For example, it is not uncommon for a psychotherapist to recommend some form of physical exercise to the client who is experiencing symptoms of depression. It is much easier to intervene at the physical level than at the cognitive level; thus, the recommendation to exercise is one approach to alter the conditions and increase the ways a client can manage their depression. The confluence of all factors is bound to change and collapse. Situations are impermanent.

To fully comprehend a moment in consciousness (*citta*) that has arisen dependently, the conditions that nourished such an arising need to be enumerated and fully understood. Therefore, examine the conditions closely; discuss these conditions with the client. In the knowing of their conditions, the client will gain a measure of emotional distance and some ability to analyze their own situation, instead of being stuck in the emotional experience of the situation.

The reality of constant change is evident in the uncontrollable intrusion of different thoughts as the meditator tries to focus on the object of contemplation, which is usually the breath. In its extension to everyday experience, there are the constant changes in our experience of living. We change from feeling hunger at the beginning of a meal to fullness at the end of a meal and from experiencing thirst to satiation after drinking. Knowing this viscerally, experientially, will buffer one against the elations of pleasant situations and the depression of unpleasant situations and enable the psychotherapist to recognize such changes as they present in clients in the treatment room.

EMBODIED KNOWING

To truly understand impermanence, psychotherapists are encouraged to engage in their own meditation practice. Buddhist practice is experiential, aiming for that embodied knowledge. As noted by Bodhi (2016), "The Buddha does what he can by pointing out the path to liberation; the rest involves putting the path into practice" (p. 63). When engaging in silent meditation, the first thing a beginner meditator notices is change. By noticing change, the psychotherapist will experience for themselves the direct encounter with impermanence; by turning their attention inward through the act of silent meditation, it will aid in their ability to notice the incidences of when a client rejects impermanence.

CONCLUSION

The human experience of existence is one of change. Situations and our lived experiences, both internally and externally, arise depending on the confluence of multiple conditions, and these conditions are always changing. The Buddha elaborated on this idea through the conceptualization of dependent arising. In simplistic terms, dependent arising says that any given situation depends on multiple factors coexisting in a particular configuration. When the elements in the configuration change, which they are bound to do, then we humans experience impermanence (anicca).

In psychotherapy, our clients come to session talking about their experience of some unpleasant state, immersed in the sureness that it is permanent— that this moment will go on forever, like their panic attack will never end or their depression will always be there. The takeaway here is for the therapist to know that the client's state (or situation or state of mind) is impermanent. Our work as psychotherapists can facilitate the destabilization of those factors more rapidly and hopefully influence the direction that leads to changing a client's situation.

PART **III** NOT-SELF

4

THE FIVE AGGREGATES

Component Parts of How Humans Experience Existence

As we noted in the Introduction of this book, the Buddha Gotama posited that there are three marks of the human experience of existence: All conditioned things are impermanent, all conditioned things are unsatisfactory, and all things are not-self (*Dhammapada* [Dhp], 1996, 277–279: The Path). Before we can understand the rationale behind the marks of all conditioned things are unsatisfactory and all things are not-self, we need to consider how people experience existence—that is, the mechanism involved in the process of experiencing itself. Thus, Buddhism enumerates the items that must be present for the experience to occur.

Think of life as a road trip in a car. One experience, or one moment in the experience of existence, is akin to a specific car stopping at a particular gas station during one road trip. While many things arrive simultaneously (e.g., the driver, possible passengers, cargo, and all parts of the car), each entity is distinct. Each entity can be listed for the moment that specific car arrives at a particular gas station. Likewise, entities that enable a person's experience of existence in any distinct moment in time can also be listed.

https://doi.org/10.1037/0000453-005
Buddhist Psychotherapy: Connecting Early Buddhism to Mindfulness and Western Psychotherapy, by L. Tien, D. M. Kawahara, and V. Dhammadinna

In the Paññati Pañha (*Milindapañha* [Mil], 1890, 3.1.1: The Chariot Simile), the monk Nāgasena compares the self to a chariot. To update this metaphor for the 21st century, the notion of a self can be likened to the concept of a car. Using the car analogy, this chapter provides an overview of the parts needed to construct a car and then describes each part in greater detail. The Buddhist conceptualization of the list of car parts is mentality-materiality (*nāmarūpa*) plus consciousness (*viññāna*). How the car parts work together is the topic of the next chapter.

A PERSON DEFINED: MENTALITY-MATERIALITY PLUS CONSCIOUSNESS

One of the three marks of existence states that all conditioned things are not-self. The concept of a self (*attā* in Pali) is different from the concept of a person (*puggala*; Pali Text Society, n.d.). A person, conceptualized in Buddhism as mentality-materiality (nāmarūpa) plus consciousness (viññāna), exists in the universe. The self (*attā*), as conceptualized in Buddhism, is a mental construct, while existing in the person's world does not exist in the universe. The construction of the notion of a self is taken up in much greater detail in later chapters.

On the topic of a person, Buddhism starts with some self-evident observations. First, it is observed that there is matter that is external to and autonomous from humans. This philosophical debate has occupied many thinkers through the ages. Theravāda Buddhism believes firmly that there are things in the universe that are external to and autonomous from a person's experience. Taking this stance implies, for therapists, that regardless of what a client reports as their experience, there is a reality that is external and independent of the client's experience of that event. This stance gives therapists a measure of theoretical assurance that a client's perception and experience are not the only valid way to consider a situation. The importance of this assertion for psychotherapy is that regardless of what the client thinks is going on around them, things do occur that are independent of the client: This means there is a reality that exists in its own right. The reality that there are things that are autonomous from the person's experiences counters their experienced reality—which is, experientially speaking, "I am the center of the universe, and things occur relative to and in relation to me." In other words, this is the manifestation of the ever-present unarticulated primary narcissism.

In congruence with the stance that there is a universe that is external to and autonomous from a person's experience, Buddhism makes another self-evident observation: Humans are composed of the same material base elements as the material of the universe. This means that humans share the same features as the basic elements of the universe (e.g., oxygen, carbon, hydrogen, nitrogen, and calcium) as well as characteristics found in nature and named in the sutta (e.g., solidity, temperature, coherence, and fluidity). Additionally, because we are composed of the same material elements, we humans share the same fate as other animals around us. This stance is the basis of meditation that takes the breath as its object of contemplation. For example, the Satipaṭṭhāna Sutta (*Majjhima Nikāya* [MN], 1995, 10.5.12: The Foundations of Mindfulness) gave instructions for meditation on this observation by saying:

> Again, bhikkhus, a bhikkhu reviews this same body, however it is placed, however disposed, as consisting of elements thus: 'In this body there are the earth element, the water element, the fire element, and the air element.'. . . Just as though a skilled butcher or his apprentice had killed a cow and was seated at the crossroads with it cut up into pieces; so too, a bhikkhu reviews this same body. . . . In this way he abides contemplating the body as a body.

Humans experience existence from and through their own body; that is, ours is an embodied existence. Buddhism is especially concerned with analyzing those parts and processes that, when taken together, are a person and their experience of existence. The Buddha referred to several conceptual frameworks for a person versus a self. Of those parts that are relevant to a person's experience of existence, the conceptual framework for a person is mentality-materiality (nāmarūpa) plus consciousness (viññāna). The formulation for this is given in the Naḷakalāpī Sutta (*Saṃyutta Nikāya* [SN], 2000, 12.67: Two Sheaves of Reeds), where Venerable Mahākoṭṭhita asked Venerable Sāriputta the following:

> How is it, friend Sāriputta: Is birth . . . Is existence . . . created by oneself, or is it created by another, or is it created both by oneself and by another, or has it arisen fortuitously, being created neither by oneself nor by another?

Venerable Mahākoṭṭhita, in the lexicon of the sutta, was asking whether humans come to be and exist through some divine intervention, like god or Brahmā, or whether humans are born and exist solely based on the material of the universe without some type of divine intervention. The Venerable Sāriputta answered with a simile:

> Just as two sheaves of reeds might stand leaning against each other, so too, with name-and-form (Nāmarūpa) as condition, consciousness (viññāna) [comes to be]; with consciousness as condition, name-and-form [comes to be]. With name-and-form as condition, the six sense bases [come to be]; with the six sense bases as condition, contact. (SN, 2000, 12.67; Pali words added)

This simile rejects the stance of materialism, in which the self arises at birth and ceases at the demise of the body. The simile also rejects theism, where the self is created by another such as god or Brahmā. Nor is human existence a cocreation of god and humans, nor serendipity from the elements that compose life on earth. Venerable Śāriputta gave a conceptualization of a person as dependently arising, mutually dependent on mentality-materiality (nāmarūpa) and consciousness (viññāna).

The conceptual framework for a person is the mutual coarising of mentality-materiality (nāmarūpa) and consciousness (viññāna), as shown in Figure 4.1. This framework specifies all of the parts that comprise the conceptual formulation of mentality-materiality and consciousness. Nāmarūpa is a compound Pali word: *Nāma* has been variously translated as "mind," "name," and "mentality," and *rūpa* has been translated as "form," "body," and "materiality." Some have translated this compound word as "mind-body," "mind and body," or "materiality-mentality." The concept of nāmarūpa is not quite the same as any of these translations. The complexity of translating the terms nāma and rūpa separately is reflected in the following definitions:

[*Rūpa* is defined as] form, figure, appearance, principle of form, . . . better (philosophical) terms "matter," "material quality" are recommended . . . as the representative of sensory or material existence: (a) universally as forming the corporeal stratum in the world of appearance or form . . . as compared with the incorporeal . . . where in contrast with *nāma* (as abstract, logical, invisible or mind-factor) *rūpa* represents the visible (material) factor.

[*Nāma* is defined as] to give a name . . . to call by name, to enumerate . . . as metaphysical term is opposed to *rūpa*, and comprises the four immaterial factors of an individual (vedanā saññā sankhārā viññāna; see khandhā). (Pali Text Society, n.d.)

The combined word, nāmarūpa, is translated as "individuality, individual being. . . . These two are inseparable . . . Nāma+rūpa form an elementary pair" (Pali Text Society, n.d.). There is no comparable concept of nāmarūpa in English. Compound words often connote a completely different concept from the parts of the word. For example, when the English word "scarecrow" is dissected into its component words "scare" and "crow," the result is not an inanimate object in the shape of a person with straw stuffed into human clothing. Likewise, a person, conceptualized in the formulation of nāmarūpa, cannot be dissected into its individual component words of "mind" and "body" or "mentality" and "materiality." Nāmarūpa is more akin to the strands of the double helix of DNA. Each side of the double helix strand is different, and the strands function together; neither exists nor functions without the other. Karunadasa (2015a) referred to nāmarūpa as a psychosomatic complex of mentality and materiality. For the sake of simplicity and referencing,

FIGURE 4.1. Conceptual Form

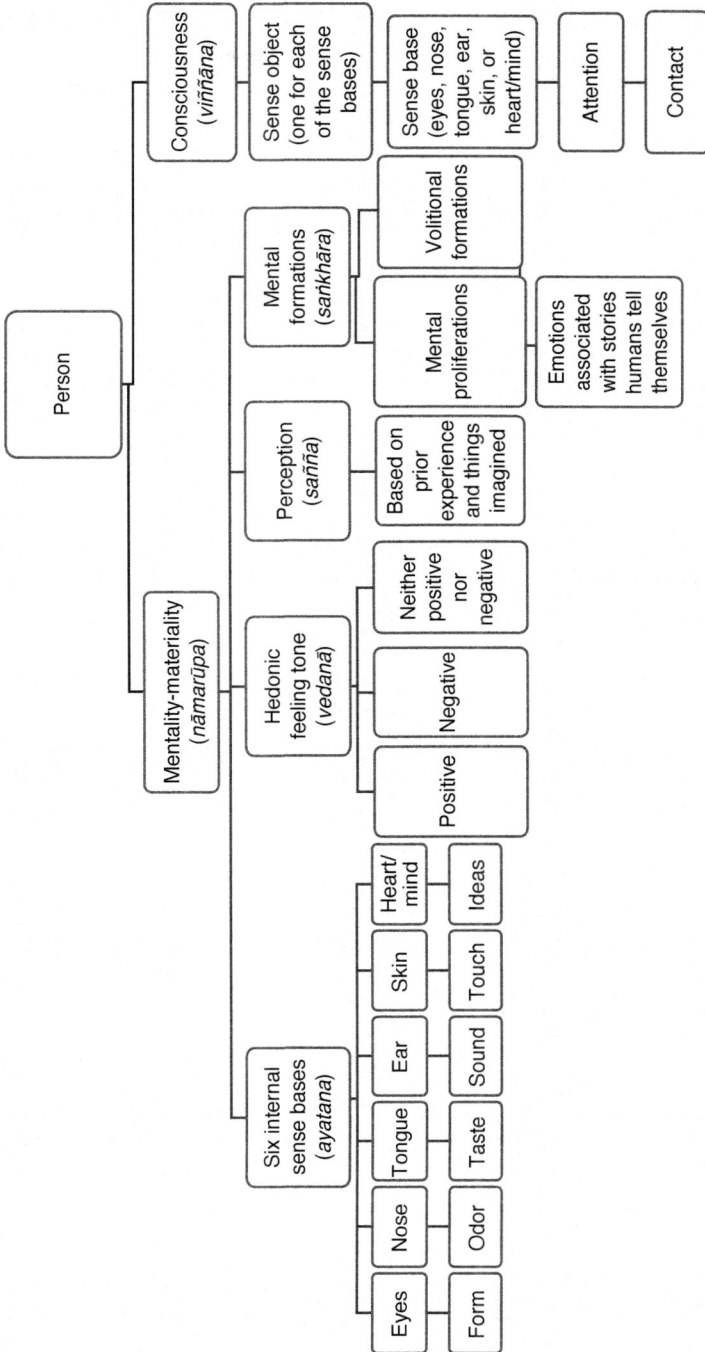

the English term *mentality-materiality* will be adopted for nāmarūpa in this volume.

The clinical application of mentality-materiality (nāmarūpa) is to know that the soma and the psyche, or mentality, are intimately connected. That is, altering the soma affects the psyche and vice versa. Examples are seen in treatment approaches based on self-regulation studies, which are grounded in the interlocking workings of the soma and the psyche or mentality. As Gendolla (2015) stated:

> Popular notions of self-regulation have traditionally been dualistic, portraying self-regulation as the product of a detached mind that in some mysterious way makes contact with the body and its needs, drives, and habits. . . . Self-regulation unfolds within the living tissue of our biological organism. It is therefore vital for behavioral theorists to heed the fundamental embodied, biological nature of self-regulation. (p. 2)

Altering the soma to affect the mental condition can be seen when practitioners recommend exercise for people who experience depression or systematic relaxation for individuals with difficulty managing anger. In general, Buddhism posits that it is easier to work with the soma to affect the mental condition because the soma is usually much more accessible for intentional manipulation.

The second part of Venerable Śāriputta's conceptual framework for a person is consciousness (viññāna). Before we undertake further examination of the concept of consciousness, linguistic clarification regarding the term *consciousness* is needed. There are several different concepts in the Pali *Nikāya* that are usually translated using the English word "consciousness," as listed in Exhibit 4.1. General use of the word consciousness encompasses all of these types of awareness and the knowing of a thing. For the sake of clarity in this book, when there is the need for specification of the word consciousness, it will be followed by the term *citta, cetasika, mano, nāma, manasikāra,* or viññāna. When the word consciousness is used without an accompanying Pali word, then it is understood to conform to the combined definition as follows: The *APA Dictionary of Psychology* defines consciousness as "the state of being conscious," "an organism's awareness of something either internal or external to itself," or "the waking state" (American Psychological Association, n.d.), whereas the *Cambridge Dictionary* defines it as "the state of being awake, aware of what is around you and able to think; the state of understanding and realizing something" (Cambridge University Press & Assessment, n.d.).

As Exhibit 4.1 shows, consciousness (viññāna) is the bare knowing of an object at the point of sense contact. One example is the eye receiving the color wavelength for blue but before the person applies the label "blue" from the eye stimuli; this is the moment prior to the labeling of the object being associated with the stimuli. As defined in the *Pali Text Society's Pali–English*

EXHIBIT 4.1. Types of Consciousness

1. *Mano* is the mind organ. The mind organ is at the same level or equivalent to the eye organ knowing the presence of sight stimuli and receiving the sight stimuli, the ear organ receiving sound stimuli, the nose organ receiving smell stimuli, the tongue organ receiving taste stimuli, and the touch organ receiving tactile stimuli. The mano is the receiver of noncorporal stimuli, such as ideas and memories. The human nervous system is most likely the closest similitude to the mano.

2. *Viññāna* is the bare knowing of an object at the point of sense contact, prior to its labeling as being associated with the stimuli. An example is the eye receiving the color wavelength for blue before the person labels the eye stimuli as "blue."

3. *Citta* is the totality of conscious acts.

4. *Cetasika* refers to the mental properties and factors collectively at work with consciousness. Cetasika is a collective functioning of mental factors, such as attention and perception in the mind, that give a sense object sufficient familiarity to give it a label or name. This ranges from the simplicity of the perception of "blue" to the complexity of repeated mental proliferation linked with complex feelings and mental states.

5. *Nāma* is part of the accompanying compounded or coordinated condition in nāmarūpa for the arising of consciousness. The term *nāmarūpa* has been translated as "mind plus body," "mentality plus materiality," and "name plus form." The *nāma* portions of the various translations are the "mind," "mentality," and "name," as in naming or labeling a sense consciousness.

6. *Manasikāra* in the sutta refers to attention, as in consciously drawing one's attention to stimuli.

Dictionary, viññāna is "a mental quality as a constituent of individuality, the bearer of (individual) life, life-force . . . principle of conscious life, general consciousness (as function of mind and matter) . . . the bare phenomenon of aroused attention" (Pali Text Society, n.d.). Hereinafter, the English word consciousness will be adopted for viññāna with the combination consciousness/viññāna.

Mentality-materiality (nāmarūpa) can be thought of as a person in the vegetative state, alive but not aware. Adding the function of consciousness/viññāna brings the person in a vegetative state alive, in the sense of being awake and conscious. Venerable Śāriputta's conceptual framework for a person is the mutual coarising of nāmarūpa (mentality-materiality) and viññāna (consciousness).

THE FIVE AGGREGATES

Buddhism dissects mentality-materiality (nāmarūpa) and consciousness (viññāna) into more detailed component parts. For the nāmarūpa portion of a person, there are four parts: *rūpa* (materiality, form), *vedanā* (hedonic feeling tone), *saññā* (perception, naming, labeling), and *saṅkhāra* (mental

formations). In combination with viññāna, a person consists of five categories or aggregates (khandhā). The Pali Text Society's Pali–English Dictionary
defines khandhā as "bulk, massiveness (gross) substance . . . the body of,
a collection of, mass, or parts of; in collective sense 'all that is comprised
under'; forming the substance of" (Pali Text Society, n.d.). Think of each
aggregate as referring to a class of things (e.g., liquids as a class comprising
all sorts of chemical compounds that can flow).

The five aggregates, when combined in their coordinated functioning, comprise a conceptual framework for a human person and are as follows:

- rūpa (materiality, form)
- vedanā (hedonic feeling tone)
- saññā (perception, recognition, naming, labeling)
- saṅkhāra (mental formations or mental fabrications, mental proliferations,
  and/or volitional formations)
- viññāna (consciousness)—arising from the act of turning the mind's
  attention/manasikāra to the sense object to make contact with the stimulus

Table 4.1 illustrates each aggregate with an excerpt from the Khajjanīya
Sutta (SN, 2000, 22.79: Being Devoured). Next, we examine each aggregate
in greater detail.

The First Aggregate: Form (Rūpa)

The first aggregate, materiality or form (rūpa), consists of internal and
external materials. Among all the elements within the human body that
comprise a person, there are only six internal senses that are involved in the
experience of existence. These six internal senses, or bases, interact with six
external elements, or objects. The six external sense objects are those items
existing in the universe that are detectable by the six internal sense bases.
These six internal sense bases and six external sense objects are collectively
referred to as the āyatana.

> There are [sets of] . . . six internal sense-spheres: eye-, ear-, nose-, tongue-,
> body-, mind-sense sphere . . . six external sense-spheres: sight-, sound-,
> smell-, taste- tangible-, mind-objects. (Sangiti Sutta; Dīgha Nikāya [DN],
> 1987/1995, 33.2.2: The Chanting Together)

> The six internal bases should be understood. . . . There are the eye-base, the
> ear-base, the nose-base, the tongue-base, the body-base, and the mind-base. . . .
> This is the first set of six. The six external bases should be understood. . . .
> There are the form-base, the sound-base, the odor-base, the flavor-base, the
> tangible-base, and the mind-object-base. So it was with reference to this that it
> was said: The six external bases should be understood. (Chachakka Sutta; MN,
> 1995, 148: The Six Sets of Six)

TABLE 4.1. The Five Aggregates

Aggregate	Excerpt from sutta
1. Form (*rūpa*): the material universe, to which the human body belongs	It is called "form." Afflicted with what? With cold & heat & hunger & thirst, with the touch of flies, mosquitoes, wind, sun, & reptiles. Because it is afflicted, it is called form.
2. Hedonic feeling tone (*vedanā*): a psychosomatic hedonic reaction to a sense contact, which is different from the English word "feeling"	And why do you call it "feeling"? Because it feels, thus it is called "feeling." What does it feel? It feels pleasure, it feels pain, it feels neither-pleasure-nor-pain. Because it feels, it is called feeling.
3. Perception (*saññā*): also translated as "recognition" and "naming"; the mental associations to the sense contact	And why do you call it "perception"? Because it perceives, thus it is called "perception." What does it perceive? It perceives blue, it perceives yellow, it perceives red, it perceives white. Because it perceives, it is called perception.
4. Mental formations (*saṅkhāra*): also translated as "mental fabrications" or "volitional formations"; the stories humans tell themselves about the sense contact and the derivative emotions associated with those stories	And why do you call them "fabrications"? Because they fabricate fabricated things, thus they are called "fabrications." What do they fabricate into a fabricated thing? For the sake of form-ness, they fabricate form as a fabricated thing. For the sake of feeling-ness, they fabricate feeling as a fabricated thing. For the sake of perception-hood. . . . For the sake of fabrication-hood. . . . For the sake of consciousness-hood, they fabricate consciousness as a fabricated thing. Because they fabricate fabricated things, they are called fabrications.
5. Consciousness (*viññāna*): arising from the act of turning the mind's attention/*manasikāra* to the sense object to make contact with the stimulus	And why do you call it "consciousness"? Because it cognizes, thus it is called consciousness. What does it cognize? It cognizes what is sour, bitter, pungent, sweet, alkaline, non-alkaline, salty, & un-salty. Because it cognizes, it is called consciousness.

Note. Excerpts are from the Khajjanīya Sutta (SN, 2000, 22.79: Being Devoured).

The six internal sense bases consist of the eye, ear, nose, tongue, skin of the body, and mind. The six internal bases should be understood in terms of the human experience of existence. They involve knowing that our knowledge of the universe is derived from information collected by the internal sense bases and external sense objects. In the *Nikāya*, the Buddha Gotama had a formulaic presentation of the āyatana. This formulaic presentation lists (a) the sense bases, (b) what type of sense object (as in stimuli) activates that sense bases, and (c) what sense consciousness arises from linking the sense base and the sense object.

For the internal sense base of the eye, the external sense object is light. One section of the light spectrum stimulates the receptors in the eye. It is the eye that perceives colors and shapes. Imagine being in total darkness in a furnished room: There is no light detectable to the human eye. Functionally, there is no visual sense object, even though there are objects in the room, such as a table that one could bump into or a chair one could trip over if one were to start moving around the room. Like the furniture that is not visible in the dark room, there are objects in the universe that are not detectable by humans but nonetheless are there. For example, we cannot see infrared light without the aid of a mechanical device, and we cannot see the dark matter that exists all around us. Items that are detectable by humans are referred to as the external sense objects. Items that are not detectable by the human sense bases are outside of the human experience of existence.

For the sense base of the ear, the sense objects are certain sound waves. When the sense object of a sound wave meets the sense base of the ear, the person perceives sound. The type of sound humans can detect is limited by the physical mechanism of the ear. There are sound waves that the human ear cannot detect and to which we do not react. For example, dogs have a wider range of sound detection than humans and are known to react to sounds that humans cannot hear.

For the sense base of the nose, the sense objects are certain particles in the air. When the sense object of airborne particles meets the sense base of the nose, the person perceives smell. Again, the range of odors is limited to those particles that stimulate the receptors in the human nose. For example, dogs have a much better sense of smell. We take advantage of dogs' better sense of smell to help find people in disaster areas or to find contraband, such as drugs and explosives, in airports.

For the sense base of the tongue, the sense objects are certain chemicals. When the sense object of select chemicals meets the sense base of the tongue, the person tastes things. The tongue receives stimuli that is then described with words such as "sweet," "sour," "bitter," and "salty." Again, human tastes are limited to the range of stimuli that stimulate the receptors in the tongue.

The largest sense base in the human body is the skin. The skin is sensitive to pressure, texture, and temperature. It perceives hard and soft, rough and smooth, and hot and cold. Although it is not named in the suttas, this category could also include proprioception, which allows us to sense muscle movement, balance, and our position in space.

The one sense base that is included in Buddhism but is not commonly included as a Western sense base is the mind. The mind/citta, acting as a sense base, in the Buddhist worldview has two main functions at a concrete level: The mind/mano receives noncorporal items, like ideas, whereas the mind/citta processes the information from the āyatana (internal sense bases and external sense objects). Additionally, the mind/citta (not the mind/mano) holds a very special place in the worldview of Buddhism. The Buddha considered the mind/citta as follows:

> I don't envision a single thing that, when undeveloped, leads to such great harm as the mind. The mind, when undeveloped leads to great harm. I don't envision a single thing that, when developed, leads to such great benefit as the mind. The mind, when developed, leads to great benefit. (*Aṅguttara Nikāya* [AN], 2012, 1)

In addition to processing sense objects (mind/mano), the mind/citta is the instrument that generates mindfulness, concentration, and insight that leads to the unconditioned state of *nibbāna*, or total liberation from suffering (*dukkha*).

The six external bases include the knowledge that the human experience of existence is limited to the stimuli from the six types of sense objects perceptible by the six sense bases. There are many more objects in the universe but because humans do not have the internal sense bases to detect those objects, they are nonexistent to the human experience of existence. At the same time, research on perception is continually discovering the limits and the extraordinary capabilities of the sense bases; thus, carefully consider the assertion from either other cultures or some unique individuals who report experiences either beyond or outside of the six sense bases. Do not automatically relegate these types of reported experiences into the category of psychotic hallucinations without careful consideration and exploration.

In conclusion, the Buddha was saying that all of a person's experience of existence is confined to the information obtained from the āyatana (six internal bases and six external sense objects) when he said,

> Bhikkhus, I will teach you the all. . . . And what, bhikkhus, is the all? The eye and forms, the ear and sounds, the nose and odors, the tongue and tastes, the body and tactile objects, the mind and mental phenomena. This is called the all. (Sabba Sutta; SN, 2000, 35.23: The All)

The Second Aggregate: Hedonic Feeling Tone (*Vedanā*)

The second aggregate, hedonic feeling tone (*vedanā*), was described in the Khandhā Sutta (SN, 2000, 22.48: Aggregates) as follows:

> And, bhikkhus, why do you call it feeling? 'It feels,' thus it is called feeling. And what does it feel? It feels pleasure, it feels pain, it feels neither-pleasure-nor-pain. 'It feels,' bhikkhus, therefore it is called feeling.

Accompanying every sense contact is an association referred to as vedanā, a psychosomatic hedonic reaction of the whole person to a sense stimulus. The *Pali Text Society's Pali–English Dictionary* defines vedanā as "feeling, sensation" (Pali Text Society, n.d.).

This overall reaction is akin to how babies react with their whole body. When babies experience something pleasant, they react by moving their arms and legs and wiggling their body, accompanied by a big smile. When babies experience something unpleasant, they react with stiff arms and push their legs out, accompanied by a grimace. The sutta names vedanā as a way of knowing the object by one's reaction (pleasant, unpleasant, and neither pleasant nor unpleasant). This reaction involves both the soma and the psyche, thus the conceptual translation of vedanā is hedonic feeling tone.

Vedanā consists of three nominal variables: pleasant, unpleasant, and neither pleasant nor unpleasant. The pleasant and unpleasant categories have ordinal gradations, like on a Likert scale. For pleasant, there is extremely pleasant (e.g., consensual sex) on one end and mildly pleasant (e.g., a morning cup of coffee) on the other. The category of unpleasant is also ordinal, with one end being extremely unpleasant (e.g., a panic attack) and the other being mildly unpleasant (e.g., tripping without falling). The category of neither pleasant nor unpleasant is not ordinal—something is neither pleasant nor unpleasant, or it is not. If not, then it is either pleasant or unpleasant.

Vedanā is the bridge linking the soma and the psyche. Vedanā influences the psyche as well as behavior in specific ways. When there is a pleasant vedanā, it pushes the psyche toward wanting to retain the experience and repeatedly chase after it when that hedonic pleasant sense experience is lost. At a very simplistic level, think about having that first bite of delicious chocolate cake. For a clinical application, think of someone who remembers and longs for the first blush of infatuation, the heady feeling of being in love. Then when the love object is lost, the same infatuation can turn into the disturbing behavior of stalking as a way to chase after that pleasant feeling when the love object is lost.

When there is an unpleasant vedanā, it pushes the psyche to remove the experience of that sense contact, wishing for it not to be. At a simplistic level, think of a dog barking in the middle of the night that wakes you up from sleeping soundly. The sound of the dog barking is accompanied by an intense wish for the sound to stop, and then the psyche pushes you to get out of bed to make the dog stop barking. For a clinical application, think of someone who badly wants to be rid of their panic attacks, to not experience the hyperventilation accompanied by rapid heart rate and dizziness.

When something is neither pleasant nor unpleasant, there simply is not any awareness of the stimulus. The mind slides over stimuli that are neither pleasant nor unpleasant. The mind does not attend to these stimuli; the mind skips and slides over them until it finds and grabs on to something that is pleasant or unpleasant. By the very nature of neither pleasant nor unpleasant vedanā, the person is not aware and does not know that they have simply skipped over the item.

The Third Aggregate: Perception (*Saññā*)

The third aggregate, perception (*saññā*), was described in the Khandhā Sutta (SN, 2000, 22.79: Being Devoured) as follows:

> And why, bhikkhus, do you call it perception? . . . And what does it perceive? It perceives blue, it perceives yellow, it perceives red, it perceives white. 'It perceives,' bhikkhus, therefore it is called perception.

Armed with a sense contact, accompanied by hedonic feeling tone, the mind then engages in a process to identify, make sense of, understand, and label the sense contact. This process is referred to as saññā, which has been variously translated as "perception," "recognition," "naming," or "labeling." The *Pali Text Society's Pali–English Dictionary* defines saññā as "sense, consciousness, perception, . . . discernment, recognition, assimilation of sensations, awareness" (Pali Text Society, n.d.). Let us return to our example of color perception. According to the sutta definition of saññā (perception, naming, labeling), the person perceives the color blue (SN, 2000, 22.79). The explanation for this perception states the result of a process. What occurs in this phase ends with the person recognizing that what is encountered through the sense contact is "blue." The process of recognizing something, such as the color blue, requires the mind to go into memory to match any previous knowledge of the stimulus with the current stimulus. Recognition necessarily relies on past experience. Based on one's past encounters with that stimulus, the mind gives the current stimulus a label, like "blue."

The Fourth Aggregate: Mental Formations (*Saṅkhāra*)

The fourth aggregate, mental formations (*saṅkhāra*), was described as follows:

> Whatever kind of mental formation or mental fabrications/saṅkhāra there is, whether past, future or present, internal or external, gross or subtle, inferior or superior, far or near: this is called the mental formation or mental fabrications/ saṅkhāra aggregate. . . . And why do you call them "fabrications"? Because they fabricate fabricated things, thus they are called "fabrications." What do

they fabricate into a fabricated thing? For the sake of form-ness, they fabricate form as a fabricated thing. For the sake of feeling-ness, they fabricate feeling as a fabricated thing. For the sake of perception-hood. . . . For the sake of fabrication-hood. . . . For the sake of consciousness-hood, they fabricate consciousness as a fabricated thing. Because they fabricate fabricated things, they are called fabrications. (SN, 2000, 22.79)

The term saṅkhāra has been most often translated as "mental formations" and sometimes as "mental fabrications" and "mental proliferations." In its definition and comments, the Pali Text Society (n.d.) pointed to the inadequacy of this translation for saṅkhāra:

[Saṅkhāra is] one of the most difficult terms in Buddhist metaphysics, in which the blending of the subjective-objective view of the world and of happening, peculiar to the East, is so complete, that it is almost impossible for Occidental terminology to get at the root of its meaning in a translation. We can only convey an idea of its import by representing several sides of its application, without attempting to give a "word" as a definition. . . . 1. Aggregate of the conditions or essential properties for a given process or result—e.g., (i.) the sum of the conditions or properties making up or resulting in life or existence; the essentials or "element" of anything . . . (ii.) Essential conditions, antecedents or synergy (co-ordinated activity), mental coefficients, requisite for act, speech, thought . . . sankhārā are in the widest sense the "world of phenomena," all things which have been made up by pre-existing causes.

The world of phenomena, or saṅkhāra (mental formations, mental fabrications, mental proliferations), can be thought of as the stories we tell ourselves about the encountered sense stimuli. After the process of saññā (perception, naming, labeling) has been completed (i.e., a sense contact has been recognized, identified, perceived, named, and labeled), then we tell ourselves a story about the external sense object that initiated the sense contact. This is the place where intention inserts itself. These constructed stories can be the bases for intentions that lead to actions of body, speech, and mind. Saṅkhāra consists of the stories and those accompanying emotions derived and based on these stories we form or fabricate. For the purposes of psychotherapy, think of saṅkhāra as the story we tell ourselves about any specific sense stimulus at any specific time. For some, there may be a tendency to construct stories that attempt to meet one's innermost yearnings and desires. Regardless, like any engaging story, saṅkhāra usually has a cast of characters, a plot line, some foreshadowing, and scenes that evoke an emotional state (e.g., anxiety, sadness, or foreboding doom). Or, in a simplified version, saṅkhāra can be thought of as the process of thinking. Saṅkhāra is what comes into the psychotherapy treatment room when the client starts talking.

The Fifth Aggregate: Consciousness (*Viññāna*)

Buddhaghosa (1956/2010) described the fifth aggregate, consciousness (*viññāna*), as follows:

> The eye does not see a visible object because it has no mind. The mind does not see a visible object because it has no eyes. . . . So the meaning here is this: On seeing a visible object with eye-consciousness. . . . He only apprehends what is really there. (p. 81)

The six internal sense bases and six external sense objects (āyatana) by themselves are equivalent to the human body in a vegetative state, which does not enable humans to experience existence. To experience existence, consciousness (viññāna) needs to be present. Viññāna is a cognitive process that occurs only in the presence of mentality-materiality (nāmarūpa). If a person does not have a body with any functioning sense bases, that person would not be conscious. At the same time, if there were no viññāna, then humans would not experience existence. Without viññāna, the person would be in a medical vegetative state, which would not be considered being alive and experiencing life. Viññāna is the awareness of an object without any name or story attached to it. It is mere awareness. Each of the āyatana has an accompanying viññāna.

> Bhikkhus, consciousness is reckoned by the particular condition dependent upon which it arises. When consciousness arises dependent on the eye and forms, it is reckoned as eye-consciousness; when consciousness arises dependent on the ear and sounds, it is reckoned as ear-consciousness; when consciousness arises dependent on the nose and odors, it is reckoned as nose-consciousness; when consciousness arises dependent on the tongue and flavors, it is reckoned as tongue-consciousness; when consciousness arises dependent on the body and tangibles, it is reckoned as body-consciousness; when consciousness arises dependent on the mind and mind-objects, it is reckoned as mind-consciousness. . . . Consciousness is reckoned by the particular condition dependent on which it arises. (Mahātaṇhāsankhaya Sutta; MN, 1995, 38.8: The Greater Discourse on the Destruction of Craving)

Consciousness (viññāna) arises when three items function together, and they must be present simultaneously. These items include (a) one of the six internal sense bases, (b) an external sense object perceptible by one of the six internal sense bases, and (c) the mind's attention/manasikāra turning toward the sense object. The moment when the external sense stimulus comes through the sense base and makes contact with the processing function of the mind is the first moment of viññāna of a stimulus, and it is also the first moment of a human lived experience in interaction with that specific stimulus.

CONCLUSION

People experience existence through the functioning of the five aggregates (khandhā). These aggregates include rūpa, the material things of the universe, or the ayatana, the six internal sense bases and the six external sense objects; vedanā, the hedonic feeling tone of how humans know a sense object; saññā, the process of labeling a sense object; saṅkhāra, the stories people tell themselves about the sense object, which contain the content of the story as well as the emotions associated to the story; and viññāna, consciousness.

Returning to our earlier car analogy, the khandhā are like the car parts that, when assembled, allow a car to function as a mode of transportation. This is akin to what the monk Nāgasena referred to as the collection of the parts that make up a chariot (Mil, 1890, 3.1.1). The Buddhist conceptualization of such a list of parts is mentality-materiality (nāmarūpa) plus consciousness (viññāna).

In the application of mentality-materiality plus consciousness to psychotherapy, the psychotherapist is tasked with discerning the five aggregates as they function during the psychotherapy session. In the application of mentality-materiality plus consciousness to the treatment goal, the psychotherapist's job is to discern and then to relay to the client each of the aggregates occurring at the critical moment of their presenting problem.

Clients usually report a disturbing situation when they present for treatment. The psychotherapist using the functioning of the five aggregates would first pinpoint the internal sense bases and external sense objects (āyatana) that initiated the disturbing situation. Lest they take the client's report of the stimuli that started it all at face value, the psychotherapist must use their own embodied knowledge of what constitutes a sense contact learned from their own meditation practice. After the psychotherapist determines the sense contact, they would then identify and articulate the other three aggregates of hedonic feeling tone, the labeling, and the fabricated story told about the sense contact. The next chapter examines how all of these parts fit together, similar to how an instruction manual describes how to assemble the parts of a car to construct a functioning car that moves.

5 HOW THE FIVE AGGREGATES WORK TOGETHER

Chapter 4 defined and described each of the five aggregates (*khandhā*). This chapter explores how the aggregates fit together and coordinate to generate our experience of existence. The Buddha Gotama described the coordinated process of the five aggregates in the Khandhā Sutta (*Saṃyutta Nikāya* [SN], 2000, 22: Connected Discourses on the Aggregates). The process of experience starts with making contact with the universe. This contact is made from the information provided by the six internal sense bases and the six external sense objects (*āyatana*). To experience existence requires all five aggregates to function in coordination with each other. The coordinated function of the aggregates is referred to as the *pañcakkhandhā*; the translation for this term is relatively straightforward, with *pañca* meaning "number 5" and *khandhā* meaning "aggregates" (Pali Text Society, n.d.).

The simultaneous coordinated functioning of the five aggregates generates the experience of existence. It can be said that we humans experience the universe by way of the workings of the five aggregates. What humans know of an object is not the object, or *noumenon*; what a person knows and experiences of that sense object is a representation of that object processed through the functioning of the five aggregates. Essentially, humans do not experience

https://doi.org/10.1037/0000453-006
Buddhist Psychotherapy: Connecting Early Buddhism to Mindfulness and Western Psychotherapy, by L. Tien, D. M. Kawahara, and V. Dhammadinna

an object of the universe, or a stimulus; instead, what humans experience is a representation of that object, the product of the coordinated workings of the aggregates.

CONSCIOUSNESS (VIÑÑĀNA)

The experience of existence starts with the arising of consciousness (viññāna). The arising of consciousness depends on the interconnection between the external sense object, the internal sense base, and the mind's (citta's) attention (manasikāra in Pali). The relationship that creates the consciousness of the object is described as follows:

> The eye does not see a visible object because it has no mind. The mind does not see a visible object because it has no eyes. . . . So the meaning here is this: On seeing a visible object with eye-consciousness. (Buddhaghosa, 1956/2010, p. 81)

We offer a brief aside about the author of this quote, Bhadantácariya Buddhaghosa. He was a Buddhist scholar-monk who lived and wrote in Sri Lanka during the 5th century (C.E.). His best known and often used book is the Visuddhimagga, translated as The Path to Purification. Bhikkhu Ñáóamoli, translator of the Pali version of Visuddhimagga to English, said of Buddhaghosa's work: "This author's work is characterized by relentless accuracy, consistency, and fluency of erudition. . . . The Visuddhimagga itself extracts from the Tipitaka all the central doctrines . . . welded into an intricate edifice" (Buddhaghosa, 1956/2010, p. xxxvii). The writings of Bhadantácariya Buddhaghosa are often used as a primer to understand the Nikāya.

In the earlier quote, Buddhaghosa (1956/2010) explained the arising of consciousness (viññāna), the first moment of a lived experience in regard to a particular stimulus. Consciousness arises with the meeting of the sense object with the sense base at the sense door plus attention (manasikāra). The Pali word manasikāra, usually translated as "consciousness," is more appropriately translated as "attention." The Pali Text Society's Pali–English Dictionary defines the noun manasikāra as "attention pondering fixed thought" (Pali Text Society, n.d.).

The first phrase in the quote from Buddhaghosa (1956/2010), "The eye does not see a visible object because it has no mind" (p. 81), calls our attention to a process that requires a mind (citta) to process the information. The interaction between a person and the universe starts when a stimulus of the material universe, or a sense object, contacts an internal sense base. At this point, it is said that the sense object is knocking at a person's sense door, trying to catch the mind's attention (manasikāra).

The next phrase in the quote from Buddhaghosa (1956/2010), "The mind does not see a visible object because it has no eyes" (p. 81), calls our attention to the conditions that influence whether the mind's attention is turned to the sense object. In order for a sense object that is knocking at the sense door to catch the mind's attention, that sense object must be within the range of a human sense receptor and must be loud (in volume, proximity, or both) to stimulate a human sense base. A sense stimulus can either be intrusive (e.g., a very loud noise, like an ambulance siren) or a person can decide to turn their attention to that stimulus. This volitional act of deciding to turn one's attention to something is the basis of mindfulness meditation. Humans are constantly bombarded by hundreds of stimuli. Some of these stimuli register in the mind's attention; most of them do not. When a sense object does not register in the mind's attention, that sense object essentially does not exist for the person.

The meeting of the external sense object, the internal sense base, and the mind's attention (manasikāra) generates contact (*phassa*) between the external and the internal (Figure 5.1). The Pali word phassa has a very uncomplicated translation and is the English equivalent of "contact" and "touch" (Pali Text Society, n.d.).

Once contact is made, then the mind/cetasika, in its processing function, commences the first instance of a cognitive mental process. This is the moment when a sense consciousness/viññāna arises. It is the first moment of a human lived experience of that specific stimulus.

In its application to psychotherapy, all experiences start with a sense object impinging on the person's sense door. In the in-session dialogue with a client about their troubling experience, there will always be a sense object that starts the whole thing. For Buddhism, the mind is also a sense base, so the sense object can be a stray thought that floats across the mind and triggers a cascade of follow-up thoughts to which the person attends. This means that whatever a client complains about, worries about, is troubled by, and brings into therapy sessions for discussion, it all starts with a sense

FIGURE 5.1. Contact Between the Internal and the External

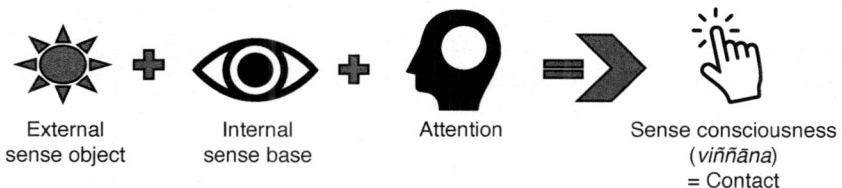

| External sense object | Internal sense base | Attention | Sense consciousness (*viññāna*) = Contact |

contact. Take the time to uncover the sense object and the first moment of consciousness (viññāna) of the troubling situation. These are moments that the client has lived, not something to guess at or hypothesize about. The training in meditation to observe the mind aims at this level of awareness. Psychotherapy may stand as an enactment of meditation, with the psychotherapist acting as mindfulness. The in-session line of inquiry by a psychotherapist will help with a person's ability to notice these first moments of contact that precipitate their troubling situation.

A PSYCHOSOMATIC HEDONIC ASSOCIATION (*VEDANĀ*)

Contact immediately elicits a hedonic feeling tone (*vedanā*). Consider the following from the Madhupindika Sutta (*Majjhima Nikāya* [MN], 1995, 18: The Honeyball):

> [W]ith the six sense bases as condition, contact. . . . With contact as condition there is . . . feeling . . . perception . . . mental proliferations . . . lust . . . aversion . . . views . . . ignorance . . . rods and weapons . . . quarrels, brawls, disputes, recrimination, malicious words, and false speech.

The phrase, "With contact as condition there is . . . feeling" (MN, 1995, 18), means that once a sense consciousness (viññāna) has arisen, there is hedonic feeling tone (vedanā), a psychosomatic hedonic association regarding that sense contact. The term vedanā is most often translated as "feeling." The term *feeling*, in its colloquial usage, is not equivalent and does not impart the totality of the meaning for vedanā. Vedanā is a psychosomatic hedonic reaction of the whole person to a sense stimulus that includes both the soma and the psyche. Hedonic feeling tone influences the soma as well as the psyche. If the person experiences a pleasant vedanā, then that experience acts as a force on the psyche pushing for behavior that will continue the pleasant experience. Once that pleasant experience stops, which it is bound to do because of impermanence (*anicca*), the hedonic feeling tone acts as a force to have the person chase after that lost pleasant experience. What might first appear as unpleasant, like anger, may have at its base a pleasant hedonic feeling tone. This anger may be the reaction to losing the state that generated the initial pleasant hedonic feeling tone, like the anger behind jealousy that may arise when one loses a desired love object. This force that grabs on to and chases after a pleasant experience is called *lobha* in Pali and has been translated as "desire," "lust," "greed," "craving," and "attachment." The *Pali Text Society's Pali–English Dictionary* defines lobha as "covetousness" and "greed" (Pali Text Society, n.d.). For the purposes of psychotherapy, think of lobha as the urge to grab on and retain. The object of covetousness or greed (lobha) may be a material object, a person, a situation, an experience, or a symptom of some psychological pathology, such as relief experienced after performing some compulsive sequence of actions. What might first appear as distasteful, like stalking a lost love, may be a manifestation of the desire for a pleasant state; the act of stalking may be in pursuit of the once pleasant state of being in love.

When the person experiences an unpleasant hedonic feeling tone, the experience will influence the psyche to act in such a way as to push the unpleasant experience away, to make that unpleasant state disappear; the person is influenced toward aversion. What might first appear as grasping for a pleasant state, like stalking a lost love in pursuit of the once pleasant state of being in love, may be a reaction to the inability to stop an unpleasant hedonic feeling tone. The pursuer continues to call, text, and find ways to interact with the past romantic partner, even when the partner has communicated that the relationship is over, to avoid the pain of being rejected or feeling abandoned or lonely. This unpleasant experience and the motivating force on the psyche pushing for behavior that will make the unpleasant go away is called *dosa* in Pali, which is usually translated as "hate." The *Pali Text Society's Pali–English Dictionary* defines dosa as "anger, ill-will, evil intention, wickedness, corruption, malice, hatred" (Pali Text Society, n.d.). For the purposes of psychotherapy, think of dosa as the urge to push away, to make something disappear. As with greed and covetousness (lobha), the object of anger and ill will (dosa) may be a material object, a person, a situation, an experience, or a symptom of some psychological pathology, such as a panic attack.

When the sense contact is neither pleasant nor unpleasant, then the mind (citta) tends to lose interest. The person tends to lose engagement with the stimulus and drift. In meditation, the person stops attending to the object of contemplation, like the breath, and grabs on to whatever might be more stimulating, regardless of whether the topic is pleasant or unpleasant. In daily activity, the person loses track of what they are doing and drifts to the mind's default mode in which rumination becomes active. The mind, in its untrained, undisciplined state, is like a 2-year-old. It is in constant motion, getting into all sorts of trouble. Like a 2-year-old, the mind does not stop; when it is forced to be still, as when one starts to train the mind in meditation, it tends to lose interest and gravitate toward ruminating about things that are more stimulating. These unattended-to constructed stories do not need to be pleasant. Sometimes, the stories a disinterested mind conjures up can be quite unpleasant. The stories just need to be stimulating. This mind state is called *moha* in Pali, which has been translated as "ignorance" and sometimes as "delusion." The *Pali Text Society's Pali–English Dictionary* defines moha as "stupidity, dullness of mind & soul, delusion, bewilderment, infatuation" (Pali Text Society, n.d.). By its nature, the mind does not know that it is under the influence of neither pleasant nor unpleasant hedonic feeling tone (vedanā). In its not knowing, the mind is ignorant of the fact that it is not attending to something that it should; it is tricked, or deluded, into not attending. For the purposes of psychotherapy, think of moha as the urge to distract oneself with something more interesting, not attending to some very dull matter at hand. It does not matter whether the distraction is pleasant or unpleasant or is foreseeably problematic or not, so long as it is distracting. Think of the person who, without much thought, opens the pantry to look for something to eat and then mindlessly eats a bag of potato chips. The matter at hand may be something that does not need much attention, like watching that television show while eating that bag of potato chips. On the other hand, the matter might be justifiably in need of doing. For example, an employee needs to categorize their receipts for reimbursement from a business trip, but they find this task so boring that they distract themself by going on social media instead. Psychotherapists, acting as mindfulness, can select unnoticed but significant items for attention and further discussion.

Buddhism posits that greed and covetousness (lobha), anger and ill will (dosa), and dullness of mind, delusion, and ignorance (moha) are the motivators to all actions of body, speech, and mind. In our earlier car analogy, hedonic feeling tone (vedanā) can be thought of as the driver, the force that directs where the car goes. This idea is reflected in the three states of hedonic feeling tone being depicted at the center of the Buddhist wheel of life (*bhāvacakka* in Pali and *thangka* in Tibetan). In the center of the wheel, at the hub around which the wheel of life turns, there is pictorial representation of the three afflictive states shaped by hedonic feeling tone. For greed and covetousness, the usual image is a bird; for anger and ill will, it is a snake; and for mental dullness and delusion, it is a pig.

Hedonic feeling tone is present in all moments of experienced existence. If one looks with sufficient attention and sensitivity, one can always find which of these three forces is at the root of any experience. In its application to psychotherapy, this psychosomatic hedonic association to a stimulus is important in two ways. The first is that hedonic feeling tone is the bridge between soma/body (*rūpa*) and psyche/mind (*nāma*). The second is that hedonic feeling tone has characteristic patterns in its influence on the mind (citta) and human behavior. When a client complains of a somatic discomfort, or what might be considered a psychosomatic disorder, look for its influence on the mind. When the client complains about a psychic experience, like anger, look for its influence on the body.

Let us consider an example from psychotherapy. A client walked in to session as she was ending a call with her ex-husband. She was obviously agitated but she had not wanted to talk about her ex-husband, thus doubling her agitation with him for disturbing her immediately before a therapy session. I (Tien) asked her, "Where is your breath when you are agitated?" The client gave me a puzzled look, to which I responded, "Right now, my breath is high up on my chest, and I hold it a bit between the inhale and the exhale." She then said, "Wait a minute," and closed her eyes. Then she opened her eyes and said, "My breath is high up on my back, and there is muscle tension around my shoulders. Oh, I know what to do. I will do abdominal breathing for a minute." After the client completed her breathing, she opened her eyes and said, "I don't need to deal with him; after all, that is why he is my ex-husband." At that point, she went on to discuss what she had been planning to talk about in the therapy session.

Sometimes, it is easier to impact a psychoemotional experience by talking to the client about making changes in their body, such as taking deep breaths or going for a walk when they report experiencing high anxiety. The Buddhist theory of hedonic feeling tone (vedanā) would indicate that changes in the somatic state, like exercise, would impact a psychological state. Conversely, changes in the psyche, such as focusing the mind during meditation, would impact the soma, like the body relaxing.

Thus far, we have linked six items: (a) an external stimulus, or a sense object, with (b) the internal sense base by way of (c) turning the mind's attention (manasikāra) to make (d) contact, thus (e) generating consciousness (viññāna) and (f) eliciting a hedonic feeling tone (vedanā). Meditation is a technique that trains the mind to be attentive enough to notice these six items at play. A psychotherapist can also enact the same type of inquiry by slowing down the action in session enough to notice each of these six items. It is especially important to identify the sense object that started the whole situation. For example, a client came to psychotherapy trying to decide whether to get a divorce. He was very busy talking about his tendency toward indecision, that his being unable to follow through with his wish for a divorce was yet another example of his indecisiveness. The immediate actionable topic of concern was divorce, not necessarily the client's tendency toward indecision. Therefore, the psychotherapist inquired about the last time this client experienced the wish for a divorce. He reported that it was the previous day when he got home from work. On further exploration to pinpoint the exact moment the client became aware that he was thinking about a divorce, he reported that he was walking up to the front door of his house. Slowing down the action even more, the in-session dialogue focused on what the client noticed as he approached the door of his house. With considerable animation and a change in his tone of voice, the client exploded: "There was another box from Amazon Prime!" This sense contact of seeing the box from Amazon Prime was accompanied by an extremely unpleasant hedonic feeling tone. The client and the therapist then discussed the client's anxiety about not earning enough money to pay the bills that his wife generated from all the things she ordered online, which was a very different direction than the client's earlier notion of himself being indecisive.

Hedonic feeling tone has a characteristic pattern of influence on the soma, the psyche, and one's behavior of body, speech, and mind. Buddhism postulates that there is fluid communication between the psyche and the soma, indicating that intervention can be targeted at either the somatic or the psychic level. Although the client may be discussing these situations primarily at a cognitive or emotive level (or both), each situation has a large quantity of somatic elements associated with it. Thus, the psychotherapist needs to assess for the somatic as well as the cognitive association with a sense contact.

PERCEPTION, NAMING, AND LABELING (*SAÑÑĀ*)

After contact, armed with a hedonic feeling tone to a sense stimulus, mentality initiates with *saññā*.

> [With] the six sense bases as condition, contact. . . . With contact as condition there is . . . feeling . . . perception . . . mental proliferations . . . lust . . . aversion . . . views . . . ignorance . . . rods and weapons . . . quarrels, brawls, disputes, recrimination, malicious words, and false speech. (MN, 1995, 18)

> And what, bhikkhus, is perception? There are these six classes of perception: perception of form, perception of sound, perception of smell, perception of taste, perception of tactile sensation, [and] perception of mental phenomenon. This is called perception. With the arising of contact there is the arising of perception. With the cessation of contact there is the cessation of perception. (Sattaṭṭhāna Sutta; SN, 2000, 22.57: The Seven Cases)

> [T]his is called the perception/saññā aggregate. . . . And why do you call it "perception/saññā"? Because it perceives, thus it is called "perception." What does it perceive? It perceives blue, it perceives yellow, it perceives red, it perceives white. Because it perceives, it is called perception/saññā. (MN, 1995, 18)

The phrase, "What one feels, that one perceives" (MN, 1995, 18), describes perception, naming, and labeling (saññā), the process of identifying the sense object. Once a stimulus is noticed, the mind's (*cetasika's*) identifying processing function commences. In Pali, this process is called saññā and it is the stage where the mind (citta), in its processing function, must figure out what is being experienced through the sense door.

As shown in Figure 5.2, the process of perception, naming, and labeling (saññā) ends with a label. Using our earlier example with color, the eye receives a certain wavelength of light. The process of saññā goes from the wavelength of light to labeling that wavelength as the color blue. Thus resulting in the color blue (MN, 1995, 18) is the thing being experienced. That process starts with consciousness (viññāna) of a sense object. The Theravāda Abhidhamma analyzes the activities of saññā into the following stages (Karunadasa, 2015b).

Once the sense consciousness (viññāna) is activated, the mind (cetasika) in its processing function investigates the activated viññāna. This investigation stage is referred to as *consciousness (santirana)*, and it involves the activity of repeatedly scanning the object to encode the object into short-term memory. These scans of the sense object have the function of sinking the mind into the stimulus to figure out what it is. The investigative stage starts with an initial scan of the sense object. Think of it like an artist painting a landscape. The artist studies the landscape by repeatedly scanning it in order to encode the scene long enough to transfer what they see to paint on canvas. This same repeated scanning of the sense object is done in perception, naming, and labeling (saññā). This initial scanning is to encode the sense object in short-term memory. The mind then goes into the long-term memory to match the current sense contact with any previous knowledge of the same thing. When there is a match between the current sense contact with any previous experience of that same or a similar sense contact, then a label is made.

The process of going back into memory to match previous experiences of a sense object with the current encounter involves more than just recognizing and labeling an object. Recognition includes the material naming of an object, such as a table or the color blue. In addition, this scanning also pulls up not only the name of an object, like blue, but also the hedonic feeling tone (vedanā) associated with that object and any past experiences associated with that sense object. If the past knowledge of that object stored in memory has no particularly strong emotional loading, then perception, naming, and labeling (saññā) ends with a benign label, like "blue." However, if the contact has a strong affective loading from the past experience associated with it, then the label or perception is not confined to the name of the object. Consider the example of a person with a history of struggling with

FIGURE 5.2. The Process of Labeling

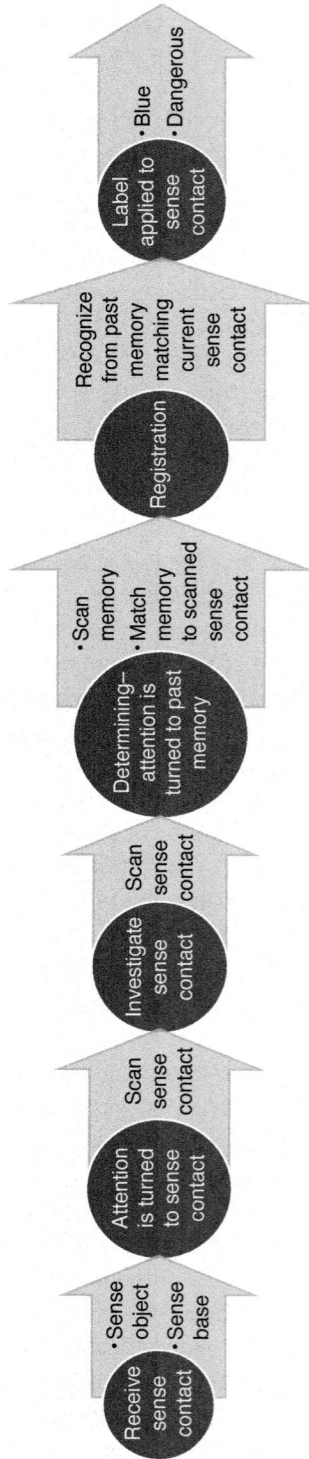

Receive sense contact

• Sense object
• Sense base

Attention is turned to sense contact

Scan sense contact

Investigate sense contact

Scan sense contact

Determining— attention is turned to past memory

• Scan memory
• Match memory to scanned sense contact

Registration

Recognize from past memory matching current sense contact

Label applied to sense contact

• Blue
• Dangerous

obesity and repeated dieting: Upon seeing an especially well-made chocolate cake, the person may label the sense object not only as "cake" but also as "bad object." In addition, the person may associate cake with danger, seduction, and evidence of poor impulse control.

In its application to psychotherapy, the process of labeling is where memories of past experiences influence present associations with a sense contact. Because it is based on a person's past experiences, perception of any given stimulus or situation will be idiosyncratic to that person's past lived experience.

The process of labeling, clinically speaking, deserves meticulous attention. It is important for the psychotherapist to take the time to slow down the action in session to understand how the client went from point A, a sense contact, to point B, like a phobic reaction. Theravāda Abhidhamma postulates six discrete steps in this process (Karunadasa, 2015b). In everyday life, this process from sense contact to labeling occurs so quickly that it seems simultaneous, and those six discrete steps go by unnoticed. In-session dialogue has the capacity to unpack and articulate each step of the process of arriving at a label for the sense contact. When the label is uncovered, it is usually evidenced by two characteristics: One is that the naming, or labeling, is short—usually one word or one phrase. It is never a long explanation with a logical rationale. The other characteristic is that the client will exhibit a noticeable change in some somatic aspect, like a change in tone of voice, body posture, facial expression, or some other somatic expression.

Exploration of labeling starts with this question: "What is that sense contact?" The exploration ends with a label, such as "danger" or "blue." Consider this clinical example: A client reported persistent insomnia accompanied by the paranoid ideation that his neighbor will come into his room to beat him once he falls asleep. It took a few sessions and a detailed homework assignment for observing, noting, and reporting on this process of saññā (perception, naming, labeling). It turned out that the sense stimulus was the sound the mattress made when the client sat down on the bed. He would physically tense up and think of all sorts of danger, like the neighbor coming into his room to beat him up. In tracking this process, the client identified labels associated with the sound as a sense of danger. In doing the many scans of linking the sound of the mattress to this sense of danger, the link that emerged was the client's childhood memory of his father coming home late at night after he had gone to bed. As a disciplinary method, his mother would say, "Wait until your father gets home." When his father got home, he would get a litany of all his son's misbehavior of the day. His father would then go into the client's room, sit down on the bed, and proceed to dole out his punishment. As in classical conditioning, this client eventually associated the sound of the mattress with danger, like being punished.

The last step in the process of saññā is naming and labeling. At the end of this process of recognition, the mind (citta) comes up with a label and an accompanying psychosomatic affective quality. Fully articulating the process of labeling will result in understanding the link between a sense object (sense contact) and a client's past experience with that sense object.

MENTAL FORMATIONS, MENTAL PROLIFERATIONS, AND VOLITIONAL FORMATIONS (SAṄKHĀRA)

Once a sense stimulus has been identified and given a name or label, then we try to make sense by telling ourselves a story about the stimulus; that is, we engage in the process of saṅkhāra:

> [W]ith the six sense bases as condition . . . the meeting of the three [sense object, sense base, and attention] is contact. . . . With contact as condition there is feeling. What one feels, that one perceives. What one perceives, that one thinks about. What one thinks about, that one mentally proliferates. (MN, 1995, 18)
>
> [T]hinking . . . arise[s] from elaborated perception and notions. When elaborated perceptions and notions are present, thinking arises. (Sakkapañha Sutta; Dīgha Nikāya [DN], 1987/1995, 21: Sakka's Questions)

As shown in Figure 5.1, the process of making contact with the external world, as laid out in the Sakkapañha Sutta (DN, 1987/1995, 21), can be summed up with the following equation: Sense Object + Sense Bases + Attention = Sense Contact. Building on this equation, Figure 5.3 shows the process by which sense contact leads to mental formations, which are the stories we tell ourselves. When sense contact is linked with a hedonic feeling tone and a label, mental formations result. These formations lay out the links between a sense contact and the story we tell ourselves about that stimulus.

FIGURE 5.3. The Creation of Mental Formations

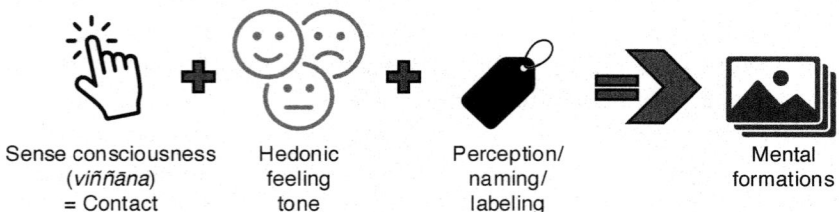

| Sense consciousness (viññāna) = Contact | Hedonic feeling tone | Perception/ naming/ labeling | Mental formations |

This process is called saṅkhāra, which is a Pali term for "the multifarious mental factors involving volition, choice, and intentions" (Bodhi, 2005, p. 305). The closest equivalent to saṅkhāra (mental formations, mental proliferations, volitional formations) in English is the process of thinking with its linked affect. Saṅkhāra is the story we tell ourselves—or the stories our clients tell us in therapy—about any specific sense contact at any specific time and the accompanying emotions attached to that story. For Buddhism, the stories we tell ourselves about the sense contact are just that, stories we tell ourselves. We fabricate these stories from the hedonic psychosomatic associations with the sense contact, from our past experiences, and from whatever ideas may be floating through our mind.

What are usually thought of as feelings and emotions are what tags along with these stories that we tell ourselves about the sense contact. Here is an example: I (Tien, a short-statured female) see a person walking toward me as I exit the library late in the evening. That visual object of a person does not give me comfort; I experience an unpleasant hedonic feeling tone (vedanā). I avoid looking directly at the person walking toward me but keep the person within the periphery of my sight. My past experience with strangers on a dark street is from cautionary tales of strangers, especially in the dark, as being dangerous. The story I tell myself about this person walking toward me is that the person holds ill intent toward me. I move to the far side of the sidewalk, clutching my backpack and mentally taking a tally of what I hold in my hands and which of my backpack contents can be used as a weapon to defend myself from a physical attack by this stranger. My body is tense in anticipation of a dangerous physical confrontation. From the sense contact of seeing a person, linked with an unpleasant hedonic feeling tone (vedanā) and that sight labeled as a stranger (saññā) with ill intent toward me (mental formation [saṅkhāra]), I experience fear and anxiety. In actuality, the other person may be fabricating the same story about me.

Buddhism recognizes that there is a constant stream of thought that goes through the mind. Some of these thoughts pass through with very little effect on one's action of body, speech, or mind. Embedded among all of the thoughts that float through the mind are potential volitional thoughts. Volitional formations generate actions of body, speech, or mind. Actions of mind are those thoughts that initiate a cascade of thoughts in the mind. For example, the thought "I am alone in a dark street with a stranger approaching" is accompanied by a cascade of mental fabrications about all the disasters that will follow: "I will be attacked. I will need to figure out a way to defend myself. This person approaching is dangerous." From within the process of saṅkhāra (mental formations) comes volition formations. Here is one such example: "I need to cross the street now so as not to be within reach of the dangerous stranger approaching me." Those thoughts that initiate actions of body, speech, or mind are referred to in Buddhism as *cetanā*, which is usually translated as "volitional thoughts." The *Pali Text Society's Pali–English Dictionary* defines cetanā as "thinking as active thought, intention, purpose, will" (Pali Text Society, n.d.). For psychotherapy, volitional thoughts are of greater importance because they are the very beginning of action.

Buddhism categorizes actions as actions of body, actions of speech, and actions of mind (cetanā). Here are a few examples, from coarser to finer grained: an action of body could be crossing the street to avoid potential contact with a stranger; an action of speech could be saying a hateful word when you are angry; and an action of mind could be a client who is depressed from relentlessly reprimanding themself for some imagined failing. As a psychotherapist listening to the client's report of their troubles, listen for the volitional thought that may have initiated a cascade of internal self-talk.

Circling back to the concept of dependent arising (*paṭiccasamuppāda*) discussed in Chapter 3, saṅkhāra (mental formations, mental proliferations, volitional formations), or phenomena in consciousness, do not occur without rhyme or reason. What arises is dependent on a confluence of conditions, or "when this exists, that comes to be; with the arising of this, that arises; when this does not exist, that does not come to be; with the cessation of this, that ceases to be" (SN, 2000, 12.21.1). The amalgamation of so many necessary circumstances congeals into a phenomenon that experienced in consciousness is a fragile structure bound to dissolve, which sets the stage for impermanence (aniccā). In its application to psychotherapy, we can work with our clients to remove elements or conditions in their life, which in turn would disrupt the confluence of conditions that give rise to their suffering (*dukkha*), or whatever it is that the client is not okay with.

CONCLUSION

The human experience of the world is a mental representation of sense objects filtered through the five aggregates: rūpa (materiality, form), vedanā (hedonic feeling tone), saññā (perception, naming, labeling), saṅkhāra (mental formations or mental fabrications, mental proliferations, and/or volitional formations), and viññāna (consciousness, attention). What humans know of a sense object is not the object itself. Rather, what humans know of a sense object is a representation of that object. Therefore, what humans know of the universe are phenomena, not noumena.

What comes into the psychotherapy room is the phenomena, the mental representations, of the interchange between the client's internally constructed world with the external sense object. Phenomena in consciousness (citta) are conditioned and thus impermanent (aniccā). In the next chapter, we further explore the construction of a notion of a self.

6 HOW WE CONSTRUCT A NOTION OF A SELF

Buddhism is concerned with the nature of the phenomenologically lived experience of an empiric existence. Buddhism analyzes the experience to its component parts and then synthesizes those component parts to explain the experience of existence. The *five aggregates* system names the building blocks for the experience of living. The five aggregates, without clinging, are referred to as not-self (*anattā*). Chapters 4 and 5 discussed the most elementary system of analysis, which is the five aggregates.

The synthesis of those component parts is the five aggregates subject to clinging (*pañcupādānakkhandhā*). The *five aggregates subject to clinging* can be said to be a definition of a self or, more accurately, the building blocks for the construction of a notion of a self (*attā*).

> Bhikkhus, I will teach you . . . the five aggregates subject to clinging. . . . And what, bhikkhus, are the five aggregates subject to clinging? Whatever kind of form there is, whether past, future, or present . . . far or near, that is tainted, that can be clung to: this is called the form aggregate subject to clinging. Whatever kind of feeling there is . . . that is tainted, that can be clung to: this is called the feeling aggregates subject to clinging. Whatever kind of perception there is . . . that is tainted, that can be clung to: this is called the perception

https://doi.org/10.1037/0000453-007
Buddhist Psychotherapy: Connecting Early Buddhism to Mindfulness and Western Psychotherapy, by L. Tien, D. M. Kawahara, and V. Dhammadinna

aggregate subject to clinging. Whatever kind of volitional formations there are . . . that are tainted, that can be clung to: These are called the volitional formations aggregate subject to clinging. Whatever kind of consciousness there is, whether past, future, or present, internal or external, gross or subtle, inferior or superior, far or near, that is tainted, that can be clung to: this is called the consciousness aggregate subject to clinging. These, bhikkhus, are called the five aggregates subject to clinging. (Khandhā Sutta; *Saṃyutta Nikāya* [SN], 2000, 22.48: Connected Discourses on the Aggregates)

The five aggregates subject to clinging, or the constructed notion of a self, is how humans experience the universe. This chapter explains how we construct that notion of the self. Chapter 7 examines what that constructed notion of a self experiences of existence.

THE FIVE AGGREGATES PLUS CRAVING (*TAṆHĀ*)

The five aggregates are, by themselves, the parts that work together to generate the experience of human existence. It is the addition of craving (*taṇhā*) that transforms an impersonal functioning of the five aggregates into the five aggregates subject to clinging. As noted earlier, the five aggregates subject to clinging can be said to be a definition of a self or, more accurately, the building blocks for the construction of a notion of a self/attā.

Before we examine the construction of a notion of a self, linguistic clarification regarding the terms *craving* and *desire* is needed. There are several different concepts in the Pali *Nikāya* that are usually translated using the English words "desire" and "craving." For the sake of clarity in how the five aggregates are transformed into a notion of a self, clarification is needed for the Pali words *taṇhā*, *chanda*, and *lobha*, all of which have been translated as "desire."

The cause of suffering or unsatisfactoriness (*dukkha*) as stated in the Second Noble Truth is *taṇhā*:

> Now this, bhikkhus, is the noble truth of the origin of suffering: it is this craving which leads to renewed existence, accompanied by delight and lust, seeking delight here and there; that is, craving for sensual pleasures, craving for existence, craving for extermination. (Dhammacakkappavattana Sutta; SN, 2000, 56.11: Setting in Motion the Wheel of the Dhamma)

The cause of dukkha, as stated in the Bhadraka Sutta (SN, 2000, 42.11: With Bhadraka), is chanda: "Whatever suffering arises all that arises rooted in desire (chanda), with desire as its source; for desire is the root of suffering."

Chanda, often translated as "desire," is defined as "impulse, excitement; intention, resolution, will; desire for, wish for, delight in. As virtue: striving after righteousness, ardent desire, zeal. Often combined with other good qualities" (Pali Text Society, n.d.). Chanda (desire) is value neutral: It can be desire for enlightenment or desire for sensual pleasures. Taṇhā, also often translated as "desire" or "craving," is not value neutral. Taṇhā is defined as "drought & thirst; craving, hunger for, excitement, the fever of unsatisfied longing" (Pali Text Society, n.d.). Taṇhā can be desire for the experience of pleasant hedonic feeling tone (*vedanā*), desire for avoidance of unpleasant hedonic feeling tone, or desire for existence. One significant difference between chanda (desire) and taṇhā (craving) is that chanda can be satisfied. For example, when it is chanda (desire) for enlightenment, that desire can be satisfied and resolved. In contrast, taṇhā (craving) tends to have the characteristic of not being able to be resolved. For example, taṇhā (craving) for the existence of an eternal permeant self (attā) cannot be satisfied and resolved. This differentiation can be seen in the Chandasamādhi Sutta:

> Bhikkhus, if a bhikkhu gains concentration, gains one-pointedness of mind based upon desire, this is called concentration due to desire. He generates desire for the non-arising of unarisen evil unwholesome states. . . . He generates desire for the abandoning of arisen evil unwholesome states. . . . He generates desire for the arising of unarisen wholesome states. . . . He generates desire for the maintenance of arisen wholesome states. . . . Thus, this desire and this concentration due to desire . . . this is called the basis for spiritual power that possesses concentration due to desire. (SN, 2000, 51.13: Concentration Due to Desire)

A third Pali word that is also often translated as "desire" is *lobha*, which is defined as "covetousness, greed" (Pali Text Society, n.d.). Lobha is the desire for things and experiences that are driven by the pursuit of pleasant hedonic feeling tone (vedanā). Lobha is the instigator of many difficult and problematic situations. The topic of lobha (covetousness, greed) and chanda (desire) will be discussed more extensively in subsequent chapters in this volume.

For the construction of a notion of a self, or the five aggregates subject to clinging, craving (taṇhā) is of interest because its addition to the five aggregates animates the five aggregates into a notion of a self that is the cause of suffering or unsatisfactoriness (dukkha). The notion of a self is discussed next.

THE BUDDHIST NOTION OF A SELF

Equation of the five aggregates subject to clinging to suffering is stated in the formulation of the First Noble Truth.

> Now this, bhikkhus, is the noble truth of suffering: . . . in brief, the five aggregates subject to clinging are suffering. (Dhammacakkapavattana Sutta; SN, 2000, 56.11: Setting in Motion the Wheel of the Dhamma)

Taṇhā (craving) animates the five aggregates to five aggregates subject to clinging. The five aggregates subject to clinging is the designation for a notion of a self. It is the notion of self that manifests human suffering and populates the client's complaints in psychotherapy.

In the Paññati Pañha (*Milindapañha* [Mil], 1890, 3.1.1: The Chariot Simile), the dialogue between King Milinda and the monk Nāgasena when they first met speaks to the Buddhist notion of a self (attā). Indo-Greek King Milinda, named King Menander in the West, ruled Bactria around 150 BCE. Bactria was located in what is now Afghanistan, Uzbekistan, and Tajikistan. Parts of the ancient Silk Road traversed Bactria. Nāgasena, a Buddhist monk, and King Milinda had the following conversation upon meeting (Pesala, 2001):

KING MILINDA: How is your Reverence known, and what, Sir, is your name?

NĀGASENA: O king, I am known as Nāgasena but that is only a designation in common use, for no permanent individual can be found.

KING MILINDA: If, most venerable Nāgasena, that is true, . . . a man were to kill you there would be no murder. . . . You say that you are called Nāgasena; now what is that Nāgasena? . . . I can discover no Nāgasena. Nāgasena is an empty sound. Who is it we see before us? It is a falsehood that your reverence has spoken.

NĀGASENA: How did you come here, by foot or in a chariot?

KING MILINDA: In a chariot, venerable sir.

NĀGASENA: Then, explain sir, what that is. Is it the axle? Or the wheels, or the chassis, or reins, or yoke that is the chariot? Is it all of these combined, or is it something apart from them?

KING MILINDA: It is none of these things, venerable sir.

NĀGASENA: Then, sir, this chariot is an empty sound. . . . Just as it is by the existence of the various parts that the word "Chariot" is used, just so is it that when the aggregates of being are there we talk of a being. . . . That being is called Nāgasena. And Nāgasena is but a collection of aggregates.

The five aggregates (*khandhā*) are the equivalent of the parts that make up a chariot or, using our previous 21st century analogy, the parts that comprise what is called a car. The label "car" is a shorthand reference to an assemblage of nuts, bolts, metal, plastic, spark plugs, an engine, and many other components used to construct the car. Similarly, the conventional label "self" is a shorthand reference to the five aggregates. This assemblage of parts is, by convention, referred to as *a being* or as *a notion of a self*. The naming of a car is a fabricated notion. Likewise, the naming of a self is a fabricated and constructed notion.

Schematically, human experiences are processed through the coordinated function of the aggregates. All five of the aggregates—*rūpa* (materiality, form), *vedanā* (hedonic feeling tone), *saññā* (perception, labeling, naming), *saṅkhāra* (mental formations or mental fabrications, mental proliferations, and/or volitional formations), and *viññāna* (consciousness)—function simultaneously, like a functioning car that has all parts moving simultaneously.

The ignition that starts the car or activates the aggregates is sense contact (*phassa*). As shown in Figure 5.1, sense contact can be summed up in the following formula: external sense object + internal sense bases + attention = sense contact. "The meeting of the three is contact" (*Majjhima Nikāya* [MN], 1995, 18: The Honeyball). The driver directing where the car goes is hedonic feeling tone (vedanā). The pleasant hedonic experience, or lobha (greed, covetousness), has the function of motivating a person to retain that pleasant hedonic experience; if the condition for that pleasant hedonic experience is lost, then lobha pushes the person to behave in such a way as to regain that pleasant experience. *Dosa* (anger, ill will) functions to motive toward aversion of an unpleasant hedonic experience. *Moha* (dullness of mind, delusion) is experienced as disinterest and pushes for stimulation. This process that synthesizes the functioning of the aggregates is delineated in the Madhupindika Sutta:

> Dependent on the eye and forms, eye-consciousness arises. . . . Dependent on the ear and sounds. . . . Dependent on the nose and odors. . . . Dependent on the tongue and flavors. . . . Dependent on the body and tangibles. . . . Dependent on the mind and mind-objects, mind-consciousness arises. The meeting of the three is contact. With contact as condition there is feeling. What one feels, that one perceives. What one perceives, that one thinks about. What one thinks about, that one mentally proliferates. With what one has mentally proliferated as the source, perceptions and notions [born of] mental proliferation beset a man with respect to past, future, and present mind-objects cognizable through the mind. (MN, 1995, 18)

THE FOUR INVERSIONS

The five aggregates, in its coordinated information processing system, exhibits four types of biases. These four types of preprogrammed biases systematically alter the experience of the sense contact. Think of the biases as types of software. For example, entering the number 1 in a data processing program (e.g., Microsoft Excel) is processed differently than entering a 1 in a word processing program (e.g., Microsoft Word), even though the same stimulus (i.e., entry of the numeric 1) is entered in both programs. These four types of processing biases, the *four inversions*, are named in the Vipallāsa Sutta:

> Bhikkhus, there are these four inversions of perception, inversions of mind, and inversions of view. What four? (1) The inversion of perception, mind, and view that takes the impermanent to be permanent; (2) the inversion of perception, mind, and view that takes what is suffering to be pleasurable; (3) the inversion of perception, mind, and view that takes what is non-self to be self; (4) the inversion of perception, mind, and view that takes what is unattractive to be attractive. These are the four inversions of perception, mind, and view. . . . Perceiving permanence in the impermanent, perceiving pleasure in what is suffering, perceiving a self in what is non-self, and perceiving attractiveness in what is unattractive, beings resort to wrong views, their minds deranged, their perception twisted. (*Aṅguttara Nikāya* [AN], 2012, 4.49: Inversions)

Think of this same passage in outline form:

> These are the four inversions of perception, mind, and view. . . .
> perceiving permanence in the impermanent,
> perceiving pleasure in what is suffering,
> perceiving a self in what is non-self, and
> perceiving attractiveness in what is unattractive. (AN, 2012, 4.49)

Remember the three marks of existence: all conditioned things are impermanent (*aniccā*), all things are not-self (*anattā*), and all conditioned things are unsatisfactory (dukkha; *Dhammapada* [Dhp], 1996, 277–279: The Path). As an anecdotal aside, remember the *Aṅguttara Nikāya: The Numerical Discourses of the Buddha* (2012). One might observe that Buddhism does love counting—with the three marks of existence and the four inversions. The three marks of existence are categorically different from the four inversions. The four inversions are occurrences that happen within the mentality portion of processing a stimulus, whereas the three marks of existence are statements about the universe that are independent of the human experience of existence. The two are related in that the inversions state how we misperceive the three marks of existence.

The first processing bias, or misperception, is "inversion of perception, mind, and view that takes the impermanent to be permanent" (AN, 2012, 4.49). This is when the person experiences a transient situation and believes that situation will never end. Consider a clinical example of a client having a panic attack. Although the client may know intellectually and cognitively that panic attacks do not last forever, the client experiences that panic attack as never-ending. A longer-lasting situation may be that of marriage. In the

Christian faith, marriage is not expected to end in this lifetime. Catholics and Protestants take the vows of marriage "until death do us part"; Presbyterians and Quakers take the vows for "as long as we both shall live" (Copeland, 2024). Many people enter into marriage with the expectation of permanence; that is, their married status is permanent for life. However, the U.S. Census Bureau (2021) reported that among "ever-married adults 20 years and over, 34% of women and 33% of men had ever been divorced; the percentage ever-divorced was highest (about 43%) for adults of both sexes ages 55 to 64." This means almost half (43%) of marriages will end in divorce by age 64. Expecting the permanence of a marriage is an instance of taking what is "impermanent to be permanent" (AN, 2012, 4.49). When divorce does occur, many are disquieted, disturbed, disillusioned, and possibly depressed.

The second misperception is to take "what is suffering to be pleasurable" (AN, 2012, 4.49). This is when the person experiences a situation to be pleasurable when, in all probability, that situation will bring suffering. A clinical instance of this is seen with addiction. For example, many individuals who drink alcohol or ingest other mood-altering substances report they experience a very pleasurable state. Although the person experiences a temporary pleasurable state, the long-term effects on one's life are most often unpleasant and cause much suffering. Many drug treatment interventions incorporate examination of the long-term ill effects of drug use on a person's life. While under the influence of the mood-altering substance, the person takes what is suffering to be pleasurable.

The third misperception is to take "what is non-self to be self" (AN, 2012, 4.49). This is when the person experiences any one of the five aggregates as self/attā. For example, many people in the United States identify with one of the U.S. Census Bureau (2024) race categories, such as Asian, Black, or White. To look at me (Tien), most in the United States would categorize me as Asian American. If I identified myself as Asian American as well, then individuals in the United States would agree that I am Asian American, along with all the stereotypes attached to the label "Asian American." In this instance, I experience my existence based on my phenotype, such as the shape of my eyes and nose and the color of my hair and skin, which are stereotypically Asian. A person has very little to no control over how others categorize their race; for me, to mistake this seemingly arbitrary use of a physical feature as who and what I am would be an instance of taking what is non-self to be self (AN, 2012, 4.49)—that is, taking the shape of my eyes to be who I am.

The fourth misperception is to take "what is unattractive to be attractive" (AN, 2012, 4.49). Typically, this is when the person is attracted to and possibly falls in love based on the other person's physical appearance. Entering into and sustaining a romantic relationship involves many aspects of relating between two people. To pursue a romantic partner based on societal standards of beauty is to ignore different aspects of the person that may be unattractive. Consider this clinical example: A man in his early 60s fell in love with a woman in her early 40s who, by societal standards, was physically beautiful. They entered couples therapy when they started to argue about her drug use. He became despondent when this relationship ended, thinking that he was too old and unattractive to keep her in this romantic relationship. He chose to ignore her daily use of mood-altering illegal drugs and her inability to remain employed as a result of her inebriation while on the job. His infatuation with this physically beautiful younger woman was a case of taking what is unattractive to be attractive.

Buddhism considers all humans to suffer from these processing biases and misperceptions. The Fourth Noble Truth and the Noble Eightfold Path are aimed at altering this pattern of misperception to one of realizing the three marks of existence—that being impermanence, not-self, and unsatisfactory nature of conditioned existence. To shift from the four processing biases named in the Vipallāsa Sutta (AN, 2012, 4.49), one needs to train the mind. *Vipassanā* is one of the techniques used in Buddhism to train the mind to see through the preprogrammed biases and to notice and understand that the functioning of the aggregates is not the self/attā. Vipassanā is defined as "inward vision, insight, intuition, introspection" (Pali Text Society, n.d.). Vipassanā (insight) meditation is the technique used in many mindfulness-based treatment programs.

The untrained mind misidentifies the workings of the aggregates and construes them to be one solid unit. This solid unit, colloquially referred to as a self, is a notion that is constructed from the misinterpretation of and identification with the functioning of the five aggregates. For the purpose of explicating empiric reality and for the purpose of psychotherapy, the five aggregates subject to clinging (*upādānakkhandhā*) is the functional definition of a self that experiences life.

CLINGING ASPECT OF THE FIVE AGGREGATES SUBJECT TO CLINGING

The five aggregates (*pañcakkhandhā*) can be thought of as the individual ingredients in split-pea soup, for example. To make any type of soup, one needs several categories of ingredients, such as liquids, protein, vegetables, and spices. Think of the aggregates of rūpa (materiality and form), vedanā (hedonic feeling tone), saññā (perception, labeling, and naming), saṅkhāra (mental formations), and viññāna (consciousness) as categories of ingredients, such as liquids, protein, vegetables, and spices. Applying taṇhā (craving, the fever of unsatisfied longing) to the five aggregates is like applying heat to the ingredients when making split-pea soup.

In our split-pea soup example, the construction of a notion of a self begins when heat is applied to the ingredients. It generally takes time for the soup ingredients to blend. Time on the fire can be thought of as upādāna, which is usually translated as "clinging, attachment." The *Pali Text Society's Pali–English Dictionary* defines upādāna as "material substratum by means of which an active process is kept alive or going, fuel, supply, provision; drawing upon, grasping, holding on, grip, attachment; finding one's support by or in, clinging to, taking up, nourished by" (Pali Text Society, n.d.). The manifestation of upādāna that produces the notion of a self can be thought of as the inevitable merging of the individual ingredients in the split-pea soup when heat is applied. Stewing of the soup ingredients (five aggregates [pañcakkhandhā]) with the application of heat (craving, the fever of unsatisfied longing [taṇhā]) over time (clinging, attachment [upādāna]) results in a mixture in which the individual ingredients are no longer easily identifiable (five aggregates subject to clinging [upādānakkhandhā]), and the resultant concoction is called split-pea soup (notion of a self). Figure 6.1 depicts this process. Upādānakkhandhā is defined in the *Pali Text Society's Pali–English Dictionary* as "the factors of the fivefold clinging to existence" (Pali Text Society, n.d.). This process in the construction of a notion of a self through craving (taṇhā) and then clinging or attachment (upādāna), which gives rise

FIGURE 6.1. The Constructed Notion of a Self

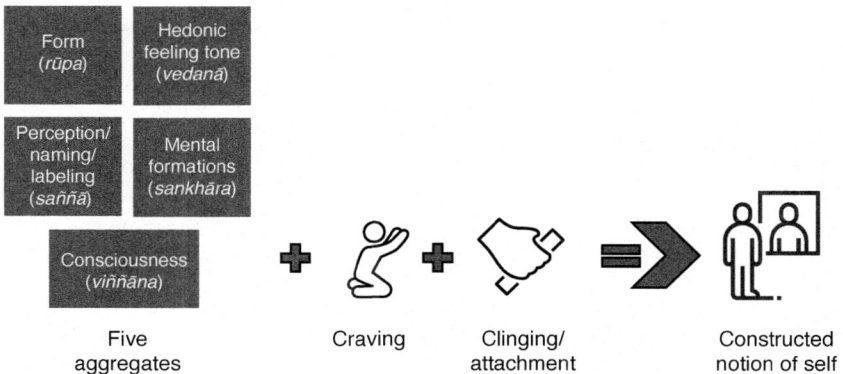

Form (rūpa)	Hedonic feeling tone (vedanā)
Perception/ naming/ labeling (saññā)	Mental formations (sankhāra)
Consciousness (viññāna)	

Five aggregates   Craving   Clinging/ attachment   Constructed notion of self

to suffering (dukkha), and is described in the Upādāna Sutta (SN, 2000, 12.52: Clinging) as follows:

> Bhikkhus, when one dwells contemplating gratification in things that can be clung to, craving increases. With craving as condition, clinging comes to be; with clinging as condition, existence; with existence as condition, birth; with birth as condition, aging-and-death, sorrow, lamentation, pain, displeasure, and despair come to be. Such is the origin of this whole mass of suffering.

Different kinds of soup contain different ingredients, but all soups contain similar categories of ingredients (e.g., liquids, protein, vegetables, and spices). Each of the five aggregates subject to clinging/upādānakkhandhā can be thought of as a different category of soup ingredients (five aggregates/pañcakkhandhā). In making soup, the categories of ingredients remain similar while individual ingredients within the category change, resulting in different kinds of soup. Likewise, the five aggregates/pañcakkhandhā are the categories for the construction of the notion of a self. Different configurations from each of the categories change what manifests, distinguishing differences in people, like changing the type of vegetables or spices to make different kinds of soup.

The untrained mind cannot detect the five aggregates/pañcakkhandhā, similar to how most people cannot distinguish different ingredients in soup. However, those with well-trained palettes are able to distinguish individual ingredients in any food dish. Likewise, those with well-trained minds are able to distinguish the functioning of each of the five aggregates/pañcakkhandhā at the time a person experiences a sense object. Such a well-trained mind is able to discern that the actuality of the notion of a self, not the misidentification or the misinterpretation, is the five aggregates subject to clinging/upādānakkhandhā. The Buddha usually referred to humans as being composed of the five aggregates, subject to clinging. For the purpose of explicating empiric reality and for the purpose of psychotherapy, the five aggregates subject to clinging/upādānakkhandhā is the functional and operational definition of a notion of a self that experiences life.

PERSONIFICATION

Buddhism posits that personification is the mechanism for mistaking the parts (five aggregates/pañcakkhandhā) for an infrangible whole (a self/attā).

> Bhikkhus, there are these six standpoints for views. What are the six? Here, bhikkhus, an untaught ordinary person . . . regards material form thus: "This is mine, this I am, this is my self." . . . Regards feeling thus: "This is mine, this

I am, this is my self." . . . Regards perception thus: "This is mine, this I am, this is my self." . . . Regards formations thus: "This is mine, this I am, this is my self." . . . He regards what is seen, heard, sensed, cognized, encountered, sought, mentally pondered thus: "This is mine, this I am, this is my self." And this standpoint for views, namely, "That which is the self is the world." (Alagaddūpama Sutta; MN, 1995, 22.15: The Simile of the Snake)

In this sutta, an "untaught ordinary person" describes a category of individuals. The term "untaught" refers to someone who has not been taught the *dhamma*, the teachings of the Buddha Gotama. The term "ordinary" refers to someone who has not practiced living as recommended by the Buddha Gotama, which in general refers to the Noble Eightfold Path.

The act of clinging to the five aggregates (pañcakkhandhā) results in the formation of the notion of a self that is experienced as follows:

etaṃ mama (this is me)
eso'ham asmi (this is mine)
eso me attā (this I am). (MN, 1995, 22)

Although Buddhism acknowledges the conventional existence of a self, just like the conventional existence of a car, there is not an ultimate existence of a solid unified self (attā) that contains the essential nature of a person. The Buddha poses that what humans experience and what is conveniently labeled as the self/attā/being is constructed from the five aggregates subject to clinging. It is by convention and for convenience of communication that Buddhism refers to the five aggregates subject to clinging as a notion of a self, a being.

The construction of the notion of a self is accomplished by personifying the processing of the sense contact by the five aggregates. The mind misconstrues, misinterprets, and exaggerates the aggregates by the process of personification. *Personification*, as defined in the *APA Dictionary of Psychology*, is "a figure of speech in which personal or human characteristics are attributed to an . . . abstraction, as in saying *Fortune smiled on her*" (American Psychological Association, n.d.). A notion of a self is constructed by attributing personal identity to the natural functioning of the aggregates, arriving at an individualistic personality.

The pathway for this personification is elucidated in the Cūḷavedalla Sutta (MN, 1995, 44: The Shorter Series of Questions and Answers). Two different translations of the sutta are presented next to give a sense of the topic:

How does identity view come to be? . . . Regards (material form . . . feeling . . . perception . . . formations . . . consciousness) as self, or self as possessed of (material form . . . feeling . . . perception . . . formations . . . consciousness), or (material form . . . feeling . . . perception . . . formations . . . consciousness) as in self, or self as in (material form . . . feeling . . . perception . . . formations . . . consciousness). That is how identity view comes to be. (MN, 1995, 44.7)

[H]ow does a substantialist view come about? . . . They regard (form-rūpa . . . feeling-vedanā . . . perception-saññā . . . mental choices-saṅkhāra . . . consciousness-viññāna) as self, self as having (form-rūpa . . . feeling-vedanā . . . perception-saññā . . . mental choices-saṅkhāra . . . consciousness-viññāna), (form-rūpa . . . feeling-vedanā . . . perception-saññā . . . mental choices-saṅkhāra . . . consciousness-viññāna) in self, or self in (form-rūpa . . . feeling-vedanā . . . perception-saññā . . . mental choices-saṅkhāra . . . consciousness-viññāna). That's how substantialist view comes about. (MN, 2018)

In this sutta, "identity view" refers to the construction of the I/self/attā. To handle this concept in psychotherapy, it may be easier to consider this process as the development of a personality, or the sense of a personhood, rather than identity. This sutta lists the types of relationships the self can have with the five aggregates in the development of an individual personality: namely, (a) the aggregates as self, (b) self as having aggregates, (c) the aggregates in self, and (d) self in the aggregates.

The phrase, "This is mine" (MN, 1995, 22), regards self as "having (material form . . . feeling . . . perception . . . formations . . . consciousness)" (MN, 1995, 44). This is the act of appropriation, taking any of the functioning of the five aggregates to be oneself. An individual who appropriates form considers themself to be represented by form, or material possessions, such as the type of car one drives, the neighborhood one lives in, the brand-name clothing one owns and wears, and one's material body. This person mistakes possession of material form to be the self and typically considers their body to belong to the self.

The phrase, "This is my self" (MN, 1995, 22), regards "(material form . . . feeling . . . perception . . . formations . . . consciousness) as self" (MN, 1995, 44). This is the act of identification. Some individuals think of themselves as their diagnosis. For example, a client was basically functional and had received a diagnosis of bipolar disorder. Although the client's symptoms were disturbing to her, they did not significantly interfere with her function at work. However, after the client received the diagnosis, she came to a psychotherapy session and asked the therapist what she should change, whether she should quit her job, whether she should move to a different living situation, and so on. When the therapist asked the client why she was considering all of these changes, she said, "I have to figure out how to live as bipolar." The client had identified with her diagnosis.

The aggregates in self or the self in the aggregates (MN, 1995, 44) addresses the question of parts and whole. Self in the aggregates is the question of whether the whole is greater than the parts. If the self is in the aggregates and the aggregates taken together is the self, then the whole is greater than the parts; this is similar to the idea of the whole self, as in the saying "to bring your whole self to work." Self in the aggregates is the idea of an essence that is surrounded by things that obscure the true essence, such as smog blocking the view of a mountain or grime tarnishing the brilliance of a gem. This is the belief that there is a true/essential self that is different from the aggregates.

The phrase, "This I am" (MN, 1995, 22), is the act of projection. "That which is the self is the world" (MN, 1995, 22) is the mind's mistaken assumptions based on the residual unexamined primary narcissism that the impersonal functioning of the five aggregates is the essential self/attā, and that essential self, in turn, is the center of the universe. Thus, this self-centered experience of existence is projected out. In this projection, the person, without much awareness or examination, expects that everything and everyone should accommodate their wishes and desires. An example based on projection of one's mental formations is taking the stance that what one thinks of any given situation is the totality of truth. As it applies toward the individual, it might sound something like this: "I am what I think," or "I am what I feel."

Buddha Gotama posited that what humans experience and what is conveniently labeled as the self/attā/being is constructed from the five aggregates, just like split-pea soup is made of different categories of ingredients. The difference between the aggregates and the clinging aspect of the aggregates is the *self-view*, often stated as "this is me, this is mine, this I am" (SN, 2000, 22.151.2). Buddhist interventions, such as meditation, work primarily on the clinging aspect of the five aggregates.

CONCLUSION

Humans experience existence by way of the processing function of the five aggregates. The unexamined experience of existence is by way of the notion of a self, or the five aggregates subject to clinging. The self, or a being, is just as Nāgasena said to King Melinda:

> this chariot is an empty sound. . . . Just as it is by the existence of the various parts that the word "Chariot" is used, just so is it that when the aggregates of being are there we talk of a being. . . . That being is called Nāgasena. And Nāgasena is but a collection of aggregates. (Mil, 1890, 3.1.1)

This assemblage of parts is, by convention, referred to as a being or as a self/attā. The naming of a chariot is a fabricated notion. Likewise, the naming of a self/attā is a fabricated and constructed notion.

Having explained the construction of a notion of a self, next we will examine what that notion of a self experiences of existence. The experience is typified by dukkha (suffering, unsatisfactoriness). The next chapter describes the types of dukkha; what each type of dukkha looks like, including how it manifests in therapy; and what Buddhism prescribes to alleviate the experience of dukkha (suffering, unsatisfactoriness), with the hope of increasing *sukha* (happiness, satisfaction).

PART **IV** DUKKHA

7 DUKKHA DEFINED

Having established the how of experienced existence, the next several chapters examine what humans experience of existence. What humans—or to be exact, the five aggregates subject to clinging—experience of existence is said by the Buddha Gotama as, "All conditioned things are unsatisfactory" (*Dhammapada* [Dhp], 1996, 277–279; The Path). This unsatisfactoriness is described in the concept of dukkha. The Buddha enumerated several types of *dukkha* (suffering, unsatisfactoriness) in the First Noble Truth. The term dukkha has been generally translated across a variety of texts as "suffering," "unpleasant," "painful," "causing misery," and "unsatisfactoriness." However, as discussed in Chapter 1 (this volume), the full meaning is more nuanced:

> There is no word in English covering the same ground as Dukkha does in Pali. Our modern words are too specialized, too limited, and usually too strong. Sukha & dukkha are ease and dis-ease (but we use disease in another sense); or wealth and ilth from well & ill (but we have now lost ilth); or wellbeing and ill-ness (but illness means something else in English). We are forced, therefore, in translation to use half synonyms, no one of which is exact. Dukkha is equally mental & physical. Pain is too predominantly physical, sorrow too exclusively mental, but in some connections, they have to be used in default

https://doi.org/10.1037/0000453-008
Buddhist Psychotherapy: Connecting Early Buddhism to Mindfulness and Western Psychotherapy, by L. Tien, D. M. Kawahara, and V. Dhammadinna

of any more exact rendering. Discomfort, suffering, ill, and trouble can occasionally be used in certain connections. Misery, distress, agony, affliction and woe are never right. They are all much too strong & are only mental. (Pali Text Society, n.d.)

Humans tend not to see, understand, acknowledge, or accept the ever-changing nature of dependent arising of phenomena in consciousness that are constructed from the five aggregates subject to clinging. Instead, humans tend to experience an infrangible self existing in nonchanging everlasting situations. Clinging to and identifying with the notion of a nonchanging infrangible self (*attā*) results in dukkha (suffering, unsatisfactoriness).

Clients enter psychotherapy with their complaints, expecting the psychotherapist to intervene in such a manner that their complaints are resolved. The request for intervention can be either implicit or explicit and may come in the form of a complaint. Some examples (expressed in a reductionist manner) are as follows:

- "It is not okay that I feel depressed, so fix it so I am not depressed anymore."

- "It is not okay that my mother-in-law is inconsiderate, so fix it so I don't continue to argue with my spouse about their mother."

- "It is not okay that I procrastinate, so fix it so I do all tasks immediately with ease."

For psychotherapy, dukkha (suffering, unsatisfactoriness) can be thought of as anything that a client complains about that is not okay in their life, regardless of what that complaint may be.

THE DART (*SALLA SUTTA*)

As we discussed in Part I (this volume), the cause of suffering or unsatisfactoriness in life (dukkha) is craving (*taṇhā*). Craving (*taṇhā*), when added to the five aggregates (*khandhā*), and then clinging or attachment (*upādāna*) to the craving, leads to a constructed notion of self. It is this constructed notion of self through which we experience existence. That life lived from within a constructed notion of the self has the characteristic of dukkha (suffering, unsatisfactoriness; refer to Figure 6.1). A life lived from the functioning of the five aggregates (not-self) instead of through the constructed notion of a self has the characteristic of *sukah* (happiness, satisfactoriness).

The five aggregates alone do not cause suffering, nor does desire (*chanda*). All humans need chanda (desire) to be alive, and chanda for individual and collective benefit adds nobility to the human endeavor. The addition of craving (taṇhā) is problematic, especially when that craving develops into clinging or attachment (upādāna). It is the addition of taṇhā and upādāna that results in the five aggregates subject to clinging, which generates the notion of a self.

This clinging to the functioning of the five aggregates manifests itself not only in how people react to life's events but also in how the preprogrammed biases distort noumena. *Noumena* was discussed extensively by philosopher Immanuel Kant and is defined as "a posited object or event as it appears in itself independent of perception by the senses" (Merriam-Webster, n.d.). The preprogrammed biases distort noumena, or reality as it is. These preprogrammed biases are listed in the Vipallāsa Sutta (*Aṅguttara Nikāya* [AN], 2012, 4.49: Inversions). Combining the mistakes of "perceiving permanence in the impermanent" (AN, 2012, 4.49) with "perceiving a self in what is non-self" (AN, 2012, 4.49) leads to the type of suffering and unsatisfactoriness described in the First Noble Truth. This distortion and its consequences are described in the Salla Sutta (*Saṃyutta Nikāya* [SN], 2000, 36.6: The Dart):

> Bhikkhus, when the uninstructed worldling is being contacted by a painful feeling, he sorrows, grieves, and laments; he weeps beating his breast and becomes distraught. He feels two feelings—a bodily one and a mental one. Suppose they were to strike a man with a dart, and then they would strike him immediately afterwards with a second dart, so that the man would feel a feeling caused by two darts. So too, when the uninstructed worldling is being contacted by a painful feeling . . . he feels two feelings—a bodily one and a mental one.

In the Buddha's analogy, the human experience of existence is like being hit by two darts. The first dart represents events that occur in life, such as getting married, getting divorced, getting a job, losing a job, being in a car crash, having a tree fall on a newly purchased car, or any number of other events. The first dart is inevitable because life happens. From the simplest of events to the most complex, life happens. A simple event would be a pedestrian who trips and falls on an uneven patch of pavement in the sidewalk—a simple trip that happens to almost everyone at some time in their life. A complex event would be a person losing their job due to automation in manufacturing. For example, automation in refrigerator manufacturing means both a decrease in the cost of making a refrigerator, thus enabling more people to purchase home refrigerators, and a decrease in the number of employees needed to manufacture refrigerators. Even though more refrigerators are produced, fewer people are employed in the job of manufacturing refrigerators. From the simple trip on the sidewalk to the complex process leading to the loss of jobs in manufacturing is, figuratively speaking, the first dart.

The second dart, which mistakes life's events to being related to oneself, is dukkha (suffering, unsatisfactoriness). The second dart is what usually presents in psychotherapy. The person who trips on the sidewalk thinks of themselves as clumsy, ungraceful, or unattractive, then feels embarrassed and despondent and withdraws from their walking companion. This person, being actively aware of their unpleasant feeling of embarrassment, would have (more likely than not) discussed the discomfort of embarrassment or characterized themselves as being clumsy and socially awkward in a treatment session, with an implicit request for the psychotherapist to help them change their social awkwardness and to give them ways to stop the experience of the unpleasant feeling of embarrassment. The person who has lost their job at the refrigerator factory imagines the decline of their usefulness due to an inability to earn a livelihood; thinks themselves unjustly punished; reacts with anger, resentment, and despondency; and wishes to avoid these unpleasant feelings and seeks escape into the momentary pleasure of drinking alcohol to feel better. This person would likely bring their alcoholism as the problem needing to be treated in psychotherapy. These hypothetical sequences of events are the second dart.

For the aforementioned hypothetical person complaining of their social awkwardness, the first dart is tripping on the uneven sidewalk. The second dart is the moment of embarrassment and then deciding to avoid painful feelings of embarrassment by withdrawing socially so as not to deal with the friend's imagined negative judgment for their clumsiness as evidenced by their tripping and falling. For the person who drinks alcohol to excess, the first dart is the loss of the job; the second dart is the moment when the person decides to escape the painful feelings of their imagined uselessness and feelings of anger by seeking sense pleasure through drinking alcohol. Buddhist interventions, and by extension those interventions used in Buddhist psychotherapy, are designed to separate the experience of the first dart from the self-inflicted harm of the second dart.

THE FIRST NOBLE TRUTH: ENUMERATION OF FOUR TYPES OF DUKKHA

Two renditions of the First Noble Truth are presented next. There is very slight variation in the types of dukkha (suffering, unsatisfactoriness) listed. Because all these types of dukkha show up in treatment, this section will include the types of dukkha listed in both suttas. The first rendition of the First Noble Truth is as follows:

And what, friends, is the noble truth of suffering? Birth is suffering; aging is suffering; death is suffering; sorrow, lamentation, pain, grief, and despair are suffering; not to obtain what one wants is suffering; in short, the five aggregates affected by clinging are suffering. (*Saccavibhaṅga Sutta; Majjhima Nikāya* [MN], 1995, An Analysis of the Truths)

The following is the second rendition of the First Noble Truth:

Birth is suffering, ageing is suffering, death is suffering, sorrow, lamentation, pain, sadness, and distress are suffering. Being attached to the unloved is suffering, being separated from the loved is suffering, not getting what one wants is suffering. In short, the five aggregates of grasping are suffering. (Mahāsatipaṭṭhāna Sutta; *Dīgha Nikāya* [DN], 1987/1995, 22: The Greater Discourse of the Foundation of Mindfulness)

In the traditional interpretation of the First Noble Truth, three types of dukkha are named: dukkha-dukkha, vipariṇāma-dukkha, and saṅkhāra-dukkha. For use in a theory for psychotherapy, the summation from DN (1987/1995, 22), "in short, the five aggregates of grasping are suffering," will be treated as a fourth type of dukkha.

Dukkha-dukkha is the suffering and unsatisfactoriness that are linked to an embodied existence. The *Pali Text Society's Pali–English Dictionary* defines dukkha-dukkha as follows:

painful sensation caused by bodily pain, illnesses & all bodily states of suffering; pain & bodily discomfort through outward circumstances, as extreme climates, want of food, gnat—bites etc. (Mental) distress & painful states caused by the death of one's beloved or other misfortunes to friends or personal belongings. (Pali Text Society, n.d.)

Vipariṇāma-dukkha is the suffering experienced when situations change, which is defined as "being caused by change" (Pali Text Society, n.d.). *Saṅkhāra-dukkha* is the suffering that is inflicted on oneself from one's own mental formations, fabrications, or proliferations; it is defined as "having its origin in the saṅkhāra" (Pali Text Society, n.d.).

The traditional interpretation of the First Noble Truth names only the three types of suffering just described. However, the last phrase in MN (1995, 141), "in short, the five aggregates affected by clinging are suffering," describes the suffering that often presents in psychotherapy and is one that can be said to be the most fundamental. Therefore, for the purpose of a Buddhist theory of psychotherapy, the last phrase in the sutta is added as a fourth category of dukkha (suffering, unsatisfactoriness). This fourth category is the five aggregates subject to clinging, which is a designation for the notion of a self (Exhibit 7.1).

EXHIBIT 7.1. Types of Dukkha

- *Dukkha-dukkha:* suffering due to birth, aging, and death
- *Viparināma-dukkha:* suffering due to situational change
- *Saṅkhāra-dukkha:* suffering due to mental formations
- *Five aggregates subject to clinging:* suffering due to the notion of a self

In the remaining chapters of Part IV (this volume), we will examine each type of suffering. Each chapter follows the Buddha Gotama's format of (a) naming and describing the type of dukkha (suffering, unsatisfactoriness), (b) identifying the type of processing bias and misconception that conditions the dukkha, (c) possible topics for the in-session dialogue with a client, and then (d) the meditation interventions specified in the Satipaṭṭhāna Sutta (MN, 1995, 10: The Foundations of Mindfulness) to ameliorate the type of dukkha under discussion.

There are different types of approaches for meditation and any number of nonmeditation-based interventions discussed by the Buddha. Some of these nonmeditation-based interventions are discussed in the Sabbāsava Sutta (MN, 1995, 2: Discourse on All the Taints), which is examined in Chapter 17 (this volume). Only meditation taught in the Satipaṭṭhāna Sutta (MN, 1995, 10) will be the intervention discussed in the chapters related to the First Noble Truth, primarily to explicate the link between meditation as it is used in the mindfulness-based intervention programs in mental health practice and the ideas found in early Buddhism.

CONCLUSION

Buddha's observation of the human world is that of *anicca* (impermanence) when he said, "All conditioned things are impermanent" (Dhp, 1996, 277–279). Humans are conceptualized as *nāmarūpa* (mentality-materiality, a psychosomatic complex) plus *viññāna* (consciousness). How humans experience existence is via the five aggregates. The clinging to, appropriating, and identifying with the functioning of the five aggregates generate a notion of a self. Said another way, the five aggregates subject to clinging exist in a world of *anicca* (impermanence).

How humans experience existence is by way of the processing function of the five aggregates. The personification, appropriation, and identifying with the processing function of the five aggregates results in the five aggregates subject to clinging, which is the mechanism for the construction of a notion of a self. Humans experience the universe from the standpoint of that notion of the self.

What do the five aggregates subject to clinging experience in a world of impermanence? Posited another way, what does a person experience when their constructed infrangible permanent self meets the ever-changing universe? The Buddha said that what humans experience has the characteristic of dukkha (suffering, unsatisfactoriness). That is, dukkha is characteristic of the human lived experience when the constructed infrangible permanent self meets the ever-changing universe. For psychotherapy, dukkha is the oppressiveness of anything that is not okay with the client; that not-okayness is what comes into the psychotherapy treatment room.

There are four types of suffering (dukkha-dukkha, vipariṇāma-dukkha, saṅkhāra-dukkha, and five aggregates subject to clinging). Subsequent chapters will describe each type, identify the type of processing bias and misconception that characterizes it, and then offer interventions to ameliorate it to increase the experience of sukha (happiness, satisfactoriness).

8

THE FIRST DUKKHA

Suffering Due to Birth, Aging, and Death

In the Dhammacakkapavattana Sutta (*Saṃyutta Nikāya* [SN], 2000, 56.11: Setting in Motion the Wheel of the Dhamma), Buddha Gotama said, "Now this, bhikkhus, is the noble truth of suffering: birth is suffering, aging is suffering, illness is suffering, death is suffering." The first type of *dukkha* (suffering, unsatisfactoriness) is *dukkha-dukkha*, which is related to and based on the human material existence of our embodied being. That is, dukkha-dukkha is the suffering due to the birth of a body, the experiences of that body, and the inevitable changes to the material form of the body. Table 8.1 presents sutta excerpts relating to the three stages of the body: birth, aging, and death.

The human existence as an embodied being brings its uniquely characteristic experiences. Examples include the oppressiveness of physical pain such as a back injury, the delight of sense pleasure like listening to one's favorite song, the hopefully temporary misery of constipation, the all-consuming pleasure of consensual sex, the discomfort of physical and mental fatigue, and on and on. These are various experiences of dukkha-dukkha, the suffering and unsatisfactoriness linked to an embodied existence. This chapter discusses the

https://doi.org/10.1037/0000453-009
Buddhist Psychotherapy: Connecting Early Buddhism to Mindfulness and Western Psychotherapy, by L. Tien, D. M. Kawahara, and V. Dhammadinna

TABLE 8.1. Suffering Based on Having a Body

Stage of body	Sutta excerpt
Birth	And what, friends, is birth? The birth of beings into the various orders of beings, their coming to birth, precipitation in a womb, generation, the manifestation of the aggregates, obtaining the bases for contact–this is called birth.
Aging	And what, friends, is ageing? The ageing of beings in the various orders of beings, their old age, brokenness of teeth, greyness of hair, wrinkling of skin, decline of life, weakness of faculties–this is called ageing.
Death	And what, friends, is death? The passing of beings out of the various orders of beings, their passing away, dissolution, disappearance, dying, completion of time, dissolution of aggregates, laying down of the body–this is called death.

Note. Excerpts are from the Saccavibhaṅga Sutta (MN, 1995, 141: The Analysis/Exposition of the Truths).

misperceptions involved in this type of suffering, along with ways to manage the unpleasantness of dukkha-dukkha.

PERCEIVING AN IMPERMANENT FORM (I.E., A BODY) TO BE PERMANENT

As stated in SN (2000, 56.11), "birth is suffering, aging is suffering, death is suffering." This is what happens when the constructed infrangible permanent self meets the reality of an interdependently existing, ever-changing body. The mind, in its processing function, systematically personifies the body and then appropriates the personified body into an infrangible self. The human experience of suffering or unsatisfactoriness (dukkha) is conditioned by the mind (*citta*) mistakenly taking "what is impermanent to be permanent, what is suffering to be pleasurable, and what is not-self to be the self" (Vipallāsa Sutta; *Aṅguttara Nikāya* [AN], 2012, 4.49: Inversions). In this process, the notion of the self usually appropriates the body into their notion of the self; as such, that body does not exist independent of that notion of themself.

This whole process of existence and the human experience of existence starts with birth. Remember the sutta formulation of impermanence, which states, "When this exists, that comes to be; with the arising of this, that arises" (SN, 2000, 12.21.1). The First Noble Truth states that "birth is suffering" (SN, 2000, 56.11). Stated within the formulation for impermanence, "When this [birth] exists, that [dukkha—suffering, unsatisfactoriness] comes to be" (SN, 2000, 12.61). A human being "comes to be" with "birth, precipitation in a womb, generation, the manifestation of the aggregates, obtaining the bases for contact—this is called birth" (Saccavibhaṅga Sutta; *Majjhima Nikāya* [MN], 1995, 41: The Analysis/Exposition of the Truths). Such birth necessitates the experiences of change, such as disease and injury, in a body that is impermanent.

The usual experience of the body is in the moment, with that moment extending permanently over time. Imagine the experience of the body in the moment of panic during an anxiety attack. The experience of that body amid a panic attack is that the moment will never end; the experienced panic will last forever. While healthy, a person does not recall the discomforts of the physical body when experiencing the symptoms of illness, like influenza; or while physically fit, the person does not permit the possibility of pain from a sprained ankle or broken bone or chronic pain from a spinal cord injury. When the body succumbs to disease, such as a simple cold or a serious illness like cancer, there is incredulity, there is suffering, and there is dukkha (suffering, unsatisfactoriness).

The normal course for the body is to age. As the body evolves over time, it will undergo changes such as "brokenness of teeth, greyness of hair, wrinkling of skin, decline of life, weakness of faculties—this is called ageing" (MN, 1995, 141). And finally, in the realm of physical changes to the body, there is death. The sutta turns our attention to death and defines death as "their passing away, dissolution, disappearance, dying, completion of time, dissolution of aggregates, laying down of the body—this is called death" (MN, 1995, 9). Although everyone knows, in theory, that one day this body will die, people usually do not know exactly when or how this body will cease to be. Thus, this theoretical event of death is usually envisioned to maybe occur in some infinitely distant future. While there is cognitive and theoretical knowledge that everyone will die, there usually is not the embodied knowledge that "this body of mine too, is of the same nature as that [lifeless deceased] body, is going to be like that body" (Satipaṭṭhāna Sutta; MN, 1995, 10: The Foundations of Mindfulness).

In general, most people avoid thinking about death, whether about one's own death or the death of others. It is rare that a person does the necessary planning for this momentous event. Most people do more planning for a vacation than for the death of their own body. In the collective avoidance and the experiential rejection of the inevitable event of death, humans generally consider death as suffering.

That physical body is also the source of sense contact. The sutta's description of birth is "the manifestation of the aggregates, obtaining the bases for contact—this is called birth" (MN, 1995, 141). With sense contact, a person may experience their body with a pleasant or unpleasant hedonic feeling tone (*vedanā*) or they may be largely unaware of the body. Many clients come to therapy with complaints about their body. Some feel offended by their body being too big, too fat, too skinny, too tall, too short, lopsided, or any number of bodily traits that do not match their notion of their preferred body and their image of the bodily self. Many also feel betrayed by their body when it succumbs to illness, regardless of whether the illness is temporary (e.g., a cold), chronic (e.g., diabetes), or life-threatening (e.g., a brain tumor). Then there is the inevitable event of death or the untimely death of a loved one, such as a spouse, parent, child, or friend.

Most notable is the actuality of physical pain that is present when there is an injury to the body. Many feel hopeless in the face of chronic pain and endlessly seek medical, physical, and psychological intervention to either mitigate or extinguish the oppressive experience of the pain.

Dukkha-dukkha (physical and emotional pain from the body) is the emotional disturbance, the oppressiveness, that results from the mind's habitual lock on a permanent infrangible self/*attā*, of which a nonchanging body is part and parcel of that self/*attā*, meeting the reality of a changing body that is independent of the self/*attā*. The various Buddhist interventions are designed for the person to gain an embodied experiential knowledge that the body is the body and that the body is not-self (*anattā*).

INTERVENTION

In the normal course of a person's life, birth, aging, and death happen. Yet most people struggle against the reality of birth, aging, and death. In the Salla Sutta (SN, 2000, 36.5: The Dart), the Buddha said that "when the uninstructed worldling is being contacted by a painful feeling . . . he feels two feelings—a bodily one and a mental one."

Birth, aging, and death comprise the first dart, which comprise those inevitable events of life. A person's reaction to the normal and inevitable events of birth, aging, and death is the second dart. Most people do not usually confine the experience of life to the first dart. The Buddha Gotama indicated that the untrained person adds to that life event with the second dart by adding reactions ("sorrow, grieve, lamentation, weeps, beating their breast and becomes distraught" [SN, 2000, 36.5]) to that life event.

The body functions and changes of its own accord. These functions and changes can be thought of as the first dart, as a sense contact. Although the person, to some measure, has influence over the body, they do not own or control the body. In its application to psychotherapy, the client will typically focus on the problems, difficulties, and frustrations in their attempts to control the functioning of the body. The struggle to control the body is the second dart. The mind is the medium through which humans focus on that second dart. The location for all the machinations is in the mind. The target for psychotherapy is to loosen the bond between the first dart and the second dart. Said another way, the goal is for some measure of separation from the identification with the body, where the body is appropriated into the self. To separate the second dart from the first dart, one has to train the mind. Thus, the site of intervention is the mind.

The Buddha described the mind in several ways:

> I don't envision a single thing that—when untamed, unguarded, unprotected, unrestrained—leads to such great harm as the mind. The mind—when untamed, unguarded, unprotected, unrestrained—leads to great harm. (Akammaniyavagga Sutta; AN, 2012, 1.23: A Single Thing)

The Buddha's description of an untrained mind (i.e., a mind without the training from meditation) is found in the Cittavagga (*Dhammapada* [Dhp], 1996, 33–43: The Mind):

> Quivering, wavering, hard to guard, to hold in check: the mind.
> Like a fish pulled from its home in the water & thrown on land: this mind flips
> & flaps about to escape Mara's sway.
> Hard to hold down, nimble, alighting wherever it likes: the mind.
> So hard to see, so very, very subtle, alighting wherever it likes: the mind.
> Wandering far, going alone, bodiless, lying in a cave: the mind.

Meditation is one of the Buddhist methods for training the mind to notice the functioning of the mind that gives rise to dukkha.

Buddhism indicates that all experience starts with a sense contact, which would be the first dart in the complaints that our clients bring to psychotherapy. That first dart will consist of a stimulus that is noticed by one of the internal sense bases, which is the form aggregate, and is attended to by mentality/processing functioning of the mind/cetasika. In its typical presentation, a client will probably start reporting on their *sankhāra* (mental formations, mental fabrications, and mental proliferations) with elaborations of accompanying emotions. Instead of immediately attending to the client's mental formations or their proliferated emotions, it would be informative for the psychotherapist to get a clear idea of the sense contact that started the whole chain of mental proliferations and emotions that resulted in the client's complaint. The psychotherapist might respond by first asking, "What happened?" in the process of tracking down the sense contact. In most cases, the client will most likely be unable to name the event of that first dart. The psychotherapist will most likely have to engage the person in a meticulously lengthy inquiry to identify the event of the first dart. The Buddhist practice of meditation is designed to be sufficiently aware of the functioning of the mind to notice the event of that first dart. The lengthy process of mastering the mind sufficiently to notice the sense contact that generated the client's difficulties may be cut short by engaging in such an inquiry with the psychotherapist in their therapy sessions.

Introduction to Silent Meditation as a Means to Development of Mindfulness

To aid in the psychotherapist's training for understanding and utilizing the ideas of the Buddha, it is essential for a psychotherapist using Buddhist ideas to have their own daily meditation practice. This is because it is easier to recognize the nuanced ways that sense contact appears and how the aggregates manifest in a client when one has some experience of the direct contact with *rūpa* (materiality, form), at least, and thus knows how it manifests in the stream of the client's words.

Any technique that can be of great benefit, like mindfulness meditation, can also be of great harm. To prevent the known harm of silent meditation, it is essential for the psychotherapist to have their own meditation practice with a live, well-trained Buddhist meditation teacher. It is not advisable for the psychotherapist to learn this technique by self-study with meditation apps readily available online. The traditional Theravāda Buddhist meditation techniques are different from the meditation approaches available in the United States and readily available online. Most online meditation apps are primarily aimed for calming and relaxation. The traditional Theravāda Buddhist meditation technique, when used as designed, holds the promise of *nibbāna*, or total liberation from dukkha (suffering, unsatisfactoriness). It also has the potential, if used without proper training, to precipitate psychotic states as well as suicide. In their everyday life, clients with a disturbed state of mind/citta, such as preoccupation with suicide, use various means of distraction to reduce the destructiveness of their disturbing mind. Think of this traditional Theravāda Buddhist meditation technique as an invitation for the client to go unaided into the turbulent world of their mind/citta. Assigning meditation as homework is like instructing the client to enter that destructive disturbed mind state unaided and unguarded. If the psychotherapist chooses either to use meditation as homework or to integrate a silent meditation sitting during their sessions, they must be very selective for whom and how this is used.

Although Buddhist psychotherapy is not a course in religion nor a manual for meditation, it does use the ideas and the meditation techniques from

Buddhism for psychotherapy. This book is not intended to teach meditation; it addresses theory and techniques linked to the theory. More detailed instructions for insight (*vipassanā*) meditation can be found in various publications as well as in the manuals for some mindfulness-based intervention programs. The sections on meditation in this volume are meant to give the reader a framework that can be taken into the in-session dialogue with the client. The meditation techniques described by the Buddha can be used by a Buddhist psychotherapist as a guide in how to function as mindfulness (*sati*) in their treatment session and as topics for in-session discussion.

The purpose of Buddhist meditation is to train the mind. It does not aim to train the body on the appropriate ways to breathe, walk, sit, or perform any other bodily functions. Various suttas discuss how best to train the mind in silent meditation. The main meditation suttas that are the bases for many mindfulness-based treatment programs are the Mahāsatipaṭṭhāna Sutta (*Dīgha Nikāya* [DN], 1987/1995, 22) and the Satipaṭṭhāna Sutta (MN, 1995, 10). It is not unusual for the *Nikāya* to have two versions of a sutta: The difference is that the sutta with the *mahā* prefix is longer and contains more information than the sutta without the prefix. Thus, the Mahāsatipaṭṭhāna Sutta (DN, 1987/1995, 22) is a longer version of the Satipaṭṭhāna Sutta (MN, 1995, 10); the type of meditation addressed in both suttas uses sati (mindfulness) for the purpose of vipassanā (insight).

Sati used for the purpose of vipassanā is the basis for most mindfulness-based intervention programs. Jon Kabat-Zinn (1984) used this approach in his Stress Reduction and Relaxation Program where he said, "Mindfulness meditation has roots in Theravāda Buddhism where it is known as sattipatana [*sic*] vipassanā or insight meditation" (p. 34). Two key words in the work by Kabot-Zinn are "sati," the root word in Satipaṭṭhāna, and "vipassanā." The *Pali Text Society's Pali–English Dictionary* defines sati as "memory, recognition, consciousness" (Pali Text Society, n.d.). The Pali word vipassanā is defined as "inward vision, insight, intuition, introspection" (Pali Text Society, n.d.). Sati used for the purpose of vipassanā can be translated as "insight meditation." This means meditation is a technique to gain insight. For Buddhism, meditation is used to gain insight on the three marks of existence: *aniccā* (impermanence, transitory), *dukkha* (suffering, unsatisfactoriness), and *anattā* (not-self).

The word sati has also been translated in English as "mindfulness." In the Nagaropama Sutta (AN, 2012, 7.67: The Fortress), the Buddha likened sati (mindfulness) to that of a "gatekeeper in the king's frontier fortress."

> Furthermore, the royal frontier fortress has a gate-keeper—wise, experience[d], intelligent—to keep out those he doesn't know and to let [in] those he does.

> With this sixth requisite of a fortress, it is well provided for the protection of those within and to ward off those without.
>
> Just as a citadel has a gatekeeper who is astute, competent, and intelligent, who keeps strangers out and lets known people in, in the same way a noble disciple is mindful. They have utmost mindfulness and alertness and can remember and recall what was said and done long ago. A noble disciple with mindfulness as their gatekeeper gives up the unskilled and develops the skillful, they give up the blameworthy and develop the blameless, and they keep themselves pure. This is the sixth good quality they have. (AN, 2012, 7.67)

This gatekeeper is "one who keeps out strangers and admits acquaintances, for protecting its inhabitants and for warding off outsider[s]" (AN, 2012, 7.67). This means that if the instruction is to pay attention to the breath, then the meditator is to remember/sati to focus on the breath. Sati (mindfulness) is constantly on guard identifying the activities of the mind. Sati acts like the frontier fortress gatekeeper by asking of every activity in the mind whether it is on the task of paying attention to the breath, which is the object of contemplation, or is the mind/citta's attention on something else. If the mind/citta is not on the breath and is instead thinking about something else, like planning the day's dinner menu, then sati tells the mind to abandon that thought. If the mind is on the breath, like noting the temperature of the breath as the air travels into the nose, then that activity is to be indulged, not abandoned.

In the Satipaṭṭhāna Sutta (MN, 1995, 10), the Buddha started off with a rhetorical question: "And how, bhikkhus, does a bhikkhu abide contemplating the body as a body?" He then gave instructions on how to take the body as the object of contemplation. The instructions start with preparation for meditation. The first instruction in the sutta is for finding a location for sitting meditation. The Satipaṭṭhāna Sutta (MN, 1995, 10) says that a monk "gone to the forest, to the root of a tree, or to an empty hut, sits down, having folded his legs crosswise, set his body erect, and established mindfulness in front of him, ever mindful he breaths in." To translate the ideal environment from the Indian subcontinent of 2,500 years ago to the present day, the equivalent of "gone to the forest" (MN, 1995, 10) is to remove oneself from daily life. In India 2,500 years ago, social life occurred in a village that was usually at the edge of a forest. Thus, going to the forest meant leaving the village and all of the social interactions that occurred in a village. For the present day, this translates to isolating oneself in a place where there will be no social interactions. The phrase, "[gone] to the root of a tree" (MN, 1995, 10), in the context of a forest, means to find a place where one is protected from the elements and secluded. Thus, one would find a protected space where one will not be visited by their pets, baked by the sun (e.g., a beach), or exposed to rain and wind (e.g., one's backyard). The phrase, "[gone] to an empty hut" (MN, 1995, 10), would mean to be isolated from all social contact. In the present-day context, this means that no distractions (e.g., computers, mobile phones with mindfulness apps, music playing in the background) are present. The instruction is to find a quiet place where one can sit and will not be disturbed.

The next instruction in the sutta regards setting the position of the body. The meditator "sits down, having folded his legs crosswise" (MN, 1995, 10), which is the instruction for a sitting meditation position. The cross-legged lotus position is ideal for providing the upper body with the most support. Sit on a cushion, or anything sufficiently cushioned for comfort, that is high enough for the knee to easily touch the floor without putting weight on the knee. Set the legs crossed with one ankle in front of the other ankle or wherever is comfortable for the body, depending on the flexibility of the legs. For knee comfort and support, rest the knees on cushions. For many societies in the Asian subcontinent, most of life is lived at the level of the floor, with cushions and bedrolls instead of chairs and desks. For our 21st-century bodies that are not accustomed to lounging on the floor, the equivalent of "sits down, having folded his legs crosswise" (MN, 1995, 10) may be sitting on a chair.

The next instruction in the sutta is to "set his body erect" (MN, 1995, 10). The erectness of the body enhances the mind/citta's alertness. When the torso is slouched and the shoulders are hunched, there is a tendency for the mind toward dullness and sleepiness. For the equivalent position of sitting in a chair, the best type of chair for meditation may be a stool; the meditator may also sit perched on the edge of a chair. This position allows the spine to be placed in the equivalent position of legs crosswise. Do not rest on the back of the chair; sit perched on the edge of the chair with the knees slightly below the hip, in line with the heels and toes. This position allows for a slight tilt of the hips that sets the spine in its most natural curvature. Regardless of what position one places the legs and arms, the instruction for "sets the body erect" (MN, 1995, 10) is to position the spine with its natural curvature to allow the body's skeletal structure to set the body erect, not to rely on the muscles to keep the torso erect.

Once a suitable place and time are found, then as one approaches the designated place for meditation, one has "established mindfulness in front of him" (MN, 1995, 10). Arousing mindfulness starts at the point when the meditator walks toward the reserved location for meditation. As the meditator walks, they tell themselves, "It is time to meditate; it is not time to hurry up and meet my New Year's resolution of self-care by doing daily meditation so that I can then go on with something more productive." Establishing mindfulness is telling the meditator to first state the intentions for the meditation session, as follows:

> I will pay attention to the breath and bring the mind back to the breath when the mind wanders. I will not follow the mind wandering, though it is bound to wander. I will go back to the breath when the mind wanders.

The first object of contemplation given in the Satipaṭṭhāna Sutta (MN, 1995, 10) is the breath. The phrase, "ever mindful he breaths in" (MN, 1995, 10), establishes the thing to which the mind is to attend, to the exclusion of all other activities in the mind. This directs the meditator to tell the mind to pay attention to all things that are part and parcel of the breath. Once one sits on the meditation cushion, then one directs the mind to the breath. The breath is the traditional object, primarily because everyone has a breath, and that breath is dynamic enough to allow for multifaceted exploration. Throughout the meditation sitting, one is to keep the mind's attention/manasikāra on the breath (over and over again, because the mind/citta will wander) and to remember that the exercise is to train the mind to be tethered to the breath, not to have the mind wandering hither and yon.

In daily practice, there is a great deal of leeway for selecting the object of contemplation in meditation. For psychotherapy, there may be reasons to select different objects of contemplation. It is advisable for the psychotherapist to carefully select the object of contemplation for the client if daily meditation is used as homework. The selection of the object of contemplation needs to be guided by the instructions on how the meditator should consider their object of contemplation, which is "ardent, fully aware and mindful" (MN, 1995, 10). In regard to the selection of the object of contemplation, "fully aware" means the meditator is aware of the reason the object of contemplation is selected and the insight to be gained from its selection.

For example, for someone who is hostile toward their body, as in many forms of body disorders, it may be counterproductive to select the breath as the object of contemplation. If one of the purposes for meditation is to have the insight that one's body is not an enemy to subdue, it may be more useful to select a part of the body that does not give rise to hostility. It may take some time to find such a location, and the results can be rewarding. The traditional resort is to go to the extremities, like the foot. One example of finding an object for contemplation with a client who experienced symptoms of an eating disorder turned out to be the client's big toe on the right foot. It was the only part of the body that was neutral. For this client, they would set their intentions thus:

I will pay attention to the sensations in my big toe and return the mind there if it wanders, which it is bound to do; all with the clear knowledge that the exercise is to experience the body as its own thing, not as a bad part of myself.

The first set of topics for meditation is on the body. As explicated and numerated in the Satipaṭṭhāna Sutta (MN, 1995, 10), contemplation of the body starts with the breath, goes on to the four bodily postures and then the four material elements, and ends with death in the contemplation of the corpse. The Satipaṭṭhāna Sutta then goes on to three other general topics for object of contemplation.

For the purposes of psychotherapy, it is not necessary to take up every item listed in the Satipaṭṭhāna Sutta. Various items may be selected depending on the specific concerns of the individual client. A listing of the topics, not the full description of each item for meditation, is provided next. The instruction given in the sutta is quoted, followed by a brief discussion of how to implement those instructions. For the purposes of psychotherapy, if silent meditation is chosen as a homework assignment, then take care to select the object of contemplation for the client.

Contemplation of the Body: A Counter to Identification With and/or Appropriation of the Body

In the first section of the First Noble Truth, the Buddha points out the mind's tendency to appropriate the body as permanent and a nonchanging part of oneself. When the body does change, which it is bound to do, the person experiences dukkha (suffering, unsatisfactoriness) because they are not expecting the body to age, become ill, be injured, or die.

The first section of the Satipaṭṭhāna Sutta (MN, 1995, 10) provides instructions on what to take as the object of contemplation for meditation as an exercise with two goals or two insights (vipassanā). One vipassanā (insight) is to see through the mind's erroneous bias to take what is impermanent to be permanent, which is that the body does not change; that the body will always be healthy, fat, thin, damaged, and so on. The second vipassanā (insight) is to see through the bias of taking what is not-self/anattā to be self/attā. The vipassanā is that it is erroneous to identify with and appropriate an image of a body as self/attā. The intervention for contemplation of the breath in meditation is to gain embodied knowledge that the body has its own nature; it is not under the control of the meditator.

As an aside, have you ever told yourself to hold your breath? If so, you have had the experience that, sooner or later, the body will assert its own nature, independent of what you want, and start breathing. The contemplation of the breath is to experientially gain the embodied knowledge that the body is its own entity; that it does not belong to the self/attā; and that (a) there is a body, (b) that body is its own entity, and (c) the body is not the self/anattā.

The first object in the contemplation of the body is contemplation of the breath in the body, where the aim is for the meditator to understand:

"I breathe in long"; or breathing out long, he understands; "I breathe out long." Breathing in short, he understands: "I breathe in short"; or breathing out short, he understands: "I breathe out short." He trains thus. (MN, 1995, 10)

Contemplation of the breath starts with remembering to observe the breath, to notice what the breath is doing, to not control the breath, and to not stray from the breath.

The first encounter of the mind in meditation is usually one of inattentiveness to the object of contemplation—that mind is often referred to as "monkey mind," because it jumps from topic to topic like monkeys jump from tree to tree. Noticing this jumpy mind can give one the insight and experienced knowledge that the occurrences in the mind are anicca (impermanent, transient), which is probably good to know during a panic attack. Applying the experience of the wandering mind to everyday life, for example, one notices the constant changes in life situations and in the mind, from the unpleasant feeling of hunger to the pleasant experience of eating food that satiates the hunger. Also notice the change from the pleasant satiation to the unpleasant experience of feeling stuffed from overeating. Noticing the constant change in the mind while in meditation, as well as outside of meditation, is the lived experience for one of the marks of existence, where it is noted that "all conditioned things are impermanent" (Dhp, 1996, 277–279).

Eventually, the meditator will experience the body relaxing of its own accord. Because the mind and the body are linked, when the mind is constantly roaming—like a herd of wild horses—the body will not be still. When the mind is tethered by being reminded constantly to focus on the breath, it is like tethering those wild horses. Once tethered, the mind (like a wild horse) tends to settle. When the mind is settled, the body is composed. The decreased tension in the body is a symptom of a concentrated mind.

Many of the mindfulness apps on the market and some of the mindfulness exercises in treatment aim for this side effect of bodily relaxation that comes with a concentrated mind. If meditation is to be used for relaxation, it may be more efficacious to use systematic relaxation techniques instead of meditation. The main effect for systematic relaxation techniques is to reduce bodily physical muscular tension and is much easier to learn then meditation. Although relaxation is a pleasant side effect, the aim of meditation is not for relaxation. The aim is to train the mind; in this case, to notice what the breath is doing.

The Satipaṭṭhāna Sutta (MN, 1995, 10) gives successive objects for the mind to contemplate, all with the aim for the meditator to gain the experientially embodied knowledge that the body exists, independent of the self/attā. The first section of Satipaṭṭhāna Sutta focuses on the body. The specific objects of contemplation are, in sequential order: the breath, the four postures, the four great elements, the body's anatomical parts, and the body's decay in the charnel grounds. In the mindfulness practice that has reached the United States, it is the first two portions of the contemplation of the body that are commonly practiced.

The vipassanā (insight) to be gained for the contemplation of the body is the experiential knowledge of the impermanence of the body, the inappropriateness of sustaining the image of an unchanging body, the oppressiveness of the body in its constant demands, and the misguidedness of identification with the body. The goal is the experiential knowledge that there is a body and that the body is its own entity: the body does not belong to the self/attā, nor is it the self/attā. The vipassanā (insight) is that the body is not the self/anattā. The way out of suffering is to experientially know that the body has its own nature. When a person lives with the experienced, embodied knowledge that the body is the body and is subject to its own rhymes and reasons and not subject to what the self wishes, then the person is not dysregulated when the body does not perfectly reflect the person's image of their wished-for body or when the body inevitably changes from aging, illness, or death. In all likelihood, the person will be able to pay clearer attention to the functions and needs of the body.

The embodied knowledge and experience of the body as the body is the basis for the Buddha's proclamation of not-self/anattā. In the various objects for the contemplation of the body, the vipassanā (insight) to be gained is the experiential knowledge that the body is the body, it has its own nature, it is impermanent, and it is not the self/attā. For psychotherapy, this acknowledgment of the fact that the body is not the self/attā can be held as an undeniable fact by the psychotherapist. Taking this stance conveys the message, in the many ways one conveys a belief, that it is inappropriate for anyone to identify with the body as if the body is part and parcel of the self/attā. In the Suññataloka Sutta, Ānanda asked what the Buddha meant by saying, "Empty is the world," and the Buddha responded:

[E]mpty is the world? It is, Ānanda, because it is empty of self and of what belongs to the self that it is said, "Empty is the world." And what is empty of self and of what belongs to the self? Forms are empty of the self and of what belongs to the self. (SN, 2000, 35.85: Empty Is the World)

Form is synonymous with anything that has material for its basis of existence, which includes one's body, house, car, clothing, hairstyle, and so on. In its application to psychotherapy, knowing that the body is the body, and that the body is not the self, would guide the psychotherapist to help separate the client's identification and appropriation of their body and possessions into their identity.

In-Session Dialogue

In its utilization for psychotherapy, the meditation method of the Satipaṭṭhāna Sutta (MN, 1995, 10) cannot be transposed without some alteration to fit the demands of a psychotherapy session. For one thing, meditation is done in solitude. Even if one meditates sitting next to someone else who is meditating, there are no interactions between meditators. Psychotherapy is done with at least two people in constant interaction with each other. Additionally, clients may consider meditation a religious practice; thus, they may not appreciate their psychotherapist suggesting that they practice Buddhism. Finally, not everyone should engage with their mind unmediated. Inviting someone experiencing certain mental states, like an active psychotic episode or suicidality of clinical depression, to engage internally will exacerbate a difficult mind state.

Instead of recommending sitting meditation, or even meditating with a client in session, the psychotherapist could engage the client in conversation with the psychotherapist acting in the role of sati (mindfulness), functioning as mindfulness would function. Conceptually, the operational application of Buddhist concepts to in-session dialogue is for the psychotherapist to take on the function of mindfulness. The psychotherapist needs to have their own meditation practice to know how to function as the observing mind of mindfulness to the client's communications. In the capacity of mindfulness, the psychotherapist notices what is occurring in the client's mind within the framework of the five aggregates subject to clinging as they manifest in their discourse with the psychotherapist in session as well as in any other means of communication. While the client is caught in the suffering of their experience, the psychotherapist detects and recognizes the functioning of the aggregates, the type of dukkha (suffering, unsatisfactoriness), and the type of hindrance that is showing up in the treatment room. The therapeutic process allows the conversation to go into a more detailed experience of the client's world. The goal for using any of the instructions from the Satipaṭṭhāna Sutta (MN, 1995, 10) is to help the client gain a small measure of distance between their experience and their body—just enough distance not to be in the grip of suffering.

CONCLUSION

How humans experience existence is through the five aggregates subject to clinging. That is, we encounter the universe through a world constructed from within the notion of a self. What that notion of the self experiences has the characteristics of dukkha (suffering, unsatisfactoriness). The description of the four types of dukkha is listed in the First Noble Truth. The first type listed is dukkha-dukkha, which is described as "birth is suffering, aging is suffering, death is suffering" (SN, 2000, 56.11). Dukkha-dukkha pertains to the human material existence of an embodied being—that is, the suffering due to the birth of a body, the experiences of that body, and the inevitable changes to the material form of the body. Ordinarily, without examination, we appropriate material forms as part and parcel of the self. These material forms may include the body, a car, a real estate property, a wardrobe, and any other material items that may be owned. To reduce dukkha-dukkha, Buddhism invites an examination of the appropriateness and the consequences of appropriating and/or identifying with the material side of existence. One method of examination is through meditation. The instruction for such meditation is given in the first section of the Satipaṭṭhāna Sutta (MN, 1995, 10) with the contemplation of the breath, the four bodily postures, and the four material elements, and ends with death in the contemplation of the corpse.

The vipassanās (insights) to be gained from the contemplation of the body are to see through the mind's erroneous bias to take what is impermanent to be permanent and to see through the bias of taking what is not-self/anattā, meaning the material form of the body, to be self/attā. The goal for undertaking these objects for meditation is to know that the body is the body, the body is not-self—that the world we construct is empty of the self.

> Then the Venerable Anada approached the Blessed One (the Buddha) . . . and said to him: Venerable sir, it is said, "Empty is the world, empty is the world." In what way, venerable sir, is it said, "Empty is the world?" It is, Ānanda, because it is empty of self and of what belongs to the self that it is said, "Empty is the world." And what is empty of self and of what belongs to the self? Forms are empty of the self and of what belongs to the self. (SN, 2000, 35.85)

9

THE SECOND DUKKHA

Suffering Due to Situational Change

The second type of *dukkha* (suffering, unsatisfactoriness) described in the First Noble Truth is suffering due to situational change (*vipariṇāma-dukkha*). The Pali word *vipariṇāma* means "to change, alter" (Pali Text Society, n.d.). Vipariṇāma-dukkha is the category of suffering that is related to and based on not recognizing, acknowledging, and/or realizing that situations change, that the reality of human existence is *anicca* (impermanence), and that "whatever is subject to origination is all subject to cessation" (Dhammacakkapavattana Sutta; *Saṃyutta Nikāya* [SN], 2000, 56.11: Setting in Motion the Wheel of the Dhamma). Vipariṇāma-dukkha is what occurs when the constructed infrangible self meets the reality of anicca of situations. Table 9.1 presents excerpts from the sutta describing potential outcomes when one is faced with recognizing, acknowledging, or accepting changes in one's situation.

https://doi.org/10.1037/0000453-010
Buddhist Psychotherapy: Connecting Early Buddhism to Mindfulness and Western Psychotherapy, by L. Tien, D. M. Kawahara, and V. Dhammadinna

TABLE 9.1. Potential Outcomes of Vipariṇāma-Dukkha (Suffering Due to Situational Change)

Outcome	Sutta excerpt
Sorrow	And what, friends, is sorrow? The sorrow, sorrowing, sorrowfulness, inner sorrow, inner sorriness, of one who has encountered some misfortune or is affected by some painful state—this is called sorrow.
Lamentation	And what, friends, is lamentation? The wail and lament, wailing and lamenting, bewailing and lamentation, of one who has encountered some misfortune or is affected by some painful state—this is called lamentation.
Pain	And what, friends, is pain? Bodily pain, bodily discomfort, painful, uncomfortable feeling born of bodily contact—this is called pain.
Grief	And what, friends, is grief? Mental pain, mental discomfort, painful, uncomfortable feeling born of mental contact—this is called grief.
Despair	And what, friends, is despair? The trouble and despair, the tribulation and desperation, of one who has encountered some misfortune or is affected by some painful state—this is called despair.

Note. Excerpts are from the Saccavibhaṅga Sutta (MN, 1995, 141): The Analysis/Exposition of the Truths.

PERCEIVING IMPERMANENT SITUATIONS TO BE PERMANENT

Vipariṇāma-dukkha examines the suffering resulting from mistaking situations that are impermanent to be permanent, or suffering based on the inability and/or unwillingness to acknowledge situational changes. This is one of the four types of processing errors, or inversions, that the mind systematically commits. As we discussed in Chapter 6 (this volume), the four types of inversions named in the Vipallāsa Sutta (*Aṅguttara Nikāya* [AN], 2012, 4.49: Inversions) are as follows:

• perceiving permanence in the impermanent,
• perceiving pleasure in what is suffering,
• perceiving a self in what is non-self, and
• perceiving attractiveness in what is unattractive.

The type of processing error that conditions vipariṇāma-dukkha (suffering due to situational change) occurs when "beings resort to wrong views, their minds deranged, their perception twisted . . . perceiving permanence in the impermanent" (AN, 2012, 4.49). The mind (*citta*) is biased to experience situations as permanent. Humans usually experience situations as if they are and will be forever. The mind incorporates what it experiences as a permanent situation into its infrangible self. When the infrangible self meets the reality of anicca (impermanence), where all conditioned things are impermanent (Dhp, 1996, 277–279: The Path), the person experiences "sorrow, lamentation, pain, grief, and despair" (*Majjhima Nikāya* [MN], 1995, 141). Vipariṇāma-dukkha (suffering due to situational change) occurs when the mind takes what is impermanent for permanent.

There are pleasant and unpleasant changes. Pleasant experiences will eventually come to an end, but unpleasant experience will also cease. When an unpleasant situation ceases, very few people will complain or seek psychotherapy to understand the change. However, when a pleasant and desirable situation changes, a mental phenomenon usually occurs: "he worries and grieves he laments, beats his breast, weeps and is distraught" (Sallatha Sutta; SN, 2000, 36.6: The Dart). The conditions for those desirable pleasant experiences shift from the small inconsequential situations to weighty ones. For example, that wonderful experience of taking the first sip of coffee in the morning does not last—not even for the duration of drinking the full cup. Conversely, the condition for an undesirable unpleasant experience also disappears. Using our coffee example, the 3 days of headache from caffeine withdraw also disappear. The disappointment that follows the joy in the first sip of coffee in the morning disappears quickly and is usually deemed nonconsequential for daily existence.

For situations that last for longer periods, such as identifying with a family role (e.g., a child, spouse, or partner), a profession or career (e.g., a police officer, firefighter, teacher, administrator, manager, or any number of other jobs), or a group of people (e.g., a marathon runner, mountain climber, dancer, or a member of any number of group activities), its cessation is more consequential in a person's daily life. The role of a child is impermanent because, at some point, one's parents or caregivers pass away. Deriving one's identity from an activity (e.g., "I am a runner") is impermanent because, at some point, one will likely experience the body aging or a bodily injury that precludes the person from running. When the role or activity with which one identifies as the self (*attā*) no longer exists, one reacts with "sorrow, lamentation, pain, grief, and despair" (MN, 1995, 141).

The grief experienced at the end of a marriage or the despair experienced at the loss of a job, in turn, leads to a sense of being obsolete and therefore leading a useless life. This sense does not disappear quickly because the mind repeatedly returns to that situation, as if that situation is occurring in the present and not in the past. The mental pain may be so unpleasant and agonizing that it leads to the intense wish for the dukkha (suffering, unsatisfactoriness) to cease. This is the oppressiveness of mental pain that pushes the person toward actions to alleviate the pain. The behavior likely involves seeking sense pleasure, as noted in the Sallatha Sutta (SN, 2000, 36.6):

> Being contacted by that same painful feeling, he harbors aversion towards it. When he harbors aversion towards painful feeling, the underlying tendency to aversion towards painful feeling lies behind this. Being contacted by painful feeling, he seeks delight in sensual pleasure. For what reason? Because the uninstructed worldling does not know of any escape from painful feeling other than sensual pleasure. When he seeks delight in sensual pleasure, the underlying tendency to lust for pleasant feeling lies behind this.

Most people who engage in psychotherapy are those who seek relief from, if not total elimination of, this kind of suffering. With depression, the person does not question their assumption that their despair is absolutely permanent. Although it is not advisable to dismiss a client's suffering and concern with a cavalier attitude (e.g., "Don't take yourself so seriously. Things will change on their own accord"), psychotherapists must both acknowledge the real suffering of the client and take the stance that the client's situation will change, so as not to be caught up in the same misconception of taking an impermeant situation as permeant.

INTERVENTION

In the normal course of a person's life, situations inevitably change. Yet most people struggle against the reality of impermanence—the reality that life happens, and things change. Consider the language of the Salla Sutta (SN, 2000, 36.5): "when the uninstructed worldling is being contacted by a painful feeling . . . he feels two feelings—a bodily one and a mental one." The first dart is a pleasant desirable situation that inevitably changes, and the person experiences the second dart of "sorrow, lamentation, pain, grief, and despair" (MN, 1995, 141). That second dart is where the client talks about what the changed situation indicates about their self/attā. Here are some examples of the second dart: "A divorce means I am unlovable," "The loss of a job means I am a loser," and "Not getting that perfect score on the exam means I am stupid." That second dart are the machinations of mentality that construct a notion of the self. The target for psychotherapy is to loosen the bond between the first dart and the second dart where a situation, like divorce, is not a direct link to the notion that "I am unlovable" with its accompanying unpleasant emotions.

More concretely, "sorrow, lamentation, pain, grief, and despair" (MN, 1995, 141) results from identifying with the unpleasant hedonic feeling tone (*vedanā*) of the ending of the desirable state of marriage, having appropriated the social status of being married into the notion of oneself. The contemplation of vedanā is designed for the person not to sink into the hedonic feeling tone and to identify with the change in their social status of being married, just enough to insert another thought (e.g., "I am more than my marriage" or "Being rejected by my spouse does not mean I am unlovable").

Meditation

Taking our meditation instructions from the Satipaṭṭhāna Sutta (MN, 1995, 10: The Foundations of Mindfulness), we are directed to take the body as the first category of contemplation to counter the oppressiveness of *dukkha-dukkha*, as discussed in Chapter 8 (this volume). After the contemplation of the body, the Satipaṭṭhāna Sutta directs the meditation to the contemplation of vedanā (hedonic feeling tone). The instruction in the sutta states the following:

> Here, when feeling a pleasant feeling, a bhikkhu understands: "I feel a pleasant feeling"; when feeling a painful feeling, he understands: "I feel a painful feeling"; when feeling a neither-painful-nor-pleasant feeling, he understands: "I feel a neither-painful-nor-pleasant feeling." . . . He abides contemplating in feelings their nature of arising, or he abides contemplating in feelings their nature of vanishing, or he abides contemplating in feelings their nature of both arising and vanishing. (MN, 1995, 10)

The meditation intervention for contemplation of vedanā is designed to address the suffering of "sorrow, lamentation, pain, grief, and despair" (MN, 1995, 141) in its struggle against the impermanence (anicca) of situations. The target is to experientially acknowledge that "there is feeling" (MN, 1995, 10) by training the mind to notice the hedonic feeling tone (vedanā)—the hedonic embodied pleasant, unpleasant, or neither pleasant nor unpleasant sensation—associated with a sense stimulus. The instruction for meditation of feeling is for mindfulness that "there is feeling" is simply established in the meditator "to the extent necessary for bare knowledge and mindfulness" (MN, 1995, 10). This is training the mind to notice and be able to recognize the embodied hedonic quality of the sense contact. The insight (vipassanā) is that the hedonic feeling tone (vedanā) is not the self (attā).

Insight Into Not-Self (*Anattā*)

The insight (vipassanā) that the hedonic feeling tone (vedanā) is not the self (attā) is the basis for the Buddha's proclamation of not-self (*anattā*). In the contemplation of hedonic feeling tone, the insight to be gained is the experiential knowledge that hedonic feeling tone is impermeant (anicca) and it is not the self (anatta). Thus, it is inappropriate to identify with the psyche and the soma's hedonic feeling tone association with a sense contact. In the Suññataloka Sutta, when asked what the Buddha meant by saying, "Empty is the world," the Buddha said to Ānanda:

> It is, Ānanda, because it is empty of self and of what belongs to self that it is said, "Empty is the world." And what is empty of self and of what belongs to self? . . . Whatever feeling arises with mind-contact as condition—whether pleasant or painful or neither-painful-nor-pleasant—that too is empty of self and of what belongs to self. (SN, 2000, 35.85: Empty Is the World)

In its application to psychotherapy, this would guide the psychotherapist to help separate the client's identification and appropriation of their affective response to a sense stimulus (i.e., "I am my feelings, and my feelings are my self").

In-Session Dialogue

To utilize the knowledge that a hedonic feeling tone is fleeting in psychotherapy, it helps to manage the negative mental states when the client can identify the discomfort as hedonic feeling tone (vedanā) to the sense stimulus, and then for them to know that they are not their feelings ("I am not my feeling") and they can tolerate the transient nature of the unpleasant mental state. The misconception of "taking what is impermanent for permanent" (AN, 2012, 4.49) can be explored through dialogue about the client's expectations for the changed situation. For example, in-session dialogue about a divorce may explore the client's beliefs about marriage, including (but not limited to) the following:

- what they were told about marriage when they were growing up;
- what they believe about marriage from their culture, their subculture, and their society;
- what their expectations were when they married;
- what changes will occur to their social status as a result of divorce;
- what impact the divorce will have on their financial situation; and
- anything else that could have contributed to the client's mental status in relationship to the divorce.

These types of exploration would allow the client and the psychotherapist to gain a clearer understanding of the conditions that supported the experience of an unpleasant hedonic feeling tone (vedanā) connected to the divorce.

A way to think about the areas of exploration is to state an observation. For example, not everyone who gets divorced is despondent or disturbed or experiences unpleasant hedonic feeling tone. For some, a divorce supports the condition for a pleasant situation. Thus, to fully understand the conditions, seek to answer the question of what it is about this client's situation that gives rise to the unpleasant hedonic feeling tone in regard to divorce.

CONCLUSION

How humans experience existence is through the five aggregates subject to clinging. That is, we encounter the universe through a world constructed from within the notion of a self. What that notion of the self experiences has the characteristics of dukkha. The four types of dukkha (suffering, unsatisfactoriness) are described in the First Noble Truth. The second type of dukkha (suffering, unsatisfactoriness) is viparināma-dukkha, which is described as follows: "sorrow, lamentation, pain, grief, and despair are suffering" (MN, 1995, 141). Viparināma-dukkha is the category of suffering that is related to and based on not recognizing, acknowledging, and/or realizing that situations change, that the reality of human existence is aniccā (impermanence), and that "whatever is subject to origination is all subject to cessation" (SN, 2000, 56.11). Humans usually sink into the experience of a situation as if it is and will be forever. This includes the vedanā (hedonic feeling tone) that is associated with a sense contact: The mind misidentifies the vedanā as a permanent state of being and incorporates it into its infrangible self. To reduce viparināma-dukkha, Buddhism invites us to identify the vedanā, to acknowledge its presence, and then to experience that it is fleeting. The vipassanā (insight) to be gained from the contemplation of vedanā, as specified in the Satipaṭṭhāna Sutta (MN, 1995, 10), is "their nature of arising . . . their nature of vanishing."

> Then the Venerable Anada approached the Blessed One (the Buddha) . . . and said to him: Venerable sir, it is said, "Empty is the world, empty is the world." In what way, venerable sir, is it said, "Empty is the world?" It is, Ānanda, because it is empty of self and of what belongs to the self that it is said, "Empty is the world." And what is empty of self and of what belongs to the self? . . . Whatever feeling arises with mind-contact as condition—whatever pleasant or painful or neither-painful-nor-pleasant—that too is empty of the self and of what belongs to the self. (SN, 2000, 35.85)

10 THE THIRD DUKKHA

Suffering Due to Mental Formations

The third type of *dukkha* (suffering, unsatisfactoriness) described in the First Noble Truth is suffering due to mental formations (*saṅkhāra-dukkha*). Saṅkhāra-dukkha is a result of not realizing that the human experience of existence is phenomena in consciousness, not the noumena of the universe. It is taking our constructed world, or *saṅkhāra*, to be the only reality there is. It is mistaking our mental formations, which result from our perception of the external sense contact, to be reality itself (for a review of how mental formations are constructed, see Chapters 5 and 6 in this volume). It is "the inversion of perception, mind, and view that takes what is non-self to be self" (Vipallāsa Sutta; *Aṅguttara Nikāya* [AN], 2012, 4.49: Inversions).

The Pali word saṅkhāra is defined as "in the widest sense the 'world of phenomena'" (Pali Text Society, n.d.). As is the usual case in translating a complex concept, there is not one word in English that can convey the full meaning of the word saṅkhāra or the full array of saṅkhāra-dukkha. Considering a few other definitions from various translators may provide a fuller sense of the idea for saṅkhāra-dukkha. Karunadasa (2015a) translated the concept as follows: "[T]here is suffering as constructed (saṅkhāra-dukkha).

https://doi.org/10.1037/0000453-011
Buddhist Psychotherapy: Connecting Early Buddhism to Mindfulness and Western Psychotherapy, by L. Tien, D. M. Kawahara, and V. Dhammadinna

This aspect corresponds exactly to the suffering involved in grasping the five aggregates" (p. 75). Kalupahana (1992) translated it as, "He (Buddha Gotama) was referring to the dispositions as implied in the statement 'All dispositions are impermanent' (sabbe saṅkhāra aniccā), because all dispositions, unless they are appeased or de-solidified, lead to suffering (sabbe saṅkhāra dukkha)" (p. 89).

PROJECTION FROM THE STANCE OF PRIMARY NARCISSISM

We experience mental phenomena as the stories we tell ourselves about the world we live in. The world of phenomena in consciousness is the domain of saṅkhāra, the aggregate of mental formations, mental fabrications, mental proliferations, volitional formations, and/or dispositions. In the widest sense of the concept, clinging to saṅkhāra, in the lexicon of psychology, is identifying with the world one has constructed from one's thinking and its iterations. This is where one believes that "I am my thoughts, my thoughts are me." Or when the constructed infrangible self believes in its own construction, it is believed to be the only true reality. In Western psychology, saṅkhāra-dukkha is the projection from the stance of primary narcissism. The suffering is because the universe does not conform to one's constructed world when what one wants is not realized.

It is from the mind's mistaken assumption based on the residual unexamined primary narcissism that somehow the essential self (*attā*) is the center of the world and that the universe should or would, of course, accommodate to one's wishes and the desires of the self/attā. From the mundane (e.g., the inconvenience of long grocery store checkout lines) to the significant (e.g., being passed over for a promotion), there is unpleasantness associated with these experiences. That residue of primary narcissism shows up in displeasure when having to be associated with, deal with, or just acknowledge something or someone that gives one displeasure. This displeasure can be with a person (e.g., the office gossip who relishes in telling us unflattering stories about another person in the office) or a situation (e.g., thinking this same office gossip has been spreading very unflattering and untrue stories about us).

A person does not realize or recognize that their constructed phenomenon in consciousness, their construction of reality, is created from the stance of their primary narcissism where the self is the center of the universe. From that stance, one then projects their world out to others. The usual conventional stance is that the only true reality is how the self has constructed that reality. For instance, if we think someone is out to get us, then, of course, that someone really is out to get us because that person is evil incarnate, whereas we are innocent victims of their ill will toward us.

Essentially, saṅkhāra dukkha (suffering inflicted from one's own mental formations) arises from having constructed a world and a reality from the stance of primary narcissism; that constructed reality is then projected out to the world. When the world does not comply with what one has constructed, what one expects, then there is incredulity, there is dis-regulation, and there is suffering (dukkha). Dukkha occurs when the world challenges the narcissistic centrality of self/attā by way of us having to associate with people, things, and situations we do not love (i.e., being attached to the unloved); by being separated from people, things, and situations we love (i.e., being separated from the loved); and, even more so, by not getting what we want (i.e., not getting what one wants). Table 10.1 sums up these challenges, and each is described next.

TABLE 10.1. The World's Challenges to Primary Narcissism

Challenge	Sutta excerpt
Being attached to the unloved	And what, monks, is the suffering from being joined to what is not liked? Here, for that one who has unwanted, unlovely, unpleasant forms, sounds, smells, tastes tangibles, and thoughts; or, for that one who has those who do not desire his welfare, benefit, comfort and security–(and then) having meetings, assembly, connection, and interaction with then: this, monks, is called the suffering from being joined to what is not liked. (*Mahāsatipaṭṭhāna Sutta*, 2011; SN 22)
	And what, monks, is being attached to the unloved? Here, whoever has unwanted, disliked, unpleasant sight-objects, sounds, smells, tastes, tangible or mind-objects, or whoever encounters ill-wishers, wishes of harm of discomfort, of insecurity, with whom they have concourse, intercourse, connection, union, that, monks, is called being attached to the unloved. (DN, 1987/1995, 22)
Being separated from the loved	And what, monks, is the suffering from being parted from what is liked? Here, for that one who has wanted, lovely, pleasant forms, sounds, smells, tastes, tangibles, and thoughts; or, for that one who has those who do desire his welfare, benefits, comfort and security–mothers, or fathers, or brothers, or sisters, or friends, or companions, or blood relatives–(and then) not having meeting, assembly, connection, and interactions with them: This, monks is called the suffering from being parted from what is liked. (*Mahāsatipaṭṭhāna Sutta*, 2011; SN 22)

(continues)

TABLE 10.1. The World's Challenges to Primary Narcissism (*Continued*)

Challenge	Sutta excerpt
	And what is being separated from the loved? Here, whoever has what is wanted, liked, pleasant sight-objects, sounds, smells, tastes, tangibles or mind-objects, or whoever encounters well-wishers, wishers of good, of comfort, of security, mother or father or brother or sister or younger kinsmen or friends or colleagues or blood-relations, and then is deprived of such concourse, intercourse, connection, or union, that, monks is called being separated from the loved. (DN, 1987/1995, 22)
Not getting what one wants	Now what, monks, is the suffering from not obtaining what one longs for? To those beings subject to birth, monks, a longing like this arises: "Oh, might we not be subject to birth, may birth not come to us!" But that cannot be attained merely by longing for it: this is the suffering from not obtaining what one longs for. (*Mahāsatipaṭṭhāna Sutta*, 2011; SN 22)
	And what is not getting what one wants? In beings subject to birth, monks, this wish arises: "Oh that we were not subject to birth, that we might not come to birth!" But this cannot be gained by wishing. That is not getting what one wants. In beings subject to ageing, to disease, to death, to sorrow, lamentation, pain, sadness and distress this wish arises. "Oh that we were not subject to aging . . . distress, that we might not come to these things!" But this cannot be gained by wishing. That is not getting what one wants. (DN, 1987/1995, 22)
	And what, friends, is "not to obtain what one wants is suffering"? To beings subject to birth there comes the wish: "Oh, that we were not subject to birth! That birth would not come to us!" But this is not to be obtained by wishing, and not to obtain what one wants is suffering. To beings subject to ageing . . . subject to sickness . . . subject to death . . . subject to sorrow, lamentation, pain, grief, and despair, there comes the wish: "Oh, that we were not subject to sorrow, lamentation, pain, grief, and despair! That sorrow, lamentation, pain, grief, and despair would not come to us!" But this is not to be obtained by wishing, and not to obtain what one wants is suffering. (Saccavibhaṅga Sutta; MN, 1995, 141: The Analysis/Exposition of the Truths)

Being Attached to the Unloved

In the everyday activities of life, one accepts without question what one experiences as reality, and that view is shared by everyone else on the planet. Thus, when one thinks someone does "not desire his welfare, benefit, comfort and security" (*Dīgha Nikāya* [DN], 1987/1995, 22: The Greater Discourse of the Foundation of Mindfulness), it surely must be that the other person is evil. Not only is it unthinkable, but it is surely unbearable to then have "meetings, assembly, connection, and interaction with" (DN, 1987/1995, 22) that evil being. It goes against the grain for most people to think, being the recipient of such ill will, that hostility from others is well deserved based on what one has done. The actuality of having to endure people, things, and situations that (one thinks) harbor ill will toward oneself goes against the image of oneself as a person who would not do anything that warrants any dislike from anyone or anything.

Clients often talk about having to deal with people they do not like, such as that new boss who does not appreciate their work, that snippety colleague who is jealous of them, or that rude relative who challenges their sensibilities during holiday dinners. Clients may also refer to material objects they do not like. For example, a client may dislike having to live in a dark basement apartment because they cannot afford to rent a better place while living on student loans in graduate school; or they may dislike the computer that keeps crashing because they cannot afford to purchase an updated laptop. To all of the incidents of having to associate with the unloved, life is just not fair.

Being Separated From the Loved

The flip side in which people are separated from their likes, or separated from what they love, is also untenable; it also seems unfair. These situations range from the trivial to the consequential as well. An example of a trivial situation that many encounter in the computer age is the suffering people experience when their beloved laptop malfunctions and they are forced to be separated from it for the duration of having it repaired. It is not unusual for the owner of said computer to worry over it for days (e.g., What kind of backup is needed so that nothing will be lost? How will work be accomplished for the 48 hours that the laptop will be in the repair shop? Will the computer come back with all of files intact?). This is an example of such oppressiveness from the suffering of being separated from the loved.

Clients usually do not seek psychotherapy for help to deal with the temporary inconveniences such as separating from a beloved item, like a computer or car while it is being repaired. Clients usually come into psychotherapy seeking relief from the suffering and experience of significant losses—death of a loved one, loss of health from a chronic illness, divorce, and so on. They are dysregulated, not knowing how to go on without something or someone they have a significant association with. These individuals are beset with life's many assaults to their sense of order as having to be separated from their loved ones.

Not Getting What One Wants

Finally, there is the frustration of not getting what one wants or wishes. Much irritation and indignation arise when it seems unfair that one did not get what one wants, such as being passed over for that expected promotion at work, having to cancel a much-anticipated vacation because of illness, or not getting that perfect grade on the last assignment. It seems that life is just not fair and that one does not get what is due to oneself.

INTERVENTION

A first-level intervention is to name the type of dukkha experienced by the client. Many times, realizing that all of one's machinations are due to not getting something that one wanted can be illuminating, giving people a chance to step back and examine their underlying expectations. It is from those expectations that one constructs the reasons surrounding any given event experienced in the person's life. Having an in-depth discussion focused on expectations of a situation clarifies the conditions that give rise to saṅkhāra-dukkha (suffering inflicted from one's own mental formations).

Mind is that which notices the sense contact. Mind is that which notices the hedonic feeling tone of the sense contact. Mind is that which constructs phenomena in consciousness. The task of the psychotherapist is to notice the workings of the mind and to introduce the mind's constructed phenomenon in consciousness to the client in the treatment room. Then the psychotherapist's task is to coconstruct an alternative phenomenon in consciousness, one that is less hurtful and, hopefully, one that the client is more able to manage.

Meditation: Contemplation of Mind to Address *Saṅkhāra-Dukkha* (Suffering Inflicted From One's Own Mental Formations)

The objects of contemplation specified in the Satipaṭṭhāna Sutta (*Majjhima Nikāya* [MN], 1995, 10: Foundations of Mindfulness) follow the formulation of the types of dukkha listed in the First Noble Truth. For *dukkha-dukkha*, the Satipaṭṭhāna Sutta provides instruction on the contemplation of the body. For *vipariṇāma-dukkha*, the Satipaṭṭhāna Sutta provides instruction on the contemplation of feelings or hedonic feeling tone (*vedanā*). For the third category of saṅkhāra-dukkha, the Satipaṭṭhāna Sutta provides instruction on the contemplation of mind. It instructs the meditator on how to notice the mind in its activity of saṅkhāra (mental formations), not by focusing on the thoughts in constructing a world in which the person is immersed and from which the person acts, but by discerning the underlying hedonic feeling tone that pushes the mind, however subtle. The instruction in the sutta simplifies this activity of observing one's mind by describing the influence of the three types of hedonic feeling tone. The sutta says:

> And how, bhikkhus, does a bhikkhu abide contemplating mind as mind? Here a bhikkhu understands mind affected by lust as mind affected by lust, and mind unaffected by lust as mind unaffected by lust. He understands mind affected by hate as mind affected by hate, and mind unaffected by hate as mind unaffected by hate. He understands mind affected by delusion as mind affected by delusion, and mind unaffected by delusion as mind unaffected by delusion. He understands contracted mind as contracted mind, and distracted mind as distracted mind. . . . He understands concentrated mind as concentrated mind, and unconcentrated mind as unconcentrated mind. . . . In this way he abides contemplating mind as mind internally, or he abides contemplating mind as mind externally, or he abides contemplating mind as mind both internally and externally. Or else he abides contemplating in mind its nature of arising, or he abides contemplating in mind its nature of vanishing, or he abides contemplating in mind its nature of both arising and vanishing. Or else mindfulness that "there is mind" is simply established in him to the extent necessary for bare knowledge and mindfulness. And he abides independent, not clinging to anything in the world. That is how a bhikkhu abides contemplating mind as mind. (MN, 1995, 10)

How does the mind contemplate itself? The Buddha Gotama told us to notice the hedonic feeling tone that is influencing the mental formations, as well as the emotions that are associated with that constructed world. There are characteristic influences of hedonic feeling tone on mental activities. The sutta names (a) mind affected with lust and without lust, (b) mind affected with anger and without anger, (c) mind affected with delusions and without delusions, and (d) mind that is contracted and distracted as well as concentrated and not concentrated.

Saṅkhāra-dukkha (suffering due to mental formations) is what usually populates the content of client's concerns. Instead of focusing on the content of the client's concerns, the directive from the Buddha is to notice "mind affected by lust . . . mind affected by hate . . . mind affected by delusion" (MN, 1995, 10). The directive is to notice the influence of hedonic feeling tone on cognition.

In-Session Dialogue

As the client is reporting their concerns, the psychotherapist may act as mindfulness armed with meta-cognition by labeling the category of the suffering. Recall the example in Chapter 5 of the client who came to psychotherapy talking about his indecisiveness, with the latest incident of his indecision manifesting in his inability to decide whether to carry through with his wish for a divorce. His was a mind affected by lust—wanting to decide, wanting clarity that could relieve him from indecision, wanting a marriage that he did not have, wanting his wife to be different; a mind full of wants is a mind affected by lust. His was also a mind affected by hate—hating that his wife spent so much money, hating that he could not earn enough money to comfortably support his wife's spending habits; a mind affected by hate is one that is filled with aversion. The aversion motivated this client's question about divorce.

This client constructed a world in which he was not getting what he wanted. The sutta's (MN, 1995, 10) instruction to notice the mind affected by lust is to take note of what it is that the person wants. Conversely, to notice the mind affected by hate is to take note of what it is that the person wants to avoid. In the case of this client, he had wanted his wife to be different and was avoiding the evidence that he was not getting what he wanted.

Having the psychotherapist bring the in-session dialogue to this client's wanting his wife not to spend money and not getting what he wanted is much more focused, and probably more productive, than having the client contemplating the notion of himself as being indecisive. The directive for implementation of contemplation of mind is not to focus on the content of the mental formations and proliferations—in this case, whether the client is an indecisive person and whether he should divorce his wife. Instead, it is to attend to the mind state of lust, which would involve a discussion about what the client wants, and to attend to the mind state of hate, which is about what the client does not like about his wife.

There is a large element of soma in the manifestation of hedonic feeling tone. It may be easier to focus on the interplay between the soma and the psyche for contemplation of the mind. Noting the interconnectedness of one's physical (tense, relaxed) and mental (anxious, happy) states addresses how to detect our primary narcissism at work influencing the mind state and our actions. In noticing a mind affected by lust, we come to realize and appreciate the forces acting on cognition, that pleasant hedonic feeling tone influences the mind toward lust or acquisition of the object of desire; that unpleasant hedonic feeling tone influences the mind toward aversion; and that neither pleasant nor unpleasant hedonic feeling tone tends to influence the mind toward apathy, boredom, and distractedness. In the state of neither pleasant nor unpleasant hedonic feeling tone, the client may not notice things that are significant, but the psychotherapist may notice and bring them into the in-session dialogue. Noting these mind states may allow for some meta-cognition to be focused on a person's ruminations, thus allowing room for alternative interpretations, another point of view, or another course of action.

It is necessary and unavoidable that a measure of primary narcissism is functioning at all times. To the extent that a person does not function as if they are the center of the universe by making a shift to see situations from another person's viewpoint, there is less suffering, a greater level of maturity, and greater flexibility in handling interpersonal conflicts. Many times, psychotherapy helps reduce a client's suffering by helping them take a wider perspective or an alternative perspective on a difficult situation. This is not a negation of the client's experience of that situation. But by adding more information, the client's experience of the situation is altered. To the extent that a person stays within the confines of their primary narcissism, thinking themselves to be the center of the universe, then there is difficulty when one has to be "attached to the unloved . . . separated from the loved . . . [and] not getting what one wants" (DN, 1987/1995, 22).

Noting a mind affected by lust, hate, and/or delusion can allow the person to surface from the immersion in their experience of the suffering. Analyzing instead of experiencing provides a bit of distance with one's created reality, just enough to take on other points of view that may be a bit more functional in the client's life situation.

CONCLUSION

How humans experience existence is through the five aggregates subject to clinging. That is, we encounter the universe through a world constructed from within the notion of a self. What that notion of the self experiences has the characteristics of dukkha. The description of the four types of dukkha (suffering, unsatisfactoriness) is listed in the First Noble Truth. The third type of dukkha (suffering, unsatisfactoriness) is sankhāra-dukkha:

> And what, monks, is the Noble Truth of Suffering? . . . Being attached to the unloved is suffering, being separated from the loved is suffering, not getting what one wants is suffering. (Mahāsatiputtāna Sutta; DN, 1987/1995, 22)

Sankhāra-dukkha is the category of suffering that is related to and based on not recognizing, acknowledging, and/or realizing the constructed nature of the world, but instead identifying with the world one has constructed from one's thinking and its iterations. It is the dukkha that comes when one believes that "I am my thinking, what I think is me." Or when the constructed infrangible self believes in its own construction as the only true reality. In Western psychology, saṅkhāra-dukkha is the projection from the stance of primary narcissism; not that the reality of human existence is anattā (not-self), and that all things are not-self (*Dhammapada* [Dhp], 1996, 277–279). The mind misidentifies the stories we tell ourselves about a sense stimulus as real, not as a representation. To reduce sankhāra-dukkha, Buddhism invites us to notice the push of vedanā (hedonic feeling tone) of how the mind constructs the stories we tell ourselves about the centrality of ourselves in the universe, to understand our construction of the world is from the stance of primary narcissism, and to recognize a "mind affected by lust . . . mind affected by hate . . . mind affected by delusion as mind affected by delusion. . . . He understands contracted mind as contracted mind, and distracted mind as distracted mind" (MN, 1995, 10).

11

THE FOURTH DUKKHA

Suffering Due to the Notion of a Self

Traditionally, Buddhism names three types of *dukkha* (suffering, unsatisfactoriness): *dukkha-dukkha*, *vipariṇāma-dukkha*, and *saṅkhāra-dukkha*, which are detailed in Chapters 8 to 10, respectively. The last phrase of the First Noble Truth is traditionally not considered a type of dukkha, but a summary. The last phrase is usually stated as "in brief, the five aggregates subject to clinging are suffering" (Dhammacakkapavattana Sutta; *Saṃyutta Nikāya* [SN], 2000, 56.11: Setting in Motion the Wheel of the Dhamma). However, what enters the psychotherapy treatment room is usually the five aggregates subject to clinging. Therefore, for the purpose of formulating a Buddhist-based theory of psychotherapy, the last phrase of the First Noble Truth will be treated as a fourth type of dukkha. Because this is formulated only for the purpose of psychotherapy, the coverage in this chapter is adjusted for application to psychotherapy and is very narrowly focused on the process of providing treatment to a client. In the section on hindrances in this chapter, the discussion does not represent Buddhism's overall coverage; rather, it specifically addresses what the psychotherapist would be listening for, which is a specific underlying desire in the hindrance.

https://doi.org/10.1037/0000453-012
Buddhist Psychotherapy: Connecting Early Buddhism to Mindfulness and Western Psychotherapy, by L. Tien, D. M. Kawahara, and V. Dhammadinna

DIFFERENTIATING THE FIVE AGGREGATES SUBJECT TO CLINGING FROM THE FIVE AGGREGATES

The fourth category of dukkha (suffering, unsatisfactoriness) is an overarching summation in reference to the human experience of an embodied existence. The five aggregates subject to clinging (*pañcupādānakkhandhā*) in the Buddhist lexicon is the constructed notion of a self. We experience existence through this constructed notion of a self. This notion of a self does not see the impermanence (*anicca*) embedded in dependent arising (*paṭiccasamuppāda*); it does not understand that the functioning of the five aggregates (*pañcakkhandhā*) is not the self (*anattā*); that the five aggregates function independent of a self; and that as long as we experience existence through this notion of a self, we are bound to experience dukkha.

The Buddha Gotama stipulates that how humans experience is by the five aggregates, and that what humans experience of existence is characterized by dukkha when life is experienced through the five aggregates subject to clinging (pañcupādānakkhandhā). The following are examples of the same thing being said in different suttas of the *Nikāya*:

> Now this, bhikkhus, is the noble truth of suffering: . . . in brief, the five aggregates subject to clinging are suffering. (SN, 2000, 56.11)

> And what, friends, is the noble truth of suffering? . . . In short, the five aggregates affected by clinging are suffering. (Saccavibhaṅga Sutta; *Majjhima Nikāya* [MN], 1995, 141: An Analysis of the Truths)

> And what, monks, is the Noble Truth of Suffering? . . . In short, the five aggregates of grasping are suffering. (Mahāsatipuṭṭāna Sutta; *Dīgha Nikāya* [DN], 1987/1995, 22: The Greater Discourse of the Foundation of Mindfulness)

A fuller statement is found in the Saccavibhaṅga Sutta:

> And what, friends, are the five aggregates affected by clinging that, in short, are suffering? They are: the material form aggregate affected by clinging, the feeling aggregate affected by clinging, the perception aggregate affected by clinging, the formations aggregate affected by clinging, and the consciousness aggregate affected by clinging. These are the five aggregates affected by clinging that, in short, are suffering. This is called the noble truth of suffering. (MN, 1995, 141)

The Saccavibhaṅga Sutta is where dukkha is explicitly tied to *upādāna*, the act of clinging to, the identifying with, and the appropriation of any or all of the five aggregates into a constructed notion of a self (*attā*). It is formulated as follows: "This is mine, this I am, this is my self" (Alagaddūpama Sutta; MN, 1995, 22: The Simile of the Snake).

The five aggregates subject to clinging (pañcupādānakkhandhā) are to be differentiated from the five aggregates (pañcakkhandhā). The five aggregates are, by themselves, the constituent parts of the coordinated functioning that enables humans to experience existence. Recall from Chapter 5 (this volume) in the discussion of the five aggregates plus craving (*taṇhā*) that when a person appropriates the five aggregates, then a notion of a self is constructed. Specifically, the experience of existence through that constructed notion of the self is characterized by dukkha.

THIS IS MINE, THIS I AM, THIS IS MY SELF

Functionally, in the construction of the notion of a self, clinging (upādāna) evolves from craving (taṇhā). This evolution is a two-step manifestation of dependent arising:

> When this exists [in this case, sense contact], that comes to be [in this case, desire/chanda];
> with the arising of this [desire/chanda], that arises [craving/taṇhā]. (SN, 2000, 12.21.1: The Ten Powers)

Then in the next step of the evolution,

> When this exists [in this case, craving/taṇhā], that comes to be [clinging/upādāna];
> with the arising of this [clinging/upādāna], that arises [the constructed notion of a self, or "This is mine, this I am, this is my self"]. (SN, 2000, 12.21.1; Pali terms added)

The first step is a reaction to a sense stimulus. Consider this example: A person accidentally touches a hot stovetop while cooking. The skin senses heat. The person's immediate response, without any consideration, is to withdraw their hand from the hot stovetop. This immediate response of aversion is an unpleasant hedonic feeling tone (*vedanā*); it is generated from a desire (*chanda*) to continue existence unharmed. The desire manifests itself in craving (taṇhā) for safety in the form of the person clinging (upādāna) to protect their body. For this person, "my body" is the first instance of self-referencing in relationship to the sense contact of heat from the hot stove. This self-referencing is the emergence of a notion of a self from appropriation of the body.

This process is what the sutta refers to as the five aggregates subject to clinging (pañcupādānakkhandhā). Furthermore, the five aggregates subject to clinging is the designation for the constructed notion of a self as, "This is mine, this I am, this is my self" (MN, 1995, 22).

The Alagaddūpama Sutta links each of the five aggregates to its appropriation and identification for the result, "This is mine, this I am, this is my self," or the construction of notion of a self.

> Bhikkhus, there are these six standpoints for views. What are the six? . . . person . . . regards material form thus: "This is mine, this I am, this is myself." He regards feelings thus: "This is mine, this I am, this is myself." He regards perception thus: "This is mine, this I am, this is myself." He regards what is seen, heard, sensed, cognized, encountered, sought, mentally pondered thus: "This is mine, this I am, this is myself." And this standpoint for views, namely "That which is the self is the world"; . . . this too he regards thus: "This is mine, this I am, this is myself." (MN, 1995, 22)

The first aggregate, *rūpa* (materiality, form), refers to the material composition of the universe, of which the human body belongs. Material form in this sutta can be taken to mean the body, material possessions (e.g., car, house, or articles of clothing), or another person. The hedonic feeling tone (vedanā) of a stimulus is translated as "feelings" in this sutta. Perception in this sutta is the aggregate of perception, naming, recognition, and labeling (*saññā*). Being "seen, heard, sensed, cognized, encountered, sought, [and/or] mentally pondered" (MN, 1995, 22) is the aggregate of *saṅkhāra* (mental formations). Finally, "that which is the self is the world" (MN, 1995, 22) refers to the totality of one's world as constructed by appropriation of and identification with the functioning of the five aggregates, or notion of the self. The five aggregates subject to clinging (pañcupādānakkhandhā), fueled by craving (taṇhā) and personified by clinging (upādāna), can be thought of as the underlying mechanism for the constructed notion of a self. It is the notion of the self that is the framework from within which human suffering occurs and shows up for psychotherapy (Figure 11.1).

The phrase, "This is mine," can be thought of as appropriating the aggregates into a notion of a self. Examples for appropriation of material form may sound like this: "No daughter of mine will go out dressed like that! You will go back upstairs and change into something decent before you leave the house." In this example, the daughter's appearance is an extension of the parent, meaning this parent has appropriated their daughter's physical form into their notion of themself. This notion of a self is constructed through appropriating any of the five aggregates, not just material form. An example of appropriation of mental formations into a notion of a self might sound like this: "My wife was curt and demanding in asking me a question as we were on our way to meet her family for dinner at a restaurant. She was rude, and

FIGURE 11.1. Conceptual Map Combining the Elements of Bronfenbrenner's Ecological Systems Theory, Social Positionality, and the Five Aggregates Subject to Clinging

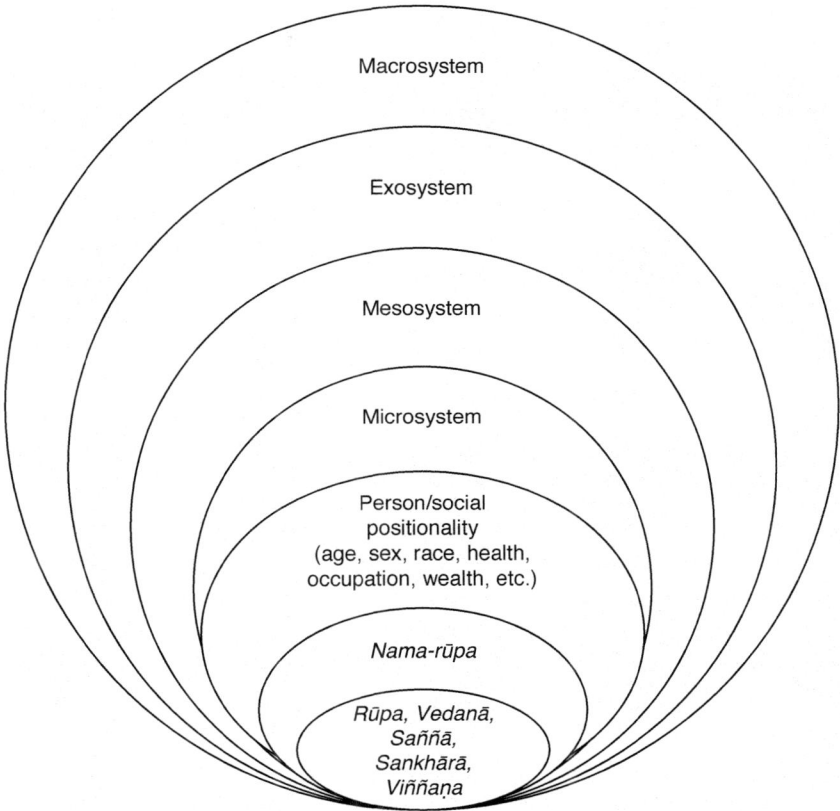

I felt insulted. So, I turned around and went home." As in this situation, having formulated a story about the wife's tone of voice, the person felt insulted, having appropriated his mental formations into a self and thus equating the story he told himself about his wife's tone of voice with his self. He constructed a world in which his wife did not respect him, and he was not going to tolerate anyone who showed disrespect toward him. The client's indignation was what came into the treatment room, having identified with his mental formation and its accompanying emotion of anger. In reality, the client's wife was driving them in rush hour traffic; she was trying to navigate a difficult left turn into the parking lot of the restaurant while the client insisted that she respond to his question at that moment.

The phrase, "This I am," can be thought of as identification with any of the five aggregates. This is akin to labeling oneself with either a social position or personality trait (e.g., male/female/nonbinary, student, professor, person of color, partner/spouse/husband/wife, or any number of social positions with which the person identifies). This notion of a self is constructed through appropriating the aggregate. For Buddhism, the labels are constructed. An example of constructed labels for me (Tien) is Asian American with all of its stereotypes when I am in residence here in the United States. Me, the same person, is not labeled Asian American with its associated stereotypes when I am in residence in China. Thus, if I appropriate Asian American and the associated stereotypes into my constructed notion of a self, when I move to China where I would not be labeled the same, then I would experience disorientation and dysregulation. A clinical example of what enters the psychotherapy treatment room could sound like this:

> I'm turning 30 soon and still don't have a steady partner. I know it is because I am overweight, old, and not attractive. I can't help myself from eating, but afterward I feel so bloated that I have to throw up. How else am I going to be attractive enough to find a partner?

In this example, the appropriation and identification with the body with all of the client's conventional social associations is what came into the treatment room, accompanied by mental proliferations around that body. In abbreviated form, the phrase "This I am" equates to the following: "I am unlovable because I am 30 and still don't have a partner, I am overweight, I am old, I am unattractive, I am female; thus, I need to be pretty to attract a partner."

The phrase, "This is my self," can be thought of as that constructed notion of a self/attā, projected outward. The stance, "That which is the self is the world" (MN, 1995, 22), projects the constructed world of the self/attā onto the universe. The constructed notion of a self that is projected onto the universe presents as "I want to be seen as who I am." The following is an example of what this may sound like when the client enters the psychotherapy treatment room:

> I know I am not smart, but I am a motivated self-starter. I passed my exams and got that graduate degree only because I studied very hard, unlike my brother who sailed through without even having to study. So, I know why my father does not listen to my opinion like he listens to my brother's opinion. My father thinks it is dumb for him to leave the family business to me, but instead he will leave it to my brother. My brother does not even like the family business! That is why I must start my own company; I will have to show them that even though I am not smart, I am a self-starter who can make a million dollars.

The constructed world is projected onto this client's family and mediates his interpretation of their actions. The client's projection of the notion, "I know I am not smart, but I am a motivated self-starter," shows up in the treatment room with the wishing for the universe to see the client as he sees himself.

DETECTING THE NOTION OF A SELF AS IT MANIFESTS IN THE MIND

The Satipaṭṭhāna Sutta's (MN 10: The Foundations of Mindfulness) instruction for detecting the constructed notion of a self is through contemplation of mind objects:

> the direct path for the purification of beings, for the surmounting of sorrow and lamentation, for the disappearance of pain and grief . . .—namely, the four foundations of mindfulness. . . . What are the four? Here, bhikkhus, a bhikkhu abides contemplating the body as a body, . . . feelings as feelings . . . mind as mind . . . **mind-objects as mind-objects**. (MN, 1995, 10: The Foundations of Mindfulness; *Note:* Boldface was added to terms in the sutta to direct the reader to key concepts.)

The Satipaṭṭhāna Sutta is usually translated as the "Foundations of Mindfulness" but is sometimes also translated as the "Four Foundations of Mindfulness." These four foundations name the objects of contemplation, or what the meditator is to notice in their silent meditation. Traditionally, the contemplation of "mind-objects as mind-objects" (MN, 1995, 10) includes all six sense bases (*āyatana*) and the seven factors of enlightenment; for the purpose of psychotherapy, the contemplation of mind objects will only address phenomena or hindrances.

The Buddhist method to understand the nature of one's suffering is to observe the mind. The mind is that which notices the sense contact; the mind is that which notices the hedonic feeling tone of the sense contact; the mind is that which notices the mind and mind objects. In the contemplation of mind objects, or phenomena in consciousness, the meditator is considering the functioning of the mind and the mind culture. The methodology for observing the mind is in the activity of silent meditation. During meditation, obstructions arise when the meditator tries to see through the manifestations of craving (*taṇhā*) and clinging (*upādāna*) to the construction of the notion of a self, then through the constructed notion of a self to the functioning of the five aggregates. The obstruction is experienced as mental states that pervade the mind. They serve the function of hindering, blocking the ability to clearly apprehend the self as a constructed notion. These obstructions are referred to as *hindrances*.

In the contemplation of mind objects, or phenomena in consciousness, the meditator is considering the functioning of the mind and the mind culture. In meditation, the meditator takes the mind objects or the culture of the hindrances as the object of contemplation. In this task, the meditator's attention is turned toward the hindrance. This *turning toward* is to first recognize the presence of the hindrance. Once the meditator has identified the type of hindrance in the mind, the meditator examines that mind state in order to understand the conditions that enabled that mind state to arise and then determines how to abandon that mind state.

Hindrances can be thought of as a state of mind with distinct patterns and characteristics. Each hindrance, while functioning as obstruction, has its own characteristics. A function is different from a characteristic. For example, all cities anywhere in any country function the same way by sheltering a large number of humans in a small geographical area; within this small geographical area, all cities include similar features, like buildings and roads. Yet each city is unlike any other city with its own characteristics and reputation. For example, the first author's (Tien's) hometown of Seattle, Washington, functions much like any other city, with its buildings, shopping districts, and roads as well as its intangible institutions, such as city government offices and the police force. Aside from these similarities, Seattle has its own unique character. It is said to have what is called the "Seattle freeze." This term describes the often-encountered initial smiles, warm welcome, and friendliness from longtime residents of Seattle, but this same warm and friendly greeting will probably never extend to an invitation to the newcomer for a social gathering at the longtime resident's home. These same functions and characteristics, like in cities, are found in each of the five hindrances.

A person, on their own, will most likely encounter these hindrances the first moment they sit down to silent meditation. Once a hindered mind state is known, the person is able to identify its functioning at all moments, on or off the meditation cushion. These internal mind states are most obvious when they engage in meditative contemplation of a chosen designated object, like the breath. Their topology is less obvious when off the meditation cushion. Nonetheless, mind states of the hindrances function at all times. Sometimes, the hindrance mind state is obvious as soon as a person starts to talk in psychotherapy; for others, depending on the nature of their presenting complaint, the hindrance mind state will be less obvious. Regardless, all hindrances have the same function, which is to hinder the person from detecting the constructed notion of a self/attā and the construction of their world.

Although each hindrance has unique nuances in different individuals, the function and general characteristics of the hindrances generalize into what comes into the psychotherapy room. The hindrances manifest as the world-view, disposition, or mind culture out of which the client reports their experiences. Identifying and articulating the client's worldview, disposition, or mind culture often enables the client to conceptualize and analyze their presenting complaint, instead of being immersed and overwhelmed with the experience of that complaint.

In the Satipaṭṭhāna Sutta (MN, 1995, 10), Buddha Gotama invites the meditator—and, in turn, the psychotherapist—to direct one's attention toward the mind objects, the hindrances. This means to look at the patterns of the mind, not the content of the thoughts, as the object of contemplation in meditation and as the topic of discussion in the in-session dialogue. This turning toward is to recognize the presence of the hindrance, then to examine the characteristic manifestations in order to understand the conditions that enabled that mind state to arise in the mind/citta, and then to determine how to abandon that mind state. For the psychotherapist, it is of less benefit to consider the content of a client's concern because the specifics of the concern shift from session to session, and they sometimes even shift several times in a session. Instead, it is more helpful to look at the pattern of the client's mind state, meaning to identify the hindrance at play.

The Buddha likened the way that hindrances manifest in consciousness to a magic show (SN, 2000, 22.95: A Lump of Foam). This magic show conjures up a mind culture with its own topography. When the beginner meditator sits down, closes their eyes, and turns inward, they first encounter this magic show. The mind object is the magician's act. Like a magician who creates illusions of seemingly impossible occurrences, a mind object is the illusion created by the mind that hinders the noticing of the sense contact. This magician's show is also what populates the content of the client's in-session deliberations.

A magician's show is the foreground that hides the functioning of the five aggregates and the constructed notion of the self.

> Suppose, bhikkhus, that a magician or a magician's apprentice would display a magical illusion at a crossroads. A man with good sight would inspect it, ponder it, and carefully investigate it, and it would appear to him to be void, hollow, insubstantial. For what substance would there be in a magical illusion? So too, bhikkhus, whatever kind of consciousness there is, whether past, future, or present, internal or external, gross or subtle, inferior or superior, far or near: a bhikkhu inspects it, ponders it, and carefully investigates it, and it would appear to him to be void, hollow, insubstantial. For what substance could there be in consciousness? (Pheṇapiṇḍūpama Sutta; SN, 2000, 22.95)

What the magician conjures up for the audience, the meditator, is the magic show of the hindrances. Like a magic show, if one is knowledgeable about how the illusion is created, one can see through the illusion to the actuality of the trick. The contemplation of the mind object is the method to allow the person to see through the constructed notion of the self to the actuality of a situation. The magic show, or the hindrances, is the illusion that hinders the noticing of the functioning of the five aggregates, the working of the mind/citta, and the preprogrammed misconceptions of the sense contacts. Although these mind states that hinder piercing through the illusion of the magic show are most obvious when one turns inward in meditation, these hindered states of mind are present in everyday activities and thus can be evident at any time, including during psychotherapy in-session dialogue.

In theory, there may be any number of mind states that hinder the person's ability to discern the functions of the pañcakkhandhā (five aggregates) and the construction of the pañcupādānakkhandhā (five aggregates subject to clinging). The psychotherapist is encouraged to develop a label for states of mind commonly experienced by a client. An example of such a label is one that is experienced often by many, that being the *planning mind*. For some, this planning mind intrudes into daily life as well as during meditation, where the mind spends some time problem-solving and planning for upcoming events or projects. The planning mind spends time rehearsing, for example, every detail of going to pick up someone from the airport (e.g., the time needed to drive from home to the airport, when to leave home, and the route to take depending on the time of day in order to avoid traffic delays). Some states of mind are commonly found, and others are unique to individuals. It may be useful for the client to have a handy label for their most troublesome states of mind.

The likelihood is high that a person will often experience a specific type of mind state, a specific hindrance. This habituated hindrance can be the preferred pervasive stance within a person's internal world. However, this does not mean that the other mind states are absent. A preferred mind state is the one that predominates the mind most of the time. While clients describe the content of their problems, the psychotherapist is listening for the pattern in the mind state to identify and label which hindrance is at work. Identifying the type of hindrance that the client exhibits by way of how the client describes their difficulties may be an avenue into the root of the client's craving. It is of greater importance to examine the mind object as a mind state. It is less important to attend to the content of what the client talks about because the contents are changeable, depending on the concern of the day.

Hindrance mind states are present during meditation as well as other daily activities; thus, they can be evident at any time, including during psychotherapy in-session dialogue. To combat the gaslighting effect of the hindrances, one has to be engaged in this "endeavor during one's ordinary life" (Thera, 2013). As stated by Thera Nyanaponika (2013),

> This widespread harmful influence of the five hindrances shows the urgent necessity of breaking down their power by constant effort. One should not believe it sufficient to turn one's attention to the hindrances only at the moment when one sits down for meditation. Such last-minute effort in suppressing the hindrances will rarely be successful unless helped by previous endeavor during one's ordinary life. (para. 6)

The endeavor to combat the harmful influence of the hindrances can start during the in-session dialogue and then extend to the client's daily activities. The Buddha gave very specific and precise meditation approaches to address the mind states that hinder a person's ability to directly experience the functioning of the pañcakkhandhā (five aggregates). It is useful for psychotherapists to be familiar with these meditation approaches so they can comprehend the links between the theory and the meditation intervention techniques. Additionally, these meditation approaches can be taken as directives for the psychotherapist in their functioning as mindfulness when conducting in-session dialogue with the client.

While in principle, there is the possibility of any number of mind states that hinder, the sutta names five commonly found hindered states of mind. The first hindrance is based on materiality, and the remaining four are based on mentality. These hindrances, as listed in the Nivāraṇa Sutta (SN, 2000, 46.40: The Chapter on Hindrances), are as follows:

- sensual desire (*kamacchanda*)
- ill will (*vyāpāda*)
- sloth and torpor (*thīna-middha*)
- restlessness and remorse (*uddhacca-kukkucca*)
- doubt (*vicikicchā*)

The hindrances have only one function—to hinder a person from being able to see through the five aggregates subject to clinging to the functioning of the five aggregates. The remainder of this chapter discusses the characteristics of each of the five types of hindrances, the types of desire that underly those different hindrances, and thus what the psychotherapist would be listening for in their in-session dialogue with the client. Although the Buddha gave extensive instructions on how to handle the hindrances in meditation, they will not be addressed in this chapter. The meditation methods to counter the hindrances will be collectively discussed in Chapters 15 and 16 (this volume). Table 11.1 summarizes the hindrances at a glance.

TABLE 11.1. The Five Hindrances

Hindrance	Description	Example	Underlying desire	Therapist's task
Sensual desire (*kamacchanda*)	Being contacted by painful feeling, one seeks delight in sensual pleasure (Salla Sutta [SN 36.6]: The Dart)	Addiction	To experience no pain, either somatic or psychological	Listen for what the client is avoiding
Ill will (*vyāpāda*)	Making bad, doing harm: desire to injure, malevolence (Pali Text Society, n.d.)	Critical self-talk	Have the universe be as it should be	Listen for the unrequited desires
Sloth and torpor (*thīna-middha*)	Lack of driving power (Buddhaghosa, 1956/2010)		To be	Listen for what is being avoided
Restlessness and remorse (*uddhacca-kukkucca*)	Sorrow about what has and what has not been done; worry about how that will affect the future (Buddhaghosa, 1956/2010)	Anxiety	To be safe	Listen for the real danger in the situation
Doubt (*vicikicchā*)	Uncertainty, as in the following example: "Thus, as the traveler in the desert is uncertain whether robbers are there or not, he produces in his mind, again and again, a state of wavering and vacillation, a lack of decision, a state of anxiety; and thus, he creates in himself an obstacle for reaching the safe ground of sanctity" (Commentaries; Thera Nyanaponika, 2013)		To be blameless	Listen for the underlying fear of disapproval with the accompanying desire for approval

The Buddha likens a mind state that is absent of hindrances to that of clear water (SN, 2000, 46.55). If one were to look at one's own reflection in a still pool of clear water, one would see the reflection without distortion. Without the hindrance, there would be clarity, not a distorted view of any situation under discussion in the treatment session. The goal for meditation is to be able to see through the hindrances and notice the functioning of the aggregates; to experientially know that the aggregates are nonpersonal functions; and to see through the mind's appropriation and identification with the aggregates of form, feeling, perception, mental formation, and consciousness. The counter to the suffering of an embodied existence is to see through the hindrances to the craving and the structure of the five aggregates.

To introduce the idea of pervasive mind states, the psychotherapist can start with the observation of a mind state and identify features of hindrances in the treatment sessions. Characteristics of hindrances can often be seen in the foreground when the client describes the details of their troubles. The in-session dialogue holds the time and space for the client to take a more considered view of themselves, their situation, and their problems.

It is beneficial for the psychotherapist to narrate the client's struggles during their in-session reports of their concerns. The challenge for the psychotherapist is to not get caught up in the content of the client's problems, as if the psychotherapist is sharing the experience with the client and also sharing in the client's urge to solve the problem. This stance inhibits the psychotherapist's ability to help the client analyze their experience and thus be able to figure out a more personal and lifestyle-congruent way out of their struggles. In Buddhist psychotherapy, the task at hand is to create a space for in-session dialogue about each of the elements in the aggregate, the dukkha, and the hindrances. The therapeutic process allows the conversation to go into the client's internal world in greater detail. The in-session intervention enables both the psychotherapist and the client to cocreate a different platform from which a different worldview can fully emerge.

In the treatment sessions, the psychotherapist is listening for the characteristics of the client's internal landscape. The psychotherapist is advised to be sufficiently familiar with the characteristics and manifestations of each, so as to be able to discern the mind state of a hindrance when listening to their client's report of their problems. The best method to familiarize oneself with the hindrances is to observe them in one's own meditation practice. Each hindrance is described next.

THE FIRST HINDRANCE: SENSUAL DESIRE (*KAMACCHANDA*)

The hindrance of sensual desire is the only one of the five named hindrances that is based on the materiality of the body.

> Being contacted by that same painful feeling, he harbors aversion towards it. When he harbors aversion towards painful feeling, the underlying tendency to aversion towards painful feeling lies behind this. Being contacted by painful feeling, he seeks delight in sensual pleasure. For what reason? Because the uninstructed worldling does not know of any escape from painful feeling other than sensual pleasure. When he seeks delight in sensual pleasure, the underlying tendency to lust for pleasant feeling lies behind this. (Salla Sutta; SN, 2000, 36.6: The Dart)

The compound word *kāmacchanda* is usually translated as "sensual desire." In the *Pali Text Society's Pali–English Dictionary*, *kāma* is defined as "pleasantness, pleasure—giving, an object of sensual enjoyment" and "enjoyment, pleasure on occasion of sense, sense—desire"; *chanda* is defined as "(impulse) . . . expressing the active, clinging, and impulsive character of desire" (Pali Text Society, n.d.). When these words are combined, kāmacchanda refers to the sense of impulsively, perhaps at times compulsively, turning to pleasure of the six sense bases to escape the various suffering that is inevitable in life.

The mind filled with sensual desire has an internal landscape likened to the distortions we observe when we look through colored lenses. In the Saṅgārava Sutta (SN, 2000, 46.55: With Saṅgārava), the Buddha compared each of the five hindrance mind states to bowls of water. For the hindrance of sensual desire, the Buddha said,

> Suppose, brahmin, there is a bowl of water mixed with lac, turmeric, blue dye, or crimson dye. If a man with good sight were to examine his own facial reflection in it, he would neither know nor see it as it really is. So too, brahmin, when one dwells with a mind obsessed by sensual lust . . . on that occasion even those hymns that have been recited over a long period do not recur to the mind, let alone those that have not be recited. (SN, 2000, 46.55)

Characteristics of Sensual Desire

The Salla Sutta (SN, 2000, 36.6) describes the use and function of sense pleasure as a way to escape experiencing dukkha (suffering, unsatisfactoriness); the oppressiveness of the body; the oppressiveness of emotions; the pains, displeasure, and dissatisfactions of life; the loss of things pleasant and desired; the fear of not having; and so on. To do this, the mind state of sensual desire seeks pleasant experiences in relation to the *āyatana* (any of the six sense bases) as a way to distract itself from the experience of dukkha.

The hindrance of the sensuous mind state is focused on grabbing and hanging on to pleasant sense-based experiences. In its benign manifestation, these sense-based experiences are ones that most of us would consider as making life enjoyable:

- desire for pleasurable sight—as in fine art, or panoramic vistas from a mountain top;

- desire for pleasurable sound—as in a grand symphony played by an excellent orchestra, or the sound of a gentle breeze rustling through the trees;

- desire for pleasurable smell—like freshly baked bread or pine trees in a forest;

- desire for pleasant taste—such as a delicious slice of moist chocolate cake or one's favorite meal from childhood;

- desire for the pleasant touch—as in consensual sex, or a fuzzy warm blanket on a cold winter evening; and

- the sense stimulation of the mind when introduced to new and novel ideas.

Addiction is an example of the more problematic manifestation of this mind state. The desire is for the pleasant state induced by the intoxicant, be it chemical (e.g., alcohol) or situational (e.g., gambling).

The mind state of sensual desire is full of wants. It is engaged with planning for getting what one wants, the complaints of not having or being able to get what one wants, and the fear of losing what one wanted and acquired. The topology of the mind is imbued with wants accompanied by fear of losing what one has. That fear shows up in the psychotherapy treatment room as anxiety, with content full of what one does not have, what one has but does not want, or the possibility of losing what one has already.

Desire That Underlies Sensual Desire

In the Salla Sutta, the Buddha described the motivator behind sensual desire: "Being contacted by painful feeling, he seeks delight in sensual pleasure" (SN, 2000, 36.6). Although desire for the continued experience of a pleasant state is generated by any contact with sensual pleasure, the motivator mentioned in this sutta phrase is particularly applicable to the psychotherapy treatment room. The hindrance of the sensuous mind is focused on grasping and attaching to the sense experience for the purpose of escape from dukkha.

Buddhism posits that underlying the mind state of sensual desire is aversion, that humans seek relief from life's suffering by distracting themselves through indulging in the pleasures derived from pleasant experiences of the six sense bases. In the midst of the experience of sensual pleasures, the Buddha says that

> when one dwells with a mind obsessed by sensual lust, overwhelmed by sensual lust, and one does not understand as it really is the escape from arisen sensual lust, on that occasion one neither knows nor sees as it really is one's own good, or the good of others, or the good of both. (SN, 2000, 46:55)

Having that immediate sense-based pleasant experience is like an addict seeking the pleasant state induced by the intoxicant, which enables them to escape painful life situations. Like an addict, that person is not focused on the long-term consequences of indulging in these pleasant distractions.

The underlying desire is to escape from all forms of dukkha. Buddhism, in the Third Noble Truth, posits that escape from dukkha is possible. However, the mind state of sensual desire is a problematic and dysfunctional method for such escape.

Intervention for Sensual Desire: In-Session Dialogue
The in-session dialogue for a client with the mental state of sensual desire has the following basic sentence structure:

- "I want [fill in the blank]." (e.g., "I want to be loved by that person," "I want a healthy, slim, and attractive body," "I want a rewarding job," "I want a car that reflects who I am," "I want to be free of this headache," "I want to be released from this depression," or "I want to be carefree like I was before these anxiety attacks.")

- "I don't want [fill in the blank]."

If a person has what they want, is not suffering from the presence of things they do not want, is satisfied with what they have, and/or is able to manage their wants so as not to be sufficiently unhappy to be bothered by the absence of the things they want but don't have, they will most likely not be seeking psychotherapy.

A person with an internal landscape filled with sensual desire will present to the psychotherapist with complaints containing the underlying theme of either (a) wanting something they do not have or (b) experiencing fear, anxiety, or worry of losing something they do have or the grief of having lost something they had. Wanting something they do not have might sound like complaining about their job not paying enough money to afford a cruise, where they could be pampered through access to well-prepared food 24 hours a day, entertainment and shows, casinos, body massages, swimming pools, theater shows, and a whole host of sensual indulgences that are available on a luxury cruise. Lest we get the wrong impression that Buddhism advocates for purging of all desire, recall the discussion of the five aggregates plus craving (taṇhā) in Chapter 6, which examined the various Buddhist concepts that are uniformly translated as "desire" in English. Not all desires are dysfunctional and unwholesome. Chanda (desire) is value neutral. It can be desire for enlightenment, or it can be desire for sensual pleasures. Taṇhā, also often translated as "desire" or "craving," is not value neutral. One significant difference between chanda (desire) and taṇhā (craving) is that chanda can be satisfied, and thus is not usually dysfunctional. This type of desire (chanda) can and should be encouraged. Taṇhā (craving) cannot be satisfied; therefore, it causes all sorts of unpleasant experiences.

Conversely, the client may be wanting something they had but lost. This usually shows up in psychotherapy with clients who have lost someone or something—maybe a loved one, either to a terminal illness or involuntary separation—and do not want the dukkha (suffering, unsatisfactoriness) of that loss. Or it is the client not wanting something they do have, like fear of a panic attack. This is wanting to get rid of something unpleasant.

The mind state of sensual desire hinders noticing the underlying desire to get away from life's difficulties. As psychotherapists, our task during deep listening in treatment sessions is to first hear the client's pain/dukkha (suffering, unsatisfactoriness) and then to hear the underlying wish and desire in the client's presenting complaint. That underlying desire is the client's implicit request to us psychotherapists.

The job of the psychotherapist is not only to figure out the underlying desire but also to name the avoidance strategy—what the client is doing to avoid the painful feelings, the unpleasant experiences. This avoidance mechanism is most likely the ways that the person has used to cope with their presenting complaint. Finding a way to fulfill that underlying desire is the client's implicit request to the psychotherapist. In other words, once the mind state of sensual desire is detected, listen for the client's underlying desire and their avoidance strategies to deal with the inability to acquire their underlying desire. Having a dialogue about the underlying desire may allow the client to consider other methods to satisfy that desire.

The Buddha gives explicit and extensive instructions on how to handle the mind state of sensual desire in the Satipaṭṭhāna Sutta (MN, 1995, 10). Discussion of this will be included in Chapters 15 and 16 (this volume) on concentration and meditation.

HINDRANCES BASED ON MENTALITY

In the application to psychotherapy, the underlying impetus for the hindrances of ill will, sloth and torpor, restlessness, and remorse and doubt can be motivated by one of the three hedonic feeling tones linked to a sense stimulus. The meditative consideration, as specified in the Satipaṭṭhāna Sutta, is as follows:

> And how, bhikkhus, does a bhikkhu abide contemplating feelings as feelings? Here, when feeling a pleasant feeling, a bhikkhu understands: "I feel a pleasant feeling"; when feeling a painful feeling, he understands: "I feel a painful feeling"; when feeling a neither-painful-nor-pleasant feeling, he understands: "I feel a neither-painful-nor-pleasant feeling." (MN, 1995, 10)

The Second Hindrance: Ill Will (*Vyāpāda*)

In the Kesaputtiya Sutta, the Buddha stated, "Kālāmas, a person who is full of hate, overcome by hatred, with mind obsessed by it, destroys life, takes what is not given" (*Aṅguttara Nikāya* [AN], 2012, 3.65: Kesaputtiya). The *Pali Text Society's Pali–English Dictionary* defines *vyāpāda* as "making bad, doing harm: desire to injure, malevolence, ill-will" (Pali Text Society, n.d.). Vyāpāda is most often translated as "ill will," sometimes as "hatred," and less often as "anger." The mind filled with vyāpāda has an internal landscape of turbulence, as described in the Saṅgārava Sutta:

> Imagine a bowl of water, heated on a fire, boiling up and bubbling over. If a man with good eyesight were to look at the reflection of his own face in it, he would not know or see it as it really was. (SN, 2000, 46.55)

In other words, considering any situation through a mind filled with ill will is like looking for one's reflection on the surface of a pot filled with boiling water. One would get a distorted view of what is there.

Characteristics of Ill Will

The mind state of vyāpāda is one of being critical, either inwardly toward the self or outwardly toward the other (or to both the self and the other), constantly comparing the self and/or the universe with what the self and/or the universe should be. The mind state of vyāpāda (ill will, hatred, anger) is filled and overwhelmed with rage at one extreme and with mild frustration at the other, regardless of whether that ill will is directed toward oneself or another person. If ill will is directed inwardly, typically it will be a mental environment of negative criticisms.

If ill will is directed outwardly, typically it will be a mental environment of blaming. Regardless of where the ill will is directed, the primary presenting affect may be anger. Usually, the anger is narrowed to one object and intensified to an all-encompassing focus on getting rid of the object of hatred. When the hatred is directed inward toward oneself, the internal monologue is filled with critical self-talk, usually focused on clinging to a self-view that is negative and disapproving. An example is a depressed person who is ceaselessly critical (e.g., "I am [fill in the blank with a negative descriptor (e.g., lazy, stupid, fat, a worry-wart, ugly, undisciplined)]").

When the anger is directed outward, the blaming process presents first: "One should [fill in the blank]," followed by, "They should have and did not [fill in with the correct behavior or emotion]," which is the given reason for a sense of being wronged and followed by righteous justification. The internal monologue is focused on clinging to a view of the other person as dangerously evil with purposeful ill intent toward oneself.

A client with the mental state of ill will is immersed in the world of "should" (e.g., "I should," "The other person should," or both). What is verbalized in session is usually what happens when that should is not realized, meaning the client has a sense of justified righteousness in their critique of either self or other. The psychotherapist's task during deep listening is to hear the underlying desire in the client's unrelenting critique of self or other. That desire is for a self and the universe to be as it should be. The suffering is in the usually unrecognized and unarticulated demand that it is the person's burden to right that wrong and make the self and the universe as it should be.

Desire That Underlies Ill Will
The desire that underlies ill will is for the self and the universe to be as it should (e.g., as designed by the client). In the mind state of ill will, there is a deep sense that there is something irrevocably wrong with the universe and that the universe is not as it should be. In addition, there is a sense that there is something unacceptable and broken about the self and that the self is not what it should be. Both are accompanied by the dictate to right what is wrong. What is unarticulated but ever-present is the person's version of what that self and the universe should be and the sureness that it is their responsibility to make the self as well as the universe as it should be, the internal dictate to right what is wrong. The ill will is a reaction to the person's inability to right what is wrong.

The underlying desire is for the self and the universe to be as it should be, not as it is. The suffering is the unrequited love for that idealized self and the universe. The mind state of ill will is a problematic and dysfunctional method for shaping the universe to match the client's constructed world.

Intervention for Ill Will: In-Session Dialogue

A client with the mental state of ill will is immersed in the world of "should": "I should," "The other person should," or "The universe should." The Buddha Gotama lists the possible manifestations from a mind state of ill will as follows:

> What, bhikkhus, are the imperfections that defile the mind? Covetousness and unrighteous greed is an imperfection that defiles the mind. Ill will . . . anger . . . resentment . . . contempt . . . insolence . . . envy . . . avarice . . . deceit . . . fraud . . . obstinacy . . . rivalry . . . conceit . . . arrogance . . . vanity . . . is an imperfection that defiles the mind. (MN, 1995, 7.3: The Simile of the Cloth)

What is verbalized in the treatment sessions is usually what happens when the should is not realized. The inwardly directed ill will most often presents as depression with copious critical self-talk (e.g., "I should be able to meditate better," "I should not have gotten angry at my mother," "I should study harder"). There is an unarticulated conviction that something has gone wrong and a profound sense of the client not being what they should be, with an underlying fear of disapproval and the underlying desire for approval.

If the ill will mind state is directed outward, typically there will be a mental environment of being personally affronted and blaming. This affront and then blaming process presents first as "A person should," followed by "They should have, but they did not," which is the given reason for a sense of being wronged and is followed by righteous anger. These internal dialogues might sound like this:

- "They should do something about the oil industry's polluting the planet and creating global warming, but they are too greedy to do anything, and now I have to advocate for climate control."

- "He should recognize the sacrifices I have made for him and show everyone his appreciation by getting me a diamond ring."

- "They should [fill in the blank with how the universe should be] but they did not [fill in the blank with how the universe is not what it should be], and now I must not only suffer as a result of their [fill in the blank with the wrongs inflicted on the person] but I also have to [fill in the blank with actions to right that wrong]."

An example of uncontrolled hatred directed at others is seen in rage, often in acts of domestic violence. In the case of domestic violence, the client will most likely report knowing for certain that the partner purposefully and endlessly corners the client into untenable situations by doing things that the partner knows irk the client. The client has the desire to escape. The only means to escape is by violently obliterating the offending object. In the case of domestic violence, the offending object is the partner. There is a sense that the other is not what they should be, that there is something wrong with the universe, and that the universe is not what it should be. The ill will is the manifestation of the sense of affront.

That underlying desire for the world to be as "it should be" is the client's unrecognized suffering and their implicit request to us psychotherapists to right the world for them. Here, the psychotherapist is listening for the unstated anger at a hopelessly unfulfilled desire, to notice the "should" behind the critique and then the unrequited desires underneath the critique. The psychotherapist's in-session task is to accurately notice, describe, and verify with the client the content of their concern from within the framework of a landscape of vyāpāda (ill will, hatred, anger). The psychotherapist is tasked with using a line of questioning and then engaging in deep listening for the client's underlying anger (whether directed at the self or at others) at not fulfilling their desire to avoid, to escape, and/or to get rid of the offending object, be that object the unacceptable self or the other.

This line of exploration is extremely nuanced. Most psychotherapists enter this profession with a wish to be of help and assistance to others and to be instrumental in easing the other person's pain and suffering. The cautionary note here is for the psychotherapist to refrain from attempts to soothe the client's criticalness for those whose ill will is directed at the self. For the client whose ill will is directed at others, it is not for the psychotherapist to counter the client's hatred by explaining the intent of the other person's behavior. The Buddhist psychotherapist is advised not to act on this pull to soothe the client or to nullify the rage, but instead to act as mindfulness to simply notice and to make vyāpāda (ill will, hatred, anger) a topic of discussion with the client. Most people with an internal mind state of hatred rarely have anyone attend to or even cursorily listen to the complaints that manifest in the mind state of ill will. Many helping professionals find the mind state of vyāpāda to be confusing at best and abhorrent at worst. It is difficult for helping professionals to tolerate the vehemence and have sufficient self-care to patiently listen to a client in the mind state of vyāpāda.

For psychotherapists, the task during our deep listening is to hear the client's underlying desire for the world, the self, and the universe to be as it should be. The usual unarticulated implicit request is for the psychotherapist to make the world as it should be. It is amazingly healing for the psychotherapist to accurately articulate the unrequited desire for a universe, the world, and the self to be as it should be that fuels the underlying anger. Such articulation by the psychotherapist can be experienced by the client as finally being seen and heard, which can be amazingly satisfying and healing for the client.

Once the suffering is articulated, it will then be easier to address the unrequited desires for validation, acceptance, and love underneath the ill will. Part of enacting the validation, acceptance, and love is to help the client talk about the parts of their life that are going well and are experienced as pleasant. In general, little attention is given to the overall pattern of their life. To balance the unpleasant affronted items, it may be useful for the client to see the parts of their life that are going well and the things they encounter in their daily life that are pleasurable. In specifics, the client will talk almost exclusively about the items that give cause for displeasure in the situation under discussion. In dialogue with the client, the aim is to get a much fuller description of the situation being discussed; these include the things that gave rise to unpleasantness, those things that were present but neutral, and those things that were pleasant in the situation being discussed.

Consider an example. If the content of a client's in-session discussion centered around a meeting they had at work in which they felt disrespected, then it is likely that their complaint will be filled with the things said by certain individuals in the meeting. There will be attributions of ill intent from those individuals toward oneself. The client exhibits intense anger and feels justified in their ill will toward this colleague. This is what is meant by "frequently giving careless attention to it is the nutriment for the arising of unarisen ill will and for the increase and expansion of arisen ill will" (Āhāra Sutta; SN, 2000, 46.51: Nutriment).

What is missing in this client's report are things that are either pleasant vedanā (hedonic feeling tone) or neither pleasant nor unpleasant vedanā. For example, who else was in attendance at this meeting (neutral vedanā)? What responses did others give to the individual in question (neutral or pleasant vedanā)? Were there others who shared the client's position on the topic discussed at the meeting (pleasant vedanā)? This is a nuanced line of inquiry—the psychotherapist needs to be neutral in the approach, to obtain information, and to not veer toward attempts to nullify the client's anger. The nature of the psychotherapist's inquiry is to get a more comprehensive picture of the situation, not to dispute the client's position. In this fuller report, there are bound to be items that were experienced as neutral or pleasant. This is the enactment of the realization of the first mark of existence, where it is said that "all conditioned things are impermanent" (aniccā; *Dhammapada* [Dhp], 1996, 277–279: The Path). This line of inquiry is for the full understanding and articulation of *conditions*.

The nature of the psychotherapist's inquiry is to give equal weight to those pleasant or neutral items. This counters "the arising of ill will . . .

[due to the client's] giving careless attention" (SN, 2000, 46.51) to the repulsive, through giving equal attention to the pleasant and the neutral in any given situation.

The Third Hindrance: Sloth and Torpor (*Thīna-Middha*)

Buddhaghosa (1956/2010) described *thīna* (stiffness; also sloth) and *middha* (torpor) as follows:

> The meaning is, paralysis due to lack of urgency, and loss of vigour. The compound thìnamiddha (stiffness-and-torpor) has the characteristic of lack of driving power. Its function is to remove energy. It is manifested as subsiding. Torpor has the characteristic of unwieldiness. Its function is to smother. (p. 477)

The Pali term for sloth and torpor is the compound *thīna-middha*. The *Pali Text Society's Pali–English Dictionary* defines thīna as "stiffness, obduracy, stolidity, indifference" and middha as "torpor, stupidity, sluggishness." Together, thīna-middha "is one of the five hindrances (*nīvaranāni*) to Arahantship" (Pali Text Society, n.d.).

Thīna-middha is often translated as "dullness" and "drowsiness," and sometimes as "sloth" and "torpor." One can liken this state to the physical experience of stiffness, as in muscles being stiff after too much exercise. When stiff, the muscles tend to be sluggish in response, accompanied by a sense of tiredness, as if it takes a monumental effort to move. Thīna is more physical, whereas middha is more mental. In meditation, thīna-middha is the mental experience of drifting toward sleepiness. When it is a pleasant state of sloth and torpor, it is more like being in a sedated state; think of the pleasant placidness of resting on a soft couch after vigorous exercise. When it is an unpleasant state of sloth and torpor, it is more like sinking in quicksand; think of those same muscles aching from being overworked but needing to move the body. In the state of sloth and torpor, it is a mind that, for any variety of reasons, does not engage. In the Saṅgārava Sutta, the Buddha likened the hindrance of the mind state of sloth and torpor to algae-filled water.

> Again, brahmin, when one dwells with a mind obsessed by sloth and torpor, overwhelmed by sloth and torpor, and one does not understand as it really is the escape from arisen sloth and torpor, on that occasion one neither knows nor sees at it really is one's own good, or the good of others, or the good of both. . . . Suppose, brahmin, there is a bowl of water covered over with water plants and algae. If a man with good sight were to examine his own facial reflection in it, he would neither know nor see it as it really is. . . . In the same way, when one's mind is possessed by sloth and torpor, overpowered by sloth

and torpor, one cannot properly see the escape from sloth and torpor that have arisen; then one does not properly understand one's own welfare, nor that of another, nor that of both. (SN, 2000, 46.55)

Two other similes for sloth and torpor, or dullness and drowsiness, are given in the Commentaries (Thera Nyanaponika, 2013) to the *Nikāya*. One likens it to being in jail, and the other likens it to being absent.

> A person has been kept in jail during a festival day, and so could see neither the beginning nor the middle nor the end of the festivities. If he is released on the following day, and hears people saying: "Oh, how delightful was yesterday's festival! Oh, those dances and songs!" he will not give any reply. And why not? Because he did not enjoy the festival himself.
>
>   Similarly, even if a very eloquent sermon on the Dhamma is going on, a monk overcome by sloth and torpor will not know the beginning, middle or end. If after the sermon, he hears it praised: "How pleasant was it to listen to the Dhamma! How interesting was the topic and how good the similes!" he will not be able to say a word. And why not? Because, owing to his sloth and torpor, he did not enjoy the sermon. In that way, sloth and torpor are comparable to imprisonment. (Commentaries)

Characteristics of Sloth and Torpor

Often, the mind state of sloth and torpor is temporary when there is an identifiable cause. Meditation teachers for silent meditation retreats report that the mind state of sloth and torpor is what most people experience at the beginning of a retreat because the mind is tired from the constant stimulation, often overstimulation, of everyday life. When the meditator arrives at the retreat, the mind takes a respite by going into sloth and torpor for that much-needed rest in the beginning of the silent meditation retreat. The mind state of sloth and torpor is like the body's sluggishness after a period of intense exercise. That sluggishness dissipates on its own accord with a bit of rest. It is a normal state for the mind to float and perhaps sleep when given a chance to be still, as in meditation. This too should dissipate after a short period of time. This kind of temporary fatigue and restoration is different from the habitual torpor.

The mind state of torpor will usually manifest in meditation as sleepiness. Sloth and torpor refer to the mind state of a meditator where there is mental sluggishness and lethargy. This is more a lack of energy, as if the person's energy to engage has been withdrawn. Some Buddhist traditions describe this as laziness and, at times, as cowardness due to the mind's unwillingness to engage with challenges. The mind state of sloth and torpor does not refer to a personality of laziness; it refers to a mind that is lethargic. Some meditators describe it as a pleasant, calm, drifting cocoon from which they emerge refreshed, as if having had a very good night's sleep. However, when one has a task, like contemplation of the breath, being in the state of sloth and torpor hinders one's ability to notice the breath. Sloth and torpor, as described in the sutta (SN 46.55), is the algae in the pool that covers the water; as described in the Commentaries, it is the constraint of a jail cell; or it is being restrained from doing things that need doing and/or engaging in some pleasing activity that enhances our lived experiences. The mind filled with sloth and torpor has an internal landscape of opacity, as described in the Saṅgārava Sutta:

> Imagine a bowl of water covered over with slimy moss and water-plants. If a man with good eyesight were to look at the reflection of his own face in it, he would not know or see it as it really was. (SN, 2000, 46.55)

In other words, considering any situation through a mind filled with sloth and torpor is like looking for one's reflection in a pool of water covered over with algae. One would not get any view.

The mental state of sloth and torpor manifests in daily life as a preference for turning away from difficult situations. It is as if the person's psyche energy is working on not wanting to engage with something. In daily life, torpor is more like withdrawing, turning away. It is as if the person's psyche energy is working on not seeing something that is obviously challenging, threatening, or oppressive. The socially desirable behavior manifestation may be like having good manners, the act of politely turning away from actively noticing and commenting on a social faux pas, like a person's bad eating habits. The more benign mental manifestation can be an act of turning away from difficult situations, with the attitude that "I cannot do anything about it anyway, so why keep on paying any attention to it?" The not-so-functional manifestation is when one befuddles oneself. This may be a tendency for a person to befuddle themself as a means not to engage in something—maybe looking away from the signs of a spouse's infidelity by saying to themself that the spouse's work often takes them away on long business trips. Even if the topic comes up in some oblique form, the response is some version of "I cannot do anything about it anyway," like our collective sloth and torpor about climate change.

In the more problematic state, sloth and torpor may lead the person to shrink away from an abhorrent situation. For example, a person may run away from the site of a dead body found in the woods, and then not tell anyone about finding the dead body because they do not wish to deal with death or with the hassle of talking to the police. This type of denial is not the same as that where the person denies the existence of the difficulty. This is more an active withdrawal of one's energy from engaging. This mental state manifests in daily life as a preference for turning away from engaging and disengaging by tolerating a situation.

In psychotherapy, the client in the mental state of sloth and torpor does not usually present with complaints of laziness or a lack of energy in their daily life. Sometimes a client may complain of procrastination or a sense of being mentally and emotionally tired. The primary presenting affect might be of befuddlement and confusion or of not understanding a situation. The client may give the general impression of naivete. Usually, the person does not want to engage with an obvious and very difficult situation. There is a subtle distinction between denial and sloth and torpor. In the defense mechanism of denial, the client actively asserts that something is false: For example, a person diagnosed with cancer says that there is no cancer and the medical system is out to defraud them of their hard-earned money; thus, this person refuses to engage in cancer treatment. In sloth and torpor, the person does not deny the existence of the cancer. Rather, they may refuse to change any of their daily routine because they assert that the next treatment will work or that their body knows how to heal itself; thus, this person does not have to change anything in their life because of the cancer. Torpor is also like a friend shrinking away from the presence of the person with cancer. They internally shrink away from contacting their friend undergoing cancer treatment, reasoning that they can do nothing to help the friend anyway. Often, clients will talk about difficult situations, such as a chaotic family environment; they reference these difficult situations and environments with a strong conviction that they do not want to be involved with their crazy family, but they instead want to work on finding their own life. Or clients may present with a situation and wonder why or how they ever got into such a conundrum.

Desire That Underlies Sloth and Torpor

Here, the psychotherapist is listening for what the client finds to be both abhorrent and intractable, thus using tactics of aversion. During our deep listening, our task as psychotherapists is to hear the unpleasant situation with which the client is befuddling themself so as to avoid having to grapple with a difficult situation and the wish for it to simply disappear from their environment.

A personal situation may shed light on the pattern in sloth and torpor. As you may guess from my name, I (Tien), am a person with Asian ancestry. All my life, I had expressed a sense of not belonging. I excused my tendency to withdraw from social situations by saying that I am an introvert, just so that I do not have to experience the feeling of not belonging. It was not until the Trump presidency and the COVID-19 pandemic when I was forced to not befuddle myself from a painful social reality that the reason I do not feel like I belonged in this country is because I was treated as the unwanted other, regardless of whether the behavior was benign benevolent racism or hostile racism. I actively struggled not to see the racism directed toward me or the racism evident all around me. For the psychotherapist who would have had me as a client, their task during deep listening would be to hear the wounds of racism and have me turn toward and engage with the racism that I faced every day. Turning away from the reality of racism was what was taking away all my energy from engaging with people. For me, the mind state of sloth and torpor was an act of not wanting to engage with racism, searching for a way to pull back from racism by saying that something was not right with me. Some members of U.S. society at times collectively collude in the tactic of turning away from racism by attributing the problem to what they perceive as an offense (e.g., stigma around receiving social safety net benefits, perpetration of gang violence) by another group.

Intervention for Sloth and Torpor: In-Session Dialogue
Buddhism gives extensive advice on how to handle sloth and torpor, or dullness and drowsiness. Although some of the instructions are for meditation, many strategies are for handling dullness in daily life, which translate easily into topics for in-session dialogue. In the Bojjhaṅgasaṃyutta Sutta, the Buddha suggested the following with regard to the sluggish mind:

> When the mind is sluggish, it is the proper time for cultivating the following factors of enlightenment: investigation of reality, energy and rapture, because a sluggish mind can easily be aroused by them. (SN, 2000, 46.53.3ii: Connected Discourses on the Factors of Enlightenment, Fire)

Alternatively, the same sentence is translated as follows:

> When the mind becomes sluggish, it is timely to develop the enlightenment factor of discrimination of states, the enlightenment factor of energy, and the enlightenment factor of rapture. (SN, 2000, 46.53)

For the purpose of psychotherapy, both phrases "investigation of reality" and "discrimination of states" mean to engage with the client to determine what is their current situation, what is distasteful about their situation, their wish for the difficult situation to simply not be, and what it means to not engage with their unpleasant abhorrent situation.

Consider the following clinical example of a client in his early 20s who still lived at home. He reported witnessing, when he was a child, extensive drug use by both his mother and father; he also witnessed his father and his uncle physically beating each other repeatedly, and then his uncle shooting his father. There continues to be extensive drug use, as well as occasional physical altercations, in the client's living environment. The client presented with complaints of fatigue and the wish to learn meditation to find internal calm. The fatigue is a manifestation of the mind state of sloth and torpor. His wish to learn meditation to achieve an internal state of calm is the voice of torpor, a wish simply to not engage with the ugliness that pervades his living environment. The in-session dialogue is an opportunity for the psychotherapist and the client to discuss the nature of the sloth and torpor mind state, then to invite this client to engage in an investigation of reality in regard to his living situation with his family of origin. It is virtually impossible for this client to manage his life situation without acknowledging the dysfunction of his family of origin and the inevitable chaos associated with drug abuse. The Buddha tells us that to counter the mind state of sloth and torpor, it is appropriate to engage in an investigation of reality (SN, 2000, 46.53.3ii).

The Fourth Hindrance: Restlessness and Remorse (*Uddhacca-Kukkucca*)

Buddhaghosa (1956/2010) described worry as follows:

> The state of that [restlessness and remorse] is worry (kukkucca). It has subsequent regret as its characteristic. Its function is to sorrow about what has and what has not been done. It is manifested as remorse. Its proximate cause is what has and what has not been done. It should be regarded as slavery. (p. 478)

The Commentaries (Thera Nyanaponika, 2013) referred to the mind state of restlessness and remorse (*uddhacca-kukkucca*) as follows:

> Hereby the Blessed One shows the unabandoned hindrance of [restless and remorse] . . . should be understood as follows: A slave who wants to enjoy himself at a festival is told by his master: "Go quickly to such and such a place! There is urgent work to do. If you don't go, I shall have your hands and feet cut off, or your ears and nose!" Hearing that, the slave will quickly go as ordered, and will not be able to enjoy any part of the festival. This is because of his dependence on others.

The *Pali Text Society's Pali–English Dictionary* defines *uddhacca* as "overbalancing, agitation, excitement, distraction, flurry" and *kukkucca* as "bad doing, misconduct, bad character, in its literal sense it is bad behavior with hands and feet"; it states that "together with kukkucca 'flurry or worry' is the 4th of the 5th nīvaraṇāni" (Pali Text Society, n.d.). The combined term, uddhacca-kukkucca, has been alternatively translated as "restlessness and remorse," "worry and flurry," or "restlessness and anxiety." In the Saṅgārava

Sutta, the Buddha likened the hindrance of the mind state of restlessness and remorse as follows:

> Suppose, brahmin, there is a bowl of water stirred by the wind, rippling, swirling, churned into wavelets. If a man with good sight were to examine his own facial reflection in it, he would neither know nor see it as it really is. So too, brahmin, when one dwells with a mind obsessed by restlessness and remorse. (SN, 2000, 46.55)

Characteristics of Restlessness and Remorse

The mind state of uddhacca-kukkucca (restlessness and remorse) is where the mind cannot settle down; the mind is constantly traveling away from the body. This mind state does not live in the present. Restlessness is a mind that travels to the future; remorse travels to the past. This constant movement in the mind of restlessness and remorse is different from the biologically based attention-deficit/hyperactivity disorder (ADHD), which often manifests as inattention and constant movement and looks like restlessness. In ADHD, the mind's movement is usually jumping from one thing to another in the present time. To the outside observer, it may appear as loose associations. However, unlike loose associations, the ADHD mind is usually jumping from one stimulus to another stimulus present in the environment at the time. The mind of restlessness and remorse is in constant motion, traveling back and forth in time. On the meditation cushion, restlessness is like the urge to get off the meditation cushion to get on with more important things beside sitting and doing nothing. In daily activities, restlessness manifests as feeling an urgent need to be arranging things so that the future unpleasant eventualities do not manifest.

Remorse is the mind's travels to the past. The mind ruminates on past events where one did something that one did not approve of, wishing one could go back and redo that thing. The mind obsessively thinks about past occurrences and worries about their effects on the person's future.

A mind beset by restlessness and remorse traverses fluidly from past to future without ever stopping in the present. When time traveling to the past, the mind scans past deeds for faults, generating remorse for paths taken and wishes for paths not taken. When time traveling to the future, the mind is moving to future possibilities with worrying and a constant flurry of thoughts planning for all what-ifs that could come to pass. The anxiety is usually of a feared future that one imagines is undesirable but inevitable. It may express itself in thoughts like these:

> I should be better at self-care, but I don't have time for that right now. I should have started the term project earlier so that I would not be so pressed for time and end up handing in a bad project. If I take time for self-care now, I will for

sure get a bad mark on my term project and not get a good grade in the class. I cannot afford to get a bad grade. If I get a bad grade, then my future will be ruined; I will not be able to graduate, then what would become of my life?!

The Commentaries (Thera Nyanaponika, 2013) refer to this mind state as that of slavery. The assumption is that a slave does not command their own agenda, their own time, or their own activity. A slave is constantly looking to their master for what will please the master, so as to not encounter the master's displeasure and be punished. The slave constantly worries about what they should do now, to anticipate the master's needs and have them fulfilled before the master can experience any discomfort; or the slave worries about the possibility that they had not done something they should have or they did something they should not have that, when noticed by the master, will generate punishment. In this state, the mind is jumpy and unable to settle down and the body is tense, anticipating the need to be doing some bidding at a moment's notice.

Desire That Underlies Restlessness and Remorse

Clients in the mind state of restlessness and remorse will often engage in ruminations of the many what-ifs, traversing easily from the past to the future. Behind those ruminations is a fear that some future danger will manifest. The assumption is that the danger is not real; it is an unreasonable worry. In all likelihood, the danger is real. For example, a graduate student experiences anxiety when ruminating about having submitted an ill-prepared assignment. For the student, there is the real possibility of receiving a poor mark from the instructor, which will result in a failed course; as a result, the many troubles generated from a course failure could lead to the student's dismissal from their degree program. The analogy to slavery from the Saṅgārava Sutta (SN, 2000, 46.55) refers to the student putting their fate in the hands of another; here, the student's fate is in the hands of the professor who will evaluate the submitted assignment and will either fail or pass the student.

Although it is probable that there may have been a real danger in the past, as in severe punishment for some slight disobedience or imperfection from a demanding or abusive person, the task during psychotherapy is to navigate the present situation. During the psychotherapist's deep listening, their task is to hear the real danger behind the ruminations and to differentiate the real danger from the experienced past danger. The intervention can then address ways to manage the current situation to prevent foreseeable unpleasant consequences and let go of imagined unforeseeable consequences. Additionally, for clients who have experienced past trauma, the psychotherapist deeply listens to hear their generalized fear and costrategizes actions in the present that will increase the likelihood of a desirable outcome when the past danger materializes again. This is like learning defensive martial arts so one knows what to do if they are physically threatened, thus having some hope of preventing the harm from materializing to reality.

As in all hindrance mind states, with uddhacca-kukkucca (restlessness and remorse) that is not a consequence of biological nervous system dysfunction, the psychotherapist is listening for the underlying taṇhā (craving) and the motivating desire. Here, the psychotherapist is faced with a habitual pattern of uddhacca-kukkucca and is listening for the underlying fear of disapproval with the accompanying desire for approval.

Intervention for Restlessness and Remorse
Consider the following case example. A client who was constantly beset by the mind state of restlessness came into a treatment session with this opening remark: "I have been procrastinating again. I know I am a procrastinator, and it's because I am a lazy person." Upon the psychotherapist's inquiry into what evidence the client had that supported her conclusion that she is lazy, this client essentially said,

> I have a big work assignment that I have not been doing. When I get a big assignment, I procrastinate until it's too late, then I will stay up all night and work all weekend to get it done. I have horrible work/life balance all because I am lazy and don't get around to the assignment until I cannot put it off any longer; though I know I should not pull all-nighters, I also know that I will have to in order to get the project done. I know I should start the project as soon as I was assigned it a few weeks ago, but I was too lazy to get started on it. I know I am a lazy person.

This client is usually physically restless, tapping her feet, shaking her leg, twitching her fingers, and so on. In this session, she reported feeling like she could not sit still during her many hours of work meetings, because she was thinking about the need to get started on her large assigned project. Her mind resides in a future date, the date when the project comes due, while fluidly traveling back to a past event, the time when she was handed the assignment and the days that passed when she did not work on the project. Having imagined that she handed in a sloppy product, she then constructed a notion of a self that is lazy to explain the less than satisfactory product while simultaneously constructing a reality where she could control her time, as if she were not lazy and she would have had sufficient time to work on her project.

In the in-session dialogue, it may be tempting to collude with the client in focusing on a self (in this case, a self that procrastinates and is lazy). This would involve the psychotherapist turning the dialogue toward examining how the client might feel about being lazy and what prevents the client from not being lazy, the cost and benefits of laziness, and possibly how the client is enacting her mother's image of her as being lazy from when she was a little girl who was severely and constantly berated for not immediately doing as she was told. In chasing after her laziness, the conditions and realities of the present situation are lost.

The Theravāda Abhidhamma principle of *paṭṭhānanaya* (conditional relations or causal relationships) tells us that:

> Nothing arises without the conditions necessary for its arising.
> Nothing arises from a single cause.
> Nothing arises as a single effect, as a solitary phenomenon.
> From a plurality of conditions arises a plurality of effects. (Karunadasa, 2015b, p. 276)

If the psychotherapist colludes with this client to discuss her laziness, then they would be ignoring the idea that "nothing arises from a single cause." Furthermore, a formulation that the client's laziness caused this procrastination would essentially claim that a single cause (the laziness) had a single effect (procrastination). Contrary to this client's proposition, the dependent arising formulation would have the psychotherapist exploring the multiple factors in the present conditions that gave rise to the client's procrastination; then the psychotherapist would explore the various effects of the client's procrastination. To follow the dictates of the formulation that "nothing arises without the conditions necessary for its arising," the in-session dialogue focused on the nature of the client's project (which was to develop a fix for a software glitch), the conditions required for addressing the project (which was to have large blocks of uninterrupted time to delve into a very complex software package), and the conditions of her daily work (which is filled with meetings, so there are, at most, only 1-hour allotments of nonmeeting times at various points in her workday). All of these factors required the client to stay late, work on weekends, or both when she had blocks of uninterrupted time to delve into this complex project. Because the client loathes giving up her weekends and her evening activities, she is left with not starting the project until such time when she feels enough pressure, manifesting in the mind state of restlessness, to work all night and throughout a weekend to complete the project. As the in-session conversation progressed and the client and the psychotherapist delved into the conditions at work, the client visibly became less agitated, and her fidgeting stilled as she engaged in the task of problem-solving to gain large blocks of time at work necessary to delve into her complex assignments. This line of inquiry is the enactment of the first mark of existence that "all conditioned things are impermanent"

(Dhp, 1996, 277–279). The psychotherapist is acting as mindfulness attending to conditions.

It is much more productive and much easier to address the client's need for large blocks of time at work for big complex projects, instead of focusing on her notion of a lazy self. For the psychotherapist, the in-session task is to not collude with the client in hunting for origins (traveling to the past) to explain the present self ("I am lazy") that will cause future catastrophes (not finishing projects on time or producing a quality product). The in-session dialogue, in a variety of approaches, helps to develop that quietude of mind for problem-solving, as indicated in the Āhāra Sutta for the denourishment of restlessness and remorse, where the Buddha said,

> There is quietude of mind; frequently giving wise attention to it—that is the denourishing of the arising of restlessness and remorse that have not yet arisen, and of the increase and strengthening of restlessness and remorse that have already arisen. (SN, 2000, 46.51)

By repeatedly directing the in-session dialogue back to the current situation of needing to work on her assignment, the client is forced to examine the present conditions. The psychotherapist is not colluding with the client by traveling to the past and speculating on the origin of the client's procrastination and laziness, or to traveling to the future and acknowledging the client's worry about receiving an unsatisfactory evaluation that possibly leads to her being laid off the next time there is a reduction in the labor force.

The Fifth Hindrance: Doubt (*Vicikicchā*)

Recall that in Chapter 1 (this volume), we described the Kālāmas, who had been exposed to the beliefs and teachings of many different wandering ascetics and were experiencing doubt. The Buddha said to the Kālāmas (Kesamutti Sutta; AN, 2012, 3.65), "It is fitting for you to be in doubt. Doubt has arisen in you about a perplexing matter." In the Kesamutti Sutta, the Buddha told the Kālāmas, and by extension all of us, how to settle arisen doubt. It is reasonable to look for information to resolve doubt. However, the Buddha said the following with regard to when one does not act to resolve the doubt:

> There are things causing doubt; frequently giving unwise attention to them—that is the nourishment for the arising of doubt that has not yet arisen, and for the increase and strengthening of doubt that has already arisen. (SN, 2000, 46.51)

> A man traveling through a desert, aware that travelers may be plundered or killed by robbers, will, at the mere sound of a twig or a bird, become anxious and fearful, thinking: "The robbers have come!" He will go a few steps, and then out of fear, he will stop, and continue in such a manner all the way; or he

may even turn back. Stopping more frequently than walking, only with toil and difficulty will he reach a place of safety, or he may not even reach it. . . . Thus, as the traveler in the desert is uncertain whether robbers are there or not, he produces in his mind, again and again, a state of wavering and vacillation, a lack of decision, a state of anxiety; and thus, he creates in himself an obstacle for reaching the safe ground of sanctity (ariya-bhumi). In that way, skeptical doubt is like traveling in a desert. (Commentaries; Thera Nyanaponika, 2013)

The *Pali Text Society's Pali–English Dictionary* defines *vicikicchā*, one of the hindrances (*nīvaraṇas*), as "doubt, perplexity, uncertainty" (Pali Text Society, n.d.). With doubt, there is uncertainty. The mind state of doubt is apprehension regarding the precariousness of one's abilities, the assessment of a situation, and the correctness of taking action. The classic Buddhist rendition on the mind state of doubt is questioning the efficacy of the Buddha's teachings, the knowledge base of their dhamma teacher's instructions, and their own ability in engaging in correct meditative practice. In the Saṅgārava Sutta, the Buddha likened the hindrance of the mind state of doubt thus:

If there is a pot of water which is turbid, stirred up and muddy, and this pot is put into a dark place, then a man with a normal faculty of sight could not properly recognize and see the image of his own face. In the same way, when one's mind is possessed by doubt, overpowered by doubt, then one cannot properly see the escape from doubt which has arisen; then one does not properly understand one's own welfare, nor that of another, nor that of both. (SN, 2000, 46.55)

Characteristics of Doubt

In the mind state of doubt, the mind is tying itself in knots waiting for the next disaster, knowing with certainty that disaster will come if the wrong action is taken. This doubt is different from the uncertainty that comes from engaging in a new venture where it is appropriate for the beginner to doubt themselves. The doubt in starting a new venture motivates the person to seek guidance, to learn, and to become competent. This is a state I (Tien) often experience when engaged with my leisure pastime of do-it-yourself home fixer projects. My current undertaking is the building of my first built-in bookcase. A space in the house needs a bookshelf, so I have decided to undertake the adventure of building my first bookcase. As with any new endeavor, I constantly doubt my skills to build this bookcase. This doubt motivates me to attend workshops, to research online, to watch do-it-yourself videos, to talk to carpenters—all of which I have done in preparation for building this bookshelf. It is also normal for this type of doubt to stop at some point and transition to decision for a course of action, like purchasing the wood to start building the bookshelf. It may also be appropriate for whole groups of people to be in doubt. Graduate students in mental health training programs live with the mind state of doubt—wondering if they are able to give aid and comfort to their future clients. The many markers in a training program are designed to signal mastery over certain skills, such as passing the comprehensive examination or practicum placements. This kind of doubt would naturally end at some point, and the graduate student would warm to the idea that they might actually be of assistance to their clients.

As doubt is applied to a mind state off the meditation cushion, it is a mind that has the habit of uncertainty, of doubting the success of doing (anything). The habit of doubting one's ability might sound the same in meditation as in daily life activities. A Western take on this mind state of doubt might be to label such a person as having low self-esteem. They question their own evaluation of a situation (including what they want) and, therefore, are never solidly committed to their own opinion or a course of action.

This mind state of doubt serves to inhibit the person from taking action. The internal dialogue might sound something like this: "I don't know what I am doing. I am inadequate." That person would be constantly second-guessing themselves, thinking "on the other hand," and thus might never actually commit themselves to a course of action.

Desire That Underlies Doubt

Our task as psychotherapists during deep listening is to hear the fear—the fear of committing to a course of action that would turn out to have some negative consequences. It is as if the person needs a guarantee that things will be okay and that things will turn out in the desired way before they commit to any course of action. This is craving for blamelessness. Behind that craving for blamelessness is fear of being blamed for some future disaster. There is usually some history of severe punishment or abuse; thus, the person is reluctant to act, so as to escape the possibility of future blame and abuse. The underlying affect is one of fear. There is a constant need and an abiding desire for external validation as a means to allay that fear.

Intervention for Doubt: In-Session Dialogue

The sentence stem for the in-session dialogue would be something like this: "If I . . ., then . . . but then . . . well . . . maybe." During deep listening, the psychotherapist is listening for the real danger and the desire for validation. The therapeutic relationship may be used as the source of external validation: first confirming the client's direct experience, and then validating the client's perceptions and decisions.

This in-session dialogue might take its direction from what the Buddha said when the Kālāmas approached him with their minds full of doubt, as discussed in Chapter 1 (this volume). The Kesaputtiya Sutta is the recounting of the dialogue between the Buddha and the residents of Kesaputta, a town in Kālāma. The Kālāmas said to the Buddha:

> there are some ascetics . . . who come to Kesaputta. They explain and eluci-
> date their own doctrines, but disparage, denigrate, deride, and denounce the
> doctrines of others. But then some other ascetics . . . come to Kesaputta, and
> they too explain and elucidate their own doctrines, but disparage, denigrate,
> deride, and denounce the doctrines of others. We are perplexed and in doubt,
> Bhante, as to which of the good ascetics speak truth and which speak false-
> hood. (AN, 2012, 3.65)

The Kālāmas were basically asking the Buddha what to do when one is perplexed and in doubt. What the Buddha said to the Kālāmas, as discussed next, can serve as a directory of topics for the in-session dialogue between a psychotherapist and a client whose mind is habitually beset with doubt.

The first phrase from the Āhāra Sutta (SN, 2000, 46.51) that was quoted at the beginning of this section says, "There are things causing doubt." This refers to the same situation in the first phrase of the Buddha's response to the Kālāmas in the Kesaputtiya Sutta (AN, 2012, 3.65), where the Buddha said, "Doubt has arisen in you about a perplexing matter." Both of these lines call our attention to the fact that the Buddha is making a distinction between things that appropriately cause doubt versus the hindrance of doubt. For those situations where doubt is appropriate, the Buddha is saying, "There are things causing doubt" (SN, 2000, 46.51), and "It is fitting for you to be perplexed, Kālāmas, fitting for you to be in doubt" (AN, 2012, 3.65). In its application to psychotherapy, the psychotherapist and the client, in dialogue, need to make a determination as to whether the situation calls for doubt. One way to make this determination is to ascertain whether the client has the necessary information to decide on a course of action or whether there needs to be a period of investigation to acquire the necessary informa-tion before any decisive action can or should be taken. For individuals who are habitually hindered by doubt, it is too easy to dismiss the possibility that their doubt is appropriate.

The psychotherapist may be instrumental in making the delineation between experiencing doubt due to insufficient information versus dealing with the hindrance of doubt. Further, the psychotherapist can help the client to ascertain when sufficient information has been gathered and the time for deciding on a course of action has come. If, at this point, the client continues to be indecisive and to have doubt, then the person is most likely experiencing the hindrance of doubt.

To address the hindrance of doubt, the in-session dialogue may venture into examination of how to establish a course of action. In this regard, the Buddha advised the Kālāmas as follows:

> do not go by oral tradition, by lineage of teaching, by hearsay, by a collection of texts, by logic, by inferential reasoning, by reasoned cogitation, by the acceptance of a view after pondering it, by the seeming competence of a speaker, or because you think, the ascetic is our teacher. (AN, 2012, 3.65)

In the aforementioned sutta, the Buddha covered a lot of ground in what not to do. The psychotherapist can decipher whether the client is using any of the 10 insufficient methods described in the sutta. Probabilities are high that the client would be engaging is using more than one or two of these unsuitable methods. Most items on the list of 10 unsuitable methods are self-explanatory. For review, refer to Chapter 1 (this volume).

For getting beyond habitual doubt, the last item ("because you think, the ascetic is our teacher" [AN, 2012, 3.65]) is significant. In its application to psychotherapy, it is important that the therapeutic relationship be firmly established and that the client has sufficient trust in the psychotherapist before both try new approaches to address the client's difficulties.

In the in-session dialogue that explores different options the client might consider, the psychotherapist would follow the guidance that the Buddha gave to the Kālāmas: to look past the surface appearance of things and examine the motivations at play in any given situation. While the sutta refers to examining the motives of those who urge a course of action, in psychotherapy, the exploration might be to examine the client's motivation behind the various options under discussion. Those options that are motivated by "greed, hatred, or delusion" (AN, 2012, 3.65) are best avoided. Those changes required for the adoption of options that are kusalā (skillful, wholesome, which has a higher probability of pleasant future fruition, can be further explored between the psychotherapist and the client.

CONCLUSION

How humans experience existence is through the five aggregates subject to clinging. That is, we encounter the universe through a world constructed from within the notion of a self. What that notion of the self experiences has the characteristics of dukkha. The description of the three types of dukkha (suffering, unsatisfactoriness) is listed in the First Noble Truth; for the purpose of psychotherapy, the summation in the last phrase of the First Noble Truth (i.e., "the five aggregates subject to clinging are suffering") is the fourth type of dukkha.

The last phrase of the First Noble Truth, "in brief, the five aggregates subject to clinging are suffering" (SN, 2000, 56.11), is an overarching summation in reference to the human experience of an embodied existence. The pañcupādānakkhandhā (five aggregates subject to clinging) in the Buddhist lexicon is the constructed notion of a self. The construction of the notion of a self/attā is adding taṇhā (craving) and upādāna (clinging, grasping) to the functioning of the pañcakkhandhā (five aggregates) for pañcupādānakkhandhā (five aggregates subject to clinging) that conditions the development of "this is mine, this I am, this is my self" (MN, 1995, 22). It is that constructed notion of a self that experiences the dukkha (suffering, unsatisfactoriness) of existence.

The mind is where we encounter the constructed notion of a self. The mind/citta raises obstructions that function as hindrances in blocking the person's ability to detect their constructing their notion of a self/attā. The Buddha likens the obstructions to that of a magic show, creating the mind culture of the hindrances. Seeing the mechanisms in the construction of the notion of the self/attā is often blocked by the magic show of the mind/citta. The magic show concocts the mind culture of the hindrances. The hindrances have the function of obstructing the person from seeing through the pañcupādānakkhandhā (five aggregates subject to clinging) of "this is mine, this I am, this is my self" (MN, 1995, 22) to the functioning of the five aggregates (pañcakkhandhā) and the actuality of experienced existence. In principle, there may be any number of mind cultures that hinder the person's ability to clearly, knowingly, and directly experience the functioning of the aggregates. The Buddha names the five most common mind cultures of hindrances as follows: (a) sensual desire (kāmacchanda), (b) ill will (vyāpāda), (c) sloth and torpor (thīna-middha), (d) restlessness and remorse (uddhacca-kukkucca), and (e) doubt (vicikicchā).

This chapter discussed the five mind cultures of hindrances as if they are static; this static approach was used only for the purpose of explication. In the functioning of the five aggregates, all mind states can and do manifest at various times, on or off the meditation cushion, in daily life, and in psychotherapy sessions. Use the static description as a point of reference and be prepared for manifestations of any of the hindrances in the actual in-session dialogue, although a certain type of hindrance usually predominates for a person. Although these mind states that hinder piercing through the illusion of the magic show are most obvious when one turns inward in meditation, these hindered mind cultures are present in everyday activities and thus can be evident at any time, including during psychotherapy in-session dialogue.

One of the purposes of psychotherapy is to illuminate the hindrances obstructing the detection of the constructed notion of the self/attā so the person can more clearly see the process that is occurring. While the hindrances are more fluid, the notion of the self tends to be more stable over time, and people may hold multiple descriptions of themselves. Because it is the notion of the self/attā that manifests human suffering and shows up for psychotherapy in the form of the hindrances, the in-session dialogue can be directed to identifying the hindrances, then analyzing them, and thus deconstructing the five aggregates subject to clinging. This process will include articulating for the client the type of hindrance and labeling the client's notion of the self. Once named, it becomes easier to analyze, instead of sinking into, the disturbances of the hindrance and the iterations of the notion of self. The in-session dialogue needs to take the necessary time to engage in the exploration of the topology of the hindrances, as well as their content, to get to the root craving behind the hindrances.

This notion of the self can be determined by the psychotherapist asking the client for confirmation of something the client has said about themselves. For example, the psychotherapist could ask, "So, you think you are [characteristic]?" The psychotherapist would use one word to summarize a characterization of the client within the context of what the client has been talking about (e.g., "So, you think you have a temper?" "So, you think you are deficient?" or "So, you think you are lazy?"). The clarification and articulation of this notion of the self can provide the client some structure to bind the client's suffering and then to start analyzing the situation instead of being emersed in the suffering.

This chapter discussed the characteristics of each of the five types of mind culture of the hindrances, the types of desire underlying those different hindrances, and the manifestation of them or how they might show up in dialogue with the psychotherapist. Although the Buddha gave extensive instructions on how to handle the hindrances, those were not addressed in this chapter. The method to counter the hindrances will be collectively discussed in the subsequent chapters in Part V (this volume) on concentration, meditation, and mindfulness.

12

THE CAUSE AND REMEDY OF DUKKHA

The Second and Third Noble Truths

Recall from Chapter 2 (this volume) our discussion of the Buddha Gotama's research question: "What is the human experience of existence?" The Buddha found that humans suffer due to not acknowledging the three marks of existence:

- All conditioned things are impermanent (*aniccā*).
- All things are not-self (*anattā*).
- All conditioned things are unsatisfactory (*dukkha*). (*Dhammapada* [Dhp], 1996, 277–279: The Path)

As discussed previously, impermanence (aniccā) is that our experience of any given situation depends on multiple conditions coexisting in a particular configuration; when the elements in the configuration change, which they are bound to do, then we humans experience impermanence (aniccā). Not-self (anattā) explicates how we experience existence, which is through the five aggregates subject to clinging. The five aggregates function as an interrelated system driven by contingencies. However, constructing a notion of a self by clinging to the five aggregates manufactures a seemingly solid entity of

https://doi.org/10.1037/0000453-013
Buddhist Psychotherapy: Connecting Early Buddhism to Mindfulness and Western Psychotherapy, by L. Tien, D. M. Kawahara, and V. Dhammadinna

"this is mine, this I am, this is my self" (Alagaddūpama Sutta; *Majjhima Nikāya* [MN], 1995, 22: Simile of the Snake). It is through this notion of a self that we experience existence. What humans experience of existence through that notion of a self has the characteristics of dukkha (suffering, unsatisfactoriness).

Having presented the oppressiveness of the human embodied existence with a detailed examination of dukkha, Buddha Gotama goes on to posit that the cause of dukkha is craving (*taṇhā*) in the form of the Second Noble Truth. The Buddha does not leave us with the bleak assessment of human existence described in the First and Second Noble Truths. He tells us that there are ways to ameliorate the experience of dukkha (suffering, unsatisfactoriness) in the form of the Third Noble Truth. This chapter discusses the Second and Third Noble Truths as they relate to a theory for psychotherapy.

THE SECOND NOBLE TRUTH: CRAVING IS THE CAUSE OF SUFFERING

Consider the following excerpts from the Dhammacakkapavattana Sutta:

> Now this is the truth of the origins of suffering. It's the craving [taṇhā] that leads to future lives, mixed up with relishing and greed, taking pleasure wherever it lands. That craving for sensual pleasures (kāmataṇhā), craving to continue existence (bhavataṇhā), and craving to end existence (vibhavataṇhā). (*Dhammacakkapavattana Sutta*, 2018, para. 5)

> Now this, bhikkhus, is the noble truth of the origin of suffering: it is this craving [taṇhā] which leads to renewed existence, accompanied by delight and lust, seeking delight here and there; that is, craving for sensual pleasures, craving for existence, craving for extermination. (*Saṃyutta Nikāya* [SN], 2000, 56.11: Setting in Motion the Wheel of the Dhamma)

The addition of craving (*taṇhā*) transforms an impersonal functioning of the five aggregates (*pañcakkhandhā*) into the notion of a self (*attā*). Notice that the Second Noble Truth says it is taṇhā (craving) that originates suffering: "craving for sensual pleasures . . . craving to continue existence . . . craving to end existence" (SN, 2000, 56.11). Craving has desire behind it, but it is not the same as desire. Desires are not all unwholesome. Recall that in the discussion of the five aggregates plus craving (taṇhā) in Chapter 6, we made the linguistic distinction between the Pali words *taṇhā*, *chanda*, and *lobha*, all of which have been translated in English as "desire" and "craving." Chanda can indicate an element of virtue, as in "striving after righteousness, ardent desire, zeal. Often combined with other good qualities," as well as the element of iniquity, as in "desire for, wish for, delight in" (Pali Text Society, n.d.).

Chanda is value neutral and this is differentiated from desire used in the Second Noble Truth, taṇhā, which is not value neutral. For the purpose of psychotherapy, a significant difference between chanda (desire) and taṇhā (craving) is that chanda can be satisfied, whereas taṇhā has the characteristic of not being able to be resolved. A very simple example is the desire for food. Without the desire (chanda) for food, a person might not eat, which would have dire consequences for their health. This desire (chanda) for food can be satisfied with any type of food that can satiate hunger. However, if a person wakes up wanting their usual breakfast of an omelet but is on a backpacking trip and did not pack the ingredients for an omelet, then making an omelet is not possible at that time. The person thinks about this imaginary omelet. This wanting/craving (taṇhā) for the omelet may last the whole day, perhaps resulting in the formulation, "I am not a deep-woods backpacker." This wanting an omelet and the enduring experience of deprivation would make for a rather unpleasant day. In this example, it is the narrowing down of the desire (chanda) for food to craving (taṇhā) for an omelet—then to clinging (*upādāna*) to the idea of the omelet by thinking about that imaginary omelet all day—that sets up the condition for and the experience of dukkha (suffering, unsatisfactoriness), like the day-long misery of being deprived of that omelet.

The Second Noble Truth links the origin of suffering to craving (taṇhā), which are manifestations of the three unwholesome roots (*akusalā-mūlaṁ*): greed (*lobha*), hatred (*dosa*), and delusion (*moha*; Sangiti Sutta; *Dīgha Nikāya* [DN], 1987/1995, 33.1.10: The Chanting Together; Akusalamūla Sutta; *Aṅguttara Nikāya* [AN], 2012, 3.69: Roots). Each of the unwholesome roots is discussed next.

THE THREE UNWHOLESOME ROOTS OF CRAVING (*AKUSALA-MŪLAṀ*)

The forces, or the roots, behind the craving and clinging aspects of the five aggregates subject to clinging are the three unwholesome roots (akusala-mūlaṁ) of greed/lobha, hatred/dosa, and delusion/moha (DN, 1987/1995, 33.1.10; AN, 2012, 3.69). These unwholesome roots can be tied back to the aggregate of the hedonic feeling tone (*vedanā*) by which a person knows and experiences a stimulus. Pleasant hedonic feeling tone underlies and conditions the unwholesome root of greed/lobha. Unpleasant hedonic feeling tone is the unwholesome root of hatred/dosa. Neither pleasant nor unpleasant hedonic feeling tone gives rise to the action of ignoring, as in ignoring the reality of the three marks of existence. The disregard of the three marks of existence is the milieu of the unwholesome root of delusion/moha. These three unwholesome roots of clinging (upādāna) function as instigators for the actions of body, speech, and mind. Because a hedonic feeling tone (vedanā) accompanies a sense contact, the Buddha lists the sense contact through the *āyatana* (the six internal sense bases and the six external sense objects) as the stimulus that initiates and fuels the craving by way of the three unwholesome roots (akusala-mūlaṁ) of greed/lobha, hatred/dosa, and delusion/moha.

> Bhikkhus, all is burning. And what is the all that is burning? The eye is burning, forms are burning, eye-consciousness is burning, eye-contact is burning, also whatever is felt as pleasant or painful or neither-painful-nor-pleasant that arises with eye-contact for its indispensable condition, that too is burning. Burning with what? Burning with the fire of lust, with the fire of hate, with the fire of delusion. I say it is burning with birth, aging and death, with sorrows, with lamentations, with pains, with griefs, with despairs.
>
> > The ear is burning, sounds are burning . . .
> > The nose is burning, odors are burning . . .
> > The tongue is burning, flavors are burning . . .
> > The body is burning, tangibles are burning . . .
>
> The mind is burning, ideas are burning, mind-consciousness is burning, mind-contact is burning, also whatever is felt as pleasant or painful or neither-painful-nor-pleasant that arises with mind-contact for its indispensable condition, that too is burning. Burning with what? Burning with the fire of lust, with the fire of hate, with the fire of delusion. I say it is burning with birth, aging and death, with sorrows, with lamentations, with pains, with griefs, with despairs. (*Adittapariyaya Sutta*, 1981/2010, para. 2–8)

In the Adittapariyaya Sutta (1981/2010), the Buddha pointed to contact with a sense stimulus that initiates a person's interactions with the universe. Thus, this contact would be the starting point for the experience of existence. Additionally, all stimuli have an associated vedanā (hedonic feeling tone). It is the presence of the vedanā that generates the taṇhā (craving) and upādāna (clinging). The three types of vedanā are the bases for the three unwholesome roots, which are the fire of lust and greed (lobha), the fire of hate (dosa), and the fire of delusion (moha; SN 35.28). The word moha is often translated as "delusion" or "ignorance." The *Pali Text Society's Pali–English Dictionary* defines moha as "stupidity, dullness of mind & soul, delusion, bewilderment, infatuation" (Pali Text Society, n.d.). Moha can be described as the disregard of the three marks of existence. Moha (delusion) is the mind permeated with the delusion that things and situations are permanent (disregard of anicca, that all conditioned things are impermanent), that we have control (disregard of anattā, all things are not-self), and that these things will give us lasting pleasure (disregard of dukkha, all conditioned things are unsatisfactory).

The word lobha is often translated as "desire" or "greed." The *Pali Text Society's Pali–English Dictionary* defines lobha as "covetousness, greed" (Pali Text Society, n.d.). Lobha can be thought of as wanting for experiences that are linked with any of the five aggregates, like wanting to listen to one's favorite music to have the pleasant experience of sound in the ears. In general, lobha (covetousness, greed) can be wanting material as well as noncorporal objects and experiences. This is based on a vedanā (hedonic feeling tone) that is pleasant.

The word dosa often has been translated as "hatred." The *Pali Text Society's Pali–English Dictionary* defines dosa as "anger, ill-will, evil intention, wickedness, corruption, malice, hatred" (Pali Text Society, n.d.). Dosa can be thought of as the use of aversion, or pushing away, to escape unpleasant mind states and situations. One example is the use of intoxicants to avoid the unpleasant experience of grief or to escape the feeling of jealousy manifesting due to the fear of losing a love object. This is based on a vedanā (hedonic feeling tone) that is unpleasant.

The Second Noble Truth links the origin of suffering as craving (taṇhā) to the three unwholesome roots (akusala-mūlaṁ): greed/lobha, hatred/dosa, and delusion/moha (DN, 1987/1995, 33-1.10; AN, 2012, 3.69). The term akusalā-mūlaṁ is translated here as "unwholesome root." Akusalā and kusalā were discussed previously in the Kesamutti Sutta (AN, 2012, 3.65: With the Kālāmas of Kesamutta) and are ideas that have been used in some of the third-wave therapies. *Kusalā* is the Pali word translated here as "wholesome" and *akusalā* as "unwholesome." For Buddhism, behaviors are not inherently good or bad, virtuous or sinful, or moral or evil; action is either kusalā (skillful, wholesome), meeting the demand of the time and situation that then leads to a foreseeable favorable outcome; or action is akusalā (unskillful, unwholesome) that then leads to a foreseeable unfavorable outcome. It is foolish to expect that we can foresee the future in such a way that we only choose a course of action that leads to a foreseeable favorable outcome. However, there are certain categories that have an extremely high probability of generating unpleasant situations, such as murder, swindling, fraud, and the like, that are antithetical to the smooth running of a functional society. It would be favorable for a psychotherapist's recommendations to clients to, at a minimum, avoid a foreseeable unfavorable outcome.

The idea for referring to lust, greed, hatred, and delusion as mūlaṁ (root) is that when something is rooted, as in the extensive root system for a large tree, then that thing is extremely difficult to uproot and to remove. Thus, dukkha (suffering, unsatisfactoriness) that is rooted in greed, hatred, and delusion is extremely difficult to extricate. All three of the defilements have in common the root of ignorance, meaning the ignorance of how humans construct their world that mediates their experience of existence.

Desire, in and of itself, is not akusalā (unskillful, unwholesome). The vedanā, a person's hedonic response to a stimulus, occurs without too much interference from directed intentions. Everyone has desires in the service of survival. Recall the example from Chapter 11 of a person's reaction to a sense stimulus when their hand touches a hot stove while cooking: The immediate registration of physical pain and withdrawing the hand is based on the desire to safeguard the body to survive unharmed. The withdrawing of one's hand from the hot surface of the stove occurs without much intentional directive. Desires are problematic only when taṇhā (craving) is involved. It is the taṇhā (craving), not necessarily the chanda (desire), that generates the three unwholesome roots. For example, the desire for food in the service of survival can be satisfied with anything that is edible. However, when that desire for food goes beyond mere sustenance, like that picky eater who will only eat a certain food or crave an omelet while backpacking in the deep woods, then life becomes complicated. Consider a personal example from the first author (Tien): I met friends for dinner. The restaurant was pleasant, the conversation was stimulating, and the food was tasty. At the end of the meal, the waitperson asked: "Would you like any dessert?" I wanted carrot cake, my favorite dessert. To all our disappointment, the restaurant did not have carrot cake. The group decided to relocate the gathering to another restaurant that did serve carrot cake. My wish for carrot cake turned into a frustrating 2-hour hunt, going from restaurant to restaurant in search of this seemingly elusive carrot cake. The desire for sustenance where any type of food that is conveniently available narrowed into *upādāna* (clinging to the idea) for carrot cake, which disturbed what would have been an otherwise pleasant evening with friends.

INTERVENTION: THE THIRD NOBLE TRUTH

Having gone to extensive lengths to analyze the nature of dukkha and its cause, the Buddha does not leave us in the unpleasant and oppressive state of our embodied existence. The Buddha recognizes that every single human wishes to escape from all forms of dukkha. Acknowledging our universal wish for the absence of dukkha, he reassures us that escape from dukkha is possible. A way out is the promise of the Third Noble Truth. The Buddha posited in the Third Noble Truth, "Now this is the noble truth of the cessation of suffering: it is the remainderless fading away and cessation of that same craving, the giving up and relinquishing of it, freedom from it, non-reliance on it" (SN, 2000, 56.11).

The Third Noble Truth promises that there is a way out of dukkha. This promise is fulfilled in the Fourth Noble Truth, which says, "Now this, bhikkhus, is the noble truth of the way leading to the cessation of suffering: it is this Noble Eightfold Path; that is, right view . . . right concentration" (SN, 2000, 56.11).

CONCLUSION

This chapter covered the Second and Third Noble Truths. The Second Noble Truth focuses on taṇhā (craving), which is the origin of suffering: "That craving for sensual pleasures (kāmataṇhā), craving to continue existence (bhavataṇhā), and craving to end existence (vibhavataṇhā)" (*Dhammacakkapavattana Sutta*, 2018). The three unwholesome roots (akusala-mūlaṁ) of greed/lobha, hatred/dosa, and delusion/moha (DN, 1987/1995, 33-1.10; AN, 2012, 3.69) are the manifestations of taṇhā (craving). The Third Noble Truth promises a way out of all forms of suffering (dukka), which is provided by the Fourth Noble Truth through the Noble Eightfold Path.

In essence, the Noble Eightfold Path is the Buddhist intervention for the dukkha of suffering. Part V (this volume) examines the Noble Eightfold Path as it might be implemented in the mental health field. The technique of mindfulness used in the current mindfulness intervention programs is one of the interventions explicated in the Noble Eightfold Path. It is possible that more intervention programs might be developed from the other techniques mentioned in the Buddha's Noble Eightfold Path.

PART V

INTERVENTIONS
AND CLINICAL
IMPLICATIONS

13 ASSESSMENT

In Buddhist psychotherapy, the goal of an assessment is to cocreate a conceptualization of the client's presenting problem in the context of the suffering or unsatisfactoriness (*dukkha*) that is experienced in the client's embodied existence. It is for the psychotherapist and the client to construct, coconstruct, and reconstruct a fuller understanding of the client's world, as if a story is being built with the following elements:

- **Who:** the person in the treatment room (not the person about whom the client complains). This is *nāmarūpa* (mentality-materiality) plus *viññāna* (consciousness), seeing the person as they exist in the universe. This is not the constructed notion of the self.

- **What:** dukkha (more specifically for psychotherapy treatment, the client's experience of their presenting complaint for psychotherapy). Think of this as the arena of the First Noble Truth and the third mark of existence that says, "All conditioned things are unsatisfactory" (*dukkha*; *Dhammapada* [Dhp], 1996, 277–279: The Path).

https://doi.org/10.1037/0000453-014
Buddhist Psychotherapy: Connecting Early Buddhism to Mindfulness and Western Psychotherapy, by L. Tien, D. M. Kawahara, and V. Dhammadinna

- **When:** now and the moment of the client's critical incident (the specific moment is the most recent moment that gave rise to the client's awareness of their presenting complaint for psychotherapy). This necessarily needs to include a detailed analysis of the *conditions* that are at play in the moment of the client's critical incident. Think of this as the arena of impermanence in the first mark of existence that says, "All conditioned things are impermanent" (*anicca*; Dhp, 1996, 277–279).

- **Where:** in the client's consciousness. This is the constructed notion of the self and the hindrances.

- **Why:** the object of craving (*taṇhā*) and clinging (*upādāna*). What is the client grasping for and clinging to? This is the arena of the Second Noble Truth.

- **How:** the five aggregates subject to clinging. Think of this as the arena of not-self, the second mark of existence that says, "All things are not-self" (*anattā*; Dhp, 1996, 277–279).

Assessing for the who, what, when, where, why, and how is the domain of the three marks of existence and the First Noble Truth. Take all the time needed for this assessment. It is infinitely beneficial to come to a full understanding of the conditions that enable the situation of the client's presenting problem. Often, as the exploration of all the conditions evolves, clients come to an understanding of their own situation and usually craft solutions that are much more congruent for their life than anything the psychotherapist or psychology crafts.

Dukkha is described in the First Noble Truth. The cause of dukkha is given in the Second Noble Truth. Engaging in the task of assessment is the domain of the Third Noble Truth. The Third Noble Truth and the arena of psychotherapy provide the hope and the promise that there is a way for the amelioration of dukkha.

This chapter focuses on the operationalization of what to assess as directed by the Buddhist theory of psychotherapy. The assessment questions, when suggested, are designed like a qualitative research project question, which should be followed up with further detailed inquiry.

THE CRITICAL MOMENT WHEN THE PROBLEM LAST OCCURRED

The Buddhist theory of psychotherapy starts with the Buddhist doctrine of anicca (impermanence). The Theravāda Abhidhamma theory of momentariness, which is a more detailed analysis of anicca, posits that phenomena in consciousness arise and pass away from moment-to-moment dependence on conditions. The client's mind state that gave rise to their discomfort, pain, or presenting complaint is a dependently arising phenomenon in consciousness that is subject to aniccā. The theory-guided assessment approach for Buddhist psychotherapy directs the psychotherapist to conduct an analysis of momentary conditions. The goal is to fully understand the conditions occurring at any given moment. In theory, it is immaterial which moment is examined, because all elements are at play in every moment of human experience. However, psychotherapy clients seek assistance regarding a specific problem, which is usually identified in their presenting complaint. Thus, the tasks of the assessment phase of psychotherapy are (a) to engage in an analysis of the pivotal moment in the critical incident that gave rise to the client's awareness of their presenting complaint and (b) to conduct a more detailed exploration of the moment when the client's presenting problem last occurred.

The emphasis on understanding the most recent occurrence of the problem differs from searching for the first remembered moment (usually in childhood) when the client felt the uncomfortable emotion. Seeking the first moment when the client remembers experiencing their presenting problem is akin to seeking the origin or genesis of their presenting problem. Seeking origins will most likely take the in-session conversation to the client's remembered childhood experiences. The implication in such an approach is that the current presenting problem is a repeat or an echo of the original moment of the felt experience of the presenting problem. In Buddhist psychotherapy, the psychotherapist would inquire for the most recent moment and, specifically, the last time when the client became aware of their presenting complaint. This approach is based on the idea of the first mark of existence, in which we assume that the lived experience of a moment changes dependent of conditions and that the most recent moment of the experienced difficulty is not the same as the first moment of the client's presenting complaint.

The assessment phase of psychotherapy requires identifying the pivotal moment in the critical incident that gave rise to the client's awareness of their presenting complaint, and also possibly conducting a more detailed exploration of the moment when the client's presenting problem last occurred. Seeking the last time, not the first time, the client's presenting problem occurred will, hopefully, take the conversation to the present moment in the treatment room or to a relatively recent situation. Based on the identified most recent moment, then the psychotherapist would inquire for the sense contact that precipitated the discomfort. This stimulus for the sense contact in the critical moment may be a thought, a painful feeling, a physical pain, or any other form of discomfort. The psychotherapist's sentence prompt may sound something like this: "When was the last time you noticed this problem?" or "When was the last time you noticed the absence of this problem?" For example, for clients presenting with anxiety, the psychotherapist might ask: "When was the last time you felt anxious? What was the situation?" If the client cannot answer these questions, then the psychotherapist could follow with this question: "Did you wake up feeling anxious, or did the anxious feeling appear sometime after you first woke up this morning?" From the sense contact of that moment, then the psychotherapist and the client would coconstruct a full understanding of the conditions that were present at the moment of that sense contact.

To gain a full understanding of the conditions for the critical moment, the psychotherapist needs an operationalizable definition. Such a definition and operationalization need a systematized schema to contain the various items for inquiry. Although Buddhism is exquisitely attentive to the internal mental culture, it is not as focused on the contextual environmental situation that the client finds themselves in. To operationalize the conditions referred to in the idea of dependent arising, the proposed schema is a combination of the external and internal conditions. The exploration of external conditions is borrowed from other areas of social science. One framework is Bronfenbrenner's ecological systems theory (Bronfenbrenner & Ceci, 1994; Bronfenbrenner & Evans, 2000; Bronfenbrenner & Morris, 2006), and the other framework is the concept of social positionality (Gabel, 2023).

Combining the elements of Bronfenbrenner's ecological systems theory, social positionality, and the five aggregates subject to clinging, the assessment for the pivotal moment in a critical incident would include identifying and clearly articulating the following: the chronosystem, the macrosystem, the exosystem, the mesosystem, the microsystem, the person's social positionality, the client's notion of themselves, mental formations and/or proliferations (saṅkhāra) of the sense contact, the perception, name, and/or label (saññā) of the sense contact, the hedonic feeling tone (vedanā) of the sense contact, the sense contact, and the sense object or the stimulus that initiated the moment under consideration. The psychotherapist needs to ensure that both they and the client are able to articulate, identify, and describe the element in words that the client can understand; doing so helps the client grasp the relevance of the element to their situation at each level of this framework.

Figure 11.1 presents a conceptual map of this integrated framework. As viewed in the figure, it is important to understand the multiple external conditions relevant to the critical moment. Integration of the Western frameworks from the biopsychosocial model, Bronfenbrenner's ecological systems theory, and social positionality is highly recommended in the assessment of a client. As discussed previously in Chapter 3 (this volume), these frameworks provide further context (or in the Buddhist lexicon, conditions) to the understanding of the client's world. These frameworks enhance the psychotherapist's conceptualization of the multifaceted universe that conditions the client's lived experience. It is beyond the scope of this book to present them in detail. The authors assume that readers are familiar with these frameworks and their associated published assessment tools. Please refer to Bolton and Gillett (2019) for the biopsychosocial model; to Gabel (2023) for social identities, positionality, and intersectionality; and to Bronfenbrenner and colleagues (Bronfenbrenner & Ceci, 1994; Bronfenbrenner & Evans, 2000; Bronfenbrenner & Morris, 2006) for review of Bronfenbrenner's ecological systems theory and proximal processes.

The remainder of this chapter focuses on internal factors relevant to the critical moment. These internal factors include the five aggregates, the five aggregates subject to clinging, and the roots for the construction of the five aggregates subject to clinging. This process follows the layout diagrammed in the Madhupindika Sutta:

> When there is the eye, a form, and **eye-consciousness**, it is possible to point out the manifestation of **contact**. When there is the manifestation of contact, it is possible to point out the manifestation of **feeling**. When there is the manifestation of feeling, it is possible to point out the manifestation of **perception**. When there is the manifestation of perception, it is possible to point out the manifestation of **thinking**. When there is the manifestation of thinking, it is possible to point out the manifestation of being beset by perceptions and notions tinged by **mental proliferation**. Similarly, dependent on the ear and sounds. . . . Dependent on the nose and odors. . . . Dependent on the tongue and flavors. . . . Dependent on the body and tangibles. . . . Dependent on the mind and mind-objects, mind-consciousness arises. The meeting of the three is **contact**. With contact as condition there is **feeling**. What one feels, that one **perceives**. What one perceives, that one thinks about. What one thinks about, that one **mentally proliferates**. With what one has mentally proliferated as the source, **perceptions and notions** [born of] mental proliferation beset a man with respect to past, future, and present mind-objects cognizable through the mind. (Bhikkhu Bodhi, Trans.; *Majjhima Nikāya* [MN], 1995, 18: The Honeyball; Note: Boldface was added to terms in the sutta throughout this chapter to direct the reader to key concepts.)

THE SENSE CONTACT (*PHASSA*)

The assessment to uncover the start of a client's presenting complaint, as it is with any experience, starts with determining the point of contact with a stimulus. Experience is "a process of interaction between the internal sense-faculties and the external sense objects" (Karunadasa, 2015a, p. 59). Experiences start with the sense contact (*phassa*) and the process of pairing the stimulus and internal sense base. The first lived moment of an experience (i.e., client's report of a difficult situation) is when a stimulus meets the sense base and the meeting of these two attracts the attention (*manasikāra*) of the mind, bringing about consciousness (*viññāna*) of the stimulus. The Madhupindika Sutta described this process as follows:

> When there is the eye, a form, and **eye-consciousness**, it is possible to point out the manifestation of **contact**. . . . Similarly, dependent on the ear and sounds. . . . Dependent on the nose and odors. . . . Dependent on the tongue and flavors. . . . Dependent on the body and tangibles. . . . Dependent on the mind and mind-objects, mind-consciousness arises. The meeting of the three is **contact**. (MN, 1995, 18)

The first lived moment of an experience, said in a formulaic format, is as follows: Contact (*Phassa*) = (Stimulus + Internal Sense Base) + Attention (*Manasikāra*). The Pali word phassa can be translated as the "first lived moment of an experience." *The Pali Text Society's Pali–English Dictionary* defines phassa as "contact, touch (as sense or sense impression). It is the fundamental fact in a sense impression, and consists of a combination of the sense, the object, and perception . . . and gives rise to feeling" (Pali Text Society, n.d.). Contact/phassa is when one or more of the senses, such as eyesight, combines with our memory, recognition, or connection to information we hold (e.g., sense object or sense data) to then create consciousness.

Because all phenomena in consciousness start with contact/phassa between a sense object in the universe, or a stimulus, that is recognizable to one of the human internal six sense bases, the psychotherapist is looking for what exactly was seen, heard, smelled, tasted, touched, or thought at the moment immediately preceding when the client became aware of their discomfort with regard to the presenting complaint. That is, the psychotherapist is to identify the stimulus that initiated the client's reported difficult situation. Because there are numerous possibilities of sense contact, it is not possible to give exact instructions to the psychotherapist to assess for the sense contact. Although there are numerous possibilities of sense contact from the psychotherapist's vantage point, there is only one moment of contact/phassa for the client with their presenting complaint. Instead of a list of step-by-step instructions or a series of assessment questions, two examples of identifying the stimulus (or sense contact) are presented next to illustrate looking for the stimulus that immediately proceeded the moment of the person's awareness of a problem. This example is from a supervision session. Psychotherapists can extract relevant items from this example, which can then generalize to their situation with any specific client.

The inquiry for the stimulus starts with wherever the client presents and then progresses back to the point of sense contact. Consider this example from a supervision session: John is a heterosexual young male student in his fifth and last year of graduate training in a doctoral clinical psychology training program. John, who held promise to be an excellent clinician, came into supervision and was seriously considering withdrawing from the doctoral program. He reported that he does not think he is suited for treating clients and acting ethically at the same time. On further exploration for the possible reasons for what the supervisor considered an outlandish idea of John withdrawing from the training program, John said he had been struggling with his inability to handle his countertransference.

The supervisor asked a series of questions aimed at revealing the nature of said countertransference. John revealed that he experienced intrusive thoughts of engaging in sexual acts with a client. The supervisor's next series of questions were focused on determining the moment when this thought first occurred to John, which turned out to be in a client treatment session. The next series of questions were aimed at finding the first moment that John became aware of said countertransference, which led him to recount a session with a very attractive young woman. The next set of questions was for the exact moment when John felt discomfort in the treatment session with this female client. John reported that the client came to session dressed in extremely short shorts, sat with her legs spread apart, and continuously played with the shoulder strap of her flimsy shirt as she talked in the treatment session about her sexual desires for her ex-boyfriend. At one point, she leaned over and let the strap of the top she was wearing fall off her shoulder. It may be a very long and convoluted road to go from not quite knowing what to do when a client tries to seduce a psychotherapist (which occurs with some regularity) to answering the question of whether John should withdraw from the graduate program. The topic of discussion in supervision turned from whether John should or should not withdraw from his doctoral program to how to handle clients who have either fallen in love with or are sexually seductive toward the psychotherapist.

Identifying the sense object for the moment of contact/phassa is not only necessary but also extremely informative for psychotherapy. Contact/phassa, as in "the meeting of the three is contact" (MN, 1995, 18), requires an internal sense sphere, an external sense object, and the necessary level of manasikāra (consciousness, attention). For John, the internal sense sphere involved sight and sound. Based on the discussion between John and the supervisor, John was looking at an attractive seductive female teasing the psychotherapist by disrobing and talking about sexual desire. The same contact/phassa would not have arisen if John was not heterosexual or if the female client was not young, attractive, and seductive. A young heterosexual male exposed to the sight and sound of an attractive female at the first stage of possibly disrobing in a sexually seductive manner in the middle of verbally describing fantasies of sexual seduction set the conditions for sexual desire to arise. Contact/ phassa was made, and sexual desire did arise in John when his attention was drawn to the client's body at the moment her shoulder strap fell.

An analysis of the inquiry from the supervisor, who practices Buddhist psychotherapy, to John would be as follows. The first task for the supervisor conducting the assessment at this stage is to elicit from John the exact moment that he became aware of the problem. The supervisor then needs to find the sense object and to determine what John was paying attention to. John will inevitably report a situation when he was acutely aware of the presenting problem. It is typical that the client (or in this case, the supervisee) will report their internal dialogue and describe their constructed world that manifested their presenting problem. Starting with this information, the assessment process aims to get a picture of the environment and the interactions occurring at the moment John became aware of the presenting problem. Obtaining a more complete description of the situation and interactions allows for both the supervisor and John to start noticing the context and differentiating among stimuli John is acutely aware of, stimuli that John notices but does not attend to, and stimuli that are neither noticed nor attended to but are significant for the presenting problem. Once the full context of the situation is established, then one should look for contact/phassa, or the stimulus. Look for the stimulus at the juncture when one moment the presenting problem was not there and the next moment the person is aware of their presenting problem. The stimulus will be what the person noticed at that pivotal moment.

THE HEDONIC FEELING TONE (*VEDANĀ*) OF THE SENSE CONTACT

"When there is the manifestation of contact, it is possible to point out the manifestation of feeling. . . . With contact as condition there is feeling" (MN, 1995, 18). Once the stimulus that triggered the client's awareness of their presenting complaint is identified, then the next item for assessment is the type of hedonic feeling tone (*vedanā*) elicited by the sense contact.

There are some universal reactions to certain sense contact. Examples include unpleasant hedonic feeling tone to physical pain that results in not liking, pleasant hedonic feeling tone to cessation of physical pain (as in sedative drug use) that results in liking, and neither pleasant nor unpleasant hedonic feeling tone to things that are just not interesting enough to catch the mind's attention. Here, the psychotherapist is looking for the expected vedanā associated with the contact/phassa. The understandable immediate hedonic feeling tone in the earlier example of John would be one of pleasant. Indubitably, many young heterosexual men would respond with pleasant vedanā at the sight of an attractive young female making sexually suggestive physical movements. Phassa with pleasant feeling tone is the condition that underlies the tendency to grasp, cling to, or attach. John's experience of the pleasant vedanā was his felt urge to engage in sexual acts with a client. The more complicated feelings of anger, sadness, elation, despondency, or any number of feeling words are not what the psychotherapist is assessing for in the aggregate of vedanā. Those more complicated emotions are derivatives of the mental formations discussed in the later section on mental formations (sankhāra). For John, the mental formations and their derivative emotion were his subsequent judgment about his urge for sexual contact with a client, which was abhorrent to him. These mental formations led to John's more complex emotions of loathing and disgust with himself; the urge to escape these emotions was the decision to withdraw from the doctoral program and thus avoid placing himself in such complicated situations.

The contact with an unpleasant feeling tone is the condition that underlies the tendency toward aversion. In most psychotherapeutic situations, probabilities are high that the contact/phassa for the client's presenting complaint generated an unpleasant vedanā (hedonic feeling tone), which is thus the motivator for psychotherapy and an implicit request for the psychotherapist to administer interventions to eliminate those unpleasant vedanās.

Contact with neither pleasant nor unpleasant feeling tone is the condition for inattention and for the mind/citta to move toward something more interesting. There are numerous elements in most situations to which people do not attend. To attend to all elements in any situation is likely overwhelming; thus, it is useful to be inattentive to insignificant elements in one's surroundings. Probabilities are high that clients systematically ignore elements that are significant. It is the psychotherapist's task to draw the client's attention to significant elements that had elicited neither pleasant nor unpleasant feeling tone and were thus ignored.

This hedonic feeling tone associated with the sense contact, when verbalized, tends to have the effect of taking away the social judgment in a situation. When this occurs in session, the client will exhibit some change at both the soma and psyche levels. This is like the metaphorical lightbulb moment when the client knows the reason for a difficult situation and the dukkha seems to melt away. In understanding the reason, many clients do spontaneously find a lifestyle-congruent solution. The assessment for the type of vedanā (hedonic feeling tone) elicited by the sense contact will always result in only one of the three possibilities: pleasant, unpleasant, or neither pleasant nor unpleasant.

CONSCIOUSNESS (*VIÑÑĀNA*)

For the purposes of psychotherapy, consciousness (*viññāna*) can take two different focuses, depending on which definition is adopted. Considering *viññāna* as the bare knowing of an object at the point of sense contact, prior to labeling being associated with the stimulus, the psychotherapist is searching for the moment of sense contact that gave rise to the client's awareness that they have a problem. The psychotherapist would initiate a series of inquiries to find the sense contact. Depending on how aware the client is of their internal process, identifying this first moment and the sense contact can be relatively easy and straightforward, or it can take dozens of sessions to teach the client how to pay sufficient attention to their internal process to identify the sense contact.

Considering *viññāna* (consciousness) as a process, the psychotherapist tracks the general pattern and recurrent items that the person repeatedly reports as the topic of their awareness in their inner monologue. Although this focus is something slightly different than the general considerations in Buddhism for *viññāna*, we argue that it is not completely divergent. The psychotherapist is concerned with what the person is paying attention to in the general flow of mental proliferations. Usually, it is an item that is repeating. It can be a theme (e.g., "I am inadequate") or a pattern of interactions. One example is a family systems pattern in which the client takes on the responsibility for ensuring that everyone is happy and comfortable in every situation they are in, which means the client is paying attention to any discomfort exhibited by family members.

As with detecting any item, the item itself can be identified, or conversely, everything except the item can be identified; thus, what is left is the item to which the client attends. In this process, the psychotherapist is asking a series of questions to obtain a full listing of items that were present at the moment the client became aware of their presenting complaint. An example of this might be the client discussing their discomfort at a work meeting during which they experienced irritation and perhaps anger at a particular work colleague. Often, the client will focus on what this specific colleague did and said that triggered the client's anger. The assessment questions from the psychotherapist could ask the client to list everyone who attended the work meeting, thus identifying possible relevant information to which the client was not giving attention. An additional assessment question might also include the client's physical condition at the time they became irritated and angry, such as whether the client was hungry, tired, sleep deprived, or any number of physical discomforts that most likely contributed to their impatience.

PERCEPTION, NAMING, AND LABELING (*SAÑÑĀ*)

"What one feels, that one perceives" (MN, 1995, 18). Once contact is made and the stimulus is determined to be pleasant, unpleasant, or neither pleasant nor unpleasant, then the task is to label the stimulus. Think of being awakened in the middle of the night by some intrusive sound. The vedanā (hedonic feeling tone) is unpleasant, not liking being awakened from sound sleep. The mind tries to identify what that sound is, such as a dog barking, an ambulance siren, or a door opening. What label one gives the sense contact plus vedanā (hedonic feeling tone) is idiosyncratic, depending on the person's past experiences. Here, the psychotherapist is looking for one word, one phrase, or one sentence that a person would use to describe the phassa (contact) plus vedanā (hedonic feeling tone).

Perception, naming, and labeling (saññā) of contact with neither pleasant nor unpleasant feeling tone is relatively uncomplicated. For example, when presented with a cake, a person of healthy weight without a history of obesity or eating disorders would most likely report recognizing the object as a cake, something to eat. For a person with a history of obesity, years of struggling with dieting for weight loss, and a recent diabetes diagnosis, the same sight contact of cake would most likely lead them to report a pleasant feeling tone and perception of danger, recognizing the multilayer problems in the object of a cake. In conversation, this person might talk extensively about their desire for the forbidden food, their relationship with their body weight, their *attā* (sense of a self) who is diagnosed with diabetes, and their irritation at the many holiday gatherings where forbidden foods like cake abound. Seldom would such a person condense their perception to report the experience of "danger" at the sight of a cake. However, the assessment of the aggregate saññā (perception, recognition, naming, labeling) would be cake equals danger. The task for the psychotherapist would be to take all of the complexities reported by the client and condense them into one word or one phrase label for the stimulus.

MENTAL FORMATIONS (*SANKHĀRA*)

Mental formations are often the content of psychotherapy sessions where the client reports what is, metaphorically speaking, on their mind.

> When there is the manifestation of perception, it is possible to point out the manifestation of thinking. When there is the manifestation of thinking, it is possible to point out the manifestation of being beset by perceptions and notions tinged by mental proliferation. . . . What one perceives, that one thinks about. What one thinks about, that one mentally proliferates. (MN, 1995, 18)

The construction of the world surrounding a sense contact would be the closest parallel concept to mental formations, mental fabrications, and mental proliferations (*sankhāra*). The one phrase that might convey the meaning of saṅkhāra might be "the act of thinking." Thinking is differentiated from a thought. The *APA Dictionary of Psychology* defines *thinking* as "cognitive behavior in which ideas, images, mental representations, or other hypothetical elements of thought are experienced or manipulated. In this sense, thinking includes imagining, remembering, problem solving, daydreaming, free association, concept formation, and many other processes" (American Psychological Association, n.d.). It might be easier to imagine saṅkhāra as the story that is built around the sense contact. This constructed world is what is presented in psychotherapy.

Thoughts, not the process of thinking, are the content of the world that the client has built about the sense contact. The thoughts, or content, of this construction of the world are not as important as the topology of that world. There is one type of thought that is of importance for psychotherapists to notice. Normally, thoughts float by and are reported almost as a stream of consciousness. The psychotherapist is seeking one element in the continuous flow of thoughts: That one element that is of concern for the purposes of psychotherapy is volitional formations (*cetanā*). When a client is talking, their cetanā is mixed in with their saṅkhāra (mental formations, mental fabrications, mental proliferations) and the derivative emotions attached to the saṅkhāra. The reason that the psychotherapist is concerned with volitional formations (cetanā) versus all other material in the aggregate of mental formations (*saṅkhāra khanda*) is that volitional formations contain the bud of action for mind, speech, and body. In psychotherapy, mixed in among all the things that clients talk about, the psychotherapist is assessing for the one element that initiates the client's decision to act.

Actions of mind that are of special concern to psychotherapists are those that direct the client to harm either themself or others, regardless of whether the harm is lethal (e.g., suicide or homicide) or nonlethal (e.g., self-cutting or revenge of some kind). Inevitably, such a client will experience an action of the mind, like self-talk that calls the self a derogatory name followed by an urge to harm themself. It is important to flag this volitional formation and discuss its content as well as the client's normal response. It is worthwhile for the psychotherapist and the client to coconstruct possible alternative responses to those thoughts that initiate actions to harm.

THE FIVE AGGREGATES SUBJECT TO CLINGING: THE NOTION OF THE SELF

From the functioning of the five aggregates, we construct the world we live in and experience the universe. That world contains a sense of a self, or in Buddhist lexicon, a notion of a self.

> With what one has mentally proliferated as the source, perceptions and notions [born of] mental proliferation beset a man with respect to past, future, and present mind-objects cognizable through the mind. (MN, 1995 18)

Mind objects are what psychotherapy clients will usually report and discuss in treatment sessions. As in all hindered mind states, the psychotherapist is listening for the underlying craving (*taṇhā*), that is motivating the desire, and clinging or attachment (*upādāna*), as well as the more surface grasping and clinging. The assessment stage in psychotherapeutic treatment is to identify and name the steps in the process. The task in this assessment is to track the process from phassa (sense contact) to the agitated state of dukkha (suffering, unsatisfactoriness) as the client talks about their problems. The psychotherapist who listens with this process in mind will be able to pick out the client's process in the manufacturing of the agitation.

ROOTS FOR THE CONSTRUCTION OF THE FIVE AGGREGATES SUBJECT TO CLINGING

There are consistent patterns in the manifestations of craving (*taṇhā*). The suttas name three instigators for the craving, which collectively are referred to as *roots*. For the purposes of psychotherapy, we are only concerned with those roots that generate unpleasant states. These are the three unwholesome roots (*akusalā-mūlaṁ*) of greed (*lobha*), hatred (*dosa*), and delusion (*moha*; Sangiti Sutta; *Dīgha Nikāya* [DN], 1987/1995, 33: The Chanting Together).

For the purposes of defining these unwholesome roots, they are organized by four features as follows: (a) its characteristic (*lakkhaṇa*; i.e., the salient quality of the phenomenon); (b) its function (*rasa*), its performance of a concrete task (*kicca*) or achievement of a goal (*sampatti*); (c) its manifestation (*paccupaṭṭhāna*), the way it presents itself within experience; and (d) its proximate cause (*padaṭṭhāna*), the principal condition upon which it depends (Bodhi, 2013, p. 29).

Thus, listed next for each type of unwholesome desire are its characteristics, its function, its manifestations, and its proximate cause. The task for the psychotherapist is to recognize them as they present in the client's description of the moment that precipitated their awareness of the presenting complaint. The following list includes some common unwholesome desires but is not exhaustive. This list can be used in somewhat the same function as the mental status examination.

Greed (*lobha*)

The root of greed (*lobha*) shows up as wanting. It is generated from the pleasant vedanā (hedonic feeling tone) of a sense contact.

There are four types of greed/lobha (Thera Nyanaponika, 1999):

- craving for sense-gratification, sensual pleasures (*kāmatanha*)
- craving for self-preservation, existence (*bhavatanka*)
- craving for material existence (*rupavacara*)
- craving for self-annihilation, extermination (*vibbavatanha*)

Greed/lobha has the following characteristics (Thera Nyanaponika, 1999):

- will hide that fault in an attractive object and will behave accordingly,
- will overrate an attractive object, and
- identifies themself with the beloved and hence cannot bear separation from them.

Greed/lobha serves the following functions (P. Wasantha, personal communication [lecture notes], 2016):

- impulse (*chanda*)
- excitement (*raga*)
- enjoyment (*nandi*)
- love (*sineha*)
- thirst (*pipāsa*)
- consuming passion (*parilāha*)
- libidinous tendency
- sensuality (*kāma*)

- thirst (*taṇhā*)
- stinginess (*macchariya*)
- hallucinatory habits
- fraudulent
- pride in all actions
- delight in sinful actions
- unlimited desires
- unsatisfactoriness
- deep-rooted defilement in every action
- vacillation in duties
- not fearful in any sinful action
- shameful in any sinful actions
- infatuated mood in any functions

Greed/lobha has the following manifestations (Thera Nyanaponika, 1999):

- liking
- wishing for
  - wealth
  - offspring
  - fame
- longing
- fondness
- affection
- attachment
- lust
- cupidity
- craving
- passion
- self-indulgence
- possessiveness
- avarice

Root of Hatred (*Dosa*)

The root of hatred (*dosa*) shows up as aversion. It is generated from the unpleasant hedonic feeling tone of a sense contact.

Hatred/dosa has the following characteristics (Thera Nyanaponika, 1999):

- disparages an existing virtue in a disagreeable or hostile object and will behave accordingly

- identifies themself with an aversion against the un-beloved and cannot bear association with them

Hatred/dosa serves the following functions (Vatthāpnma Sutta; MN, 1995, 7: The Simile of the Cloth):

- annihilation (*vibbhavatanha*)
  - hatred directed at self (i.e., suicide)
  - hatred directed at other (i.e., violence, homicidal ideations)
- imbalance of controlling hatred
- covering others good qualities
- comparing others' good qualities with themself
- intolerance of others' wealth and progress
- hiding one's wealth from others

Hatred/dosa has the following manifestations (Thera Nyanaponika, 1999):

- dislike
- disgust
- revulsion
- resentment
- grudge
- ill humor
- vexation
- irritability
- antagonism
- aversion
- anger
- wrath
- vengefulness

Ignorance (*Avijjā*) and Delusion (*Moha*)

In psychotherapy, ignorance (*avijjā*) and delusion (*moha*) manifest as inattentiveness to items that hold significance to a client's difficulties.

There are seven types of ignorance/avijjā and delusion/moha:

- ignorance/avijjā of the Four Noble Truths (sutta)
- nonknowledge of the prenatal past (Abhidhamma)
- nonknowledge of the postmortem future (Abhidhamma)
- nonknowledge of the past and the future together (Abhidhamma)
- nonknowledge of dependent arising (Abhidhamma)
- associated with doubt (Abhidhamma)
- associated with agitation (Abhidhamma)

Ignorance/avijjā and delusion/moha have the following characteristics (Thera Nyanaponika, 1999):

- conceives things in a distorted way
- holds the true for false (the factual for nonfactual)
- four distortions of reality (*vipallāsa*)
  - seeing permanence in the impermanent/aniccā
  - happiness in what is truly suffering
  - selfhood in what is void of a self/attā
  - beauty in the unbeautiful

Ignorance/avijjā and delusion/moha serve the following functions (MN, 1995, 7):

- sloth and torpor in physical and mental performances
- restlessness
- uneasiness of doing actions
- skeptical doubts
- dogmatism
- excessive talkativeness
- dislike for wholesome practices

Ignorance/avijjā and delusion/moha have the following manifestations (Dhammasaṅgaṇī, *Abhidhamma Piṭaka*):

- stupidity
- dullness
- confusion
- ignorance/avijjā of essentials (e.g., of the Noble Truths)
- prejudice
- ideological dogmatism
- fanaticism
- wrong views
- conceit

The presence of both the clinging aspects of the five aggregates and the unwholesome roots that fuel the clinging is so pervasive that the psychotherapist does not need to probe for them. The task in the assessment phase is to sufficiently know (a) the process for the clinging aspect of the five aggregates subject to clinging and (b) the characteristics, function, and manifestations of the three unwholesome roots well enough so the therapist can identify and articulate their presence when the client talks in the treatment session about their problems.

CONCLUSION

The assessment portion of the psychotherapist's task is to discern, to eluci-date, and to enumerate all the conditions that are at play for the moment in which the first and the second darts arise. This means the psychotherapist needs to first determine both the social circumstances and the internal condi-tions that arose for this person to seek averting painful and/or uncomfortable circumstances. The focus of the assessment phase for the Buddhist psycho-therapist is not the consequence of the person's actions, but the conditions at the moment of cetanā (volitional formations). Think of deconstructing the critical moment into its component parts. Those parts include those frame-works borrowed from the biopsychosocial model, Bronfenbrenner's ecological systems theory, and social positionality. From Buddhism, those parts identify (a) the client's mind state of hindrance; (b) the type of dukkha (suffering, unsatisfactoriness) the client was experiencing at the pivotal moment; and (c) then each element of the five aggregates, which includes the sense object, the hedonic feeling tone of the sense contact, perception, mental formation and the subsequent mental proliferation and associated emotions in regard to the critical moment, and, finally, consciousness. What was the client paying attention to in the critical moment? What was the client not paying attention to in the critical moment? Focusing on the pivotal moment of the critical incident will have significance for the client's notion of the self without the psychotherapist having to address the self.

14

EMPLOYING THE FIRST TRACK OF THE NOBLE EIGHTFOLD PATH IN PSYCHOTHERAPY

Conduct

Going from assessment to intervention, we first review what Buddha Gotama did in answering the question, "What is the experience of existence?" He extensively analyzed how we experience our human existence, and then he gave us the answer of what we experience: If there is no recognition or acknowledgment of the three marks of existence, then what is experienced has the characteristics of suffering or unsatisfactoriness (*dukkha*). The Buddha recognized that every single human wishes to escape from all forms of dukkha and said, in the Third Noble Truth, that there is a way to ameliorate the experience of dukkha. In psychotherapy, this is like a client knowing they are suffering and reaching out to make that first appointment with a psychotherapist. For the client, making that appointment for psychotherapy treatment is based on the idea that there is a way out of their difficult mental and emotional state. We, as psychotherapists, have an array of interventions, which are akin to the Fourth Noble Truth that says:

> And what, friends, is the noble truth of the way leading to the cessation of suffering? It is just this Noble Eightfold Path. (Dhammacakkapavattana Sutta;

https://doi.org/10.1037/0000453-015
Buddhist Psychotherapy: Connecting Early Buddhism to Mindfulness and Western Psychotherapy, by L. Tien, D. M. Kawahara, and V. Dhammadinna

Saṃyutta Nikāya [SN], 2000, 56.11: Setting in Motion the Wheel of the Dhamma)

As mentioned previously, the Noble Eightfold Path is divided into three broad categories:

- conduct (sīla);
- concentration, mind-training, or meditation (samādhi); and
- wisdom (paññā).

The chapters in Part V examine these three parallel paths. Translating from the lexicon of Buddhism to the mental health field, the term *conduct* is used for items covered in sīla, *mindfulness* is used for samādhi, and *reframing* the client's conceptualization of their problem into a framework that is more aligned with Buddhist ideas is used for *paññā*. This chapter covers the arena of conduct.

Assessment is the first phase of psychotherapy. Assessment in the Buddhist psychotherapy approach engages in a detailed analysis of (a) the pivotal moment in the critical incident that generated the client's presenting problem and (b) the last moment when the client's presenting problem occurred.

Often, while participating in this assessment process, the client gains an understanding of the conditions that support their suffering. At that point, many clients will alter their attitudes and behaviors without specific guidance, recommendations, or directives from the psychotherapist. However, there are times when the psychotherapist will have to recommend and direct the client to change their conduct. For instance, think about telling a client who complains of insomnia not to engage with social media as their last activity before going to bed. Telling a client to refrain from social media before bed is a recommendation and a directive.

For Buddhist psychotherapy, these recommendations and directives— if and when made—are guided by two principles. The firsts principle is to make recommendations that avoid foreseeable harm to the client and harm to others. The second principle is to engage in conduct that has the highest probability of producing positive results sometime in the future. In the Buddhist approach, the surest direction for obtaining long-term peace of mind and ensuring positive favorable future situations is to engage in skillful and wholesome (kusalā) conduct, or sīla. Recall from Chapter 2, the Pali word sīla is translated as "nature character habit behavior usually as [in] . . . 'being of such a nature' like having the character of . . . stingy" (Pali Text Society, n.d.). In the context of the Noble Eightfold Path, sīla refers to adopting the habit of engaging in ethical conduct in actions and behavior of the body, speech, and mind. The guiding principle for sīla (conduct, behavior) is the cause and effect of the doing of deeds (*kamma*; often known by its Sanskrit translation, *karma*). The Pali word kamma is defined as follows:

> the doing, deed, work; . . . the act of being done . . . the deed with reference both to its cause and its effect: anything done is caused and is in itself the cause of something else . . . cause and effect: like for like—as the cause, so the result. (Pali Text Society, n.d.)

The Buddhist considerations for ethical conduct (sīla) are not based on morality with an external entity proclaiming or dictating how a person should conduct themself. The principles reflected in the cause and effect of the doing of deeds (kamma) are based on two considerations. One consideration is how a person's actions affect the environment of their mind, with a preference for actions that lead to a settled and nondisturbed mind in the long term. The other consideration is how one's actions will most likely affect other people and one's external situation in the future, with a preference for those behaviors that not only avoid foreseeable harm to both oneself and others but also have a high probability of allowing for a pleasant future in the long term.

The Buddha Gotama, and the religion of Buddhism, simplified the thinking process by listing prescribed behaviors. When appropriate, a psychotherapist may find it useful to utilize this list of prescribed behaviors. However, the idiosyncratic nature of a person's difficulties presented in psychotherapy may make using a prescribed list of behaviors difficult to administer. Psychotherapists may find using the principles of kamma (cause and effect of the doing of deeds) more flexible and thus more appropriate. These principles for kamma were articulated in the Abhiṇhapaccavekkhitabbaṭhāna Sutta:

> I am the owner of my kamma, the heir of my kamma; I have kamma as my relative, kamma as my resort; I will be the heir of whatever kamma, good or bad, that I do. . . . I am not the only one who is the owner of one's kamma, the heir of one's kamma; who has kamma as one's origin, kamma as one's relative, kamma as one's resort; who will be the heir of whatever kamma, good or bad, that one does. (*Aṅguttara Nikāya* [AN], 2012, 5.57: Themes)

Subsequent sections in this chapter are divided into (a) sīla (ethical conduct), which is the Buddha's prescribed behaviors, and (b) kamma (cause and effect of the doing of deeds), which are the guiding principles for doing of deeds. Psychotherapists may consult the list of prescribed behaviors when useful and applicable. It may be more useful to apply the principles of kamma instead of being limited to the prescribed list of behaviors. Using sīla is synonymous to using kamma, because the basis for sīla is kamma and the guiding principles for kamma are more flexible in their application for psychotherapy.

ETHICAL CONDUCT (*SĪLA*)

The Buddha described ethical conduct as follows: "Householders, there are three kinds of bodily conduct . . . four kinds of verbal conduct . . . [and] three kinds of mental conduct not in accordance with the Dhamma [law]" (Sāleyyaka Sutta; *Majjhima Nikāya* [MN], 1995, 41: The Brahmins of Sālā). The types of conduct are enumerated and articulated in the Noble Eightfold Path as follows:

1. Right view
2. Right intention
3. Right speech
4. Right action
5. Right livelihood
6. Right effort
7. Right mindfulness
8. Right concentration

Ethical conduct (*sīla*) encompasses right action, right speech, and right intention—in other words, ethical conduct of body, speech, and mind or mentality, respectively (Table 14.1). Recall the previous discussion on the Four Noble Truths in Chapter 2 (this volume), where the concept of "right" is discussed. A common interpretation of the term right is one of moral edict. However, in Buddhism, the term right refers to their accuracy in relationship to the three marks of existence. Initial implementations of sīla are primarily aimed at abstinence—that is, listing what not to do. Refraining and abstinence are followed by listing what to do. In general, in most matters pertaining to the practice of the Noble Eightfold Path, the Buddha starts with what not to do and then follows with directives of what to do. His reasoning for this pattern is based on the presumption that for most

TABLE 14.1. Ethical Conduct in the Noble Eightfold Path

Relevant aspect of the Noble Eightfold Path	Refers to
Right action	Things done with the body
Right speech	Things done for communication, regardless of whether the transmission is verbal, written, or in body language
Right intention	Things done by the mind/*citta* and mind/*cetanā*. *Cetanā* (volitional formations) initiates cascade of thoughts in the mind, or actions of body and speech

people, their problem usually stems from having engaged in some conduct that led to unpleasantness. Thus, not engaging in that problematic behavior will go a long way to eliminate the unpleasantness in their life. The Buddha then makes recommendations of what to do for those who wish to go further with engaging in behavior that will lead to more pleasant situations.

Conduct Through Action

The first type of ethical conduct is conduct through action done through the body. The Buddha provided the following directives for what not to do and what to do.

What Not to Do

The Buddha specified what not to do in conduct through action as follows:

> And how, householders, are there three kinds of bodily conduct in accordance with the Dhamma [law]. And how, householder, are there three kinds of unrighteous bodily conduct. . . . Here someone kills living beings; he is murderous, bloody-handed, given to blows and violence, merciless to living beings. . . . He takes what is not given; he takes by way of the theft [of] the wealth and property of others in the village or forest. . . . He misconducts himself in sensual pleasures; he has intercourse with women who are protected by their mother, father, mother and father, brother, sister or relatives, who have a husband, who are protected by law, and even those who are garlanded in token of betrothal. (MN, 1995, 41)

Killing, stealing, and nonconsensual sex, the named three misconducts of the body, are surely harmful to social relationships, are almost absolutely guaranteed to produce foreseeable harm, and have extremely high probability of resulting in undesirable future situations and negative unpleasant kammic resultants. These forms of misconduct are so harmful that most societies have codified prohibitions by making them unlawful. Engaging in these forms of misconduct, especially when they are unlawful, has the high probability of resulting in unpleasant and undesirable circumstances and, therefore, foreseeable harm to the client, others around them, and society in general. Regardless of the directives of the Buddha, in our opinion, it would be highly unlikely for a psychotherapist to recommend anything that would lead their client to kill, steal, or engage in sexual misconduct.

Killing. Killing, or the destruction of life, refers to the volitional, or premeditated, action of the body in which someone experiences the urge to intentionally harm another person. That kind of urge usually occurs in a mind culture full of hatred. That kind of sustained anger in the mind is not good for the body and probably not conducive to good healthy personal relationships.

Stealing. Restraining the hand from reaching out and taking something that is not freely given is slightly different from not stealing. *Stealing* is taking something that does not belong to you. It is a subcategory of taking "what is not given" (MN, 2012, 41). Consider this example of stealing: You open the refrigerator at work and use the coffee creamer that is not yours; you reason that it is only a small amount for one cup of coffee, and that no one would notice its absence from that large container. Now consider this example of stealing versus not taking what is not given: You are walking in the woods and notice an abandoned satchel. You first look around and do not see anyone else; then you open the satchel to see whether it contains any identification for the owner. To your surprise, the satchel contains stacks of one hundred-dollar bills but no identification of any kind. Keeping this abandoned satchel full of money is not stealing; however, it is taking something that is not given. You do not know who left that satchel, whether that person will come back to look for the lost item, and whether there is some way to trace the satchel to you if you take it, which would probably lead to some kind of distasteful confrontation. An alternative would be to turn the satchel over the police department. If it is unclaimed after a certain amount of time, the police might, depending on local laws governing found items, give you the satchel with all those one hundred-dollar bills. At that point, you are not taking what is not freely given; you are taking what is given to you by the police. The phrase "taking something that is not freely given" refers to the actions done through the body in which someone experiences the push of greed. That kind of urge is usually contained in a mind culture full of unrequited desire.

Sexual misconduct. Sexual misconduct is defined in the context of the chronosystem and the macrosystem (discussed in Chapter 13, this volume). Think of this as sanctioned sex. What is sanctioned differs in time and place. For Buddhism, it is acceptable to engage in socially sanctioned sexual encounters. The probability of getting into some kind of difficulty is high and probably foreseeable if the sexual act is not socially sanctioned. For example, touching an employee at work is very different from touching one's spouse, even if the touch is the same. For the most part, engaging in socially sanctioned sexual relations does not lead to harming oneself or another person.

What to Do

The Buddha specified what to do in conduct through action as follows:

> And how, householders, are there three kinds of bodily conduct in accordance with the Dhamma, righteous conduct? Here someone, abandoning the killing of living beings, abstains from killing living beings; with rod and weapon laid aside, **gentle and kindly, he abides compassionate** to all living beings. Abandoning the taking of what is not given, he abstains from taking what is not given; he does not take by way of theft the wealth and property of others in the village or in the forest. Abandoning misconduct in sensual pleasures, he abstains from misconduct in sensual pleasures; he does not have intercourse with women who are protected by their mother, father, mother and father, brother, sister or relatives, who have a husband, who are protected by law, and even those who are garlanded in token of betrothal. (MN, 1995, 41; Note: Boldface was added to terms in the sutta throughout this chapter to direct the reader to key concepts.)

Having refrained and abstained, the Buddha suggests that instead of killing living beings, one is to be "gentle and kindly" and "compassionate to all living beings" (MN, 1995, 41). For most people, it is probably much easier to not kill someone than to hold compassion for that person. While being compassionate to all living beings may be ideal, it is extremely difficult to accomplish. For psychotherapy, it is much easier to persuade a client to refrain from killing someone than to guide them toward compassion. It may be necessary for the psychotherapist to show compassion toward the client instead of directing the client to be compassionate. It is more meaningful to discuss the need for the development of compassion once a client has the experience of being the recipient of compassion. The methodology for development of compassion is described later in this chapter in discussion on the divine abodes (*Brahmā-vihāras*).

Conduct Through Speech

The second type of ethical conduct is conduct through speech. The action of speech, be it verbal or written, words or images, is the medium through which most social interactions occur. The Buddha provided the following directives for what not to do and what to do.

What Not to Do

The Buddha specified what not to do in conduct through speech as follows:

> And how, householders, are there four kinds of verbal conduct not in accordance
> with the Dhamma, unrighteous conduct? Here someone **speaks falsehood**;
> when summoned to court or to a meeting, or to his relatives' presence, or to
> his guild, or to the royal family's presence, and questioned as a witness thus:
> "So, good man, tell what you know," not knowing, he says, "I know," or knowing,
> he says, "I do not know"; not seeing, he says "I see," or seeing, he says, "I do
> not see"; in full awareness he speaks falsehood for his own ends, or for another's
> ends, or for some trifling worldly end. He **speaks maliciously**; he repeats else-
> where what he has heard here in order to divide those people from these, or
> he repeats to these people what he has heard elsewhere in order to divide these
> people from those; thus he is one who divides those who are united, a creator of
> divisions, who enjoys discord, rejoices in discord, delights in discord, a speaker
> of words **that create discord**. He **speaks harshly**; he utters such words as
> are rough, hard, hurtful to others, offensive to others, bordering on anger,
> inconducive to concentration. He is a **gossip**; he speaks at the wrong time,
> speaks what is not fact, speaks what is useless, speaks contrary to the Dhamma
> and the Discipline; at the wrong time he speaks such words as are worthless,
> unreasonable, immoderate, and unbeneficial. That is how there are four kinds
> of verbal conduct not in accordance with the Dhamma, unrighteous conduct.
> (MN, 1995, 41)

The category of speech refers to things done through communication, be it
verbal, nonverbal, or written. The specific misconducts of speech are (a) speaking falsehoods, (b) malicious speech, (c) harsh speech, and (d) gossip. Each
is described next.

Speaking falsehoods. Speaking falsehoods leads to mistrust between individuals and between groups of people. False speech includes the idea of lying
by omission as well as lying by commission. It is lying by commission to say
something that is not true. Even if one does not utter an untruth, it is lying
by omission when one leaves out certain key information that leads another
person to a false conclusion.

Malicious speech. *Malicious speech* is communication for the purpose of
ensuing division between persons or groups of people. This includes telling
one party something that is meant to create division, even if what is said
is true and accurate. For example, a client comes to session and says that
her friend told her that she saw the client's husband attending a work party
with some female. While this bit of information is accurate and true, it is
worthwhile to examine the motivation of this friend. Was that bit of information meant to create division between the wife and the husband for some

self-serving reason of the friend, or did the friend provide the information out of concern and at the request of the client? A nonclinical example of malicious speech that divided groups of people was the "Chinese virus" nickname some individuals gave COVID-19. This slur associates a deadly disease with a group of people, thus creating division between U.S. individuals and persons of Chinese descent and contributing to increased incidences of physical assault on Asian American individuals. According to hate crime statistics, there were 279 anti-Asian incidents in 2020, which was a 77% increase from 2019 (U.S. Federal Bureau of Investigation, 2020). In addition, the New York Police Department reported that "hate crimes motivated by anti-Asian sentiments jumped 1,900% in New York City in 2020" (Lang, 2021).

Harsh speech. *Harsh speech* comprises communication that is hurtful. Many clinical examples of hurtful speech are reported by children whose parents are critical, individuals whose spouses are abusive, or coworkers who are engaged in derogatory speech or are belittling to others. It is useful to identify hurtful speech and its indubitable effect, which may help the client to question the accuracy of the message.

Gossip. Finally, *gossip* and idle chatter occur when the person is talking for the sake of hearing themself talk. Most gossip is not spoken with the intent to harm. Gossip is usually done with the intent to entertain. Nevertheless, gossip can still be hurtful as well as harmful.

What to Do

The Buddha specified what to do in conduct through speech as follows:

> And how, householders, are there four kinds of verbal conduct in accordance with the Dhamma, righteous conduct? Here someone, abandoning false speech, **abstains from false speech**: when summoned to a court, or to a meeting, or to his relative's presence, or to his guild, or to the royal family's presence, and questioned as a witness thus: "So, good man, tell what you know," not knowing, he says, "I do not know," or knowing, he says, "I know"; not seeing, he says, "I do not see," or seeing, he says, "I see"; he does not in full awareness speak falsehood for his own ends, or for another's ends, or for some trifling worldly end. **Abandoning malicious speech**, he abstains from malicious speech; he does not repeat elsewhere what he has heard here in order to divide those people from theses, nor does he repeat to these people what he has heard elsewhere in order to divide these people from those; thus he is one who reunites those who are divided, a promoter of friendships, who enjoys concord, rejoices in concord, delights in concord, a speaker of words that promote concord. Abandoning harsh speech, he **abstains from harsh speech**; he speaks such

words as are **gentle, pleasing to the ear, and loveable, as go to heart, are courteous, desired by many, and agreeable to many.** Abandoning gossip, he abstains from gossip; he speaks at the right time, speaks what is fact, speaks on what is good, speaks on the Dhamma and the Discipline; at the right time he speaks such words as are worth recording, reasonable, moderate, and beneficial. That is how there are four kinds of verbal conduct in accordance with the Dhamma, righteous conduct. (MN, 1995, 41)

The community of Buddhists is known for its silence. The directive for abstaining from useless speech, idle chatter, and gossip results in less talk. In combination with the task of mindfulness, it is difficult to talk and pay attention to what one is doing (i.e., it is almost impossible to simultaneously talk and pay attention to what one is eating). Buddhist practitioners often engage in noble silence. Some clients report anxiety about social interactions; they voice fear of saying the wrong thing or not having anything to talk about, and thus experiencing that awkward silence. In-session dialogue with such a client may be taken as a blueprint for the types of speech giving in the Sāleyyaka Sutta (MN, 1995, 41). Discussing the function of speech (e.g., what kind of speech to avoid, when it is not beneficial to talk, what is hurtful to say, and what is idle chatter) supports the client in paying attention to the content of conversations instead of to their fear of not being liked or feeling socially awkward. It also encourages clients to be more attentive to the social interaction and, hopefully, to be comfortable with silence. When they decide to say something, speaking with gentle courtesy is sure to be well received. The methodology for development of gentle speech is described later in this chapter in discussion of the divine abodes (Brahmā-vihāras).

Conduct Through Mentality

The third type of ethical conduct is conduct through mentality. The Buddha provided the following directives for what not to do and what to do.

What Not to Do

The Buddha specified what not to do in conduct through mentality as follows:

And how, householders, are there three kinds of mental conduct not in accordance with the Dhamma [law], unrighteous conduct? Here someone is **covetous**; he covets the wealth and property of others thus: "Oh, may what belong to another be mine!" Or he has a **mind of ill will and intentions of hate** thus: "May these being be slain and slaughtered, may they be cut off, perish, or be annihilated!" Or he has **wrong view, distorted vision**, thus: "There is nothing given, nothing offered, nothing sacrificed; no fruit or result of good and bad actions; no this world, no other world; no mother, no father;

no being who are reborn spontaneously; no good and virtuous recluses and brahmins in the world who have themselves realized by direct knowledge and declare this world and the other world." That is how there are three kinds of mental conduct not in accordance with the Dhamma, by reason of such unrighteous conduct that some beings here on the dissolution of the body, after death, reappear in states of deprivation, in an unhappy destination, in perdition, even in hell. (MN, 1995, 41)

For Westerners, it may be a novel idea that the mind/*citta* can misbehave. In Buddhism, the mind is constantly misbehaving. Keen examples of the mind's misbehavior abound in remarks about the difficulties encountered in silent meditation. Another example of the mind's misbehavior are the seemingly continuous self-critical thoughts for those who experience depression.

The three types of misconduct by the mind/citta named by the Buddha are covetousness, ill will, and wrong view. Thoughts spontaneously occur from the push of hedonic feeling tone (*vedanā*) on the mind where pleasant vedanā influences the mind toward covetousness (*lobha*), unpleasant vedanā influences the mind toward ill will (*dosa*), and neither pleasant nor unpleasant vedanā influences the mind toward inattention. These spontaneous thoughts are an integral part of the hedonic feeling tone. The misconduct is not the presence of the thoughts; rather, it is the assent to the continuation of these thoughts and the endorsement of these thoughts by indulging in their continuation. The mind/citta goes astray when one responds to those spontaneous thoughts with assent and endorsement by indulging in their continuation in the mind.

The terms "wrong view" and "distorted vision," as described in the Sāleyyaka Sutta (MN, 1995, 41), refer to rejecting the principles of kamma (cause and effect of the doing of deeds), which will be discussed more extensively in the next section.

What to Do
The Buddha specified what to do in conduct through mentality as follows:

And how, householders, are there three kinds of mental conduct in accordance with Dhamma, righteous conduct? Here someone is **not covetous**; he does not covet the wealth and property of others thus: "Oh, may what belongs to another be mine! His free from enmity, affliction and anxiety! May they live happily!" He has right view, undistorted vision, thus: "There is what is given and what is offered and what is sacrificed"; there is fruit and result of good and bad actions; there is this world and the other world; there is mother and father; there are being[s] who are reborn spontaneously; there are good and virtuous recluses and brahmins in the world who have themselves realized by direct knowledge and declare this world and the other world. That is how there are three kinds of conduct in accordance with the Dhamma, righteous conduct. (MN, 1995, 41)

In this sutta, the Buddha suggested that refraining one's mind from being influenced by desire, hate, and delusion allows for realization of liberation or seeing reality as it is. Actions of the body and speech are initiated in the mind/cetasika. Therefore, restraining the mind/citta is equivalent to abstaining from misconducts of the body and speech.

Alternative mind states: The divine abodes (Brahmāsahavyatāya). It is easier to refrain from misconducts of the body, speech, and mind than to achieve the alternative mind states that are without covetousness or ill will. The Buddha introduces alternative mind states that counter the unpleasant mind states of covetousness and ill will with the divine mind states of (a) loving-kindness (*mettā*), (b) compassion (*karuna*), (c) sympathetic joy (*mudita*), and (d) equanimity (*upekkhā*). Engaging in these alternative mind states is the method for restraining and abandoning the misconducts of the mind/citta. These alternative mind states that are to replace the mind states of desire, hate, and delusion are listed in the Tevijja Sutta (*Dīgha Nikāya* [DN], 1987/1995, 13.76–79: The Threefold Knowledge—The Way to Brahmā). The Pali word given in the Tivijja Sutta for these alternative mind states is *brahmāsahavyatāya*. The word *sahavyatāya* means "in the company of Brahmā, gods" (Pali Text Society, n.d.). Thus, to be in the company of god, sometimes translated as "union with Brahmā" (Shults, 2013), is to live in the same mind state as the gods. A Google search (conducted on October 8, 2023) for the phrase "in the company of Brahmā" resulted in references to *Brahmā-vihāras*, the divine abodes, which is the current U.S. lexicon for the Pali textual word **brahmāsahavyatāya** (in the company of Brahmā/god). These divine abodes, as listed in the 76th to 79th paragraphs of the Tevijja Sutta, are as follows:

> the Tathagata, . . . know Brahma and the world of Brahma, and the way to the world of Brahmā, and the path of practice whereby the world of Brahmā may be gained. . . . A disciple goes forth, practices the moralities, attains the first jhānas. . . . Then, with his heart filled with **loving-kindness**, he dwells . . . always with a heart filled with loving-kindness, . . . without hate or ill-will. . . . Then with his heart filled with **compassion**, . . . with **sympathetic joy**, with **equanimity** he dwells . . . always with a heart filled with equanimity, . . . without hate or ill-will . . . so by this meditation, Vāseṭṭha, by this liberation of the heart through compassion . . . through sympathetic joy . . . through equanimity. . . . This, Vāseṭṭha, is the way to union with Brahmā. (DN, 1987/1995, 13)

When a person's mind resides in the same place where the gods reside, then the misconducts of the mind/citta and mind/cetasika are discarded. As noted earlier, these Brahmā-vihāras (divine abodes) mind states are loving-kindness (mettā), compassion (karuna), sympathetic joy (mudita), and equanimity (upekkhā). Hate is replaced by loving-kindness, ill will is replaced by compassion and equanimity, covetousness is replaced by sympathetic joy, and partiality of in-group favoring that is a by-product of the delusion of self-referencing is replaced by equanimity. Let us examine each divine abode in detail. We turn first to loving-kindness (mettā).

Loving-mindness (Mettā). *Mettā* is often translated as "loving-kindness." The *Pali Text Society's Pali–English Dictionary* defines mettā as follows:

> love, amity, sympathy, friendliness, active interest in others; desire of bringing welfare & good to one's fellow—men; to be friendly or sympathize with; kindly thought, a heart full of love; sympathetic, showing love towards; cultivation or development of friendliness (towards all living beings). (Pali Text Society, n.d.)

It is easier to refrain from misconducts of the body, speech, and mind than to achieve the mind states of loving-kindness (mettā), compassion (karuna), sympathetic joy (mudita), and equanimity (upekkhā). Additionally, the Brahmā-vihāras (divine abodes) names the destination, but not how to get there. A step-by-step instruction manual of sorts can be found in Buddhaghosa's (1956/2010) treatise, *Visuddhimagga: The Path to Purification*.

The psychotherapist can follow Buddhaghosa's instructions on development of loving-kindness, compassion, sympathetic joy, and equanimity. Buddhaghosa (1956/2010) started with developing the comportment of mettā (loving-kindness). The mind state of mettā was described in the Karaniya Metta Sutta (*Sutta Nipata* [Sn], 1995/2012, 1.8: Loving-Kindness) as follows:

> What should be done by one skillful in good
> So as to gain the State of Peace is this:
> (And let him think:) In safety and in bliss
> May creatures all be of a blissful heart.
> Whatever breathing beings there may be.
> No matter whether they are frail or firm,
> With none excepted, be they long or big
> Or middle-sized, or be they short or small
> Or thick, as well as those seen or unseen,
> Or whether they are dwelling far or near,
> Existing or yet seeking to exist.
> May creatures all be of a blissful heart.
> Let no one work another one's undoing
> Or even slight him at all anywhere:
> And never let them wish each other ill
> Through provocation or resentful thought.
> And just as might a mother with her life

Protect the son that was her only child,
So let him then for every living thing
Maintain unbounded consciousness in being;

And let him too with love for all the world
Maintain unbounded consciousness in being
Above, below, and all round in between,
Untroubled, with no enemy or foe.
And while he stands or walks or while he sits
Or while he lies down, free from drowsiness,
Let him resolve upon this mindfulness:
This is Divine Abiding here, they say.

The mind state of hate is to be replaced with the mind state of loving-kindness, as described in the Karaniya Metta Sutta (Sn, 1995/2012, 1.8). The mind state of hate is usually behind the misdeeds committed through the body and speech, regardless of whether hate is directed toward the self or toward another being. Thus, replacing hate with loving-kindness would then forestall the misconducts of body, speech, and mind. Buddhaghosa (1956/2010) started with the following:

> A meditator, who wants to develop . . . loving-kindness . . . if he is a beginner, . . . should review the danger in hate and the advantage in patience. Why? Because hate has to be abandoned and patience attained in the development of this meditation subject, and he cannot abandon unseen dangers and attain unknown advantages. (p. 291)

We psychotherapists, without naming the mind state of mettā (loving-kindness), start this practice with the client first being the recipient of mettā from the psychotherapist. The in-session dialogue would have the psychotherapist acknowledge the client's dukkha (suffering, unsatisfactoriness) and then articulate a reframe that shows understanding and kindness toward the client, with the eventuality of the client being able to show the same mettā toward themself that the psychotherapist has exhibited.

The first step in the client's development of mettā (loving-kindness) is to identify the mind state of anger and hatred. This mental state of hatred can be generalized to any experience of irritation, anger, hatred, or ill will. Helping the client identify this mind state will need to be initially done during the in-session dialogue. Whenever the psychotherapist detects anything that may be irritation, anger, hatred, or ill will (regardless of whether the client speaks about a situation, a setting, or a person), the psychotherapist, functioning as mindfulness, points out the mind state of ill will. For a person experiencing the symptoms of depression, the most frequent object of ill will is the self. The in-session dialogue is initially focused on identifying this mind state with statements like these: "You seem to be angry whenever you speak of [name the person or the situation]," "Were you irritated [label the situation]?" or "Are you angry or irritated right now?" This process may take several sessions before the client is able to recognize, acknowledge, and accurately label their mind state of anger or hatred. Some clients will deny being angry, instead using a milder term like "bothered" or "irritated." All such terms are encompassed within the mind state of ill will. It is likely that the client will discuss a different situation each session. Regardless of the content, there will most likely be the common thread of irritation, anger, hatred, or ill will, depending on the intensity of the affect.

After identifying the presence of irritation, anger, hatred, or ill will in the treatment session, then the next step is to recognize when hate is present in the mind. Identifying and recognizing the presence of the mind state of hate can be generalized from the treatment room to daily activities as a between-session homework assignment. The homework assignment would be to direct the client to observe themself in the experience of irritation, anger, hatred, or ill will in their daily activities. An example may be to have the client take notes or to journal how many times a day they experience their mind engaged in a silent recitation of the litany of their shortcomings. Needless to say, the psychotherapist needs to remember to follow up on this homework assignment at the next treatment session. It is not unusual for clients to push back on such assignments. Some common reasons for resistance may include the following: "Noticing does not tell me what to do," "Noticing is not an action plan to deal with my situation," or "If I notice it, then I have to do something about it."

When the client is able to associate the experience of irritation, anger, hatred, or ill will with the label of mind state of ill will, then the in-session dialogue can engage in a "review [of] the danger in hate" (Buddhaghosa, 1956/2010, p. 291). The dangers in experiencing the mind state of hate will be idiosyncratic to each client and need to be discussed in the context of the client's situation and life stage. One general observation may be that one's irritation, anger, hatred, or ill will usually does not affect the well-being of the other person. For example, if one driver is angry at another driver, it only stresses out that one driver but has no effect on the other driver.

Only after the client is able to associate the experience of irritation, anger, hatred, or ill will with the label of ill will and understand its effect on the well-being of the client can the psychotherapist then proceed to introduce mettā (loving-kindness). Here is a cautionary note to psychotherapists at this juncture: Do not jump too quickly to introduce mettā. The idea of mettā is like a soothing body massage if it is done before the client is able to identify the mind state of ill will and know the danger in staying in that mind state.

The idea of mettā at this stage is often taken as a platitude and is akin to a body massage that is relaxing and enjoyable for the moment but tends not to heal the injury that is causing a bodily pain. Introducing the application of mettā when the client is able to recognize the mind state of ill will allows the client to know exactly when to apply mettā toward the self. This is akin to knowing where exactly to insert an acupuncture needle. Although the insertion of a long acupuncture needle may be disquieting, it is much more effective in eliminating physical pain and healing the injury. The insertion of an acupuncture needle into an injured area is like the unpleasant task of turning toward the mind state of hate. Working with the mettā is akin to acupuncture treatment. The precision in identifying the insertion point for acupuncture is akin to the precision of accurately identifying and recognizing the mind state of hate. The insertion of the acupuncture needle is akin to interventions for the developing mettā.

After the first step of identifying irritation, anger, hatred, or ill will, the second step for the development of loving-kindness is to choose an object to which mettā (loving-kindness) is to be directed. Buddhaghosa (1956/2010) explicitly prohibited directing compassion "toward the following four kinds of persons: an antipathetic person, a very dearly loved friend, a neutral person, and a hostile person. Also, it should not be developed specifically towards the opposite sex, or towards a dead person" (p. 291). Updating these instructions to the 21st century United States, one should not choose any group of individuals to whom one has an erotic attraction. In general, do not choose any being that is erotic or elicits sexual feelings or attractions. Buddhaghosa's (1956/2010) reasoning for these prohibitions was as follows:

1. To put an antipathetic person in a dear one's place is fatiguing.
2. To put a very dearly loved friend in a neutral person's place is fatiguing; and if the slightest mischance befalls the friend, he feels like weeping.
3. To put a neutral person in a respected one's or a dear one's place is fatiguing.
4. Anger springs up in him if he recollects a hostile person.
5. If he develops it towards a dead person, he reaches neither absorption nor access.
6. Then, if he develops it specifically towards the opposite sex, lust inspired by that person springs up in him. (p. 291)

Instead, one should choose oneself as the first object of loving-kindness. Buddhaghosa (1956/2010) emphatically directed the person to first focus loving-kindness toward oneself: "First of all, it [loving-kindness] should be developed only towards oneself, doing it repeatedly thus: 'May I keep myself free from enmity, affliction and anxiety and live happily'" (p. 292).

The intervention directive is for the client to turn away from the mind state of hate and to replace it with the beginning training for mettā (loving-kindness). Each time the client notices the presence of irritation, anger, hatred, or ill will, they are to refrain from further entertaining that mind state. Instead, the client is to replace that state with mettā toward themself. For example, whenever the client notices they are calling themself some derogatory name, they are to say to themself, "May I keep myself free from enmity, affliction and anxiety and live happily," as a replacement for any thoughts of criticism, regardless of whether those thoughts are directed toward the self or the other. The first author (Tien) prefers the simpler phrase, "May I be happy. May I be well." The client is to repeat the phrase, "May I be happy. May I be well," until the hate is no longer present. Irrelevant habitual irritation, anger, hatred, or ill will usually dissipate when it is countered by self-talk phrases such as, "May I be happy. May I be well."

However, topics that surface repeatedly, in meditation and in daily activities, are of sufficient concern that they need to be discussed further in session. These repeated topics usually highlight real dangers and concerns that need to be addressed.

Compassion (Karuṇā). Often times, when someone is able to effect loving-kindness toward themself, when they witness another person's unpleasant experiences, compassion spontaneously appears. Buddhaghosa (1956/2010) said,

> For even if he developed loving-kindness for a hundred or a thousand years in this way, "I am happy" and so on, absorption would never arise. But if he develops it in this way: "I am happy. Just as I want to be happy and dread pain, as I want to live and not to die, so do other beings, too," making himself the example, then desire for other beings' welfare and happiness arises in him. (p. 293)

Development of compassion (*karuṇā*) builds on the practice of mettā (loving-kindness). When faced with suffering, one with a mind of loving-kindness would, without much effort, turn toward a mind state of compassion. The initial steps in the development of karuṇā are the same as loving-kindness (mettā):

1. The client is able to accurately identify their mind state of irritation, anger, hatred, or ill will.

2. The client is able to recognize, with some consistency, the presence of that mind state of irritation, anger, hatred, or ill will.

3. The client can reliably interrupt that mind state of irritation, anger, hatred, or ill will with the phrase, "May I be well." At some point, the client will come to realize that they can be the recipient of their own goodwill and reduce the frequency of that critical, angry mind.

4. The client can go into that state of loving-kindness with some level of ease.

At this point, the client is ready to engage with the development of karuṇā (compassion). Compassion is a response to dukkha (suffering, unsatisfactoriness), regardless of whether a person is experiencing dukkha themself or witnessing dukkha experienced by another being. The training for compassion begins with the person being able to see their own suffering. Seeing one's own suffering will most likely be done during the in-session exchanges with the psychotherapist. For the client to show karuṇā toward themself, it is necessary for the client to acknowledge that their experience is dukkha. While this might be self-evident to the psychotherapist and the client agrees that they are not happy, it is often difficult for the client to acknowledge their own experience in the framework of dukkha. However, once identified, the client can be invited to extend the wish to be free from suffering toward themself. This wish to be free from suffering is the expression of karuṇā. The introduction of karuṇā in a session is nuanced and is effective only after the client has experienced numerous instances of karuṇā from the psychotherapist toward the client. At this point, the client may be invited to say to themself whenever they encounter their own dukkha, "May I be well. May I be happy. May I be free from suffering."

The experience of karuṇā (compassion) is not as simple as being willing to say to oneself, "May I be free from suffering." At times, it may be necessary to provide the client with an experience that triggers compassion by witnessing others who they deem as suffering. Choosing the "other" is idiosyncratic and best done in collaboration with the psychotherapist. It is usually best to start with those with whom the client has no emotional involvement. Some examples of in vivo exposure might have the client volunteering to work with individuals experiencing homelessness or migrant resettlement agencies. For an exposure at a distance, the client might watch documentaries that tell the history of almost any marginalized or oppressed group in Europe or the Americas.

Depending on the nature of the client's presenting problem or their life situation, this exposure could also be done in session, with the psychotherapist reframing the client's narrative to highlight the suffering of the people around the client. Having the psychotherapist expose the suffering of others can be accomplished if the client's presenting problem involves others with whom they have a close relationship, such as their spouse, their parents, their in-laws, their supervisor, or any person with whom the client has consistent difficulties.

Once the client is able to entertain the possibility that another person is indeed suffering, the next step is to have the client entertain the idea that "just as I want to be happy and dread pain, as I want to live and not to die, so do other beings, too" (Buddhaghosa, 1956/2010, p. 293). In some Buddhist practices, this is the idea of exchanging self with the other. Compassion begins when one sees the suffering and the helplessness of another person, and then one is able to entertain the idea that the other person is just like oneself in their desire for well-being. Mettā in combination with karuṇā crowds out hate and anger when one experiences the genuine wish, "May I be well. May I be happy. May I be free from suffering," and then extends it to include "May you be well. May you be happy. May you be free from suffering."

Sympathetic joy (Mudita). Intervention to counter jealousy and covetousness is sympathetic joy or gladness (*mudita*). This is gladness at others' success, and it is sometimes rendered as "altruistic joy" and "sympathetic gladness" (Buddhaghosa, 1956/2010, p. 309). Again, the basis for mudita is the person's ability to experience and express mettā (loving-kindness) as well as karuṇā (compassion). The procedural steps start with the process from development of mettā; this is followed by the procedural steps for karuṇā, with the exception of the very last step. Instead of witnessing another person's suffering, the development of mudita is witnessing another person's happiness. Similar to the development for mettā, there are certain types of individuals to avoid in the beginning.

> One who begins the development of gladness should not start with the dear person and the rest; for a dear person is not the proximate cause of gladness merely in virtue of dearness, how much less the neutral and the hostile person. One of the opposite sex and one who is dead are also not the field for it. (Buddhaghosa, 1956/2010, p. 309)

The introduction of mudita (sympathetic joy or gladness) can, again, be done in the treatment session. The client's exposure to this state can start with witnessing their psychotherapist's genuine mudita toward them. There are certain types of individuals that are ideal to aid in development of mudita in the client. The easiest type of person to start with is someone who the client thinks is easygoing and has worked hard to earn their rewards. Again, Buddhaghosa (1956/2010) recommended:

> one who in the commentaries is called a "boon companion," for he is constantly glad: he laughs first and speaks afterwards. So he should be the first to be

pervaded with gladness. Or on seeing or hearing about a dear person being happy, cheerful and glad, gladness can be aroused thus: "This being is indeed glad. How good, how excellent!" . . . But if his boon companion or the dear person was happy in the past but is now unlucky and unfortunate, then gladness can still be aroused by remembering his past happiness and apprehending the glad aspect in this way: "In the past he had great wealth, a great following and he was always glad." Or gladness can be aroused by apprehending the future glad aspect in him in this way: "In the future he will again enjoy similar success." (pp. 309–311)

A common example of sympathetic joy used in Buddhism is what a mother feels when the child has experienced some great achievement or when the child is happy. In psychotherapy, it might be a client reporting the success of some intervention or the resolution of their presenting problem. It would be appropriate and probably much appreciated for the psychotherapist to share in the client's joy of having resolved some difficult life situation.

Equanimity (Upekkhā). Equanimity (*upekkhā*) is a stance of impartiality. This is not the same as neutrality or indifference, especially when that indifference is based on ignorance of the other person's situation. Equanimity is a stance with knowledge of the sufferings and joy of the other and allows for the independence of the other not to be altered in any way by association with oneself. This is a stance that considers all sides in any interaction, from the small dyadic interactions to international conflicts, and is able to entertain the suffering and joys of all involved. This is the abandoning of appropriation and/or identification with another person or situations or even with the five aggregates.

Upekkhā (equanimity) is facilitated by the ability to apply the workings of kamma (cause and effect of the doing of deeds). When things are contextualized within the frame of kamma, there is no room for approval or resentment; things just are. Acknowledging the other person's agency to think, feel, act, and consider independent of oneself allows room for the mind state of equanimity. Buddhaghosa (1956/2010) recommended recitation of the following:

Beings are owners of their deeds. Whose [if not theirs] is the choice by which they will become happy, or will get free from suffering, or will not fall away from the success they have reached? (p. 311)

Upekkhā is the most difficult state to achieve. For the purpose of psychotherapy, this is a state that may not be necessary for a client to live a satisfying life as a householder.

Summary of Ethical Conduct (*Sīla*)

As just described, the Sāleyyaka Sutta (MN, 1995, 41) names three categories of misconduct. These are misconduct by way of the body, speech, and mind. The format of the sutta first lists what not to do before enumerating what to do. The first set of behavior directives addresses the actions of the body. Speech can be considered a subset of the actions performed by the body. The behaviors for acting ethically, for training in sīla, are phrased as directives as follows:

• Not to kill beings
• Not to take what is not freely given
• Not to have sex with inappropriate persons
• Not to speak falsehoods, either by omission or commission
• Not to engage in divisive speech
• Not to engage in hateful speech
• Not to engage in idle chatter or gossip (MN, 1995, 41)

This set of behaviors avoids actions that have the highest probability of producing negative future situations. To mitigate the push behind the misconducts of the body and speech, one is to train the mind. One of the methods for training the mind is to replace one mind state with another mind state. The method used to train the mind is to replace covetousness, ill will, and delusion with the four divine abodes of loving-kindness, compassion, sympathetic joy, and equanimity. Hate and ill will are replaced by loving-kindness; ill will and cruelty are replaced by compassion; covetousness is replaced by sympathetic joy; and partiality of in-group favoring that is a by-product of the delusion of self-referencing is replaced by equanimity.

The Buddha gave his son, Rāhula, a good and concise summary of all the steps that result in sīla (ethical conduct). Psychotherapists might utilize the Buddha's summary, in which he helps his son to engage in right action and right speech, in their treatment intervention as well:

> Rāhula, when you wish to do an action with the [body . . . speech . . . mind] you should reflect upon that same [bodily . . . speech . . . mind] action thus: "Would this action that I [wish to do . . . am doing . . . did] with the [body . . . speech . . . mind] lead to my own affliction, or to the affliction of others, or to the affliction of both? Is it an unwholesome [bodily . . . speech . . . mind] action with painful consequences, with painful results?" When you reflect, if you know: "This action that I [wish to do . . . am doing . . . did] with the [body . . . speech . . . mind] would lead to my own affliction, or to the affliction of others, or to the affliction of both; it is an unwholesome [bodily . . . speech . . . mind] action with painful consequences, with painful results," then you definitely

should not do such an action with the [body . . . speech . . . mind]. But when you reflect, if you know: "This action that I [wish to do . . . am doing . . . did] with the body would not lead to my own affliction, or to the affliction of others, or to the affliction of both; it is a wholesome [bodily . . . speech . . . mind] action with pleasant consequences, with pleasant results," then you may do such an action with the [body . . . speech . . . mind]. (Ambalaṭṭhikāhulovadā Sutta; MN, 1995, 61.9: Advice to Rāhula at Ambalaṭṭhikā)

To aid in achieving those Brahmā-vihāras (divine abodes) is to adopt a mind state that contacts right view, which is one that holds the principles of kamma. Kamma is the topic of the next section of this chapter.

CAUSE AND EFFECT OF THE DOING OF DEEDS (*KAMMA*)

The previous section discussed the list of prescribed behaviors. As noted previously, the idiosyncratic nature of a client's difficulties presented in psychotherapy may make using a prescribed list of behaviors difficult to administer. In such a case, we turn to the principle that guided the Buddha Gotama's list of prescribed behaviors, which is the concept of kamma.

I am the owner of my kamma, the heir of my kamma; I have kamma as my relative, kamma as my resort; I will be the heir of whatever kamma, good or bad, that I do. . . . I am not the only one who is the owner of one's kamma, the heir of one's kamma. . . . All beings that come and go, that pass away and undergo rebirth, are owners of their kamma. (Abhiṇhapaccavekkhitabbaṭhāna Sutta; AN, 2012, 5.57)

The guiding principle for sīla (ethical conduct) is kamma. The general idea of kamma (cause and effect of the doing of deeds) is that one's actions, especially those motivated by greed, hatred, or delusion, have consequences, both internally and externally. Although all actions have consequences, intentional actions hold more kammic affect than nonintentional actions. This means that doing of a deed that results in unintended consequences is not as significant as doing the same deed with intentions that are fueled by greed, hatred, or delusion. One popular common misconception about kamma is reflected in the adage, "What goes around comes around." This attitude tends to be self-referencing, as in the following example:

What is happening to me is a direct result of my past actions. If nice things are happening to me, then it is because I have done good things in the past and these nice things are my reward. Or that if bad things are happening to me, it is also because of my past actions and these bad things are my punishment.

In a very general broad sense, kamma (cause and effect of the doing of deeds) does imply that what goes around comes around. However, in its narrowest sense, one's past actions do not have a 1:1 correlation with one's present situation.

The Theravāda Abhidhamma principle of conditional relations or causal relationships (*paṭṭhānanaya*), or the formulation of conditionality ("Nothing arises from a single cause; Nothing arises as a single effect"), does not support the cosmic design of a 1:1 correlation between cause and effect of the doing of deeds. The world is much too complex for such simplistic 1:1 correlation. There are conditions that influence the doing of a deed and conditions that influence the effect of that deed done. Regardless of the conditions, actions motivated by greed, hatred, and delusion influence future situations toward the unpleasant; actions motived by loving-kindness and compassion influence future situations toward pleasant experiences for the person.

Think of kamma (cause and effect of the doing of deeds) as a pebble (volitional thought [*cetanā*]) thrown (action) into a pond (the external universe) that generates ripples (effects on others) in the water. If kamma is a pebble and that pebble (a deed done) is thrown into a pond (the universe), it would generate ripples in the water. When one pebble is dropped into a small bowl of water, the ripples are distinct and easily seen. When three pebbles are successively thrown into a small pond of still water, the interacting effects of the ripples from each pebble thrown are sufficiently distinct to be seen. It is clear that the wake from each pebble affects the ripples generated from each successive pebble. When a thousand pebbles are thrown into a sea, there still are ripples from each pebble. The wake from each pebble thrown will still affect the ripples from other pebbles. However, the interactive effects are much more complex and much less discernible. There are hundreds of thousands of actions occurring at any one moment in time, each with its own ripples. The probability of one person having much control over what happens is extremely low because there are just too many moving parts at play at any one time. Instead of considering kamma (cause and effect of the doing of deeds) in terms of 1:1 correlation, think of it in terms of probabilities. In the midst of a multitude of actions done, each influencing the other, the probability of a consistent effect is increased if the same kind of action is done repeatedly. Additionally, probabilities are increased for a person to influence and be influenced by those actions done in closest proximity. Thinking in terms of probabilities, the probability of having nice, pleasant things come back to oneself is increased through increasing the number of nice, pleasant things one does, thus increasing the probabilities that the many nice, pleasant actions one does will have a repeated ripple effect. In other words, by doing nice, kind, and pleasant actions repeatedly, a person will increase the probabilities of having those actions affect others positively, and, in turn, they will react positively to the person, increasing their chances of having pleasant situations in the future.

The phrase, "I am the owner of my kamma" (AN, 2012, 5.57), says that one is responsible for one's actions, regardless of whether one accepts those responsibilities. This also means that the lack of intent (e.g., "I did not mean it") cannot be used as a way to excuse oneself from the effect of one's actions. Just because one did not intend to have a harmful effect does not somehow mean the affect is not harmful. One cannot escape the fact that one did do the deed. In general, unintentional consequences do not hold as much kammic effect as actions done with intention. This means, for psychotherapy, we can encourage clients to apologize for those harmful deeds that resulted in unintended consequences and also encourage them to be clear about their intentions before taking action.

The phrase, "I am . . . the heir of my kamma" (AN, 2012, 5.57), says that there are consequences of what one does. Regardless of one's intentions, one's actions have consequences that they cannot escape. Actions done without intent to harm, regardless of the harm done, hold less harmful consequences. For example, a person sitting and talking with a friend while cleaning a handgun has no intention of shooting and harming this friend. If, sadly, the gun accidentally fires and a bullet hits the friend, the friend is physically harmed. The person cleaning the gun cannot say, "Oh, I did not mean to shoot you," and leave the friend unattended. As such, one's actions are consequential. However, the consequence of accidentally shooting a friend will have a less harmful effect on the friendship than if the shooting was intentional. Regardless, whether the deed done has the intended or unintended effect, there is no sudden forgiveness by some divine power that wipes away all of one's past harmful actions. Those deeds done with intention hold more potential to shape the person's disposition, personality, and experiences.

The phrase, "I am not the only one who is the owner of one's kamma" (AN, 2012, 5.57), points to two things. In terms of psychotherapy, one is that what another person has experienced is due to their life situation, not necessarily caused by the client. This takes away self-referencing for another person's actions, like thinking, "If only I had been more loving, they would not have been so upset and distracted that they ran a red light and got into a car crash." The other thing it points to is that we are all alike in that all beings "are owners of their kamma" (AN, 2012, 5.57). This is the universality of consequences of action taken; deeds done. There is no such thing as avoiding consequences (i.e., "How come they get away with it?"). This is a stance that says, ultimately, this is a just world, regardless of whether that justice is dealt in such a way that is obviously observable.

Taken as a whole, kamma (cause and effect of the doing of deeds) posits that regardless of what one wants or what one intended, one's actions do have consequences. At a minimum, one's actions affect other people, and, in turn, their reaction affects oneself. Knowing that there are consequences to whatever one does precludes considering actions based solely on what one wishes and desires without regard for how it will affect others. What appears to be a reasonable action for one person does not necessarily mean the action is not harmful to someone else. Clinically, one area in which this often manifests is divorce situations. There may be persuasive and reasonable reasons why divorce is the best course of action for married couples; nonetheless, their decision to divorce has an enormous impact on their children.

Many people hold the unspoken and unexamined propositions that if they "did not mean it" and "it has nothing to do with you," then "you have no business reacting to what I do." They are often surprised or offended when there are consequences and they are somehow held accountable for their actions, regardless of their intentions.

In a broad general sense, one's past actions do have some influence on the present. Many consider their present misfortune to be caused by their past bad deeds, carrying much guilt for what they have done. Some Buddhist communities posit that even if one has committed egregious deeds in the past, and that the present misfortune is punishment for those past deeds, the event of present misfortune is like serving time in jail. Thus, when the present misfortune passes, it is like being released from jail. Once released from jail, then having paid the price for the misdeed, one is freed from past harmful deeds and is now free to establish a new and different future. This allows one then to look to the present to lay the foundations for future kamma (cause and effect of the doing of deeds).

Not only does one's past action have some influence on the present, but one's present action will have some influence on one's future. Holding on to the formula, "I am the owner of my kamma, the heir of my kamma" (AN, 2012, 5.57), points to the fact that people have agency. While the Buddha said that the experience of existence is dukkha (suffering, unsatisfactoriness), the process of individual existence is doing or kamma (cause and effect of the doing of deeds). What a person chooses to do in terms of action of body, speech, and mind does affect their situation in either the immediate or distant future.

For psychotherapy, it is more relevant to focus on the idea that kamma (cause and effect of the doing of deeds) does not just go from the past to the present. Kamma is built on the actions taken now. Actions taken now will affect a person's future kamma. The approach in psychotherapy might take the form of acknowledging that bad deeds done in the past may have contributed to the present unfortunate situation, then rejoicing in the elimination of further consequences of the past deed and focusing on present activity to build good future kamma. This mindset invites both the psychotherapist and the client to think about what to do now to influence future situations, instead of reacting to the present situation.

CLINICAL EXAMPLE OF WORKING WITH KAMMA

The idea that what one does affects their situation might appear to be such a simplistic and self-evident statement that it borders on being a platitude. However, when one listens carefully to what a client typically talks about, it is rarely about how their own behavior affects the situation. The verbal content of a client's speech is usually focused on how they feel, what they think, and how others' behaviors affect them. It is rarely, if at all, considered how their own actions of body, speech, and mind affect their situation in the past, present, or near distant future. Additionally, clients do not usually approach their difficulties with the belief that they hold agency and that they have a choice.

On the scale of platitudes, most people would, in theory, concur with the idea that they do have a choice. However, on the scale of moment-to-moment action, most people do not see that they have a choice nor do they experience the choice point. Let us consider a clinical example: A client presented with complaints of procrastination. Instead of doing her homework when she sat down in front of her computer, she would instead end up on social media, shopping or planning for some social event. The result was that she was in danger of being dismissed from college for failing too many courses for not turning in her assignments on time. She had tried all sorts of things, such as reading self-help books, talking to school counselors about how to stop being a procrastinator, and studying with friends instead of being in the library by herself. Her efforts were all to no avail. In using the Buddhist psychotherapy approach, the student was asked to recount what exactly happened in her mind when she approached her homework. The psychotherapist chose the object of contemplation as the moment when the client sat down and looked at her computer. It took about a month's worth of observing and processing what she observed. She first reported copious amounts of negative self-talk. Then she would counter these negative statements with positive affirmations, like "Believe in yourself," "Be calm," or "You can do it." Instead of being caught up in the notion of herself (being a procrastinator), the in-session focus repeatedly returned to analyzing the mind state at the moment of sitting down in front of her computer. One day, the client announced in session that she had successfully not procrastinated and instead had done all of her homework in the last few days. To the inquiry of what made the change, she said, "I noticed one whisper of a fleeting thought that said, 'I don't want to deal with this!'" She was surprised by this thought, and then noticed that at that moment, she could decide to "deal with it." That was when she decided not to log into her social media account on her laptop computer and proceeded to move it to her bedroom; then she sat down at her desktop computer with the thought, "I can decide when to do social media." She had branded herself as a procrastinator and was busy building a life around that identity. She missed noticing the moment when she held agency to do something different to change her future.

In its relevance to psychotherapy, kamma (cause and effect of the doing of deeds) has its seed in the mind. That one whisper of the fleeting thought of "I don't want to deal with this!" was the volitional mental formation that generated the client's cascade of mental proliferations resulting in the action of not doing her homework. It is those volitional thoughts that are of consequence because they lead to action, and action affects oneself, others, and thus future situations. Body, speech, and mind are the three doors to doing. The psychotherapist's task is to discern the critical moment, direct the client's attention to that specific critical moment, and then invite the client to notice what occurs in their mind at that critical moment. In the example with the young person who was in danger of failing school, the psychotherapist's job was to first select one moment in the client's daily life for her to focus on.

There are any number of moments on which to focus the client's attention. It is best to choose a moment that is very specific and occurs repeatedly. For most people who are not skilled meditators, it is difficult to catch those cetanā (volitional formations). So, it is necessary to choose a moment that tends to repeat itself, thus giving the client a chance to revisit that mind state. In the example just described, the psychotherapist chose for this client to focus on the moment when she first sat down to her computer before she started doing anything. What this client chose to do at the one moment before turning on her computer directed kamma (cause and effect of the doing of deeds) to a future in which she did not fail college.

CONCLUSION

For use in psychotherapy, the application of kamma (cause and effect of the doing of deeds) would be based on the considerations of how a person's actions and behavior affect the environment of their mind and how one's actions and behavior now will most likely affect one's situation in the future. The general concept is to avoid actions that have foreseeable negative effects on oneself and others and to pursue actions that have high probabilities of generating positive kamma. This general idea is contained in the Fourth Noble Truths and the Noble Eightfold Path and can guide psychotherapists' recommendations to clients.

15

EMPLOYING THE SECOND TRACK OF THE NOBLE EIGHTFOLD PATH IN PSYCHOTHERAPY

Mindfulness

This chapter examines the practice of concentration or mindfulness (*samādhi*), which is cultivated by engaging in meditation with the goal of training the mind to notice. The instructions for the initial stages in the development of samādhi (concentration, meditation, mental development) are the bases for many of the current mindfulness-based intervention programs. This chapter examines the Satipaṭṭhāna Sutta (*Majjhima Nikāya* [MN], 1995, 10: The Foundations of Mindfulness), one of the suttas that gives instructions on meditation technique for cultivation of mindfulness. Each section in this chapter will first present the text of the sutta, explicate the indicated techniques, name the objects of contemplation, and then end with the intended insight (*vipassanā*) from the contemplation of the chosen object.

INTRODUCTION TO SATIPAṬṬHĀNA SUTTA

The Buddha Gotama provided instructions on how to engage in silent meditation throughout the *Nikāya*, with two primary suttas that give comprehensive guidance. The Satipaṭṭhāna Sutta is one set of such instructions.

https://doi.org/10.1037/0000453-016
Buddhist Psychotherapy: Connecting Early Buddhism to Mindfulness and Western Psychotherapy, by L. Tien, D. M. Kawahara, and V. Dhammadinna

This sutta is also the one referenced and its practice used in many of the mindfulness-based intervention programs. The claim for the method given in this sutta is as follows:

> Bhikkhus, this is the direct path for the purification of beings, for the sur-mounting of sorrow and lamentation, for the disappearance of pain and grief, for the attainment of the true way, for the realization of Nibbāna—namely, the four foundations of mindfulness.
> What are the four? Here, bhikkhus, a bhikkhu abides contemplating the body as a body, . . . contemplating feelings as feelings, . . . contemplating mind as mind, . . . contemplating mind-objects as mind-objects, ardent, fully aware, and mindful, having put away covetousness and grief for the world. (MN, 1995, 10)

The name of the Satipaṭṭhāna Sutta is generally translated as the "Founda-tions of Mindfulness" and sometimes as the "Four Foundations of Mindful-ness." The four foundations, as named in Bhikkhu Bodhi's translation, are (a) contemplation of body, (b) contemplation of feelings, (c) contemplation of mind, and (d) contemplation of mind objects. Each category of objects of contemplation corresponds to the *khandhā* (five aggregates) minus *viññāna* (consciousness).

The first object is the contemplation of body (*kāyā*). The Pali word kāyā is differentiated from *rūpa* (materiality), which is one of the five aggregates that includes all material forms found in the universe, including the human body. The contemplation here is specifically on the constituent parts of the human body, not the contemplation of all material forms found in the universe.

The second object is the contemplation of hedonic feeling tone (*vedanā*). The earlier quote from the Satipaṭṭhāna Sutta (MN, 1995, 10) translates vedanā as "feelings." As discussed previously, the term feelings, especially in its colloquial usage, does not capture the meaning of vedanā. Contemplation of vedanā is to notice the whole person's response to the contact with a sense object. There is only one vedanā that accompanies one sense contact. This one response includes elements of the soma as well as the psyche.

The third object is contemplation of the mind (*citta*). The quote from the Satipaṭṭhāna Sutta translates the term citta as "mind." This is the overall dis-position of the mind, more like the colloquial meaning of the phrase "hearts and minds."

The fourth object is contemplation of mind objects (*dhammas*). The quote from the Satipaṭṭhāna Sutta translates the term dhammas as "mind objects." Based on the items included in these contemplations, dhammas might be thought of as mind states or phenomena, as opposed to noumena.

In addition to each of the four main categories of objects for contemplation, there are subcategories. Psychotherapists can choose from this extensive list of objects for contemplation (discussed later in this chapter), depending on the psychotherapist's proficiency in their own meditative practice and the specifics of their client's difficulties. For the psychotherapist, it is more useful to notice these objects of contemplation as they show up in the treatment room and to take them as topics for in-session dialogue.

Expositions of the Satipaṭṭhāna Sutta (MN, 1995, 10) are voluminous from the more than 2,500-year history that Buddhists have been practicing meditation. It is outside the scope of this book to examine the significance of the Satipaṭṭhāna Sutta or to explicate the practice of mindfulness meditation. What follows here is an extremely brief introduction, only for the purpose of and confined to the initial use of cultivating the foundations of mindfulness as given in the Satipaṭṭhāna Sutta for use with psychotherapy. This material can be useful in the psychotherapist's own meditation practice or used as a model for in-session focus where the psychotherapist takes on the function of mindfulness, as well as outside of the session meditation homework for the client. If done in session, then consider the following discussion as a directive on what to focus on and talk about in session, modeling as if the whole session is a sitting meditation session with the psychotherapist functioning as mindfulness (*sati*) accompanying the patient into their mind. If done outside of session as assigned homework, then in-session check-in and follow-up are needed. The in-session follow-up may be more informative when built on the entry into a client's meditation journal.

The approach described next is for those psychotherapists who are engaged in their own meditation practices and wish to include meditation in their treatment regime by applying some of the technique as explicated in the Satipaṭṭhāna Sutta (MN, 1995, 10). As noted previously and worth mentioning again, any technique that has great potential to heal also has great potential to harm. Meditation retreat teachers know well the harmful effects of leaving a disturbed mind to its own devices in silent meditation; it has been known to lead to psychotic episodes as well as suicidal ideation and suicide. If the approach described is used as homework or as time in session, consider using a guided meditation. Choose carefully to whom to assign silent meditation as homework.

MINDFULNESS DEFINED

The term *mindfulness*, as used in mindfulness-based interventions in U.S. psychology, is not quite the same as the term *sati* used in the Satipaṭṭhāna Sutta. The *APA Dictionary of Psychology* defines mindfulness as follows:

> Awareness of one's internal states and surroundings. The concept has been
> applied to various therapeutic interventions . . . to help people avoid destructive

or automatic habits and responses by learning to observe their thoughts, emotions, and other present-moment experiences without judging or reacting to them. (American Psychological Association [APA], n.d.)

In the APA definition, mindfulness is "awareness of their internal states . . . without judging or reacting to them." This mindfulness meditation method is often used for relaxation, with the goal of inducing a state of peacefulness. For beginning meditators, it may be the first opportunity for the mind to rest after a long period of constant activity. This resting state of stillness may be likened to the temporary quietude of an object floating in a tranquil stretch of the river. If such a state is achieved, that experience may be pleasant. Many, if not most, beginning meditators do not achieve such a state of mind, and they turn to guided meditation recordings to achieve such a state of relaxation. The meditation training to teach sati (mindfulness) is to teach the meditator to be standing on the riverbanks, safe from the occasional stillness or turbulence of the water in the river. Everyday life is like a person (consciousness) caught in the flow of a river (mental phenomenon), some-times going through a turbulent stretch and sometimes going through a calm stretch of the river. The untrained person tries to stay afloat in the river of mental phenomena by clinging to whatever convenient object floats by. In guided meditation, this is like hanging on to a piece of wood floating on the river. In daily life, the flotation device is usually the client's mental pro-liferations and those derivative feelings and, at times, changing the object of clinging as some more attractive or engaging debris floats by. In meditation, sati is the stillness of standing on the riverbank, watching the river and noting all the objects floating by.

For the purpose of using meditation in Buddhist psychotherapy, it is much more useful to take the textual meaning of the Pali word sati in the Satipaṭṭhāna Sutta. Sati is defined in the *Pali Text Society's Pali–English Dictionary* as "memory, recognition, consciousness" (Pali Text Society, n.d.). In the Nagara Sutta, the Buddha likened sati (mindfulness) to a fortress gatekeeper:

Just as the gatekeeper in the king's frontier fortress is wise, competent, and intelligent, one who keeps out strangers and admits acquaintances, for pro-tecting its inhabitants and for warding off outsiders, so too a noble disciple is mindful, possessing supreme mindfulness and alertness, one who remembers and recollects what was done and said long ago. With mindfulness as his gatekeeper, the noble disciple abandons the unwholesome and develops the wholesome, abandons what is blameworthy and develops what is blameless, and maintains himself in purity. He possesses this sixth good quality. (*Aṅguttara Nikāya* [AN], 2012, 7.67: Simile of the Fortress)

Sati (mindfulness, to remember) as the gatekeeper has the function of remembering to be vigilantly watching what arises in the mind—remembering the instructions on what to admit for further exploration, what not to dwell upon, and what to keep out. (Note: When *sati* is used in the textual meaning, it refers to "mindfulness, to remember." When *sati* is used in the psychology intervention meaning, it refers to "mindfulness." These distinctions are made throughout this chapter.) The objective is to remember what one is supposed to be doing. What one is supposed to be doing is named as the object of contemplation before the meditator begins their meditation session and throughout their daily activities. The usual and customary object of contemplation is the breath. For psychotherapists using sati (mindfulness) as an intervention, the method for choosing an object of contemplation is discussed extensively in the next section. The textual meaning of the Pali word sati (mindfulness, to remember) is to remember what task the mind should be doing. The what is the objects of contemplation, which are the body, feelings, mind, and mind objects. The task, or object of contemplation, is designated at the beginning of each meditation session.

Contrary to the APA definition of mindfulness to be aware of "one's internal states and surroundings . . . without judging or reacting to them" (APA, n.d.), the guard necessarily needs to make judgments: "Sati keeps out strangers and admits acquaintances, for protecting its inhabitants and for warding off outsiders" (AN, 2012, 7.67.3). Sati (mindfulness, to remember) needs to make judgments in order to fulfill the function of deciding what is within the scope of the assigned object of contemplation. Therefore, decisions or judgments are made about what to keep in the mind, what is not within the scope of the assigned object (therefore, what to abandon), and what to develop (therefore, what to persist). To accomplish this objective, sati (mindfulness, to remember) makes judgments. This type of judging is different from colloquial usage of the term, as used in the *APA Dictionary of Psychology* definition of mindfulness ("without judging or reacting to them"; APA, n.d.). The APA definition of *judgment* is "the capacity to recognize relationships, draw conclusions from evidence, and make critical evaluations of events and people" (APA, n.d.), which is in line with the definition and usage of the word sati (mindfulness, to remember). The colloquial usage and meaning of the term "judging" is closer to the meaning of "judgmental," which means "of, relating to, or involving judgment characterized by a tendency to judge harshly" (Merriam-Webster, n.d.). The task of sati (mindfulness, to remember) is to first remember what the task is, then to sort through the activities of the mind to determine which are on task and which are off task, then to ignore those activities in the mind that are off task, and, finally, to return the mind to the activities that are on task.

Breaking down the tasks for sati (mindfulness) as a gatekeeper is the first step to identify the object in the mind. If the breath is taken as the object of meditation, then sati (mindfulness) has to identify whether the phenomenon in consciousness is or is not part of the breath. For example, to the thought, "I wonder what is in the refrigerator that's good to eat when I am done with this meditation sitting," sati (mindfulness, to remember) has to notice that the mind/citta is thinking about food. Once noticed, then sati (mindfulness, to remember) is to identify and label that activity. Sati (mindfulness, to remember) has to decide whether thinking about what to make for dinner is about the breath or not. To the thought, "I wonder what is in the refrigerator that's good to eat when I am done with this meditation sitting," sati (mindfulness) applies the label "hindrance of sensual desire." Then sati (mindfulness, to remember) has to determine whether the observed phenomenon in consciousness is conducive to keeping the mind on the breath. Sati (mindfulness, to remember) has to notice that planning the dinner menu is not within the realm of the breath, and thus should not be dwelled upon but set aside. Finally, sati (mindfulness, to remember) has to decide whether to linger on the phenomenon, as in whether to continue contemplating the dinner menu. Because thinking about what to make for dinner is not part of the breath, sati (mindfulness, to remember) has to stop the mind from continuing to plan the dinner menu and return to the breath. If, however, the thought is "the breath is high on the chest, close to the throat," then sati (mindfulness, to remember) would judge this phenomenon in consciousness as on task about the breath and continue this line of thought and observation. The job of sati (mindfulness, to remember) is to keep the mind/citta on the task chosen at the beginning of the meditation session— be it to contemplate the breath, the vedanā (hedonic feeling tone), the mind/citta, or the mind state of hindrances.

MENTAL QUALITIES FOR UNDERTAKING MINDFULNESS MEDITATION (*SATI*)

The Buddha, in the repeating refrain throughout the Satipaṭṭhāna Sutta (MN, 1995, 10), gives instructions on how to set the mind as the meditator approaches the activity of meditation, calling forth sati (mindfulness) to guard the mind.

First, we briefly review the material covered in Chapter 8 (this volume), which introduced silent meditation as means to development of mindfulness. The Buddha's first instruction of how to prepare one's mind for meditation was as follows:

> Here a bhikkhu, gone to the forest, to the root of a tree, or to an empty hut, sits down, having folded his legs crosswise, set his body erect, and established mindfulness in front of him. (MN, 1995, 10)

A word of caution is needed here in these modern times of the internet and smartphone applications: Implementation of the phrase, "established mindfulness in front of him," does not mean for the meditator to use the numerous mindfulness applications available online and via other digital sources. Many of these applications are good at training the mind to follow instructions; however, they do not train the mind to focus.

Having found a space that is consistently private (i.e., no pets coming in to cuddle) and quiet, the repeating refrain in the Satipaṭṭhāna Sutta instructs the meditator to be "ardent (ātāpīn), fully aware (sampajāna), and mindful, having put away covetousness and grief for the world" (MN, 1995, 10). An alternative translation is to be "diligent (ātāpīn), clearly knowing (sampajāna), and mindful, free from desires and discontent in regard to the world" (Anālayo, 2018, p. 34). These two translations are referenced for the sake of getting a fuller sense of the meaning for the how one is to go about approaching the objective of meditation. The term *ātāpīn* is translated as "ardent" by Bhikkhu Bodhi (MN, 1995, 10) and as "diligent" by Bhikkhu Anālayo (2018, p. x). The *Pali Text Society's Pali–English Dictionary* defines ātāpin as "ardent, zealous, strenuous, active" (Pali Text Society, n.d.). *Sampajāna* is likewise translated as "fully aware" or "clearly knowing." The *Pali Text Society's Pali–English Dictionary* defines sampajāna as "thoughtful, mindful, attentive, deliberate" (Pali Text Society, n.d.). These translations point to the intent and will be used interchangeably in this chapter.

Ardent and Diligent (*Ātāpin*)

In the context of psychotherapy, ātāpīn (ardent, diligent) can be operationalized as repetitive effort. Within the meditation sitting, this effort can take the form of repeatedly going back to the object of contemplation. If the breath is the object of contemplation in meditation, then the meditator would try to continuously hold their attention on the breath and repeatedly go back to the breath (over and over again) when the attention shifts off the breath. In everyday life, it can take the form of a commitment to remember to pay attention to the object of meditation at any moment in time. For clients in psychotherapy, ātāpīn can be in the form of keeping the psychotherapy appointment on a regular basis and remembering to carry out any instructions from the psychotherapy session into daily activities. For psychotherapists, it can be keeping in mind that the goal of psychotherapy is to sufficiently address the client's presenting complaint in a manner that enables the client to effectively continue on the path of life and not to wander off and discuss items that are not relevant to their presenting problem. This means for the psychotherapist to hold in mind sati (mindfulness, remembering), the ever-present tasks of analyzing and reframing the client's experience within the framework of early Buddhist theory in the service of increasing flexibility in the client's ability to address their presenting problem.

Fully Aware and Clearly Knowing (*Sampajāna*)

Sampajāna (fully aware and clearly knowing) cannot be operationalized in one simple directive. For meditative contemplation, sampajāna is the precise, analytical, and comprehensive familiarity with the object of contemplation. This means, for example, if the breath is the object of contemplation, the meditation directive is to get to know anything and everything there is to know about the breath. Some of what can be known about the breath is specified in the Satipaṭṭhāna Sutta, as follows:

> Breathing in long, he understands: "I breathe in long"; or breathing out long, he understands; "I breathe out long." Breathing in short, he understands: "I breathe in short"; or breathing out short, he understands: "I breathe out short." . . . Just as a skilled lathe-operator or his apprentice, when making a long turn, understands: "I make a long turn"; or, when making a short turn, understands: "I make a short turn"; so too, breathing in long, a bhikkhu under-stands: "I breathe in long." (MN, 1995, 10)

There are, generally speaking, four aspects to sampajāna (fully aware and clearly knowing). These aspects are (a) why, (b) how, (c) generalizing into daily activities, and (d) keeping in mind that activity of contemplation itself is a product of the mind. Each aspect is discussed next.

First and foremost, the meditator needs to be clear about why they are taking the specified object of contemplation. For example, if the breath is the object of contemplation in meditation, both the client and the psycho-therapist need to know why the breath is the object in terms of the client's presenting problem. In Buddhist spiritual practice, a determining factor in deciding whether the object is appropriate for contemplation is whether this act will aid in the path of liberation. For psychotherapy, this can be trans-lated into whether the object of contemplation will aid toward the resolution of the client's presenting problem. It would be appropriate to take a calming object like the breath if the client presents with anxiety. However, the same object of the breath would be inappropriate if, for example, the client has a history of some kind of trauma. For many, memory of the trauma tends to reside in the body. Some clients with a history of trauma may guard against the experience of the trauma by cultivating a stance of inattention of the body. For these individuals, care needs to be taken in reintroducing them to their body. Contemplation of the breath may inadvertently reengage the person with their body memory of the past trauma. Instead of taking the breath as the object of contemplation, it may be more appropriate to initially take another type of object that is less encompassing for contemplation, like sound. Another example would be if a client leans toward the hindered mind state of sloth and torpor, in which case taking a calming object like the breath would most likely lead quickly and directly to nodding off in meditation. In such a case, it may be more appropriate to use, for example, sound as the object of contemplation. Or, when the person leans toward sensual desire, say for food, it may be advisable for the client to physically separate themself from the object of sensual desire (e.g., not baking a roast in the oven, which generates a rich aroma, while sitting in silent meditation).

Both the client and the psychotherapist need to be able to agree on and clearly answer the question in relationship to the client's presenting complaint: "Why am I taking, and why should I take, this object for the focus of my meditative contemplation?" Another way to phrase the question might be: "Why would contemplation of this object help with my presenting problem?"

Second to knowing the why of taking an action, sampajāna (fully aware and clearly knowing), is the how. The question to consider is: "What is the most suitable way to fulfill the goal/purpose?" For our previous example of the student struggling with procrastination (Chapter 14), instead of taking the breath as the object of contemplation, she was assigned the moment of directing the computer cursor to a website as her object of contemplation. For the example of the person with a history of trauma, the question might be phrased as follows: "What is the most suitable way to address my presenting problem without sliding back to overwhelming immersion of the traumatic incident?" A suitable topic for in-session discussion might be to explore what aspects of the soma are involved in the current presenting complaint. The determining consideration is whether this object of contemplation is conducive for the fulfillment of one's purpose without foreseeable harm to oneself or to others.

The third aspect of sampajāna (fully aware and clearly knowing) is the act of keeping the object of contemplation continuously in mind during daily activities. For the meditation of taking the breath as part of the contemplation of the body, the meditator in a silent meditation retreat is to keep the mind focused on the breath as they go about daily activities, such as eating, bathing, and preparing for bed, and not just while on the meditation cushion. A person not at a meditation retreat might be invited to periodically check in with their breath, as they go about their daily activities, especially during stressful situations. For the student struggling with procrastination, it is recommended that she keep in mind what task she has decided to undertake throughout the day, whether she is cleaning the house or talking to a friend (instead of thinking about what to post on social media).

The fourth aspect of sampajāna (fully aware and clearly knowing) is to keep in perspective that the activity of contemplation itself is a product of the mind, however one might consider the object of meditation. The mind has a tendency to create illusions of permanence. Knowing that the mind tends to see permanence in phenomena, sampajāna is to consider the impermanence of the phenomenon in the mind.

The first step in the operationalization of sampajāna (fully aware and clearly knowing) is the appropriate categorization of things occurring in consciousness. Using the metaphor of the guard at the city gate, sampajāna is the guard accurately identifying every person who comes and goes through the city gate. For psychotherapy, it would be identifying the category of the type of suffering (e.g., dukkha-dukkha, or type of hindered mind state). The second step in the operationalization of sampajāna might be to progress to a second layer of categorization. For the guard at the gate, it would be in knowing the traveler's purpose for entering the city, that being a merchant coming for trade in the market or a refugee seeking shelter in the city. Finally, the third step is to determine whether the traveler is friend or foe. For psychotherapy, it would be to determine the purpose of whatever phenomenon might be arising in consciousness.

The attitude of sampajāna (fully aware and clearly knowing), in combination with ātāpīn (ardent and diligent), is for the meditator to make a commitment to be sufficiently attentive so as to identify accurately the phenomenon that occurs in consciousness. To practice sati (mindfulness) as prescribed in the Satipaṭṭhāna Sutta (MN, 1995, 10), the meditator has to always remember what the mind is to be occupied with, like the breath, and not be wandering off to replay a disturbing conversation or to plan the dinner menu. The mindset or attitude toward one's activity is to strive for the continuous knowledge, awareness, and understanding of why a particular object is chosen for contemplation and how one's chosen activity (i.e., contemplation of the breath) serves one's goal. This is not to say that there is an expectation for one to achieve such a state of consistently accurate awareness. This is not a realistic expectation for those of us who are not an *arahant* (one who has attained a state of total liberation from life's suffering [*nibbāna*]; Pali Text Society, n.d.), let alone for a psychotherapist or a psychotherapy client. The directive is for the person to make a commitment to strive for such mastery.

Having Put Away Covetousness (Longing) and Grief (Dejection) as Well as Free From Desires and Discontent (*Vineyya Abhijjhādomanassa*)

In the lexicon of clinical mental health practice, the term *vineyya abhijjhā-domanassa*, which means having put away covetousness and grief as well as free from desires and discontent, may be to adopt a stance of meta-cognition. It is like taking the attitude of standing on the side of the river, observing the flow of the water (phenomenon in consciousness) and objects (metal forma-tions) that float by in the river. For psychotherapy, vineyya abhijjhādomanassa can be operationalized as approaching whatever is being experienced with the attitude of analyzing the experience at a meta-cognitive level and in making things impersonal. Psychotherapists might use the technique of objectifying and gaining distance from the client's presenting problem by referring to the client's problem as an object. In discussion with the client, the psychothera-pist could speak of the client's problems as a third-person noun instead of a verb or an adjective to describe the experience. With practice, one should see an increased ability to gain more emotional distance and a measure of increased resiliency.

CONCLUSION

The practice of concentration or mindfulness (samādhi) in Buddhism is to train the mind to notice. To notice anything, one is required to focus one's attention on that thing. The instructions for the cultivation of such focus are given in various suttas throughout the *Nikāya*. One of the main suttas devoted to the development of samādhi (concentration, meditation, mental develop-ment) is the Satipaṭṭhāna Sutta (MN, 1995, 10). The initial instructions given in this sutta are the bases for many of the current mindfulness-based intervention programs. There are three categories of instructions included in this sutta: (a) how to prepare the mind in approaching the task of silent medi-tation; (b) how to consider the phenomenon in consciousness that appears in the mind; and (c) on what to focus the mind, which is the listing of the objects of contemplation.

This chapter reviewed the Buddha's instructions on how to prepare the mind in approaching the task of silent meditation. The Buddha said to first find a private quiet place that is free from distraction. Then the meditator is to adopt a stance that is "ardent" (ātāpīn), "fully aware" (sampajāna), and "mindful, having put away covetousness and grief for the world" (MN, 1995, 10).

After aligning the body and focusing the mind internally, the meditator is ready to turn the mind's attention to focus on the topics covered in the sutta, which are (a) contemplation of body, (b) contemplation of feelings, (c) contemplation of mind, and (d) contemplation of mind objects. The next chapter discusses these four objects of contemplation.

16 ADVANCED MINDFULNESS IN PSYCHOTHERAPY

What to Contemplate in Meditation and Why

This chapter, like Chapter 15, is an extremely brief deliberation on the objects of contemplation in meditation. It is beyond the scope and ability of this book to conduct a comprehensive account of contemplations as specified in the Satipaṭṭhāna Sutta (*Majjhima Nikāya* [MN], 1995, 10: The Foundations of Mindfulness), because the accumulation of knowledge about meditation is voluminous and spans the thousands of years that people have been practicing Buddhist meditation and striving for mindfulness. Thus, what follows is a cursory examination, focusing only on how a select topic in the Satipaṭṭhāna Sutta might be used in psychotherapy.

FOUR OBJECTS OF CONTEMPLATION

The Satipaṭṭhāna Sutta (MN, 1995, 10) lists four objects of contemplation, which are (a) *kāyā* (body), (b) *vedanā* (hedonic feeling tone), (c) *citta* (hearts and minds), and (d) *dhammas* (mind objects, phenomena, mind states). These objects of contemplation are presented next for reader reference. Engaging

https://doi.org/10.1037/0000453-017
Buddhist Psychotherapy: Connecting Early Buddhism to Mindfulness and Western Psychotherapy, by L. Tien, D. M. Kawahara, and V. Dhammadinna

in the work detailed in the Satipaṭṭhāna Sutta would lead to a state of total liberation from life's suffering (*nibbāna*). For the purpose of psychotherapy, the majority of the objects of contemplation would rarely be used; thus, it is sufficient for the psychotherapist to briefly review the following list of the four objects accompanied by their subcategories of items to be noticed in meditation.

Body (*Kāyā*)

- Breathing
- Postures
- Activities
- Anatomical parts
- Four elements
- Corpse

Hedonic Feeling Tone (*Vedanā*)

- Pleasant
- Unpleasant
- Neutral feeling tones

Mind (or Hearts and Minds; *Citta*)

- Lust, affected and unaffected
- Hate, affected and unaffected
- Delusion, affected and unaffected
- Contracted, affected and unaffected
- Concentrated, affected and unaffected

Mind Objects, Phenomena, and Mind States (*Dhammas*)

- Five hindrances
  - Sensual desire
  - Ill will
  - Sloth and torpor
  - Restlessness and remorse
  - Doubt
- Five aggregates (*khandhā*) subject to clinging (*upādānakkhandhā*)
  - *Rūpa* (materiality, form)
  - *Vedanā* (hedonic feeling tone)
  - *Saññā* (perception, naming, labeling)
  - *Saṅkhāra* (mental formations, mental fabrications, mental proliferations, volitional formations)
  - *Viññāna* (consciousness)

- Six internal and external sense bases (*āyatana*)
  - Eye
  - Ear
  - Nose
  - Tongue
  - Skin
  - Mind
- Seven enlightenment factors
  - *Sati* (mindfulness)
  - *Dhammavicaya* (investigation of the *dhamma*, study of the Buddha's teachings)
  - *Viriya* (energy)
  - *Piti* (rapture or happiness)
  - *Passaddhi* (calm)
  - *Samādhi* (concentration)
  - *Upekkhā* (equanimity)
- Four Noble Truths
  - *Dukkha* (suffering, unsatisfactoriness)
  - The arising/cause of dukkha
  - The cessation of dukkha
  - The path leading to the cessation of dukkha

Of the objects of contemplation just listed, it would be useful for the psychotherapist to be conversant on breathing and generally on activities regarding kāya (body) and vedanā (hedonic feeling tone). It is highly advisable for psychotherapists practicing within the Buddhist theoretical orientation to engage in their own meditative practices under the guidance of a trained meditation teacher. This is so the psychotherapist can have not only cognitive knowledge but also experiential knowledge and perhaps embodied knowledge. The reason for having one's own practice is that although the instructions for Buddhist meditation are simplistic, the manifestations of the listed objects of contemplation are extremely nuanced. Based on our experience in teaching doctoral psychology students, the concepts are easily grasped but extremely difficult to have sufficient experiential knowledge to recognize in actual treatment sessions. It is advisable for those who wish to utilize this approach to have their own extensive meditative practice under the tutelage of a meditation teacher. Additionally, know that it takes time, patience, and guidance to engage in one's own meditation practice fruitfully.

At a minimum, it is necessary for the psychotherapist to have had the experience of making direct contact with the body in the object of the breath. This requires the embodied knowledge of what it is like to make direct contact, not the imagined contact, with an object. Making direct contact with the breath enables the person to differentiate between rūpa (materiality) and nāma (mentality). Rūpa is the breath, and nāma is the awareness and knowledge of contact. Direct contact with the breath is the first objective of *vipassanā* mindfulness meditation. The eventual insight to be gained from meditation on any and all of the named objects of contemplation in the Satipaṭṭhāna Sutta (MN, 1995, 10) is the embodied knowledge of the three marks of existence, which are *aniccā* (impermanence), *anattā* (not-self), and *dukkha* (suffering, unsatisfactoriness; anything that is not okay with the client). For use in psychotherapy, the substantive objective is to experience any level of aniccā, anattā, and dukkha that allows for the client to gain sufficient distance from the experience of their suffering to interject some cognitive and executive functioning before taking any actions that are of *kammic* consequence.

This chapter reviews all of the aforementioned objects of contemplation except for the Four Noble Truths, which have already been discussed at length in previous chapters.

Body (*Kāya*)

The Buddha described contemplation of the breath in the body as follows:

> Breathing in long, he understands: "I breathe in long"; or breathing out long, he understands; "I breathe out long." Breathing in short, he understands: "I breathe in short"; or breathing out short, he understands: "I breathe out short." He trains thus: "I shall breathe in experiencing the whole body"; he trains thus: "I shall breathe out experiencing the whole body." He trains thus: "I shall breathe in tranquillizing the bodily formation"; he trains thus: "I shall breathe out tranquillizing the bodily formation." Just as a skilled lathe-operator or his apprentice, when making a long turn, understands: "I make a long turn"; or, when making a short turn, understands: "I make a short turn"; so too, breathing in long, a bhikkhu understands: "I breathe in long" . . . he trains thus: "I shall breathe out tranquillizing the bodily formation." (MN, 1995, 10)

In Meditation

The first named object for contemplation in the Satipaṭṭhāna Sutta is the kāya or, more specifically, the human body. The first object in the kāya is the breath. The instruction for the appropriate setting in preparation for a silent sitting meditation session was discussed previously in earlier chapters. The verbal instruction for contemplation of the breath is, "Pay attention to the breath."

The duration for a first-time meditator can be as short at 5 minutes but is usually not longer than 30 minutes. If meditation is used for homework, ask the client to keep a meditation journal. The client may choose to write about anything they notice during their meditation sitting. However, at a minimum, the journal should contain the answer to this question: "What did you notice about the breath [or the designated object of contemplation]?" The psychotherapist is reminded to review the client's journal entries at their next treatment session. It is not unusual for the client, presumably a novice meditator, to report their thoughts (actual or imagined) in the tracking of the breath. Here is an example with a client who once refused to try meditation: The client reported that he had prior exposure to meditation on the breath, but meditating gave him insomnia instead of calm when he tried to do meditation prior to going to sleep. Upon inquiring what the client noticed, he reported that he noticed the "breath traveling from the nose through the lungs, oxygenating the blood." When asked about the physical sensations of the breath traveling and the oxygenation, he reported that he imagined the breath traveling and oxygenating. This client stayed in his mental formations without having made direct contact with any aspect of the kāya (body).

The initial exercise of noticing the breath is done to train the meditator to distinguish between a sense object (e.g., directing attention to the breath), a sense contact (e.g., direct experience of the breath), and the fanciful functioning of the mind (e.g., imagining the breath oxygenating the blood). The first step is to direct the *manasikāra* (mind's attention) to a sense object, like the breath. It is advisable to ascertain the client's direct contact with the object of the meditation, be it the breath, posture, sound, or assigned object of contemplation. As an exercise to ascertain whether the client is staying in their mental formations or whether there is direct sense contact, the psychotherapist might ask, "How do you know you are breathing?" This is not a rhetorical question; rather, it aims to determine whether the client has made a direct sense contact. The psychotherapist themself must do this exercise to gain experiential knowledge of their own ability to make direct sense contact. Statements of awareness (e.g., "I feel the cold temperature at the end of my nose when I breath in," "I can feel the shirt rubbing against my skin when I breath," or something similar) would indicate direct sense contact. Probabilities are high that if the psychotherapist can figure out when they have made direct sense contact in their own meditation practice, then they are in a much better position to notice when the client is able to track down the direct sense contact that initiated whatever problem is under discussion in the treatment session.

If meditation is used as homework outside of the psychotherapeutic treatment session, it is advisable to assign the client to keep a meditation journal as an additional homework activity. Instruct the client to write down anything they noticed during their meditation sitting. Taking the time to reflect on what was noticed helps the client pay more careful attention to what their mind was doing during meditation. As with any homework assignment, the psychotherapist should review the client's meditation journal. An incidental benefit from reviewing the client's meditation journal is the documentation of how the client approaches themself and the universe. A person who is critical may report incidents like this: "I noticed that I was not doing abdominal breathing. I know I am supposed to do abdominal breathing." A person who is anxious may report, "I kept trying to do box breathing." Or someone who tends to doubt themself may report, "I am not sure if I am doing this correctly. I am supposed to feel calm and relaxed, but I did not feel calm, so I am probably not doing this right. How am I supposed to be breathing?" In reviewing the client's meditation journal, in addition to noting whether the client made direct contact with the breath, the psychotherapist might notice and comment on how a client approached the task.

In-Session Dialogue
The breath is not the only category of body function that can be taken as an object of contemplation. Without enumeration nor belaboring the objects of meditation listed in the Satipaṭṭhāna Sutta (MN, 1995, 10), it is sufficient to say that the progression of taking different objects of the kāya (body) has a purpose and a goal. The psychotherapist is tasked with choosing the object of contemplation for the client. In choosing, the psychotherapist and the client are guided by the idea of *sampajāna* (fully aware and clearly knowing). For clients with a hostile relationship to kāya (their body), a gentle introduction to contemplation of kāya is needed. For the purpose of learning to make direct contact with the body, the psychotherapist might advise the client to direct their attention to a body part that is not problematic—that is, a neutral part of the body. Depending on the presenting problem and treatment goal, the object of contemplation may be something other than the breath.

The following are some examples of choosing objects other than the breath. A person with body dysmorphia once reported that her toes were the only part of her body that was not repulsive to her. For this client, a gentle way to ease into contemplation of the body was to pay attention to the felt sensation of her toes. For those who have a difficult relationship with their body, it is best to choose a location in the extremities, such as a part of the foot or some part of the hand.

For individuals who tend to be hyperfocused or engaged in obsessive rumination, an alternative to choosing one object (e.g., the breath or the felt sensation of the foot) may be to choose multiple *touch points* to avoid the mind's tendency to fixate. In using touch points as the object of contemplation, the person visits one part of the sense base per breath. For example, for one breath, the mind goes to sight; the second breath, the mind goes to hearing; the third breath, the mind goes to the uprightness of the torso; the fourth breath, the mind goes to touch as the hand rests on the leg; the fifth breath, the mind goes to the pressure of the bones while sitting on the cushion; and the sixth breath, the mind returns to sight.

Another method may be to direct the attention to that part of the body that is the point of contact for the patient's presenting problem. The chosen object of contemplation should lend itself to accomplishing the goal of separating the felt sense in the body from identification with the body, thus rendering "the body as a body" (MN, 1995, 10).

For the purpose of psychotherapy that addresses the client's presenting complaint, it is necessary and useful to direct the client's attention to that complaint by having the client report the sense object and sense consciousness that triggered it. More often than not, clients report their disturbed reaction to a conversation or situation. It is extremely informative to find the sense object. Often, the sense object is a phrase, a sentence said by someone in a meeting, a smell, or the sight of something. Focusing on the sense object that triggered the complaint can bypass the notion of the I/self, the mental proliferations, and their ensuing emotions.

Insight (Vipassanā)
Each of the four groups of objects for contemplation is designed for the meditator to achieve insight, or the embodied knowledge, named in the sutta. For the contemplation of the body, including the subcategory of the breath, the insight, as stated in the Satipaṭṭhāna Sutta (MN, 1995, 10), is the knowledge that the body is the body; the body is not-self. Or, as said in the sutta:

> In this way he abides contemplating the body as a body internally, or he abides contemplating the body as a body externally or both. Or else he abides contemplating in the body its arising factors, or he abides contemplating in the body its vanishing factors, or both. Or else mindfulness that "there is a body" is simply established in him to the extent necessary for bare knowledge and mindfulness. And he abides independent, not clinging to anything in the world. That too is how a bhikkhu abides contemplating the body as a body. (MN, 1995, 10)

In working with any part of the contemplation of the body, keep in mind that the purpose of the selected objects is to lead the meditator to experience "the body as a body" internally, externally, and both internally and externally (MN, 1995, 10), not as I/self. In the psychology lexicon, the purpose is to render the object—meaning any and all parts of one's own body or other people's body—impersonal. The vipassanā (insight) is to realize that the body is its own entity with its own rhythms. Regardless of however much the client identifies with the parts or events of the body, the body is its own independent entity. Not appropriating the body into the self allows the person to be clear about the needs of the body and better at listening to what the body needs. For example, when taking the breath as the object of contemplation, the psychotherapist might point out to the client that a manifestation of "the body as a body" is the fact that no matter how one tries to control the breath, one can never control the breath to the extent of not breathing; it is the nature of the body to always breath.

The intent is to enable the meditator to look beyond the external surface of the skin to the internal content of the body. The insight for this set of objects of contemplation is to know that all humans, regardless of their skin color or body shape, are made up of the same body parts. The Buddha said, "Just as though a skilled butcher or his apprentice had killed a cow and was seated at the crossroads with it cut up into pieces; so too, a bhikkhu reviews this same body" (MN, 1995, 10). This impersonal relationship is part of what is meant by anattā (not-self); the body or any material item is not-self. This type of meditation is the Buddhist method of teaching the alphabet. The methodology for learning this alphabet in Buddhism is to differentiate between the sense object, the reception of the object in the mind, and the mind's interpretation of that contact into consciousness:

> The eye does not see a visible object because it has no mind. The mind does not see a visible object because it has no eyes. But when there is the impinge-ment of door and object he sees by means of the consciousness that has eye-sensitivity as its physical basis. . . . So the meaning here is this: "On seeing a visible object with eye-consciousness. . . . He only apprehends what is really there." (Buddhaghosa, 1956/2010, p. 81)

Hedonic Feeling Tone (*Vedanā*)

The second group of objects for contemplation named in the Satipaṭṭhāna Sutta (MN, 1995, 10) is vedanā. The instruction for observing vedanā follows:

> And how, bhikkhus, does a bhikkhu abide contemplating feelings as feelings? Here, when feeling a . . . pleasant, painful, neither-painful-nor-pleasant . . . feeling, a bhikkhu understands: I feel a . . . pleasant, painful, neither-painful-nor-pleasant . . . feeling . . . In this way he abides contemplating in feelings their nature of . . . arising, vanishing, both arising and vanishing. Or else mind-fulness that "there is feeling" is simply established in him to the extent necessary for bare knowledge and mindfulness. (MN, 1995, 10)

Vedanā (hedonic feeling tone) accompanies every single contact at any of the six sense doors. Envision sense contact and hedonic feeling tone holding hands, arriving in consciousness almost simultaneously, with sense contact maybe leading no more than half a step ahead. Vedanā can be thought of as the hedonic response to the environment and is the genesis for the roots of greed, hatred, and delusion. The Buddha Gotama noted in the Satipaṭṭhāna Sutta that there are only three tonalities to the affective response to sense contact, which are pleasant, unpleasant (painful), and neither unpleasant (painful) nor pleasant (MN, 1995, 10).

In Meditation
In a meditation sitting, a pleasant vedanā (hedonic feeling tone) is the basis for desire. If the object of meditative contemplation is the breath, then notice the vedanā attached to the contact with the breath. If the meditator experiences the breath as pleasant, then they will be inclined to stay in the meditation session. If the meditator experiences the breath as unpleasant, then they will experience the push on the mind to abandon the breath. The meditator might notice thoughts of ending the meditation session (e.g., "There is a long list of things on my to-do list. I need to get on with it instead of wasting my time just sitting here"). If the meditator experiences the breath as neither unpleasant (painful) nor pleasant, they will experience the mind wandering, looking for something more interesting. The mind/*citta* may wander to thoughts in the category of greed ("What can I have for dinner tonight?") or hatred ("I'll bet that I am going to be called in for a talk at work, because I saw my arch nemesis go into my boss's office yesterday"). Or the mind/citta may wander and daydream, with the meditator finding that the meditation session has ended and they did not notice anything of the breath.

Pleasant vedanā (hedonic feeling tone) pushes the mind for more of the pleasant experience (whatever it is), the desire for permanence of that pleasant experience, followed by the inevitable fear of losing that pleasant association. Unpleasant vedanā pushes the mind toward aversion, or the desire for less of the unpleasant experience or the desire for permanent removal of that unpleasant association. Neither unpleasant (painful) nor pleasant vedanā pushes the mind toward daydreaming or any mind state that is more stimulating. In noticing the push, one sees the influence of vedanā and is thus able to trace it back to the direct experience of vedanā at the point of contact with a sense object.

In-Session Dialogue
The psychotherapist, acting as mindfulness (*sati*) in the psychotherapy session, needs to identify the vedanā (hedonic feeling tone) in order to understand

the underlying push for whatever situation the client is reporting. If the session is being conducted in English, it may be confusing to ask, "How did you feel?" when inquiring about vedanā. To get to the affective tone of a sense contact, it may be more precise to ask, "Was that [name the sense contact] pleasant?" or "Did you like that [name the sense contact]?" Because there is a large somatic element in this hedonic response, the psychotherapist can take advantage of the soma–psyche link by inquiring into the soma when the client is entangled in their own web of mental formations and mental proliferations. Here is an example of such an inquiry: "Is there tension anywhere in your body as you tell me about that difficult situation?" To follow up with the vedanā, the psychotherapist can instruct the client to speak from the soma, like this: "If that tension in your right shoulder blade area could speak, what would it say to me?"

It is advisable to be excessively precise in the link between sense contact and the accompanying vedanā (hedonic feeling tone). The more precise, the easier it will be to determine whether the push on the mind/citta (hearts and minds) was desire, hatred, or delusion. Detecting the vedanā of a situation is exceedingly consequential for psychotherapy, in that vedanā is the site of connection between the external sense object, the internal sense consciousness, and the mind/citta. For some clients, this link may be all that is needed to address a difficult situation. For others, the psychotherapist is reminded to continue exploring the ensuing mind state that arises from the vedanā of desire, hatred, and delusion.

Insight (Vipassanā)
The Buddha stated that "he abides contemplating in feelings their nature of arising, or he abides contemplating in feelings their nature of vanishing, or he abides contemplating in feelings their nature of both arising and vanishing" (MN, 1995, 10). The vipassanā (insight) to be gained from contemplation of vedanā (hedonic feeling tone) is that it is impermanent—it emerges and vanishes. That is, do not take whatever feeling tone one experiences as anything except a fleeting momentary experience of a stimulus. Experientially know that whatever one is reacting to (however intense that feeling tone is) is bound to disappear sometime in the very near future. Most people can endure a lot if they know it is temporary. Knowing that the discomfort of the unpleasant will end soon increases the probability that the client will not act based on that feeling tone, forestalling the reaction just long enough to insert some executive function into the mix.

Mind (Hearts and Minds; *Citta*)
The translation of *citta* that is most familiar to Western psychologists would be "mind," in the sense of thoughts (e.g., "What is on your mind?"). However,

Buddhism does not focus on thoughts or the content of thoughts; rather, Buddhism categorizes types of mind, similar to categorizing body types (e.g., tall, short, stocky, gangly). Thus, contemplation of mind, as guided by the Buddha Gotama, would be to distinguish the type of mind function at all times.

> And how, bhikkhus, does a bhikkhu abide contemplating mind as mind? Here a bhikkhu understands mind affected by lust as mind affected by lust, and mind unaffected by lust as mind unaffected by lust. He understands mind affected by hate as mind affected by hate, and mind unaffected by hate as mind unaffected by hate. He understands mind affected by delusion as mind affected by delusion, and mind unaffected by delusion as mind unaffected by delusion. He understands contracted mind as contracted mind, and distracted mind as distracted mind. He understands exalted mind as exalted mind, and unexalted mind as unexalted mind. He understands surpassed mind as surpassed mind, and unsurpassed mind as unsurpassed mind. He understands concentrated mind as concentrated mind, and unconcentrated mind as unconcentrated mind. He understands liberated mind as liberated mind, and unliberated mind as unliberated mind. (MN, 1995, 10)

The next listed object for contemplation is the mind/*citta*. The term *citta* has been translated with a wide variety of English words. Karunadasa (2015a) stated that "citta corresponds to the aggregate of consciousness (viññāṇakkhandha)" (p. 75). Bhikkhu Bodhi (MN, 1995, 10) and Bhikkhu Anālayo (2004) used the English word "mind" and the phrase "mind as mind" in their translation of the Satipaṭṭhāna Sutta. Bhikkhu Sujato (MN, 2018, 10) used the phrase "an aspect of the mind" in his translation of the Satipaṭṭhāna Sutta. The Chinese translate citta as "heart," as in the Heart Sutra. In the Theravāda Abhidhammic sense, citta is the totality of the human psychological experience and the source of intentional behavior. The *Pali Text Society's Pali–English Dictionary* provides a more comprehensive translation of citta:

> the heart (psychologically), i.e., the centre & focus of man's emotional nature as well as that intellectual element which inheres in & accompanies its manifestations; i.e., thought. . . . The meaning of citta is best understood when explaining it by expressions familiar to us, as: with all my heart; heart and soul; I have no heart to do it; blessed are the pure in heart; singleness of heart (cp. ekagga); all of which emphasize the emotional & conative side or "thought" more than its mental & rational side (for which see manas & viññāṇa). It may therefore be rendered by intention, impulse, design; mood, disposition, state of mind, reaction to impressions. (Pali Text Society, n.d.)

Given the variety of translated concepts, the term citta is clearly complex and there is not a simple one-word English translation for it. The nearest English term that captures the sense of citta might be the phrase "hearts and minds," which Merriam-Webster (n.d.) defines as "people's emotions and reasoning."

This task of contemplation of citta (hearts and minds) may be thought of as describing the condition of the mind. Bhikkhu Anālayo (2018) suggested that contemplation of citta can be approached by asking, "How is the mind?" (p. 127). This invites an approach to the mind as an entity that can be considered similarly to the physical body. We are used to being asked, "How is your health?" meaning the status of one's body. Most people are able to answer readily ("I have a sore throat" or "I am healthy"). Most can even go further and describe symptoms of their dis-ease ("My nose is stuffy, and I have a cough" or "I feel really tired"). We are accustomed to noticing the parts of the body that are experiencing pain or discomfort. Such a situation triggers visitation to medical clinics for interventions to end the physical pain and discomfort. We are also used to medical physicians extracting bodily fluids, such as blood, to ascertain the state of the body. We are not used to thinking of or answering the question, "How is your mind?" It is unusual for people to ask themselves similar questions ("What am I cultivating in the mind?" or "How is my mind?"). People usually know the experience of a healthy physical body, but they do not usually know the experience of a sound mind, a healthy mind. This sensitivity to the state of mind is what the sutta referred to in terms of "one knows a mind with lust to be a mind with lust" (MN, 1995, 10) or a mind with anger, delusion, contracted, or distracted.

In Meditation

The Satipaṭṭhāna Sutta (MN, 1995, 10) narrows down the possibilities for this wide-ranging concept by specifying the type of citta (hearts and minds) relevant for meditation. At some point in the meditation session, the meditator turns their attention to the question, "What is the health of my mind today? Is this a mind with lust . . . anger . . . [or] delusion . . . [or is the mind] contracted . . . [or] distracted?" (MN, 1995, 10).

In approaching contemplation of the citta (hearts and minds), one experiences the five aggregates acting in coordination in such a way that the person has the experience of a mind with anger or delusion or a mind that is contracted or distracted (MN, 1995, 10). For example, in a distracted mind, one might have loose thought associations, rapidly switching between topics, and perhaps a slightly unpleasant feeling tone and physical tension. After repeatedly approaching this question during meditation, one starts being aware of the many different states of the citta.

In-Session Dialogue

In its application to the psychotherapy in-session dialogue, it is not unusual for a client to enact the state of their citta (hearts and minds) but not be able to articulate or identify their state of mind. For example, a client came into a treatment session with her body rounded and head tilted down, saying she needed to apply for a change of location at her job. She worked for a very large company, so there was the possibility of making a parallel shift in the same job class without a loss of salary or need for physical relocation. The client proceeded to talk about how she was going to have to compose herself at work, so that she could act the same as always and not let on to anyone on her team that she would be requesting a transfer. As the session progressed and as the client tried to answer the psychotherapist's question of "What happened?" it became evident that she was trying to escape a very unpleasant situation at work. With more detailed inquiry for the sense contact that initiated the client's desire for a job transfer, she started to report, in a very disjointed manner, a conversation she had with a coworker, in which the coworker became angry and started talking to the client in a threatening manner. The client thought her coworker was enraged, and she feared that he would unleash a verbal torrent of threats toward her. She was exhibiting a distracted mind—giving vague responses to the psychotherapist's questions for the specifics of the incident and jumping from one solution to another in planning for ways to escape from having to see this coworker again. The client was caught off guard when the psychotherapist said, "You are distracted. You are scared." The observation, "You are distracted," labeled the citta, the client's state of mind. The observation, "You are scared," labeled the client's cognitive affect or *saññā* (perception, naming, labeling).

With the identification of how the client's mind was at that point, she settled. The client's report of the incident with the coworker became more specific and coherent. The psychotherapist acted as sati (mindfulness), contemplating mind as mind by identifying the state of the client's mind. Such meta-cognition in observation of the mind is useful to settle the mind.

The psychotherapist can act as sati (mindfulness) in the treatment session by taking the stance of "contemplation of mind as mind" (MN, 1995, 10). An unfailing way to identify citta (the emotional and cognitive environment of the mind) for any specific moment or situation is to go back to the initial sense object and articulate the vedanā (hedonic feeling tone) linked to that sense object. In general, a "mind with lust" is likely linked to the pleasant vedanā at the point of contact (*phassa*), a "mind with anger" is likely linked to the unpleasant vedanā, and a "mind with delusion" (MN, 1995, 10) is most likely linked to the neither pleasant nor unpleasant vedanā. For any situation that the client struggles with, there is a contact/phassa and a vedanā. There will always be a contact/phassa that initiated the cascade of constructed narratives that gave rise to the client's problematic state of mind. Articulation of the answer to the question about one's mind state ("How is my mind?") by way of describing the sense contact, the vedanā of that sense contact, and the mind's reaction to the sense contact in the client's own phrasing will, most likely, bring a great deal of relief to the client's emotional state.

Insight (Vipassanā)

When one is able to notice the state of their mind, then it is possible to experientially know the existence of the mind. In being able to identify a mind, one is thus able to say, "There is a mind that is independent of myself."

> In this way he abides contemplating mind as mind internally, or he abides contemplating mind as mind externally, or he abides contemplating mind as mind both internally and externally. Or else he abides contemplating in mind its nature of arising, or he abides contemplating in mind its nature of vanishing, or he abides contemplating in mind its nature of both arising and vanishing. Or else mindfulness that "there is mind" is simply established in him to the extent necessary for bare knowledge and mindfulness. And he abides independent, not clinging to anything in the world. That is how a bhikkhu abides contemplating mind as mind. (MN, 1995, 10)

The insight based on the experiential knowledge derived from contemplation of the mind as mind is that (a) there is a mind, (b) that state of mind is initiated from a sense contact with a sense object, and (c) that state of mind will change (impermanence/aniccā). Whatever is going on in the mind, whatever disturbances are experienced in the mind, it will change; so do not take it so seriously, and do not take it personally.

Mind Objects, Phenomena, and Mind States (*Dhammas*)

What enters the psychotherapy treatment room is most often what Buddhism labels as mind objects. Buddhism makes even finer distinctions within the categories of mind objects. These finer-grained distinctions provide easy entry into the mechanisms used in the construction of the client's presentation in the psychotherapy treatment room.

> And how, bhikkhus, does a bhikkhu abide contemplating mind-objects as mind-objects? Here a bhikkhu abides contemplating mind-objects as mind-objects in terms of the five hindrances . . . five aggregates afflicted by clinging . . . six internal and external bases . . . seven enlightenment factors . . . Four Noble Truths? (MN, 1995, 10)

The remainder of the objects for contemplation listed in the Satipaṭṭhāna Sutta (MN, 1995, 10) fall under one general category of mind objects. The list of mind objects is extensive and was presented earlier in this chapter.

For the purpose of psychotherapy, it is probably most useful to have a well-established understanding of the hindrances, the aggregates, and the sense bases. It is doubtful that psychotherapy would utilize all of the enlightenment factors, because the client would most likely have gained sufficient relief from their presenting problems to have ended the psychotherapy sessions. However, it is likely that the client will experience some of the enlightenment factors as they progress through psychotherapy and their presenting problem and difficulties begin to resolve. As for the Four Noble Truths, the whole of the ideas used in the Buddhist-based approach to psychotherapy is based on these noble truths, so they are used in every aspect of this psychotherapy approach.

The five hindrances, the five aggregates, and the six internal and external sense bases have been discussed in previous chapters; thus, their treatment here will be brief. They will be presented with slightly more explanation than merely listing them as items that are useful for psychotherapists, acting as sati (mindfulness), to observe, to notice, and to discuss with the client.

The Five Hindrances

As discussed previously, think of the five named hindrances as describing the topology of the mind.

> And how, bhikkhus, does a bhikkhu abide contemplating mind-objects as mind objects? Here a bhikkhu abides contemplating mind-objects as mind-objects in terms of the five hindrances. And how does a bhikkhu abide contemplating mind-objects as mind-objects in terms of the five hindrances? Here, there being (sensual desire . . . ill will . . . sloth and torpor . . . restlessness and remorse . . . doubt) in him, a bhikkhu understands: "There is sensual desire . . . ill will . . . sloth and torpor . . . restlessness and remorse . . . doubt in me"; or there being no sensual desire . . . ill will . . . sloth and torpor . . . restlessness and remorse . . . doubt in him, he understands: "There is no sensual desire . . . ill will . . . sloth and torpor . . . restlessness and remorse . . . doubt in me"; and he also understands how there comes to be the arising of unarisen sensual desire . . . ill will . . . sloth and torpor . . . restlessness and remorse . . . doubt, and how there comes to be the abandoning of arisen sensual desire . . . ill will . . . sloth and torpor . . . restlessness and remorse . . . doubt, and how there comes to be the future non-arising of abandoned sensual desire . . . ill will . . . sloth and torpor . . . restlessness and remorse . . . doubt. (MN, 1995, 10)

These mind objects are named *hindrances* because they hinder the mind's ability to see a situation with any clarity. The sutta names five hindrances: (a) sensual desire, (b) ill will, (c) sloth and torpor, (d) restlessness and remorse, and (e) doubt. In handling these five named hindrances, the sutta names four tasks for the meditator. The first task is to identify the presence of the hindrance. Identifying the hindrance(s) may initially be done in session by the psychotherapist. The next step is for the client to observe which hindered mind state is being experienced as they go about their daily activities. The second task is to notice when the hindrances are absent. Beyond noticing, the third and fourth tasks are to understand; that is, to know (a) how the hindrance was generated and (b) how to prevent the hindrance in the future. A way to understand the hindrance is to spot the sense contact, or the trigger, that starts the emergence of the hindrance. By extension, the way to prevent the hindrance from emerging is not to focus on the mental formations and mental proliferations that follow the sense contact. This allows the psychotherapist and the client to deal with the situation that generated the sense contact, instead of being diverted to talking about the client's mental formations and mental proliferations.

Commenting on the client's state of mind can be used as a method for calling the client's attention to what their mind is doing. For example, the psychotherapist may observe and offer comments like this:

> Oh, you are pondering what your boss did. What your boss did generated the mind state of anger, which is quite understandable given that he took you off the project without warning or explanation. Notice, you did not go into doubt, as you would have in times past, assuming that what your boss did was a justifiable response to something you had done.

The psychotherapist's statement named the sense contact (boss removed the client from a project at work), the hindrance (mind state of anger), the saññā (understandably offended when not consulted), and the absence of the hindrance of doubt (mind state of doubt). Noting the absence of doubt may be calling the client's attention to their more adaptive reaction. Not ruminating on what it is she might have done gave room for the client to inquire for her boss's reason. It turned out that the agency had lost funding for the project, instead of anything she had done. In reality, it was the boss's lack of communication of information that would be useful for workers, as opposed to the client assuming (understand how to prevent arising of doubt) they had done something wrong that justified the boss's action of removing them from the project. As instructed in the sutta for noticing, "There is no sensual desire . . . ill will . . . sloth and torpor . . . restlessness and remorse . . . doubt in me" (MN, 1995, 10); it is just as important to note the presence of the hindrance as it is to note its absence.

Following the in-session introduction to the contemplation of hindrances, the client can then be invited to structure how they touch base with their mind during their meditation sittings and in their daily activities. The client is to first notice which hindrance best describes their mind state and then to understand what sense contact led to the arising of the hindrance state of mind. In their daily activities, the client might be invited to stop every now and then to ask themself: "What is my mind doing now? Is there a mind culture of a hindrance? Which hindrance and what started it?"

We will now examine how each individual hindrance can be contemplated in meditation.

Hindrance of sensual desire. The motivator behind sensual desire is, "Being contacted by painful feeling, he seeks delight in sensual pleasure" (Salla Sutta; *Saṃyutta Nikāya* [SN], 2000, 36.6: The Dart). The hindrance of the sensuous mind is focused on grasping of and attaching to sense experience. Hindrance of sensual desire shows itself in silent meditation as wishing for the stimulation of the six sense bases. An example is when the mind wanders to topics that are sense based, either wanting or not wanting (e.g., "I wonder what is in the refrigerator that I can have for dinner" or "I wish that neighbor's dog would stop barking"). This wanting or not wanting is often accompanied by an urge to fix it (e.g., "My arm itches. It's not going to do any harm for me to scratch that itch, so I'll just go ahead and do it. No one will know").

Thus, to understand the allure of the material sensual desires, the meditative object of contemplation necessarily needs to be on various aspects of the six sense bases. To have an embodied knowledge of the actualities of the six internal sense bases and six external sense objects (*āyatana*), the Satipaṭṭhāna Sutta (MN, 1995, 10) has quite an extensive list of subjects for the meditator. The insight for this section of the sutta is for the meditator to experientially know the body as the source of both pleasant and unpleasant experiences. In other words, the insight is for an embodied knowledge that the body is the body, that the body is not the self, and that the body is not something for appropriation into or identification with the notion of the self.

The first object of contemplation in the body is the breath. The Buddha said,

> [The meditator is to be] ever mindful he breathes in, mindful he breathes out. Breathing in long, he understands: "I breathe in long"; or breathing out long, he understands: "I breathe out long." Breathing in short, he understands: "I breathe in short"; or breathing out short, he understands: "I breathe out short." (MN, 1995, 10)

This instruction tells the meditator to notice and track the rhythm of the breath. In addition to tracking the rhythm of the breath, it is not unusual for the mind to start noticing the location of the breath as well. Many beginning meditators will wish to control both the location and the rhythm of the breath, thinking that the breath should be located in the abdomen with a slow even pacing of the breath in and out. This may be a manifestation of appropriation of the body into a self, with the premise that the self and the body are one. Thus, it is perfectly normal and natural for the self to be able to dictate how the breath as part of the body should behave.

For the psychotherapist, it is useful to experientially know the difference between training the mind to observe the breath versus using the mind to train the body. Having such embodied knowledge guides the in-session discussion about the dukkha of not getting one's wishes, because the body will do what the body does and is not bound to be an attentive student that will breathe as instructed. This discussion can also touch on the distinct difference between the body and the self.

The sutta then gives instructions for taking on different functions of the body. These instructions indicate that the meditator is to take the same kind of focused attention into the daily activities of the body. The person is to have the mind be ever attentive to what the body is doing.

> [W]hen walking, a bhikkhu understands: "I am walking"; when standing, he understands: "I am standing"; when sitting, he understands: "I am sitting"; when lying down, he understands: "I am lying down"; or he understands accordingly however his body is disposed . . . when going forward and returning . . . when looking ahead and looking away . . . when flexing and extending his limbs . . . when eating, drinking, consuming food, and tasting . . . when defecating and urinating . . . when walking, standing, sitting, falling asleep, waking up, talking, and keeping silent. . . . In this way he abides contemplating the body as a body. (MN, 1995, 10)

These instructions, given in detail, can be generalized and summarized as (a) paying attention and listening to the body and (b) not ignoring the body and the body's influence on the mind.

The other instructions given in the Satipaṭṭhāna Sutta (MN, 1995, 10) are on the repulsiveness of the 32 parts of the body and contemplation of the corpse. The contemplation of the repugnancy of the body is generally utilized for reduction of erotic arousal. The contemplation of the corpse is generally utilized for dealing with declining of the body as it ages, becomes terminally ill, and ultimately dies. Although these instructions are repeated here for the reader's general exposure to the full extent of the objects of meditation on the body given in the Satipaṭṭhāna Sutta, they are not applicable to the general psychotherapy setting. The authors strongly recommend not using these objects in meditation. Contemplation of the 32 repugnant parts of the body has been known to lead to suicide. Thus, these objects are of limited use for in-session dialogue in different types of individual problems. The instructions on the repulsiveness of the 32 parts of the body are for the meditator to review:

> this same body up from the soles of the feet and down from the top of the hair, bounded by skin, as full of many kinds of impurity thus: "In this body there are

head-hairs, body-hairs, nails, teeth, skin, flesh, sinews, bones, bone-marrow, kidneys, heart, liver, diaphragm, spleen, lungs, intestines, mesentery, contents of the stomach, feces, bile, phlegm, pus, blood, sweat, fat, tears, grease, spittle, snot, oil of the joints, and urine." . . . In this way he abides contemplating the body as a body . . . mindfulness that "there is a body." (MN, 1995, 10)

The instruction on the contemplation of corpses is for the meditator to contemplate the body:

> as though he were to see a corpse thrown aside in a charnel ground, one, two, or three days dead, bloated, livid, and oozing matter, . . . being devoured by crows, hawks, vultures, dogs, jackals, or various kinds of worms . . . a skeleton with flesh and blood, held together with sinews . . . a skeleton without flesh and blood, held together with sinews . . . disconnected bones scattered in all directions . . . bones bleached white, the color of shells . . . bones heaped up, more than a year old . . . bones rotted and crumbled to dust . . . a bhikkhu compares this same body with it thus: "This body too is of the same nature, it will be like that, it is not exempt from that fate." (MN, 1995, 10)

The insight for this set of objects of contemplation is to help reconcile ourselves to the finality of the body, that death is the last act of life.

In summary, the mind state of sensual desire is seeking pleasant experiences derived from the six sense bases to avoid dukkha, which for the purpose of psychotherapy are any complaints that the client presents for treatment. Both the in-session dialogue and the meditation instructions are aimed at giving the person some psychic space between unpleasant sense-based experiences and their notion of a self, thus increasing their level of tolerance for the unpleasant and decreasing their urge toward sensual pleasure as escape from the unpleasant.

Hindrance of ill will. The mind state of ill will is immersed in hate. The hate is either directed inward toward the self or directed outward toward a person or a situation, wishing things not to be. That mind is not engaged in analyzing the efficaciousness or the harm of such a state of mind. The first thing to do to address the mind state of ill will is to notice it.

> [T]he danger in hate should be seen. . . . Thereupon he should embark upon the development of loving-kindness for the purpose of secluding the mind from hate seen as a danger and introducing it to patience known as an advantage. . . . A meditator, who wants to develop firstly loving-kindness. . . . To start with, he should review the danger in hate and the advantage in patience . . . he should embark upon the development of loving-kindness for the purpose of secluding the mind from hate seen as a danger and introducing it to patience known as an advantage. . . . First of all it should be developed only towards oneself, doing it repeatedly thus: "May I be happy and free from suffering" or "May I keep myself free from enmity, affliction and anxiety and live happily." . . . So he

should first, as example, pervade himself with loving-kindness. (Buddhaghosa, 1956/2010, pp. 291–292)

Ill will shows itself in meditation by critiquing the breath. Here is an example:

> I am not breathing correctly; I can't meditate correctly. I can't even pay attention to the breath; my breath is all wrong. I should be able to keep breathing in a four-square box pattern. I can't even pay attention to such a simple thing as my breath, so there is no way I can do the work in a doctoral program.

One of the tasks in meditation is to notice what the mind is doing, which means to pay attention to what one is paying attention to. The mind of ill will has the meditator paying attention to all those criticisms. This is the mental condition for anger and ill will to manifest. In the Āhāra Sutta, the Buddha said,

> And what, bhikkhus, is the nutriment for the arising of unarisen ill will and for the increase and expansion of arisen ill will? There is, bhikkhus, the sign of the repulsive: frequently giving careless attention to it is the nutriment for the arising of unarisen ill will and for the increase and expansion of arisen ill will. (SN, 2000, 46.51: Nutriment)

Some see the worth of paying attention to criticism directed toward the self as a way to show commitment to self-improvement. The worth in paying attention to the faults of others is a way to make the universe a better place. The worth and the effect of paying repeated attention to criticism of the self and of others may be more effectively addressed in the in-session dialogue with a psychotherapist. The meditation counter to paying attention to such criticism is simply to note that (a) one cannot pay attention to both the anger and the breath at the same time and (b) the meditation object of contemplation is the breath, not the criticisms. The counter is to not focus on the criticisms and to not argue with them; rather, notice that this is not the time for engagement with the criticisms.

In summary, the mind state of ill will starts with believing that oneself and the universe should be a certain way. In its presentation in psychotherapy, the mind state of ill will manifests as complaints of how neither oneself nor the universe is what it should be. As with the mental state of sensual desire, the in-session dialogue and the meditation instructions for ill will are aimed at giving the person some psychic space between their experience of outrage, transmuted to depression or rage, thus introducing the possibility of patience and loving-kindness toward the self, even as the self is not what it should be.

Hindrance of sloth and torpor. The comfort of a sluggish hazy mind is not productively on task; rather, it is busy being not busy. Like a driver slowly and comfortable dozing off while driving on a long stretch of highway, such is the danger of sloth and torpor.

> And what, bhikkhus, is the nutriment for the arising of unarisen sloth and torpor and for the increase and expansion of arisen sloth and torpor? There are, bhikkhus, discontent, lethargy, lazy stretching, drowsiness and after meals, sluggishness of mind: frequently giving careless attention to them is the nutriment for the arising of unarisen sloth and torpor and for the increase and expansion of arisen sloth and torpor. (SN, 2000, 46.51)

More often than not, the meditator notices that the mind has been invaded by the state of sloth and torpor only at the end of the meditation session when they emerge from the fuzziness of not having noticed anything. The Buddha advises the meditator to take the following action once they notice the mind state of sloth and torpor:

> [Y]ou should shake your ears, and rub your limbs with the palm of your hand . . . get up from your seat, and wash your eyes with water . . . look around in all directions and look upwards to the stars in the sky . . . establish the (inner) perception of light . . . walk up and down, with your senses turned inwards, with your mind not going outwards. . . . But if, by so doing, that torpor does not disappear, you may lie down on your right side, taking up the lion's posture, covering foot with foot—mindful, clearly conscious, keeping in mind the thought of rising. Having awakened again, you should quickly rise, thinking: "I won't indulge in the enjoyment of lying down and reclining, in the enjoyment of sleep!" (Capala Sutta; *Aṅguttara Nikāya* [AN], 2012, 7.58: Nodding)

Many meditators struggle to stay alert when experiencing the mind state of sloth and torpor. For those who experience this mind state, the strategies given by the Buddha in the Capala Sutta (AN, 2012, 7.58) are applicable. If the meditator does undertake these activities, they will most likely no longer experience the mind state of torpor.

The struggle is more profound when a meditator experiences torpor as a pleasant state of mind where one can take a mental rest from life's constant demand for attention to its myriad difficulties. The pull of torpor is the enactment of the meditator's desire to be left alone, metaphorically speaking; to not have to contend with the unpleasant realities of their difficult situation. The meditator might wish to point out to themself that continuing in the mental state of torpor does not advance one's progress in addressing anything.

Hindrance of restless and remorse. The hindrance of restless and remorse is the often-voiced state of worry.

> When the mind is restless, it is the proper time for cultivating the following factors of enlightenment: tranquility, concentration and equanimity, because an agitated mind can easily be quietened by them. (SN, 2000, 46.53)

The method for cultivation of tranquility is given in the Satipaṭṭhāna Sutta (MN, 1995, 10). The quality of tranquility can be achieved in the contempla- tion of the breath as given in the first directive found in the Satipaṭṭhāna Sutta. While on the meditation cushion, the traditional meditation object is to focus on the very small area immediately below the nostrils. As the meditator repeatedly returns to the sensation in this small area, the meditator brings the sensations in that area into the foreground, and other events of the body and mind fade into the background. The goal is not to empty the mind nor to push away the activities that go on in the mind. It is more like walking into a very crowded room, having spotted a dear friend among the crowd of people, and the meditator gives preference for the company with that dear friend not to fade from one's field of awareness. During meditation, the mind is essentially only attending to a calming presence of the breath, like talking to the dear friend at a social function filled with many people, thus depriving the mind of the necessary nourishment for restlessness and remorse. By repeatedly directing the mind back to the breath and not attending to the content of anything else that enters the mind, the internal environment of the meditator quiets and the experience of tranquility emerges.

Hindrance of doubt. In meditation, the internal dialogue of a meditator might sound something like this: "Am I doing the meditation correctly? Did my teacher understand me accurately so as to give me relevant instructions? Is there such a thing as equanimity, or am I really just wasting my time meditating?" The Satipaṭṭhāna Sutta states the following:

> There being doubt in him, a bhikkhu understands: "There is doubt in me"; or there being no doubt in him, he understands: "There is no doubt in me"; and understands how there comes to be the arising of unarisen doubt, and how there comes to be the abandoning of arisen doubt, and how there comes to be the future non-arising of abandoned doubt. (MN, 1995, 10.36)

The meditation counter for the mind state of doubt is, first, to recognize it. This requires the meditator to examine the mind culture to ferret out the signs and symptoms of the hindrance of doubt. The stimulus that triggers doubt is different for each person. In general, although it is good to know these triggers, for the purpose of meditation, there is nothing to decide except to remember to stay the course of noticing the breath. The ultimate goal is to know the triggers, spot them as they arise, and then not progress in further explorations, expositions, or interpretations of the thought contents.

Vipassanā (insight) for contemplation of mind objects. The Buddha said the following:

Thus, he dwells observing mental contents in mental contents . . . both internally and externally. Thus, he dwells observing the phenomenon of arising . . . and passing away in the mental contents. Now his awareness is established: "These are mental contents!" Thus, he develops his awareness to such an extent that there is mere understanding along with mere awareness. In this way he dwells detached, without clinging towards anything in the world [of mind and matter]. This is how, monks, a monk dwells observing mental contents in mental contents as regards the five hindrances. (MN, 1995, 10)

In terms of psychotherapy interventions, in addition to noticing and understanding the client's hindrance mind states, uncovering the desire underlying the hindrances allows both the psychotherapist and the client to work toward fulfilling the underlying desire with a more functional and adaptive method, thus repairing the wounds that foster the presenting complaint or the hindrance. Recall from Chapter 12 (this volume) that the unrequited wish that underlies the hindrance of sensual desire is to escape from pain; for the hindrance of ill will, it is relief from the pressure of righting what is wrong with the self or the world; for the hindrance of sloth and torpor, it is having to deal with abhorrent situations; for the hindrance of restlessness and remorse, it is recognition of the presence of real danger; and for the hindrance of doubt, it is to not be blamed should anything untoward occur anytime in the future.

The five aggregates subject to clinging. Indulging in immersion in the mind objects, or mind state of the hindrances, fosters the sense of a self. Noticing the mind objects as mind objects, one notices the presence of a constructed notion of a self.

Again, bhikkhus, a bhikkhu abides contemplating mind-objects as mind-objects in terms of the five aggregates affected by clinging. And how does a bhikkhu abide contemplating mind-objects as mind-objects in terms of the five aggregates affected by clinging? Here a bhikkhu understands: "Such is material form, such its origin, such its disappearance; such is feeling, such its origin, such its disappearance; such is perception, such its origin, such its disappearance; such are the formations, such their origin, such their disappearance; such is consciousness, such its origin, such its disappearance." (MN, 1995, 10)

This section takes up the contemplation of the notion of the self, which is the *five aggregates affected by clinging*, by breaking it down to its constituent parts of the five aggregates: rūpa (materiality, form), vedanā (hedonic feeling tone), saññā (perception, naming, labeling), saṅkhāra (mental formations, mental fabrications, mental proliferations, volitional formations), and *viññāna* (consciousness). The clinging aspect of the five aggregates is found in the Alagaddūpama Sutta:

> Regards material form thus: "This is mine, this I am, this is myself." He regards feeling thus: "This is mine, this I am, this is myself." He regards perception thus: "This is mine, this I am, this is myself." He regards formations thus: "This is mine, this I am, this is myself." He regards what is seen, heard, sensed, cognized, encountered, sought, mentally pondered thus: "This is mine, this I am, this is myself." At this standpoint for views, namely, "That which is the self is the world." (MN, 1995, 22: The Simile of the Snake)

The following is the short, abbreviated version:

> etaṃ mama (this is me)
> eso'ham asmi (this is mine)
> eso me attā (this I am). (MN, 1995, 22)

These three types of I/self are present in all humans, except maybe for a fully enlightened arahant. Psychopathologies evince in the level of rigidity to the fixed idea of the I/self. If the notion of the I/self is more fluid, then the person can adapt to changing conditions, meaning the person is more resilient. Conversely, if the person holds on tightly to a fixed notion of I/self, then they have a more difficult time adapting to changing conditions, meaning the person is more rigid. The Buddhist meditation method for addressing this fixation on the I/self is to, essentially, ignore the I/self and go directly to its constituent parts. The construction of the notion of a self is based on the primary narcissism from which the person experiences themself as the center of the universe, as in "that which is the self is the world" (SN, 2000, 22.13).

When a client says negative things about themselves (e.g., "I am an angry person," "I am ugly," or "I should be forgiving"), they are taking the I/self as the solid entity. Many psychotherapy interventions use self-affirmation statements (e.g., "I am confident," "I am powerful," or "I am successful") as counter-statements. Self-affirmation, as defined in the *APA Dictionary of Psychology*, used in psychotherapy is "a positive statement or set of such statements about the self that a person is required to repeat on a regular basis, often as part of a treatment for depression, negative thinking, or low self-esteem" (American Psychological Association, n.d.). This method targets the I/self as the site of intervention, whereas the Buddhist approach bypasses the I/self by focusing on the functioning of the five aggregates.

The meditation approach for five aggregates affected by clinging, which is the Buddhist designation for I/self, is for contemplation of the five aggregates only, not paying any attention to the affected-by-clinging process. This approach enacts anattā (not-self). Bypassing the notion of a self and focusing directly on the five aggregates is the meditative operationalization of anattā (not-self). This contemplation employs the strategy used by Nāgasena in the Paññati Pañha (*Milindapañha* [Mil], 1890, 3.1.1: The Chariot Simile), where Nāgasena equated the I/self to a chariot. If a chariot or car (in our modern-day example) had a problem, the mechanic could not fix the problem unless they disassembled that chariot or car to replace the faulty part. When a client comes into psychotherapy complaining about the I/self (e.g., "I am an angry person"), like the mechanic, the psychotherapist, using this Buddhist-based intervention, would disassemble the I/self to its constituent parts (i.e., the five aggregates) as indicated in the contemplation of mind objects in this section of the Satipaṭṭhāna Sutta (MN, 1995, 10).

In-session dialogue. The I/self/*attā* is so pervasive and dominating that it is practically invisible. To briefly recap from Chapter 6 (this volume), in the psychology lexicon, the phrase, "This is me" (MN, 1995, 22), has the functioning of the aggregates as representing I/self ("What I think represents who I am"). The phrase, "This is mine," is appropriating the aggregate into a self ("My body belongs to me"). Finally, the phrase, "This I am," is identifying with the aggregate ("The make and model of my car tells the universe who I am"). It may be useful for the psychotherapist to articulate the label that the client gives to their notion of the self. This may come in the form of the psychotherapist paraphrasing what the client has said in the format of the notion of an I/self (e.g., "So, you think you are inadequate?" "So, you think you are deeply flawed?"). Once articulated, then do not dwell on the client's notion of the self. Instead, identify each of the aggregates functioning in the situation under discussion, starting with inquiring for the exact sense object.

Let us look at another clinical example. A client came into session pondering whether to accept an invitation to the wedding reception of a work colleague's daughter. This client's immediate response on seeing the invitation was, "No, I don't want to go." Following that immediate initial response, he ruminated and debated for days about whether he should go. He reasoned that he is retired, no longer has an ongoing relationship with this colleague, and will probably never encounter this colleague ever again. However, he counter-reasoned with himself,

> It would be good to keep friendly relations with my old colleague, since we may have some future business encounter. It would be nice to reinforce my reputation as being a friendly person, and there is no reason to think I would have an unpleasant time at the reception should I attend.

In exploring the client's suffering from days of indecision, the essence of the difficulty was that he did not want to be a "not generous and sociable person." He had constructed a world in which going to the wedding reception was equal to being a generous and social person; likewise, not going to the wedding reception was equal to not being a generous and social person. The in-session dialogue bypassed this constructed notion of the self/attā as being generous or not generous and, instead, focused first on some logistics for attending this wedding reception. It turned out that this client had a long-scheduled and already paid-for vacation with his wife on the day of the wedding reception.

In meditation. For the pursuit of liberation, it is of utmost importance that one is able to recognize the presence of the I/self/attā. The dissolution of the I/self/attā is the ability to break up the solidity of the I/self/attā to its continuant parts. For the purpose of psychotherapy, it is not so important for the client, in meditation, to become aware of the I/self/attā. Per the instruction given in the Satipaṭṭhāna Sutta (MN, 1995, 10), work on identifying the constituent parts. The internal monologue might sound something like this:

> The breath is high on my chest. I don't like my breath high on the chest. I must be anxious for the breath to be high on my chest. I wonder what I am anxious about—maybe it's because I was given a new assignment at work. I am going to be found out for the fraud I am with this new assignment because I will not be able to carry through with what needs to be done about this assignment.

As the meditator catches this diversion from the breath, the meditator strives to label the aggregate as it occurs.

> The breath is high on my chest [direct contact with kāya, the body]. I don't like my breath high on the chest [vedanā, the hedonic feeling tone associated with my breath]. I must be anxious for the breath to be high on my chest [saññā, the meaning I give to breath high on the chest]. I wonder what I am anxious about [saṅkhāra, mental formation]—maybe it's because I was given a new assignment at work [saṅkhāra, mental fabrication]. I am going to be found out for the fraud I am with this new assignment because I will not be able to carry through with what needs to be done about this assignment [saṅkhāra, mental proliferations].

Insight (Vipassanā). The goal is to say, "None of this is me." Instead of experiencing an I/self/attā as anxious ("I am anxious"), the meditator gives a label to each thing that they notice arising in the mind. Then the meditator notes that they are reactions to a sense object, and these reactions are just passing phenomena in the mind.

Six Sense Bases (*Āyatana*)

To actually engage with the universe, one has to first figure out what was encountered in the universe. In other words, one has to note the stimuli in the form of the six sense bases (*āyatana*).

> Again, bhikkhus, a bhikkhu abides contemplating mind-objects as mind-objects in terms of the six internal and external bases. And how does a bhikkhu abide contemplating mind-objects as mind-objects in terms of the six internal and external bases? Here a bhikkhu understands the eye, he understands forms, and he understands the fetter that arises dependent on both; and he also understands how there comes to be the arising of the unarisen fetter, and how there comes to be the abandoning of the arisen fetter, and how there comes to be the future non-arising of the abandoned fetter. He understands the ear, he understands sounds. . . . He understands the nose, he understands odours. . . . He understands the tongue, he understands flavours. . . . He understands the body, he understands tangibles. . . . He understands the mind, he understands mind-objects, and he understands the fetter that arises dependent on both; and he also understands how there comes to be the arising of the unarisen fetter, and how there comes to be the abandoning of the arisen fetter, and how there comes to be the future non-arising of the abandoned fetter. (MN, 1995, 10).

Contemplation of the six sense bases (āyatana) is a way to notice and know how one is interacting with the universe. The objects of contemplation are the six internal sense bases and their corresponding six external sense objects. These pairings, as listed in the Satipaṭṭhāna Sutta (MN, 1995, 10), are as follows:

Internal sense base	External sense object
Eye	Forms
Ear	Sounds
Nose	Odors
Tongue	Flavors
Body	Tangibles
Mind	Mind objects (internal mind objects are the five hindrances, five aggregates subject to clinging, six internal and external bases, seven enlightenment factors, and Four Noble Truths)

The first task is to notice what has been contacted. Many clients will report psychological disturbances without clear awareness of the sense object that triggered the activation of the five aggregates. When queried about this, it is not unusual for a client to be puzzled. With enough patience and detailed inquiry, most clients are able to identify the exact sense contact.

The exercise in the contemplation of the āyatana (six sense bases) is to be aware of the exact moment when a sense consciousness is triggered by sense object.

Once contact/phassa has been made, then the sutta lists what a meditator is to do with those observations. The task involves noticing the *fetters*, which are the chains that bind the sense object in the universe to one of the internal senses of eye, ear, nose, tongue, skin, or mind.

> Bhikkhu, there are these ten fetters. What ten? The five lower fetters and the five higher fetters. And what are the five lower fetters? Personal-existence view, doubt, wrong grasp of behavior and observances, sensual desire, and ill will. These are the five lower fetters. And what are the five higher fetters? Lust for form, lust for the formless, conceit, restlessness, and ignorance. These are the five higher fetters. These, bhikkhus, are the ten fetters. (Sanyojana Sutta; AN, 2012, 10.13: Fetters)

The following tasks are associated with contemplation of the āyatana (six sense bases):

- The meditator understands the fetter that arises dependent on both; and
- understands how there comes to be the arising of the unarisen fetter,
- how there comes to be the abandoning of the arisen fetter, and
- how there comes to be the future non-arising of the abandoned fetter.

The fetters address things that are more metaphysical. For the contemplation of the āyatana (six sense bases) and its immediate application to psychotherapy, the task is to refine the ability to identify the link between the sense object, the sense base, and the client's reaction. A fuller discussion on the fetters will be presented in Chapter 17 on wisdom.

In-session dialogue. The first step in unraveling any situation presented by the client is to identify the sense base that started the client's disturbance. This task sounds much easier than it actually is. It is not unusual, verily it is the usual case, for the client to not know what starts their experienced problematic situation. The line of questioning may start with the phrase, "Tell me what happened," and will persist until the psychotherapist tracks down the sense contact. Once the sense contact is identified, the psychotherapist can help the client tell a different story (i.e., construct a different perception and mental formation about the situation).

Consider this example: A client with a history of depression came into session reporting that she was feeling a little better but had a setback yesterday, where she was crying for most of the day. The Buddhist psychotherapist pointed out that at one point, the client was feeling better; then sometime yesterday, she became more depressed. In doing some excavation work, the client was able to identify the approximate time in the day when she started to feel depressed. She reported that she remembered feeling in a lighter mood in the morning when she woke up, but then by lunch time she was depressed and crying. Continued excavation brought out the activity during which the client transitioned from feeling less depressed to more depressed. Narrowing down the events of the morning, she reported she was listening to an album and a particular song brought back memories of her singing it with her grandmother. The client's grandmother was a significant figure in her life and had passed away the year before. Instead of talking about her depression in general and maybe strategies in dealing with a depressed mood, the therapy session pivoted to the client's sense of being alone in the world without her grandmother. The ability to notice the sense base (the ear) and the sense object (a particular song) facilitated a discussion to one cause of depression, which was a feeling of being unsupported and alone in the universe.

Let us look at another example to notice the complexity of uncovering the external sense object. A client reported that she had a panic attack when her supervisor told her that he had removed all her assigned projects at work after she presented him with a letter requesting partial accommodations after sustaining an on-the-job injury. On exploration of the client's opinion of her supervisor's actions, she thought he was hyper-reactive, going way beyond what was necessary when the accommodation letter specified that she should be allowed to work remotely for half a day for 3 weeks. The client was angry at her supervisor's punitive action. She easily relayed all the supervisor's specific actions that made her angry. The psychotherapist reminded the client that she had started the session with concern about her panic attack, not her anger at the supervisor. The client was stumped when asked how she went from a panic attack to anger. Although she was able and willing to exhaustively discuss all the things she was angry about, she was no closer to knowing how she went from a panic attack to anger. After the client processed her anger, the in-session dialogue turned to the possible consequence of being removed from her projects. It was at that time that the client's fear of being terminated from her job emerged as the source of her panic attack and, more specifically, the fear of being homeless if she lost her job. The anger was tightly associated with an external event (supervisor removing her from her projects) and an understandable reaction. The fear was less associated with that event, because she worked for a large agency that could easily reassign her to other projects in 3 weeks and she had access to disability insurance. Further in-session discussion surfaced the client's fear of being homeless and was associated with an incident when she was 10 years old. Her father had locked her out of the house, telling her that she was not welcome to live with the family anymore and not to come back. The link between the supervisor removing the client from her projects to her panic attacks was the possible result (locked out of her home, homelessness) of the seemingly unpredictable and unreasonable action of someone in authority (supervisor, father).

In meditation. The task for the meditator is to keep one's attention on what each of the senses are in contact with. This can be done by having the client rotate through the touch points of seeing, hearing, and touching to get the client used to noticing direct sense contact and naming the sense object.

Insight (Vipassanā). The exercise in the contemplation of the āyatana (six sense bases) is to know the links between the sense object, the sense base, and the client's reaction. The contemplation of the āyatana is training the mind to be sufficiently observant for the exact moment when a sense consciousness is triggered by a sense object. The insight is that one's state of mind (i.e., depression or anxiety) is triggered by a sense contact.

Seven Enlightenment Factors

The seven enlightenment factors listed in the Satipaṭṭhāna Sutta (MN, 1995, 10) are (a) *sati* (mindfulness), (b) *dhammavicaya* (investigation of the *dhamma*, study of the Buddha's teachings), (c) *viriya* (energy), (d) *piti* (rapture or happiness), (e) *passaddhi* (calm), (f) *samadhi* (concentration), and (g) *upekkhā* (equanimity). For the purpose of psychotherapy, it is extremely doubtful that these contemplations would need to be assigned or cultivated. It is highly probable that the client would experience some of these enlightenment factors at some point in their psychotherapy. For instance, it is not unusual for someone to experience piti (rapture, happiness) when a difficulty is resolved during an in-session dialogue. Or the person may experience some level of passaddhi (calm) when anger transitions to understanding of some difficult situation. The majority of clients seeking psychotherapy treatment would probably experience some of the seven enlightenment factors and gain sufficient relief from their presenting problem to return to functionality. In those cases, they are no longer in need of psychotherapy.

Psychotherapy is therapy for the discomforts and disorders of the psyche. As in any therapeutic treatment, once the discomfort is addressed, the need for therapy no longer exists and psychotherapy ends. The purpose of psychotherapy does not call for dwelling on the enlightenment factors. However, it is satisfying for both the client and the psychotherapist to take a moment to celebrate the client's achievement in managing their presenting problems and their psychological discomforts.

The Four Noble Truths

A hopeful note progresses from the First Noble Truth to the Fourth Noble Truth where the Buddha Gotama shows us how to get out of our state of suffering. This is akin to the journey for a client from the initial session of assessment to the final session of discharge from psychotherapy.

> Again, bhikkhus, a bhikkhu abides contemplating mind-objects as mind-objects in terms of the Four Noble Truths. And how does a bhikkhu abide contemplating mind-objects as mind-objects in terms of the Four Noble Truths? Here a bhikkhu understands as it actually is: "This is suffering"; he understands as it actually is: "This is the origin of suffering"; he understands as it actually is: "This is the cessation of suffering"; he understands as it actually is: "This is the way leading to the cessation of suffering." (MN, 1995, 10)

Contemplation of the Four Noble Truths in the Satipaṭṭhāna Sutta (MN, 1995, 10), as opposed to the Mahāsatipuṭṭāna Sutta (*Dīgha Nikāya* [DN], 1987/1995, 22; The Greater Discourse of the Foundation of Mindfulness), is done with a light touch. Being guided by the light touch, psychotherapists might consider noting and commenting on items that have already been covered in previous sections. Items of note and worthy of comment include making real-time observations of the client's suffering as they report it in the treatment session, performing careful assessment of the conditions supporting the arising of the suffering, focusing the client's attention on the actuality of the problem (not the fabricated notion of self), and engaging the client in problem-solving the actuality of their difficult situation.

CONCLUSION

Guided by the directives given by the Buddha Gotama and by enacting the four foundations of mindfulness in psychotherapy, a client can experience some of the same healing as those who have followed the ascetic practice of Buddhism.

> Bhikkhus, if anyone should develop these four foundations of mindfulness in such a way for seven years . . . for six years . . . for five years . . . for four years . . . for three years . . . for two years . . . for one year . . . for seven months . . . for six months . . . for five months . . . for four months . . . for three months . . . for two months . . . for one month . . . for half a month . . . for seven days, one of two fruits could be expected for him: either final knowledge here and now,

or if there is a trace of clinging left, non-return. . . . So it was with reference to this that it was said: "Bhikkhus, this is the direct path for the purification of beings, for the surmounting of sorrow and lamentation, for the disappearance of pain and grief, for the attainment of the true way, for the realisation of *Nibbāna*— namely, the four foundations of mindfulness." (MN, 1995, 10)

The expected result from engaging in contemplation of all the items as directed in the Satipaṭṭhāna Sutta (MN, 1995, 10) is "final knowledge here and now, or if there is a trace of clinging left, non-return." In the lexicon of Buddhism, the term "final knowledge here and now" means enlightenment, the ultimate goal of the Buddhist practice and the Noble Eightfold Path. The term "non-return" means someone who will gain enlightenment at the end of this life.

Practicing sati (mindfulness) is to notice what is going on in the mind/citta—noticing what one is doing, noticing to what one is paying attention, and noticing one's mind state. This moment-by-moment noticing is what psychotherapists, acting as sati (mindfulness), do in in-session interactions with our clients. We help clients notice what is going on within themselves.

Once an object of contemplation has been introduced in the treatment session, the psychotherapist can invite the client to take that object as the object for their meditation session. The objects of contemplation do not need to occur in the sequence outlined in the Satipaṭṭhāna Sutta (MN, 1995, 10). The sequence will depend on the nature of the presenting problem, the temperament of the client, and the preferences of the psychotherapist. Concurrently, the characteristics of each object of contemplation are also noted by the psychotherapist and pointed out to the client during the in-session dialogue.

In conjunction with articulating the client's notion of the self/attā, the psychotherapist can paraphrase what the client has been reporting in the framework of the type of dukkha (suffering, unsatisfactoriness) and the underlying root. In this way, the client is assisted in allowing some relabeling of the self through a closer examination of their dukkha, which allows for, metaphorically speaking, some cooling of the fervor in their experience of the dukkha.

The implementation methodology for outside of the treatment session is to instruct the client to notice the occurrences in meditation. Some clients will spontaneously generalize these occurrences to their daily life. For those clients who do not spontaneously generalize, it is good to invite them to notice those occurrences when they engage in daily activities during the follow-up inquiry about their at-home meditation sittings.

It may be advisable and most useful for the psychotherapist to engage in contemplation of the body, contemplation of hedonic feeling tone, and contemplation of the mind object of the five hindrances. Gaining this type of embodied knowledge allows the psychotherapist to spot these items in their client as the client reports and discusses their presenting problem or whatever difficulties they bring into psychotherapy. With even a perfunctory noticing of the body and hedonic feeling tone, one gains a beginning ability to observe the internal working of the mind and could obtain some ability to refrain from reacting, thus enabling the client to act instead of reacting.

17

EMPLOYING THE THIRD TRACK OF THE NOBLE EIGHTFOLD PATH IN PSYCHOTHERAPY

Wisdom

This chapter addresses wisdom (*paññā*) in psychotherapy. The structure of the chapter follows the Sabbāsava Sutta (*Majjhima Nikāya* [MN], 1995, 2: Discourse on All the Taints). The topic of paññā is complex, and this sutta is compact. The approach to wisdom discussed in this sutta is multifaceted. Please recognize what thousands of meditators have known—that it takes a tremendous amount of time and patience to gain both cognitive and experiential knowledge of this intricate approach to healing. Honor yourself, your clients, and the topic with patience and grace.

INTRODUCTION TO THE SABBĀSAVA SUTTA

The Buddha Gotama also gave guidance for reduction of suffering through methods that do not involve silent meditation by addressing the mental taints (*āsavas*):

> Bhikkhus, I shall teach you a discourse on the restraint of all the taints. . . . I say that the destruction of the taints is for one who knows and sees. . . . Who knows and sees what? Wise attention and unwise attention. When one

https://doi.org/10.1037/0000453-018
Buddhist Psychotherapy: Connecting Early Buddhism to Mindfulness and Western Psychotherapy, by L. Tien, D. M. Kawahara, and V. Dhammadinna

attends unwisely, unarisen taints arise and arisen taints increase. When one
attends wisely, unarisen taints do not arise and arisen taints are abandoned.

Bhikkhus, there are taints that should be abandoned by seeing . . . by
restraining . . . by using . . . by enduring . . . by avoiding . . . by removing . . .
by developing.

Bhikkhus, when . . . the taints . . . have been abandoned—then. . . . He has
severed craving, flung off the fetters, and with the complete penetration of
conceit he has made an end of suffering. (MN, 1995, 2)

This abbreviated passage is the essence of the Sabbāsava Sutta. It defines
the topic, audience, goal, and methods for achieving that goal. The topic
is the mental taints (āsavas). The audience is "one who knows and sees"
(MN, 1995, 2). The goal is to give instructions for the destruction of the āsavas
(i.e., to make "an end of suffering," which means to reach enlightenment).
Seven methods are explicated in the sutta. These methods can be employed
within the structure of the in-session psychotherapeutic dialogue. The sections
in this chapter will follow the structure of the sutta: topic, audience, goal,
and methods.

TOPIC: ĀSAVAS (A BEFUDDLING, GASLIGHTING FORCE)

In the phrase, "Bhikkhus, I shall teach you a discourse on the restraint of
all the taints" (MN, 1995, 2), Bhikkhu Bodhi translated the term āsavas as
"taints." The Pali word *āsava* has been translated into numerous English
terms, including taint, influx, flow, inflow, outflow, cankers, influence, effluence, defilements, corruptions, intoxicants, fermentations, biases, depravity,
and misery. Like many of the concepts in Buddhism, it is difficult to find a
one-word equivalent in English for the concept of the āsava. The *Pali Text
Society's Pali-English Dictionary* defines āsava with two different concepts:
One is "that which flows (out or on to) outflow & influx," and the other is
"certain specified ideas which intoxicate the mind (bemuddle it, befoozle it,
so that it cannot rise to higher things)" (Pali Text Society, n.d.). This reference to intoxicants is likening āsavas to how alcohol affects the person, both
the mind and the body. The mind is in a state of befuddlement under the
influence of the āsavas, like the body and mind are unfit when drunk with
alcohol. Alternatively, the second definition refers to "flow." The image of
flow is referencing exchange, as in "a process of interaction between the
internal sense-faculties and the external sense objects" (Karunadasa, 2015a,
p. 59). The act of existence is what Karunadasa referred to as the interaction
between stimuli flowing into the person from encounters with the universe
and desire flowing out of the person to grasp sense objects existing out in

the universe. Combining the two definitions, the term āsavas is a befuddling, gaslighting force that exerts a subtle but ever-present persistent influence on the mind as the mind navigates the interactions that are the experience of existence.

Types of Āsavas

The Pali canon names three types of āsavas (taints): craving for sensual pleasures (*kāmāsava*), craving for existence (*bhavāsava*), and ignorance (*avijjāsava*). Kāmāsava is craving for sensual pleasures (Bodhi, 2005); it refers to the influence of the material objects on the mind and how the mind reaches out to contact objects that exist in the universe. Bhavāsava is craving for existence (Bodhi, 2005); it refers to the escape from fear of annihilation through belief in something everlasting, as in an infrangible everlasting self. Avijjāsava is ignorance (Bodhi, 2005); it refers to the idea that the mind misconstrues phenomena for noumena, where one does not realize one is deluded. In general, when the sutta references ignorance, it usually refers to ignorance of the dhamma, the Four Noble Truths, and the Noble Eightfold Path.

Occasionally, there is mention of a fourth āsava. In addition to kāmāsava (merge self with the five material senses), bhavāsava (denial of impermanence/ *aniccā*), and avijjāsava (misconstrue phenomena for noumena), there is mention of befuddlement that comes from false belief (*diṭṭhāsava*). Whereas the *Nikāya* mentions three āsavas, various publications (Burma Piṭaka Association, 2010) add diṭṭhāsava, which refers to the befuddlement that comes of false belief. The false beliefs are, at a minimum, not believing in the cause and effect of the doing of deeds (*kamma*) or the Four Noble Truths.

Kāmāsava (Influence of the Material Senses on the Mind)
The term kāmāsava refers to the influence of the six sense bases and the six sense objects on the mind. An example of this influence can manifest in the push of desire for the pleasure of listening to a well-played symphony, thus urging the person to purchase a ticket and spend time going to a renowned orchestra performing their favorite symphony. Things that are generally regarded as painful can also be experienced as pleasurable. An example is when people cut themselves (which is physically painful on the flesh) in order to escape the experience of psychological numbness (which is experienced as distressing). Just to feel anything, even the physical pain of cutting the flesh, is experienced as pleasurable because it reduces the psychological numbness. The whole class of pleasant and unpleasant sense-based

experiences would fall into this category of kāmāsava. The influence of kāmāsava manifests in the belief that things of the universe are a source of happiness. Thus, kāmāsava influences the mind by driving the person to constantly reach out for more and more pleasant sense-based experiences.

Kāmāsava (influence of the six sense bases and the six sense objects on the mind) might show up in the psychotherapy treatment room in the following ways:

- "I did not get the raise I deserve this year. I am so underpaid that I can't [buy the things I need, go on vacations with my friends, move into a bigger apartment, etc.]."

- "I am distracted from work because I am busy with arranging for meet ups with potential romantic partners on my dating app. I am lonely and would be fine if I could have a romantic partner."

Bhavāsava (Rejection of Impermanence/Aniccā or Escape From Fear of Annihilation Through Belief in Something Everlasting)

Bhavāsava is a rejection of impermanence/aniccā, one of the three marks of existence. In its traditional rendition, this is the wish to escape from fear of annihilation through belief in something everlasting. For the purposes of psychotherapy, its equivalent, stated as a declarative, is bhavāsava is the belief in the existence of and a wish for a state of everlasting happiness. The influence of bhavāsava is to believe such a state exists and to wish for it, as well as to seek out this state of happiness. This wish is reflected in some religious beliefs that there is an everlasting happy place after the death of the body, and that one can be assured of entry to such a place by following the dictates of god, the church, and the religion. The theist perspective of humans possessing a soul, or anything that is more permanent and eternal than existence in the human body, is bhavāsava, an escape from the fear of nonexistence.

This belief does not have to take the form of religiosity. Many in the United States reject the human soul–god link, professing not to be religious, but will as quickly claim that they believe there is something that is greater than their individual self and connects them to others in the world. This kind of belief in something greater can be said to be bhavāsava (escape from fear of annihilation through belief in something everlasting). The underlying desire is for something beyond the limitations of the isolated body that ends at the outer layer of the body and its disintegration at death. The psychological mechanism is the denial of impermanence/aniccā.

In its most concrete manifestation, bhavāsava is a belief that the same self exists from one moment to the next, from one day to the next, from one year to the next year, and so on. The influence of bhavāsava can manifest in the solidity of a client's belief that their current state (panic attack, depression, obese, etc.) will always be.

A more common manifestation in psychotherapy that is ever-present but seldomly articulated is that one is entitled to a state of happily ever after. One such example may be the expectation that a love relationship with another person is everlasting. In this situation, the assumption is that the material body of the loved person, as well as the romantic feelings associated with the loved person, will be eternal. Or the assumption is that the natural and normal state is for the person to be happy; if one is not happy, then there is something profoundly wrong with the universe. Thus, the urge to enter psychotherapy to right the wrongness of being unhappy is prompted.

Cultural manifestations of bhavāsava (escape from fear of annihilation through belief in something everlasting; denial of impermanence/anicca) abound. For example, jeweler De Beers uses the slogan, "Diamonds are forever," in reference to giving a diamond ring as a symbol of engagement for marriage, which is supposed to last forever. Another example is retailer Forever 21, which invokes the image of oneself as nonchanging, holding forever still at the point when one was 21 years old.

Bhavāsava might show up in the psychotherapy treatment room in the following ways:

- Negative reaction to loss of something deemed important (e.g., depression after the loss of a job or end of a romantic relationship)

- Thinking oneself as flawed because of the end of a marriage (e.g., based on the assumption that marriage is everlasting, and thus looking for self-incriminating reasons why it did not last forever)

One of the reasons for the effectiveness of group therapy may be that it connects the individual to others in the group, and the universality of their own suffering, which can be considered a method that addresses bhavāsava.

Avijjāsava (Misconstrue Phenomena for Noumena)

Avijjāsava has several meanings, including not realizing one is deluded; being ignorant of the fact that one does not perceive reality, that one only perceives a representation of that reality; and confusing phenomena for noumena. Avijjāsava (misconstrue phenomena for noumena) is the influence that leads one to believe one is connecting to reality when, instead, one is connected to the mind's representation and fabrication of reality. Under the influence of avijjāsava, one experiences the representation of the world constructed by the mind as an accurate rendition of reality. The following are some of the ways avijjāsava might show up in the psychotherapy treatment room:

- Reaction to being diagnosed with a chronic or fatal illness (e.g., this is based on the delusion of taking for granted that the body is and will always be in good health)

- Rejection from a love interest (e.g., this is based on the incorrect perception that the other person was interested in pursuing a romantic relationship or had romantic feelings for the other)

Effect of the Āsavas: Prevarication

The disquieting standpoint about the āsavas is their gaslighting effect on the mind. The objective for the psychotherapist working with the āsavas is to recognize when the āsavas are acting on the client in the development of the presenting problem. Once detected and identified, the psychotherapist can use the conceptual frame outlined in the Sabbāsava Sutta (MN, 1995, 2) to address the client's psychological pains. This conceptual frame outlines (a) the mechanism of how a client constructs their notion of themself, (b) how to loosen the client's appropriation and identification with the aggregates, and then (c) how to alter the client's notion of themself. The application can be done in a discussion with the client in which the treatment session is aimed at reframing the client's worldview away from the influence of the āsavas. Because the āsavas exert a very subtle but ever-present persistent force on the mind, these in-session discussions need to be nuanced.

AUDIENCE

In the suttas, the Buddha Gotama was usually speaking to lay people who came to ask him questions or to his group of monks. However, for the practices that address the āsavas, he said,

> Bhikkhus, I say that the destruction of the taints is for one who knows and sees. . . . Who knows and sees what? Wise attention and unwise attention. (MN, 1995, 2)

In the Sabbāsava Sutta, the Buddha's audience is "one who knows and sees." It is unusual for the sutta to define its audience. The general assumption is that the Buddha is addressing all human beings, regardless of whether that person is a monk or lay practitioner; is male, female, transgender, or gender fluid; or has any other social position. Because the people in the audience of the Buddha's talks are mostly monks, the usual salutation is "Bhikkhus." For this sutta, the Buddha spells out that the directives in the Sabbāsava Sutta are only for "one who knows and sees."

The Buddha provided the differentiating features between the individual "who knows and sees" versus one who does not: The divergence is in "wise attention and unwise attention" (MN, 1995, 2). Those who can distinguish between wise and unwise attention are people who, at a minimum, have content knowledge of the Buddha's teachings and have sufficient experiential encounters in their own practice to distinguish between wise attention and unwise attention.

The two consequential words in the Sabbāsava Sutta are "wise" and "attention." *Yoniso* is the Pali word usually translated as "wise." *Manasikāra* is the Pali word usually translated as "attention." In the context of the suttas, the word manasikāra (attention) is used to reference to various functions of the mind. The *Pali Text Society's Pali–English Dictionary* lists *mano* as the root word for manasikāra, with mano translated as "mind, thought"; manasikāra is defined as "attention, pondering, fixed thought" (Pali Text Society, n.d.). Additionally, the *Pali Text Society's Pali–English Dictionary* defines the combined phrase *yoniso manasikāra* as "pondering (over), concentration, devotion, thoroughly, orderly, wisely, properly, judiciously, fixing one's attention with a purpose or thoroughly, proper attention, having thorough method in one's thought; Opp. ayoniso manasikāra disorderly or distracted attention" (Pali Text Society, n.d.). By inference, the audience the Buddha addresses in the Sabbāsava Sutta is the subset of monks who possess a concentrated mind and are able to direct the mind's focus to items that do not increase the influence of the āsavas (a befuddling, gaslighting force).

Wise attention (yoniso manasikāra) is having the knowledge of what to pay attention to and to be able to focus the mind to give that attention. Think of the difference between a beginning student driver and an experienced trained bus driver. Both are covering the same territory; both are navigating around the same road conditions and hazards. The beginning student driver is most likely overwhelmed with the myriad stimuli. That student driver does not know what is important to pay attention to and what stimuli are irrelevant to the task of driving. Paying attention to information that is irrelevant to the task of driving is unwise attention. The experienced trained bus driver is most likely not overwhelmed by the myriad stimuli as they navigate the same stretch of roadway, because their experience with driving helps them to know what type of objects on the road are worthy of attention and they are focused enough not to be distracted by irrelevant stimuli. This bus driver is one who knows wise attention.

> When one attends unwisely, unarisen taints arise and arisen taints increase. When one attends wisely, unarisen taints do not arise and arisen taints are abandoned. (MN, 1995, 2)

Yoniso manasikāra (wise attention) is functionally defined not by the item to which one is paying attention, but by the resultant mind state. Turning the mind to and paying attention to anything that decreases the āsavas (a befuddling, gaslighting force), by definition given in the Sabbāsava Sutta, is yoniso manasikāra. Conversely, anything that increases the āsavas, by definition, is unwise attention (*ayoniso manasikāra*). There is no definitive list of things that could be said to be wise when one pays attention or attends to them. What is yoniso manasikāra (wise attention) for one person in one situation may be ayoniso manasikāra (unwise attention) for another person. For example, for individuals suffering from body dysmorphia, paying attention to certain parts of the body is extremely unwise because it feeds the distortion and increases the dysmorphia. For someone else, the exact same part of the body may hold no special meaning, so paying attention to that part has the capacity to bring a person to more neutral consideration of the body when done in conjunction with some disliked part of the body. The way to determine whether a person is giving wise or unwise attention is by the resultant state of the mind: "When one attends unwisely, unarisen taints arise and arisen taints increase" (MN, 1995, 2). This means the person's trouble will increase when attention is paid to that thing; therefore, giving attention to that thing is unwise. Clients will often obsessively recount, in session and in their own mind, wrongs done to them. The constant reiteration of offenses has the effect of increasing the client's sense of being wronged, thus increasing their anger and resentment. This is unwise attention, in that "unarisen taints arise and arisen taints increase" (MN, 1995, 2). In another example, an individual with alcohol use disorder who is trying to avoid drinking pays attention to the sense of deprivation or remembrances of the pleasant buzz of alcohol; this increases the person's longing for alcohol and decreases their ability to abstain from drinking alcohol. However, for someone who does not have alcohol use disorder and may be socially inhibited, paying attention to the pleasant buzz of having an alcoholic drink may help with socializing, thus increasing their social network.

GOALS AND OBJECTIVES

The Sabbāsava Sutta lists all the different ways the Buddha Gotama gave for the cessation of suffering.

> Bhikkhus, when for a bhikkhu the taints that should be abandoned by [seeing . . .
> restraining . . . using . . . enduring . . . avoiding . . . removing . . . developing]
> have been abandoned by [seeing . . . restraining . . . using . . . enduring . . .

avoiding . . . removing . . . developing], then he is called a bhikkhu who dwells restrained with the restraint of all the taints. He has severed craving, flung off the fetters, and with the complete penetration of conceit he has made an end of suffering. (MN, 1995, 2)

The immediate goal of the sutta is the restraint of all the āsavas (a befuddling, gaslighting force), with the aim to destroy them. The ultimate goal of the Buddhist practice is "the complete penetration of conceit" in order to make "an end of suffering" (MN, 1995, 2). The relevant goal for use in psychotherapy is not for the restraint of all the āsavas nor the complete penetration of conceit. Instead, it is the partial deconstruction of the mechanisms of the āsavas, just enough to give clients some relief from their psychological pain.

METHODS

The sutta names seven methods for the management of the āsavas (a befuddling, gaslighting force):

Bhikkhus, there are taints that should be abandoned by **seeing**. There are taints that should be abandoned by **restraining**. There are taints that should be abandoned by **using**. There are taints that should be abandoned by **enduring**. There are taints that should be abandoned by **avoiding**. There are taints that should be abandoned by **removing**. There are taints that should be abandoned by **developing**. (MN, 1995, 2; *Note:* Boldface was added to terms in the sutta to direct the reader to key concepts.)

Each of these methods (seeing, restraining, using, enduring, avoiding, removing, and developing), along with how they might be utilized in the psychotherapy treatment room, is presented next.

Taints to Be Abandoned by Seeing

Before one can abandon by seeing, one necessarily has to see the thing to be abandoned:

What taints, bhikkhus, should be abandoned by seeing? A . . . person . . . attends to those things unfit for attention and he does not attend to those things fit for attention. . . . What are the things unfit for attention . . . things such that when he attends to then, the unarisen taint of [sensual desire . . . being . . . ignorance] arises in him and the arisen taint of [sensual desire . . . being . . . ignorance] increases. (MN, 1995, 2)

The first step in seeing is (a) to know what one is looking for and (b) to pay sufficient attention to notice when the thing is detected. So, first, seeing, then what to be seen. Here the Buddha is saying that in order to see, *sati* (mindfulness) has to be functioning at all times during one's daily activities. This is like saying that in order to perceive visual objects, one has to have their eyes open; or to taste something, one has to put it in one's mouth. Sati is like having eyes open to look at the mind/citta.

Sati (mindfulness) not only has to look, but it also has to know what it is looking at and what to look for. In this case, sati has to look at the mind/citta for the presence of "sensual desire," "being," and "ignorance" (MN, 1995, 2) in the mind/citta. Sati is to monitor the activities of the mind/citta to the extent that one knows what is going on in the mind/citta, to know whether there is the presence of sensual desire, a notion of a self, and ignorance. Sati sees whether the mind attends to those things unfit for attention or does not attend to those things fit for attention. Sati then has to function like the fortress gatekeeper described in the Nagara Sutta (2004/2013). Thus, sati is to decide whether the mind is attending to something unfit or fit for attention.

It is good to pay attention to some things and not good to pay attention to other things. The defining factor in determining whether something is fit or unfit for the mind's attention is its influence on the mind. These reactions are idiosyncratic, so there is no definitive list of good stimuli or bad stimuli. But the reactions to these stimuli can definitely be judged as fit or unfit for attention.

The things to be seen are the influence of the āsavas (a befuddling, gaslighting force). Sensual desire is generated when the mind is under the influence of kāmāsava (merge self with the five material senses); when being, or identity view or the belief there is an eternal self, is generated under the influence of bhavāsava (denial of impermanence/aniccā); or when ignorance emerges under the influence of avijjāsava (misconstrue phenomena for noumena).

Sensual Desire

In the Sabbāsava Sutta (MN, 1995, 2), the Buddha defined unwise attention as that which results in an increased level of sensual desire. There are no further explanations given beyond a simple reference to sensual desire. A much more detailed definition and discussion of sensual desire is provided in the Mahādukkhakkhandha Sutta (MN, 1995, 13: The Greater Discourse on the Mass of Suffering). The discussion addresses "what is the gratification, what is the danger, and what is the escape in the case of sensual pleasure" (MN, 1995, 13). The Sabbāsava Sutta says that the allure of sensual desire is managed by seeing. The Mahādukkhakkhandha Sutta says the steps in addressing seeing of sensual desire are (a) knowing what is sensual desire; (b) being able to identify the presence of sensual desire in the mind; and (c) being able to trace the progress from (i) gratification, (ii) to the danger, and (iii) to the escape from sensual desire. The Sabbāsava Sutta points to the means for escape from the influence of sensual desire, which is seeing the gratification, the danger, and the escape route. This same process can be done relatively quickly in treatment sessions.

Gratification. Pleasantness is the allure of engaging in sensual pleasures.

> And what, bhikkhus, is the gratification in the case of sensual pleasures? Bhikkhus, there are these five cords of sensual pleasure. What are the five? Forms cognizable by the eye . . . sounds cognizable by the ear . . . odors cognizable by the nose . . . flavors cogniable by the tongue . . . tangibles cognizable by the body that are wished for, desired, agreeable and likeable, connected with sensual desire, and provocative of lust. These are the five cords of sensual pleasure. Now the pleasure and joy that arise dependent on these five cords of sensual pleasure are the gratification in the case of sensual pleasure. (MN, 1995, 13)

Identification of the sensual pleasures and desire is based on the five material senses of the eyes, ear, nose, tongue, and skin. The allure of sensual desire is stimulation of the five senses that is mostly pleasant. Withholding stimulation from the five senses is mostly unpleasant. It is so unpleasant that deprivation of sensory stimulations for "extended periods [has] detrimental effects, causing (among other things) hallucinations, delusions, hyper-suggestibility, or panic" (American Psychological Association, n.d.). The allure of the sensual pleasures is in the gratification. The encounter at the physical sense level is experienced as pleasant to the body. For example, a massage is pleasant to the skin and muscles; a well-played musical symphony is pleasant to the ear consciousness; and a spread of well-made aromatic curries is pleasant to the palate, the eyes, as well as the nose consciousness. It is pleasant to imagine these pleasures, to look forward to these experiences, and to luxuriate in the indulgence of these encounters. Experiencing the pleasure derived from stimulation of the material senses is a constant undercurrent that influences daily activities. Knowing the allure toward gratifying the sensual pleasure is the first step in seeing sensual desire (MN, 1995, 2).

Danger. The pleasantness of sense encounters is, in and of itself, not problematic. Difficulties arise when one longs for and chases after that pleasantness.

> [T]he danger in the case of sensual pleasures . . . on account of the craft by which a clansman makes a living—he has to face cold, he has to face heat, he is

injured by contact with gadflies, mosquitoes, wind, sun, and creeping things; he risks death by hunger and thirst.

If no property comes to the clansman while he works . . . crying: "My work is in vain, my effort is fruitless!"

If property comes to the clansman while he works . . . he experiences pain and grief in protecting it . . . crying: "What I had I have no longer!"

Result: . . . with sensual pleasures as the cause, . . . kings quarrel with kings . . . whereby they incur death or deadly suffering.

Result: . . . with sensual pleasures as the cause . . . men take swords . . . charge into battle . . . whereby they incur death or deadly suffering.

Result: . . . with sensual pleasures as the cause . . . men break into houses, plunder wealth, commit burglary, ambush highways, seduce others' wives, and when they are caught, . . . whereby they incur death or deadly suffering.

Result: . . . with sensual pleasures as the cause . . . people indulge in misconduct of body, speech, and mind

Result: . . . this is a danger in the case of sensual pleasures, a mass of suffering in the life to come, having sensual pleasures as its cause, sensual pleasures as its source, sensual pleasures as its basis, the cause being simply sensual pleasures. (MN, 1995, 13)

The next step in managing the push for gratification of sensual desire is to know the dangers. There is a fine line between need and want. Taking action to attain what one needs is necessary for survival. For example, in most places around the world, if one does not seek shelter from the elements, one is likely to succumb to illness and die an early death. There is inherent pleasure in taking care of the needs for food, clothing, shelter, and human connection. The danger is in indulging beyond what is needed and pursuing ego-enhancing wants, not being satisfied with what one has, and not knowing when it is enough. It is like the compulsion in the adage of "keeping up with the Joneses." The danger is not in the actuality of the experience, but what one does in the pursuit of acquiring and keeping these sensual pleasures. It is the craving for, seeking after, and the clinging to the sensual pleasures that generates all sorts of misdeeds of body, speech, and mind. For the sake of experiencing these fleeting encounters with sensual pleasure, one spends countless hours in its pursuit, with self-righteous expectation of acquiring the means to these sensual pleasures (e.g., working for wages so one has the money to satisfy the senses).

A certain level of desire for material goods is necessary. When the desire for money goes beyond what is needed for food, clothing, and shelter, then the danger of sensual desire is seen. Regardless of whether the pursuit for money is successful or fails, anguish appears. If the pursuit does not result in success, then anguish occurs for not getting what one self-righteously expects. If the pursuit does result in success, then the anguish is for the possibility that such success will all be taken away. The time and effort given, the misdeeds done in the pursuit, and the associated anguish are not considered to outweigh the fleeting encounter with the sensual pleasure. Under the influence of kāmāsava (merge self with the five material senses), one does not see the dangers to oneself nor to others.

Escape. The escape, as posed in both the Sabbāsava Sutta (MN, 1995, 2) and the Mahādukkhakkhandha Sutta (MN, 1995, 13), is to see the dangers in pursuing sensual pleasures. When the dangers are seen, then the pursuit of sensual pleasures loses its allure.

> And what, bhikkhus, is the escape in the case of sensual pleasures? It is the removal of desire and lust, the abandonment of desire and lust for sensual pleasures. This is the escape in the case of sensual. (MN, 1995, 13)

A necessary element in the removal of desire and lust is to apply the knowledge of impermanence/aniccā to the experience of sensual pleasure. An operationalization of the process for gradually introducing the experience of aniccā is to enable the client to see the dangers in pursuing sensual pleasures, to inquire about the moment when that sensual desire or craving was not present, and then to notice the moment following when that sensual desire or craving appeared. Once that pivotal moment is located, then apply yoniso manasikāra (wise attention) to that moment. Applying yoniso manasikāra to the critical moment would mean to fully explore the conditions by asking the client about the situational interactions, engaging in an ecological system analysis of the circumstances, and then enumerating and fully understanding each of the five aggregates, operations of any hindrances, the bases of the desired experience, and the dangers in the sensual desires. Methodically and continuously repeating this process introduces the client to the triggers as well as the dangers in pursuit of sensual gratification. Once all conditions of the critical moment are explored, the psychotherapist can talk to the client in terms of balance—that there is always an upside and a downside to the desire for and pursuit of sensual pleasure. In a culture with puritanical tendencies like in the United States, the pitfall is jumping to the conclusion that the pleasure itself is bad, and that one's pursuit of it is sinful. The sought-after valance here is for the client to experience the pleasure, to acknowledge the momentary fleeting nature of the pleasant experience, and to not spend psychological effort in either acquiring or retaining these fleeting pleasures.

Clients tend to selectively notice and collect certain information. They then ruminate on the bits of information that create and then support their formulation of whatever story they build for the sensual pleasure. Pointing out such bias or reframing the client's unpleasant state or discomfort as only temporary is not usually helpful. Such an interpretation might make the psychotherapist feel better but has the effect of minimizing the client's concerns. It is the repeated experience, with the psychotherapist's guidance, of seeing the moment when the pleasant experience turns to unpleasant that leads the client to the insight of impermanence in both the pleasure and the cessation of the unpleasurable distress. Here, we offer a word of advice to psychotherapists: Do not distress if this process must be repeated over and over again. The influence of kāmāsava (merge self with the five material senses) is persistent, insidious, and ever-present. Thus, the intervention of seeing must be persistent and ever-present.

Being (The Existence of a Self)

The summary phrase of the First Noble Truth, "In short, the five aggregates subject to clinging are suffering," points to how we construct the structures for our own suffering.

> This is how he attends unwisely: "Was I in the past? Was I not in the past? What was I in the past? How was I in the past? Having been what, what did I become in the past? Shall I be in the future? Shall I not be in the future? What shall I be in the future? How shall I be in the future? Having been what, what shall I become in the future?" Or else he is inwardly perplexed about the present thus: "Am I? Am I not? What am I? How am I? Where has this being come from? Where will it go?"
>
> When he attends unwisely in this way, one of six views arises in him. . . . "Self exists for me" . . . "no self exists for me" . . . "I perceive self with self" . . . "I perceive not-self with self" . . . "I perceive self with not-self." . . . "It is this self of mine that speaks and feels and experiences here and there the result of good and bad actions; but this self of mine is permanent, everlasting, eternal, not subject to change, and it will endure as long as eternity." This . . . is called . . . views. . . . Fettered by the fetter of views, . . . he is not freed from suffering.
>
> Bhikkhus, . . . disciples . . . skilled and disciplined in their Dhamma . . . [do] not attend to those things unfit for attention. (MN, 1995, 2)

One set of items of unfit attention are those that generate the belief in the existence of an "I," regardless of whether the I is eternal or annihilistic. Either way, an I is generated. The process for the development of this I, or a notion of a self, is outlined in this section of the Sabbāsava Sutta. It might be akin to the moment when a baby recognizes that the reflection in the mirror is not another baby, but a reflection of themself. Recognition of a mirror reflection of oneself can be considered operationalization of the ability to construct an I.

In the constructionist framework, the construction of the I is similar to the construction of Whiteness in the United States. White identity was constructed in relief from Negro and Black identities. Harris (1998) analyzed legal arguments to show that White in the United States is constructed as property afforded to certain individuals with White skin tone. This socially constructed Whiteness is enshrined in law as property belonging to people with White skin tone. Whiteness was something owned by White people. Some examples of how laws created and enshrined the identity of Whiteness in the United States are as follows. For the first 89 years of the United States, a White person owned his Whiteness as an inalienable property that legally granted the White person the right to be free of being kept as a slave. From 1776 to 1865, Whiteness legally defined individuals as free, not enslaved. As created and identified in law, a person who was of Black skin tone was a slave owned by a White person. Thus, by legal decree, White, Whiteness, White superiority, and White identity were created. The State of Louisiana's Separate Car Act of 1890 constructed Whiteness by granting the privilege of special seats on trains and buses to people who were White and denying those who were Negros those same special seats, regardless of whether the non-White person could afford to purchase a train ticket. Some rights commonly preserved for those identified as White, as practiced in the United States now, are things like:

- unrestricted right to purchase real estate property in any geographic location
- freedom from being stopped by police for search
- being shown leniency in the courts of law
- better schools for their White children

Whiteness is constructed from social practices and legal restrictions to those who are not White. This demonstrates how Whiteness was created and continues to be supported as an inalienable property. Similarly, an inalienable I can be created. The act of paying attention to the questions in the sutta, "Am I? Am I not? What am I? How am I?" (MN, 1995, 2), allows the mind the space to create the entity of I. When an individual pays attention these questions, the sutta says that one of six views arises in that person: (a) "self exists for me," (b) "no self exists for me," (c) "I perceive self with self," (d) "I perceive not-self with self," (e) "I perceive self with not-self," and (f) "It is this self of mine that speaks and feels and experiences here and there the result of good and bad actions" (MN, 1995, 2). These views about the self result in the belief that "but this self of mine is permanent, everlasting, eternal, not subject to change, and it will endure as long as eternity" (MN, 1995, 2).

Clients come into treatment with this unquestioned assumption that there is an I that is "permanent, everlasting, eternal, [and] not subject to change" (MN, 1995, 2). A difficult problem occurs when the client does not like the I that is permanent, everlasting, eternal, and not subject to change. Many clients come into psychotherapy with complaints about this I. Likewise, as many psychotherapists give full attention to the client's I, thus inadvertently affirming the existence of the I. The client enters into psychotherapy with an implicit request to change that I by saying things like, "I don't feel like myself. I want to feel like my old self again" or "I want to find my true self." In some way, there is an underlying assumption that there is a permanent, everlasting, eternal, and not-subject-to-change self/I that is somehow hidden. This is the belief there is an I hidden and surrounded by unpleasant things. This assumption is seen in the analogy that psychotherapists sometimes refer to treatment as peeling back the layers of an onion to eventually get to the authentic self.

Many of the psychotherapeutic interventions assume the existence of the permanent self/I. A psychotherapy approach to treatment is for the psychotherapist to interact with the client by way of their authentic self, with the task of facilitating the client's access to their true self; this can be seen in concepts like the client's authentic self, original self, or vulnerable self. There are many references in various theories of psychotherapy to a client's problems in terms of self; some of this focus on the self as the problem can be heard in terms like these: low self-esteem, fake self, idealized self, superficial self, pseudo self, tendency for self-referencing, need to integrate the parts of the self, split self, shattered self, and many other descriptions of a self.

An operationalization of the process for gradually introducing not-self to the client is for the Buddhist psychotherapist to bypass the I in the same way that the Buddha bypassed the self in the Ānanda Sutta (AN, 2012, 44.10: Ānanda Is There a Self?):

> Then the wanderer Vacchagotta approached the Blessed One . . . and said to him:
>
>> How is it now, Master Gotama, is there a self?
>> When this was said, the Blessed One was silent.
>> "Then, Master Gotama, is there no self?"
>> When this was said, the Blessed One was silent. . . .
>> Then the wanderer Vacchagotta rose from his seat and departed.
>
> Then, not long after the wanderer Vacchagotta had left, the Venerable Ānanda said to the Blessed One: "Why is it, venerable sir, that when the Blessed One was questioned by the wanderer Vacchagotta, he did not answer?"
>
> If, Ānanda, when I was asked by the wandered Vacchagotta, "Is there a self?" I had answered, "There is a self," this would have been siding with those ascetics and brahmins who are eternalists. And if, when I was asked by him, "Is there no self?" I had answered, "There is no self," this would have been siding with those ascetics and brahmins who are annihilationists.
>
> If, Ānanda, when I was asked by the wandered Vacchagotta, "Is there a self?" I had answered, "There is a self," would this have been consistent on my part with the arising of the knowledge that "all phenomena are non-self?"

No, venerable sir.
If, Ānanda, when I was asked by the wandered Vacchagotta, "Is there no self?"
I had answered, "There is no self," the wanderer Vacchagotta, already confused,
would have fallen into even greater confusion, thinking, "It seems that the self I
formerly had does not exist now."

The Buddha, rightly so, thought that to deliberate, debate, discover, and/or recover oneself will result in confusion. This is evident as psychotherapists and clients endlessly search for the client's true self, their essential self, their best self, their integrated self, and so on. Instead, the Buddha says to investigate things that cause the conceptual development of a notion of a self. The inquiry into the influence of bhavāsava (denial of impermanence/aniccā) is such an endeavor. This inquiry can be handled by directly inquiring into the functioning of the aggregates and ignoring the client's notion of their self/I. An example of the identity view may be heard when a patient says things like this: "I am fat. I am so undisciplined that I cannot stick to a diet. No one likes a fat person. I have no friends because people are repulsed by a fat person." The client's statement, "I am fat," is a manifestation of an identity view that merges the self with the body; their statement, "I am depressed," merges self with feeling. Any personality view can be substituted for "fat" or "depressed" in the sentence structure. Buddhist psychotherapists do not explore any aspect of "fat" or "depressed," thus bypassing the notion of a self. Instead, Buddhist psychotherapy would explore the conditions that gave rise to the notion of a fat or depressed self or any number of identity views of a client. Effecting changes in aspects of the conditions will alter the client's notion of the self without the psychotherapist focusing on the client's I. To explore the conditions, the psychotherapist can start a line of inquiry by looking for the most recent moment when the client generated the notion that self equals a fat body. It may be useful to approach the inquiry along the lines of the identity view with the aggregates.

> He . . . regards [form . . . feeling . . . perception . . . volitional formations . . .
> consciousness] as self, or self as possessing [form . . . feeling . . . perception . . .
> volitional formations . . . consciousness], or [form . . . feeling . . . perception . . .
> volitional formations . . . consciousness] as self, or self as in [form . . . feeling . . .
> perception . . . volitional formations . . . consciousness]. (*Saṃyutta Nikāya* [SN],
> 2000, III:22)

The sutta specifies identifying with the five aggregates in four different ways. These are (a) self is identical with it, (b) self as possessing it, (c) self as containing it, and (d) self as contained within it. Depending on the category of identity view, the psychotherapist can formulate the initial question. Keep in mind that whereas the Buddha is guiding his disciples on the path to the elimination of an identity view, the job of a psychotherapist is only to adjust the identity view, not to eliminate it.

The person who says, "I am fat," sees the self as identical with form. If the psychotherapist asks, "How do you feel about being fat?," then the psychotherapist is colluding with the client's identity view (i.e., the view that client is the same as the client's body; thus, "the body is not as thin as the client wants" is the same as "the self of the client"). For this person, the psychotherapist could ask, "What happened that gave you the idea that you are fat?" Focusing on what happened is looking for conditions, not focusing on the identification of oneself with one's body. The person who says, "I have no friends because people are repulsed by a fat person," has taken on the fourth position with self as contained within it (i.e., the "fat"). The initial question may be phrased as, "What happened that gave you the idea that people don't like you?" This client views themself as surrounded by the fat so that when others look at them, all they see is the fat. The reason this client gives for not having friends is because others are repulsed by the fat that surrounds the true self. The phrasing of the question draws attention to what happened, disregarding the identification with the body fat. The question focuses on the condition of other people's actions, which may very well have nothing to do with the client's body fat. In application, the type of identity view guides the phrasing of the opening inquiry. From there, the Buddhist psychotherapist can engage in a dialogue that focuses on the aggregates, not on the client's notion of the self.

The operationalization of the Buddhist-based approach to psychotherapy is for the psychotherapist not to collude with the client by speaking as if there is an I. This may be addressed by sidestepping the whole existence of the I and focusing directly on the aggregates. The only reference to the client's I would be to paraphrase, as in "What happened to make you think that you are [whatever the client claims]?" The psychotherapist is focusing on discovering the very last moment, not the very first moment, that gave rise to the client's notion of their self (i.e., "I am fat"). Once that moment is pinpointed, then the psychotherapist helps the client fully examine that moment in terms of the aggregates and the nature of their suffering.

The point of befuddlement in engaging clients in this manner is usually figuring out the moment that generated their notion of a self. Once that moment is located in the client's memory, it is simple to find the exact sense contact with its accompanying *vedanā* (hedonic feeling tone). However, *saññā* (perception, naming, labeling) is usually a struggle. Regardless of the struggle to identify saññā, the most fruitful dialogue usually occurs in the discussion regarding saññā. In the process of identifying saññā of the sense contact, relevant memories from the client's past that inform the client's perception usually surface. Most of the time, once the psychotherapist is able to help the client articulate saññā in one word or one phrase, their mental formations and their emotions usually shift on their own accord, followed by a shift in the client's notion of the self.

The Buddhist psychotherapist is advised to be meticulous in guiding their client to discuss each aggregate of form (*rūpa*), hedonic feeling tone (*vedanā*), and perception or labeling (*saññā*). Clients usually come into treatment sessions talking primarily from mental formations (*saṅkhāra*) and the derivative emotions based on those mental fabrications. The first task of the psychotherapist is to find the sense object, the external stimulus, that triggered the client's concern. The line of inquiry can easily start with, "What happened?" and then follow with, "What happened before that?" or "What happened then?" Questions about what happened are focusing on rūpa (form), the sense object, the sense organ, and then the sense consciousness/manasikāra. There is no end to the morass of fabrication if the psychotherapist stays with the client's identity view or their saṅkhāra (mental formations, or the stories we tell ourselves about the sense object).

The psychotherapist can make meta-cognitive comments in regard to the client's report of the aggregate and description of their mind state. In applying this approach, clients have actually reformulated their notion spontaneously as they explore the aggregates functioning in the moment where the conditions for the arising of their identified self are explored. Regardless of what that reformulated notion of the self might or might not be, it is best to let it stand as long as it is less harmful to the client. This approach differs significantly from the spiritual practice of Buddhism, in which the ultimate goal is the elimination of any identity view. Buddhist psychotherapy, the secular practice, is to reduce the client's psychological pain just enough for improved functioning; therefore, the job of a psychotherapist is only to adjust the identity view, not to eliminate it.

The client's reformulation of their self-view is usually sufficient to significantly decrease their affective distress. From there, it is easier to start discussing skillful means to respond to the arising of the conditions that triggered their notion of themself. In psychotherapy, the condition that gave rise to the client's dislike of their notion of a self is usually based on their social interactions. It is an easy step then to discuss more skillful means to navigate their social circumstance.

Avijjāsava (Ignorance, Misconstrue Phenomena for Noumena)
The third type of āsava, similar to neither pleasant nor unpleasant vedanā, is born out of ignorance of one's misperception of existence:

> What taints, bhikkhus, should be abandoned by seeing? . . . They are things such that when he attends to them, . . . the unarisen taint of ignorance arises in

him and the arisen taint of ignorance increases. . . . By attending to things unfit for attention and by not attending to things fit for attention, both unarisen taints arise in him and arisen taints increase. (MN, 1995, 2)

Avijjāsava (ignorance, misconstrue phenomena for noumena), in the most simplistic terms, is the state of not knowing that one does not know. From this seemingly simplistic concept, an overwhelmingly vast and complex network opens in the exploration of ignorance (*avijjā*). Explications of avijjā appear throughout the Pali canons, from the extremely terse Avijjā Sutta (SN 45.1: Ignorance) that covers unbelievably vast territory in its one short paragraph to longer discourses such as the section on ignorance in the Aṅguttara Nikāya (2012, 10.61). The *Pali Text Society's Pali–English Dictionary* defines avijjā as "ignorance; the main root of evil and of continual rebirth" (Pali Text Society, n.d.).

Avijjāsava (ignorance, misconstrue phenomena for noumena) is an influence on the mind's function that manifests in misinterpretation of information flow from outside stimuli into the internal sense bases. Avijjāsava is an active process that acts as a filter on all activities of the mind. When a person is not aware of this active filtering process, they systematically misidentify what is impermanent for permanent and what is unattractive for attractive. With the exception of an *arahant* (one who has attained liberation from suffering [*nibbāna*]) or a *buddha* (fully enlightened one), we believe that the stories we tell ourselves about ourselves and about the situations we find ourselves in are accurate renditions of the world. Unless we have been trained to see through the biasing influence of avijjāsava, we do not consider the stories we all tell ourselves to be manifestations of a mind under the influence of any kind of systematic bias.

For the purpose of psychotherapy, one is to assume that any and all stories clients tell themselves about themselves and their situations are to be considered to have been formulated from a mind under the influence of avijjāsava (ignorance, misconstrue phenomena for noumena). It is also reasonable to consider that all stories clients report in psychotherapy sessions are distortions filtered through the three types of āsavas (taints). To a large extent, clients come to psychotherapy knowing, at some level, that their conceptualization of their presenting problem is distorted. It is inevitable that at some point in the course of treatment, the client will either explicitly or implicitly ask the psychotherapist if what they believe about the cause and the manifestations of their presenting problem are in fact an accurate reflection of reality.

Indeed, the process that the Buddha cataloged in the Avijjā Sutta is an amazingly accurate rendition of what occurs in a client's construction of their problem.

> For an unwise person immersed in ignorance, wrong view springs up. For one of wrong view, wrong intention springs up. For one of wrong intention, wrong speech springs up. For one of wrong speech, wrong action springs up. For one of wrong action, wrong livelihood springs up. For one of wrong livelihood, wrong effort springs up. (SN, 2000, 45.1)

The amount of effort and energy that clients undertake in order to address their presenting problem can truly be said to be heroic. They suffer immensely under the weight of the following: their presenting problem by the amount of effort and time devoted to ruminations about their problem; the amount of effort to fuel the indignation poured into defending themselves against the negative estimations from either themselves or others regarding their personhood on account of their presenting problem; and the stories they fabricate and then elaborate upon to ease their discomfort. The journey clients take in psychotherapy can be likened to the hero's journey for enlightenment. The hero's journeys for enlightenment are made easier using the Buddha's words as a guide. Similarly, psychotherapists can guide their client's journey out of discomfort by using the intervention of abandoning from seeing the distortions of their own making.

In the case of helping a client to see their presenting problem in a frame that can be much more useful for addressing their presenting problem, the psychotherapist can take the same process as outlined in the Avijjā Sutta, except in the reverse order. In the in-session dialogue, the psychotherapist can start the inquiry thus:

- When wrong effort springs up (SN, 2000, 45.1), pose this question: "What all have you tried in an effort to solve your [fill in with the presenting problem]?"

- When wrong action springs up (SN, 2000, 45.1), pose this question: "What all have you done in an effort to solve your [fill in with the presenting problem]?"

It is helpful for the psychotherapist to make the distinction between what actions a client has actually taken versus what the client might think they have tried. Many times, clients believe that their worry, anxiety, and ruminations are things the person has done to address their presenting problem. Notice that experiencing the feeling of worry or anxiety does not usually produce actions that could affect those conditions that give rise to the client's presenting problem. The worry and anxiety are hindrances that enable a person to think (wrongly) and to continue in the delusional belief that something has actually been done to affect the conditions for their problem.

When wrong speech springs up (SN, 2000, 45.1), pose this question: "What did the other person say? Then what did you say in response?" It is rare for a client to fully and accurately recount an interaction. It is more likely that the client will give an account of what the client thought the other person was trying to do (not what the other person actually said or did), followed by what the client thought of the other person's intentions. For example, "I know he was tired and had been worried about losing his job, so I know he was not really angry at me when he lost his temper and yelled at me." Notice, the client did not recount what the other person actually said or did nor what the client said or did. A more precise rendition, one that is much more informative for the purpose of psychotherapeutic interventions, might sound like this:

> After he finished cooking dinner, I asked if he had soaked the pans. He said very angrily, "It is not enough that I cook for you, but now you want to tell me how I should clean up the kitchen too!" I was so scared to anger him more that I complimented him on the meal and got up to do the dishes.

When wrong intention springs up (SN, 2000, 45.1) as in this example, pose this question: "What did you want to know when you asked [restate the client's question]?" (In this case, the question for the client is "What did you want to know when you asked 'Did you soak the pans?'") Make sure that the client reports what their intentions were for whatever was said and done. It is easy to help the client formulate questions that include their intentions versus discussing the client's notion of a self that rationalizes it. If the client's notion of the self is one of "I am responsible," then the client thinks it is their fault for being yelled at (e.g., "I know he was tired and had been worried about losing his job, so I know he was not really angry at me when he lost his temper and yelled at me"). The question, "Did you soak the pans?" would be reformulated to add the intention. Here is an alternative: "I am too tired to wash the dishes tonight. It would be easier to wash the pans tomorrow if they are soaking. Did you soak the pans, or should I go and soak the pans now?"

For wrong view springs up (SN, 2000, 45.1), pose this question: "Why did you want to do that?" This question is inquiring into the desire at the base of the intention. The psychotherapist can note the type of desire, making sure to confirm whether the client is in concurrence with the category of the desire that motivated the intention. At this point in the in-session dialogue, it is useful to affirm the desire and concur that the desire itself is not harmful.

Because the goal of psychotherapy is not enlightenment, it is not necessary to examine the ignorance. However, after affirming the desire that is at the base of the intention, it is time to craft an intervention with a reframe of the situation that is congruent with the Buddhist worldview of dependent arising, *kamma,* and the not-self (*anattā*). For the intervention, design the reframe to highlight the impermanence of the situation and the dangers of craving; then suggest an alternative perspective for the client's situation. For the example of the dishes, a reframe might be:

> You were tired and did not want to do the dishes that evening but wanted to do the dishes the next morning. You knew it would be easier to clean the pans if they had been soaking the whole night, right? What could you have said to convey your intentions behind your question of "Did you soak the pans?"

Or the psychotherapist could ask the client, "What could you have said to call his attention to the fact that he had lost his temper and was yelling at you; that he had misunderstood the intent of your question?" Or they can present any other reframe, depending on the nature of the problem with this client, the nature of the relationship between the client and the partner, or both.

Taints to Be Abandoned by Restraining

When "seeing" does not spontaneously generate an alternative course of action, then other types of intervention can be utilized. The simplest may be not putting oneself in the situation where misbehavior is likely to occur.

> What taints, bhikkhus, should be abandoned by restraining? Here a bhikkhu, . . . abides with the eye . . . ear . . . nose . . . tongue . . . body . . . mind faculty restrained . . . there are no taints, vexation, or fever in one who abides with the faculties restrained. These are called the taints that should be abandoned by restraining. (MN, 1995, 2)

The phrase, "abandoned by restraining," is like the old joke about a patient that says to the doctor, "Doctor, it hurts when I do this," and the doctor responds, "Then don't do that!" In the normal course of daily activities, the six internal sense bases are continuously bombarded with stimuli from all sorts of sources. Think of the phrase, "Doctor, it hurts when I do this," like a 2-year-old indiscriminately drawn to objects in the universe; like the 2-year-old, one is overwhelmed by the senses. Consciousness (*viññāna*) cannot possibly register all of the stimuli. Only a limited number of these stimuli can register at the sense doors at any moment in time. Of these, viññāna can only process a fraction of the stimuli. The doctor saying, "Then don't do that!" is like the Buddha saying not to open oneself to being overwhelmed by the myriad stimuli and restrain the senses. Sati (mindfulness) needs to guide viññāna in selecting to which stimuli attention are given by restraining the mind/citta from reaching out to seek objects in the universe.

Examples of how this might show up in psychotherapy might start with a client reporting something like this:

> I get really upset every time I talk to my mom. She refuses to admit that at 83 she cannot live by herself in that big house of hers with no one around to help. She is so stubborn, and she accuses me of being stubborn! I was so upset that I could not go back to work. I had to take a sick day after my call with my mom. I cannot have her living by herself. One day, I am going to get a call from the police saying that she is dead in that big house of hers.

In such a situation, the psychotherapist might suggest that the client use sense restraint by not arguing with her mother. Instead, the psychotherapist might engage the client in exploring alternatives that may be more skillful, such as engaging in problem-solving with her mother on ways to get certain care-taking tasks done or talking to the mother's primary care physician, a neighbor, or the client's siblings. There are many ways to achieve a worthy goal without repeated exposure to upsetting sense contact.

Taints to Be Abandoned by Using

Consider this example: A person looks longingly at a piece of inherited jewelry that sits in the bank security box because they think it is too delicate to wear. That yearning is present in their mind for hours, disturbing the pleasure of attending a gathering. To quiet the mind, the person might consider resetting the inherited jewelry so that they can use it without the possibility of damage. At times, it is possible to quiet the disturbance in the mind to use the item.

> What taints, bhikkhus, should be abandoned by using? . . . uses the robe only for protection from [elements] . . . uses alms food . . . for the endurance and continuance of this body, . . . uses the resting place only for protection from [elements] . . . uses the medicinal requisites only for protection from arisen afflicting feelings and for the benefit of good health. . . . These are called the taints that should be abandoned by using. (MN, 1995, 2)

The phrase, "abandoned by using," is essentially suggesting that when used appropriately, no activities or objects inherently trigger sensual pleasure. Conversely, any object of activity can be used in such a way to increase sensual desire. The intervention here is to recognize the purpose of the object and use it appropriately. The determination of appropriateness is whether the activity facilitates physical and psychological health.

Examples of how this might show up in psychotherapy may be with a client reporting something like this:

> I got into this big argument with my brother last night. I know he is upset. We are all upset. Our mom just got put on hospice care because the doctor

says she has no more than a few weeks left to live. We came home last night from the hospital with vials of heroin. My brother said we should give her the heroin. I yelled at my brother for being such a pill pusher and said that if he had his way, he would make a heroin addict of my mother. I was so upset that I just walked out and went back home. I feel guilty for leaving my mother with an enabler. I don't want to argue with my brother, so I have not been back to mom's house to help take care of her.

There are many things going on with this client's report. As an example of taints to be abandoned by using (MN, 1995, 2), the item of note here in this scenario is to notice that even an extremely addictive drug like heroin, when used appropriately, can function for good, as in easing the physical pain of a terminally ill dying body. The intervention here would be to affirm the appropriate use of the heroin and perhaps to discuss (a) more skillful means for the client to interact with her brother and (b) the effect of her mother's eminent death on the client.

Taints to Be Abandoned by Enduring

Unpleasantness (e.g., postsurgical pain) will dissipate with time. Knowing the reason for such discomfort facilitates the enduring of the temporary unpleasantness.

> What taints, bhikkhus, should be abandoned by enduring? Here a bhikkhu, reflecting wisely, bears cold and heat, hunger and thirst, and contact with gadflies, mosquitoes, wind, the sun, and creeping things; he endures ill-spoken, unwelcome words and arisen bodily feelings that are painful, racking, sharp, piercing, disagreeable, distressing, and menacing to life. . . . These are called the taints that should be abandoned by enduring. (MN, 1995, 2)

The phrase, "abandoned by enduring," is essentially directing us to the fact that it really is useless to become angry at things in the world for which one has no control. No matter whether one likes or dislike things in the world, those things will continue to exist. Know this and give up trying to change things by railing against them (e.g., there is no use in being irritated at winter weather; complaining loudly about rain, fog, and short days with less sunlight will not change the weather in the Pacific Northwest).

Complaints about the weather have shown up in psychotherapy regularly in the first author's (Tien's) hometown of Seattle. Many clients have complained about their dislike of Seattle winters, with endless days of gray without sunshine, continuous days of drizzling rain, and the oppressiveness of getting up in the dark and getting home from work in the dark when sunrise is at 8:00 a.m. and sunset is at 4:30 p.m. Complaining about these conditions will not make the Seattle winters any sunnier or make the daylight last longer in winter. The psychotherapist can engage their client in finding more skillful ways to endure Seattle winters, like using light therapy lamps to counteract the effects of the short rainy days of Seattle winter.

Taints to Be Abandoned by Avoiding

In some cases, there are foreseeable difficult results for engaging in some pleasant activity. Consider the example of an individual with alcohol use disorder who cannot stop at one alcoholic beverage to loosen their social inhibition; this person should find a more skillful means of socializing with friends, such as not going out to bars.

> What taints, bhikkhus, should be abandoned by avoiding? Here a bhikkhu, reflecting wisely, avoids a wild elephant, a wild horse, a wild bull, a wild dog, a snake, a stump, a bramble patch, a chasm, a cliff, a cesspit, a sewer. Reflecting wisely, he avoids sitting on unsuitable seats, wandering to unsuitable resorts, and associating with bad friends, since if he were to do so wise companions in the holy life might suspect him of evil conduct. While taints, vexation, and fever might arise in one who does not avoid these things, there are no taints, vexation, and fever in one who avoids them. These are called the taints that should be abandoned by avoiding. (MN, 1995, 2)

This section of the sutta says not to heedlessly go into situations that will foreseeably lead to harm, either to self or others. But it is not easy to foresee harm in the types of situations that clients bring into psychotherapy. It is usually easy to see harm in hindsight. Foreseeing harm is much more difficult, especially when desire or hubris hinders paying attention to warning signs.

Here is a clinical example: A client once came into psychotherapy for treatment of depression after the death of her daughter. At first, it was easy to attribute her depression to simple grief. However, as treatment progressed, the full story gradually came to light. The client's daughter and son-in-law had separated, with her daughter accusing the son-in-law of abuse. Her daughter had successfully filed for and was awarded a restraining order in which the son-in-law was to stay at least 50 feet away from her. The client had considered her daughter to be stubborn and unreasonable ever since she was a child. This client thought the son-in-law was charming and overly accommodating to her daughter's unreasonable demands. Thinking that she knew better than her daughter what would be good for her daughter, the client had engineered a lunch date with her daughter, where unbeknownst to her daughter, the client had also invited her son-in-law. The client then left, with instructions for the two of them to "talk it over and work it out." It was at this luncheon where her son-in-law shot her daughter. The client, full of her own hubris, heedlessly set up a very dangerous situation. Her conceit, heedlessly ignoring the restraining order, blinded her to the foreseeable harm to her daughter. Treatment for this client was for the psychotherapist to initially acknowledge the depression as appropriate for the situation, and then to invite the client to take the very long road of recognizing her conceit as a way to circumvent foreseeable harm by avoiding.

Taints to Be Abandoned by Removing

There are times when one's peace of mind is facilitated by engaging in activities that are aimed at removing some unpleasant situations (e.g., participating in peaceful protest of police brutality).

> What taints, bhikkhus, should be abandoned by removing? Here a bhikkhu, reflecting wisely, does not tolerate an arisen thought of sensual desire; he abandons it, removes it, does away with it, and annihilates it. He does not tolerate an arisen thought of ill will. . . . He does not tolerate an arisen thought of cruelty. . . . He does not tolerate arisen evil unwholesome states; he abandons them, removes them, does away with them, and annihilates them. While taints, vexation, and fever might arise in one who does not remove these thoughts, there are no taints, vexation, or fever in one who removes them. These are called the taints that should be abandoned by removing. (MN, 1995, 2)

For the betterment of humanity, it is good to remove ill will, cruelty, and evil thoughts. In the implementation of psychotherapy, the method to achieve the elimination of these actions of mind is not by intolerance, but by close examination. Clients come into psychotherapy confessing thoughts of ill will and thoughts of cruelty. Often the confession is accompanied by reports of discomfort with their thoughts of ill will. Those without discomfort in the presence of ill will and cruelty would, in all likelihood, not voluntarily seek psychotherapy. To remove unwholesome desires, the psychotherapist needs to increase the level of the client's discomfort, even as the client explicitly requests assistance to reduce it.

Taints to Be Abandoned by Developing

The Sabbāsava Sutta offers the following description of abandoning taints by developing enlightenment factors:

> What taints, bhikkhus, should be abandoned by developing? Here a bhikkhu, reflecting wisely, develops the mindfulness enlightenment factor, which is supported by seclusion, dispassion, and cessation, and ripens in relinquishment. He develops the investigation-of-states enlightenment factor . . . the energy enlightenment factor . . . the rapture enlightenment factor . . . the tranquility enlightenment factor . . . the concentration enlightenment factor . . . the

> equanimity enlightenment factor, which is supported by seclusion, dispassion, and cessation, and ripens in relinquishment. While taints, vexation, and fever might arise in one who does not develop these enlightenment factors, there are no taints, vexation, or fever in one who develops them. These are called the taints that should be abandoned by developing. (MN, 1995, 2)

The purpose of the Buddha's teaching is for liberation. The enlightenment factors are worthy and necessary for the pursuit of liberation. However, these are not treatment interventions, as such. The enlightenment factors listed here may be evident as clients find relief from their disquieting symptoms and learn better ways to handle their presenting problem and life's difficulties. The enlightenment factors are not the goals for psychotherapy, even though clients most likely will experience some of them as they achieve relief from their presenting problem or problems.

CONCLUSION

This chapter concludes with some thoughts about using the Sabbāsava Sutta to guide in-session dialogue.

> When . . . contacted by a painful bodily feeling, he sorrows, grieves, and laments; he weeps and beats his breast and becomes distraught. This . . . worldling . . . has not risen up in the bottomless abyss, one who has not gained a foothold.
>
> But, . . . when the instructed . . . disciple is contacted by a painful bodily feeling, he does not sorrow, grieve, or lament; he does not weep and beat his breast and become distraught. This . . . instructed . . . disciple . . . has risen up in the bottomless abyss, one who has gained a foothold. (Patala Sutta; SN, 2000, 36.4: The Bottomless Abyss)

To help a client rise up from the bottomless abyss, the Buddhist psychotherapist does the following in the treatment session. First, the psychotherapist invites the client to verbalize their thoughts and concerns on the agreed-upon topic. Second, the psychotherapist listens and analyzes what the client is saying within the Buddhist framework. Third, the psychotherapist inquires further until a full understanding of the critical moments in the client's experience emerge. Fourth, the psychotherapist articulates what they have noticed about the client's presenting problem within the Buddhist framework. Fifth, in a variety of ways from various different angles, ideally using the client's words and terminology, the psychotherapist reframes the client's suffering within the worldview of dependent arising phenomena in consciousness, kamma (cause and effect of the doing of deeds), the five aggregates, the five aggregates subject to clinging, and hindrances. Finally, when appropriate, the psychotherapist eventually directs the client to actions that have the greatest probability of generating positive kammic resultants. Many clients spontaneously take this last step without prompting from the psychotherapist.

For the sake of structuring the psychotherapist's mapping while in session, it is proposed that they focus in-session treatment on three different arenas. The first arena is on the mechanical workings of the five aggregates. This aspect directs the psychotherapist to focus on each aggregate of rūpa (form), vedanā (hedonic feeling tone), saññā (perception), saṅkhāra (mental formations), and viññāṇa (consciousness), depending on whichever aggregate appears to be most salient within a given situation. The most common aggregate noticed by the client is saṅkhāra (mental formations) in the form of proliferating on the mental fabrications. The simplest approach may be for the psychotherapist to identify the sense contact to which the person's manasikāra (attention) is directed. This may be accomplished through inquiring about the exact moment the client became aware of their presenting problem or whatever concern is under discussion or exploration. Unlike other theories of psychotherapy that search for the first time in a client's life that the client remembers the disturbing emotion, the Buddhist psychotherapist's task is to identify the most recent moment that gave rise to the current reported incident. The psychotherapist is directed to focus primarily on revealing the rūpa (form), sense contact, and vedanā (hedonic feeling tone) of a stimulus that generated the client's concern. After firmly establishing the internal and external stimuli, hold an extensive discussion on past events, beliefs, and values that are part of the formulation for the client's saññā (perceptions, recognition). This is also the point where the psychotherapist may offer an alternative construct to the client's perceptions (but not dispute the sense contact). By introducing an alternative construct, psychotherapy essentially changes the make-up of the mental formations/*cetasika*. Having the psychotherapist noting, commenting, labeling, and framing what the client says during the treatment session is like a tutor giving real-time instruction as the client struggles with a problem.

The second arena is the five aggregates subject to clinging. This directs the psychotherapist to focus on the construction of the notion of the self (*attā*). The operationalization of such noting is to first notice and then label and comment on the workings of consciousness: citta (mind), viññāṇa (consciousness), the hindrances, and the defilements that are generated from the clinging aspect in its relationship to the five aggregates.

The third arena is the link between the Buddhist worldview of dependent arising of phenomena in consciousness and kamma (cause and effect of the doing of deeds). The dependent arising of phenomena in consciousness directs the psychotherapist to work with the stream of thoughts, paying special attention to volitional formations (*cetanā*). Kamma directs the psychotherapist to focus on interpersonal relationships and the underlying values that guide the client's actions.

The psychotherapist's observations and comments to the client would, in various combinations and varying degrees, revolve around these three arenas of (a) the mechanical workings of the five aggregates, (b) the five aggregates subject to clinging, and (c) the link between the Buddhist world-view of dependent arising of phenomena in consciousness and kamma. The arena of primary focus in any treatment session depends on the presenting problem, the temperament, and the habitual preference of the client. Regardless of the arena of focus in any particular treatment session, the general direction is toward the reduction of suffering by way of stabilizing the mind through the mind's ability to note the mind states and reframe the problem within the framework of aniccā (impermanence, transitory) and anattā (not-self), thus resetting the mind's filter.

18

THREE ARENAS FOR INTERVENTION IN BUDDHIST PSYCHOTHERAPY

A Model and Case Examples

At the end of Chapter 17, we shared the following from the sutta with regard to how Buddhist psychotherapy can be used to help a client rise up from the bottomless abyss:

> When . . . contacted by a painful bodily feeling, he sorrows, grieves, and laments; he weeps and beats his breast and becomes distraught. This . . . worldling . . . has not risen up in the bottomless abyss, one who has not gained a foothold.
>
> But . . . when the instructed . . . disciple is contacted by a painful bodily feeling, he does not sorrow, grieve, or lament; he does not weep and beat his breast and become distraught. This . . . instructed . . . disciple . . . has risen up in the bottomless abyss, one who has gained a foothold. (Patala Sutta; *Saṃyutta Nikāya* [SN], 2000, 36.4: The Bottomless Abyss)

This chapter pulls together concepts from previous chapters into an integrated model for Buddhist psychotherapy. We introduced this model at the beginning of the book, but here we will explore it in more depth and provide case examples.

https://doi.org/10.1037/0000453-019
Buddhist Psychotherapy: Connecting Early Buddhism to Mindfulness and Western Psychotherapy, by L. Tien, D. M. Kawahara, and V. Dhammadinna

THREE ARENAS OF INTERVENTION

To help a client rise up from the bottomless abyss, the Buddhist psychotherapist does the following in the treatment session: First, the psychotherapist invites the client to verbalize their thoughts and concerns on the agreed-upon topic. Second, the psychotherapist listens and analyzes what the client is saying within the Buddhist framework. Third, the psychotherapist inquires further until a full understanding of the critical moments in the client's experience emerge. Fourth, the psychotherapist articulates what they have noticed about the client's presenting problem within the Buddhist framework. Fifth, in a variety of ways from various different angles, ideally using the client's words and terminology, the psychotherapist reframes the client's suffering within the worldview of dependent arising phenomena in consciousness, *kamma* (cause and effect of the doing of deeds), the five aggregates, the five aggregates subject to clinging, and hindrances. Finally, when appropriate, the psychotherapist eventually directs the client to actions that have the greatest probability of generating positive kammic resultants. Many clients spontaneously take this last step without prompting from the psychotherapist.

To recap from Chapter 17, for the sake of structuring the psychotherapist's mapping while in session, it is proposed that they focus in-session treatment on the mechanical workings of the five aggregates. This aspect directs the psychotherapist to focus on each aggregate of form (*rūpa*), hedonic feeling tone (*vedanā*), perception (*saññā*), mental formations (*saṅkhāra*), and consciousness (*viññāna*), depending on whichever aggregate appears to be most salient within a given situation. The most common aggregate noticed by the client is saṅkhāra (mental formations) in the form of proliferating on the mental fabrications. The simplest approach may be for the psychotherapist to identify the sense contact to which the person's attention (*manasikāra*) is directed. This may be accomplished through inquiring about the exact moment the client became aware of their presenting problem or whatever concern is under discussion or exploration. Unlike other theories of psychotherapy that search for the first time in a client's life that the client remembers the disturbing emotion, the Buddhist psychotherapist's task is to identify the most recent moment that gave rise to the current reported incident. The psychotherapist is directed to focus primarily in revealing the rūpa (form), the sense contact, and vedanā (hedonic feeling tone) of a stimulus that generated the client's concern. After firmly establishing the internal and external stimuli, hold an extensive discussion on past events, beliefs, and values that are part of the formulation for the client's saññā (perceptions, recognition). This is also the point where the psychotherapist may offer an alternative construct to the client's perceptions (but not dispute the sense contact). By introducing an alternative construct, psychotherapy essentially changes the make-up of the mental formations/*cetasika*. Having the psychotherapist noting, commenting, labeling, and framing what the client says during the treatment session is like a tutor giving real-time instruction as the client struggles with a problem.

This approach has the psychotherapist bypass the client's constructed notion of the self/*attā*. The operationalization of stepping aside (e.g., side-stepping an incoming punch from a martial arts opponent, thus avoiding the harm) is to first notice and then label and comment on the workings of consciousness: mind (*citta*), viññāṇa, the hindrances, and the defilements that are generated from the clinging aspect in its relationship to the five aggregates.

The paraphrasing is the link between the Buddhist worldview of dependent arising of phenomena in consciousness and the client's constructed world. For intervention, the dependent arising of phenomena in consciousness directs the psychotherapist to work with the stream of thoughts, paying special focus on volitional formations (*cetanā*), which lays the groundwork for future kamma. Kamma directs the psychotherapist to focus on interpersonal relationships and the underlying values that guide the client's actions.

The observations and comments by the psychotherapist to the client would, in various combinations and varying degrees, pertain to three arenas (Figure 18.1):

- **Assessment:** This phase is an operationalization of "all conditioned things are impermanent" (*aniccā*), one of the three marks of existence (Dhammapada [Dhp], 1996, 277–279: The Path). In this phase of treatment, we ask and seek to answer this question: "What multiple conditions give rise to the presenting problem?" We determine the *conditions* that give rise to the client's presenting problem.

- **Diagnosis:** This phase is an operationalization of "all conditioned things are unsatisfactory" (*dukkha*). We explore all aspects of the client's experience of their suffering by asking and seeking to understand: "What is the client's experience of existence?" We determine the mechanical workings of the five aggregates, especially saṅkhāra.

- **Treatment:** This phase is an operationalization of "all things are not-self" (*anattā*). We ask and seek to understand: "How did the client's perception lead to the presenting problem, or how has the client constructed their world?" Treatment interventions are aimed at deconstructing that client's notion of the self and then, for Buddhist psychotherapy, reconstructing

FIGURE 18.1. Three Arenas of Buddhist Psychotherapy

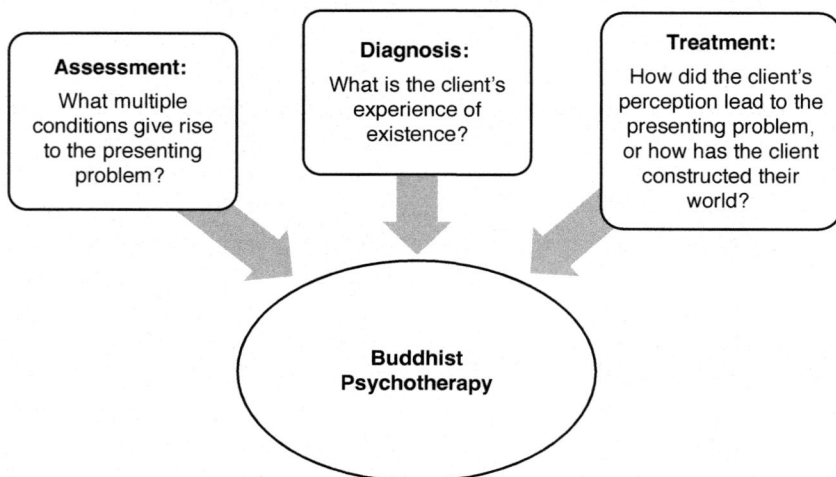

their notion of the self to something more functional. We determine the dukkha that is seeded from the five aggregates subject to clinging.

If and when directives are given, the psychotherapist strives to link the client's experience in the framework of the Buddhist worldview of dependent arising of phenomena in consciousness and kamma. The arena of primary focus in any treatment session depends on the presenting problem, the temperament, and the habitual preference of the client. Regardless of the arena of focus in any particular treatment session, the general direction is toward the reduction of suffering by way of stabilizing the mind through the mind's ability to note the mind states and reframe the problem within the framework of anicca (impermanence, transitory), anatta (not-self), and dukkha (suffering), thus resetting the mind's filter.

Vignette From the Suttas

Almost all suttas are in the format of a dialogue between the Buddha and another person. The interaction between the Buddha and the inquirer is similar to an in-session dialogue between a psychotherapist and a client. Although the dialogue from the suttas may not be of sufficient detail to use for the purpose of demonstrating psychotherapist–client interactions, it may be a simple pleasure to glance at the Buddha in the role of a psychotherapist assigning homework to a client.

There are numerous stories from the *Apadāna*, the *Thera-therī-gāthā*, and the *Nikāyas* in which a person presented with some type of mental imbalance or distress. Although these stories may not directly translate to mental health psychotherapy, it may be gratifying to take a look at a direct intervention by the Buddha. In the most common situation of mental imbalance in these stories, the distressed and grieving person has lost someone. The interventions have a common aim of demonstrating the universality of impermanence/ anicca. One of the commonly cited stories for typical interventions is found in the Kisā Gotami story, which is presented next.

Kisā Gotami

There are two distinct versions of Kisā Gotami's story in the sutta and in the Commentaries. One version of the story (Davids, 1909/1980) is briefly summarized here, with a transcript presented next: Kisā Gotami was born into a poor family but married into a rich family. She was ill favored in her husband's family and lived a rejected existence until she birthed a son. Her status was elevated by the birth of a son into her husband's family. All was well until the son died as a toddler. Fearing a repeat of the previous ill treatment from her husband's family, Kisā Gotami was distraught, unable to accept the death of her child. She was inconsolable in her grief, repeatedly seeking medical intervention to "cure" her dead son. Taking pity on her, someone recommended that she seek treatment from the Buddha Gotama. The following is a transcript of the conversations between Kisā Gotami and the Buddha.

Excerpt (Davids, 1909/1980, pp. 106–110)	Process commentary

Gotami was her name . . . she was disdainfully treated when married and was called a nobody's daughter. But when she bore a son, they paid her honor. Then, when he was old enough to run about and play, he died, and she was distraught with grief. And, mindful of the change in folks' treatment of her since his birth, she thought, "They will even try to take my child and expose him." So, taking the corpse upon her hip, she went, crazy with sorry, from door to door saying,	• Name of person: Gotami
	• Presenting problem:
	  – Fear of imagined treatment from others
	  – Grief for loss of child
	  – *Dukkha:* suffering experienced when situations change (*vipariṇāma-dukkha*); sorrow (*soka*), lamentation (*parideva*), mental pain and sorrow (*domanassa dukkhā*), and despai (*upāyāsa*)

KISĀ GOTAMI: "Give me medicine for my child!"	Presenting complaint: cannot find remedy for the undesirable condition

(continues)

Excerpt (Davids, 1909/1980, pp. 106–110)		Process commentary
CORUS:	And people said with contempt, "Medicine! What's the use?" She understood them not. But one sagacious person thought, "Her mind is upset with grief for her child. He of the Tenfold Power will know of some medicine for her." And he [the sagacious person] said, "Dear woman, go to the very Buddha, and ask him for medicine to give your child."	Source of referral: a sagacious person Reason for referral for treatment: "She understood them not"
KISĀ GOTAMI:	She went to the Vihāra at the time when the Master taught the Doctrine, and said, "Exalted one, give me medicine for my child!"	Request for treatment: implicit consent to treatment and overt request for solution to her presenting complaint
THE MASTER:	The master, seeing the promise in her, said, "Go, enter the town, and at any house where yet no man hath died, thence bring a little mustard seed."	Intervention: assign homework
KISĀ GOTAMI:	"Tis well, lord!" she said, with mind relieved; and going to the first house in the town, said, "Let me take a little mustard, that I may give medicine to my child. If in this house no man hath yet died, give me a little mustard."	Client follows through with assigned homework
CORUS:	With such mustard, then, I have naught to do.	Report of what happens when she does her homework
KISĀ GOTAMI:	So she went on to a second and a third house, until, by the might of the Buddha, her frenzy left her, her natural mind was restored, and she thought, "Even this will be the order of things in the whole town. The Exalted One foresaw this out of his pity for my good." And, thrilled at the thought, she left the town and laid her child in the charnel-field, saying,	Repeating homework assignment Attribute motive to intervention Insight: universality of impermanence

Excerpt (Davids, 1909/1980, pp. 106-110)	Process commentary
"No village law is this, no city law,	
No law for this clan, or for that along	
For the whole world—ay, sad the god in heaven—	
This is the law: ALL IMPERMANENT!"	
So, saying, she went to the Master.	
THE MASTER: And he said, "Gotami, hast thou gotten the little mustard?"	Psychotherapist: follow up on client's homework
KISĀ GOTAMI: And she said, "Wrought is the work, lord, of the little mustard. Give thou me confirmation."	Client: seeking confirmation of her attributed motive to homework assignment
THE MASTER: The Master spoke thus:	Psychotherapist: confirmation for intent of the homework assignment
"To him whose heart on children and on goods	
Is centered, cleaving to them in this thought.	
Death cometh like a grant flood in the night,	
Bearing away the village in the sleep."	
KISĀ GOTAMI: When he has spoken, she was confirmed in the fruition of the First (The Stream–entry) Path and asked for ordination [to join the ascetic community of the Buddha]. He consented, and she, thrice saluted by the right, when to the Bhikhunis, and was ordain[ed].	Resolution of presenting problem through acceptance of the impermanence of all conditioned reality

Therapy Vignette

The therapy vignette presented next is a composite profile based on many such situations. It was chosen because it is a common scenario found in Hong Kong, so there may be resemblance to many individuals' situations. Parts of this vignette have been previously submitted for the first author's (Tien's) master's thesis. This vignette demonstrates the assessment phase of Buddhist psychotherapy that seeks to explore anicca (all conditioned things are impermanent).

MeiFeng considered herself extremely fortunate to have married well to someone who is considerate of her and well regarded by her family. She had done well academically and earned a degree in finance at a highly respected university. She landed a good job after graduation and was promoted to team lead after 5 years at the company. Last year, with the support of her husband and her husband's family, she had resigned from her job after becoming pregnant. She and her husband moved into a larger apartment in order to have her mother-in-law live with them after the delivery to help take care of the baby. Everything looked perfectly prepared for the much-anticipated family.

After the birth of the baby, MeiFeng seemed to deteriorate. She did not seem to be adequately caring for her baby, was irritable and impatient with the baby, and was oppositional to her mother-in-law. A month ago, when her 1-year-old baby accidentally knocked the juice cup off the table, MeiFeng became so angry that she punched a hole in the wall. Much alarmed, MeiFeng thought she was going crazy. She discussed the situation with her husband, who thought she needed help so he suggested that she seek psychological treatment.

Applying the mark of existence that says that all conditioned things are impermanent (aniccā) in the therapy setting leads toward helping MeiFeng explore the conditions that existed at the time she punched the wall. At the simplest level, it would entail examination from the point of view that involves her in the context of her immediate social situation, with an eye on the circumstances that generated the situation of her feeding her baby.

In terms of MeiFeng's immediate social situation, one would explore the conditions that gave rise to the situation where she was at home, by herself, taking care of her baby when she was in an emotionally unstable state. The exploration might start with inquiry into childcare arrangements. This would entail questions such as these: "Where was the mother-in-law?" "Why was the mother-in-law not there to help with the care of the baby?" The focus on the mother-in-law's whereabouts is a recognition that the explicit purpose for the family moving into the larger apartment was so that MeiFeng's mother-in-law could live with the family to help with childcare. If MeiFeng was not emotionally and psychologically competent to care for the baby on that day, it would stand to reason that the mother-in-law would be feeding the baby instead of MeiFeng.

The question in terms of MeiFeng's immediate circumstance may involve finding out why her situation deviated from the usual and customary practice of Hong Kongers. For an educated young woman, the usual practice is for her to return to the workplace after childbirth. Instead, MeiFeng was at home. The reason why the mother-in-law was chosen for childcare instead of hiring a domestic helper would be of interest. In Hong Kong, it is normal and expected for a new mother and new family to hire and have the presence of someone such as a domestic helper whose job is to help with domestic chores and childcare. In MeiFeng's circumstance, instead of hiring a domestic helper, it was apparently decided to have the paternal grandmother move into their apartment and be in residence for childcare. The expected pattern would then be that either the paternal grandmother would have been taking care of the baby, thus preventing the situation of MeiFeng being present when the juice was spilled, or that MeiFeng would have handed over the care of the baby to her domestic helper when she found herself in an emotional state where she was not capable of comfortably taking care of the baby. Treatment would involve the exploration of how it was that the paternal grandmother was not caring for the baby, since the explicit purpose of the grandmother being in residence was to help with childcare.

Interviews with MeiFeng were conducted in keeping with the Abhidhamma's further explication of aniccā (all conditioned things are impermanent): (a) nothing arises without the conditions necessary of its arising; (b) nothing arises from a single cause; (c) nothing arises as a single effect, as a solitary phenomenon; and (d) from a plurality of conditions arises a plurality of effects. MeiFeng was invited to engage in explorations aimed at revealing the conditions that existed, giving rise to the circumstance of MeiFeng punching the wall. The following was revealed.

Between the events of the spilled juice incident to when MeiFeng talked to a psychologist, she decided that the condition that caused her anger at her child was her husband's general unsupportiveness. She planned to move out of their apartment to her mother's apartment, with serious considerations of seeking a divorce. However, to appease her husband and at his urging, MeiFeng agreed to seek psychological treatment from a clinical psychologist.

Upon exploration, MeiFeng reported that while the plan had been for her mother-in-law to help with the care of the baby, her mother-in-law's idea of taking care of the baby was to stand next to MeiFeng and give instructions and offer critiques. In the first few days after the birth of the baby, her mother-in-law's help consisted of telling MeiFeng how she was not breastfeeding the baby correctly. Her mother-in-law also told MeiFeng that the baby was not getting enough nutrition from the breast milk, because all MeiFeng did was lay around in her bed instead of being active in making proper meals for herself so that her breast milk would be rich enough to sustain her baby. Additionally, MeiFeng's mother-in-law repeatedly instructed MeiFeng on how to draw herself a bath and how to clean herself so as to not inflict her dirt and disease on the baby. When MeiFeng complained to her husband about his mother, his response was that she should ignore what his mother said. Then he would go off to work, leaving her to not only face the difficult task of caring for a new baby but also to fend off his mother's critiques and instructions. By the time of the wall-punching incident, MeiFeng had endured a whole year of being criticized and instructed by her mother-in-law. She had coped with the situation by isolating with her baby in her own room, trying as much as possible not to go to the kitchen to feed her baby when her mother-in-law was home. On the day of the incident, MeiFeng had stayed in her bedroom with a hungry baby. She was well into a state of irritability, and the baby was hungry and cranky, as she waited for her mother-in-law to leave the apartment for her lunch outing with a friend.

To analyze MeiFeng's situation, based on the Abhidhamma explication of anicca (all conditioned things are impermanent) stating that nothing arises without the conditions necessary of its arising, it appears that there were several immediate conditions for the arising of the wall-punching incident. These immediate conditions included (a) the critical nature of MeiFeng's mother-in-law, (b) the mother-in-law's idea of helping with childcare, (c) the absence of the husband in negotiating the relationship between his mother and his wife, (d) the husband's movement away from MeiFeng, (e) his withdrawing into his work, (f) her inability to negotiate a helpful relationship with her mother-in-law, (g) her inability to ignore her mother-in-law, and (h) her decision to hide from her mother-in-law that engendered the condition of the baby being cranky and hungry.

Regarding MeiFeng's situation based on the Abhidhamma explication of anicca (all conditioned things are impermanent) stating that nothing arises from a single cause, MeiFeng attributing the cause of her state of irritation to difficulties with her husband, specifically to him not being supportive, is insufficient. Her analysis either minimizes or ignores her mother-in-law's contributions, as well as her own, to the situation of being at home isolated and irritable instead of at work during the middle of the day. In the treatment phase for MeiFeng, she and the psychologist would necessarily need to spend time exploring the multiple causes that supported the arising of her moment of anger and punching the wall. In the process of exploration, MeiFeng would be repeatedly directed to include multiple coarising conditions.

In regard to MeiFeng's situation as it relates to the Abhidhamma explication of anicca (all conditioned things are impermanent) stating that nothing arises from a single cause "nothing arises as a single effect" or as a solitary phenomenon, again, her analysis of her state of irritation that seats the cause with her mother-in-law's presence in the apartment neglects several conditions. These conditions included (a) the timing, as the event occurred around lunch time when the baby was hungry; (b) her own decision not to venture into the kitchen when the baby became hungry; (c) the age of her baby, at which dropped cups are a common occurrence; and (d) many unknown conditions on the part of the mother-in-law.

Before the intervention phase of MeiFeng's treatment, both the psychologist and MeiFeng would need to fully understand, and MeiFeng would need to acknowledge that "from a plurality of conditions arises a plurality of effects."

Case Conceptualization

This simulated case of MeiFeng is a composite based on many such cases from clinical practice over the years. There may be an apparent resemblance to any one individual, because the situation depicted in the vignette is relatively common. However, there was effort in ensuring that no identifiable information to any one individual could be made. The names are manufactured and do not refer to any one actual person. The vignette demonstrates the intervention phase of Buddhist psychotherapy that bypasses the client's notion of self through analyzing a pivotal moment in a critical incident. The process deconstructs the client's notion of herself to the five aggregates; from the deconstruction, the client then re-constructed a different notion of herself. This is the enactment of all things are not-self (anattā).

Let us consider another case example of a client who presents with depression. Background details for this client are as follows:

- Name: Mai WONG
- Age: 34
- Sex: Female
- Nationality and ethnicity: Chinese, permanent U.S. resident (not a practicing Buddhist)
- Reason for referral: voluntary self-referral
- Presenting compliant: Mai sought psychotherapy to help eliminate her symptoms of major clinical depression.

History of Presenting Complaint

Mai reported having days where she was so tired that she could not get herself out of bed to even eat, to take a shower, or to simply brush her teeth. Having had a history of bipolar disorder, she recognized her state of major depression and knew that she needed to get professional help to come out of it. Once Mai realized she was experiencing symptoms of major depression again, she forced herself to get out of the house, go to work, and make arrangements for psychotherapy sessions.

Mai reported that the current episode of major depression was precipitated by a series of interactions with a former student that resulted in her being swindled out of $10,000 USD. She had known this American student from a Chinese class she taught at the community college about 2 years ago. He was White and was learning Chinese in preparation for a job transfer to China. This student was transferred to a position in China about a year ago. About 3 months ago, the student contacted Mai, asking for help with getting some money to his mother. Apparently, his mother lives in California and was in need of funds for a medical procedure. The student told Mai that he was unable to make the necessary bank transactions from China to his mother's bank account in the United States. Knowing that Mai had a bank account in China, this student asked if Mai would write a check to his mother for the necessary funds while he deposited the same amount of money in her account in China. Because he had been a good student in her class and she knew the difficulties of transferring funds out of China, Mai readily agreed to write a check for $10,000 to the student's mother for the medical procedure. To date, the student has not paid Mai back nor has he responded to any of her attempts to contact him. Mai became increasing despondent as she realized that she had been swindled out of $10,000, money that she had been saving up for a trip back home to Hong Kong.

Personal History
Mai's personal history is as follows.

Social and developmental. Mai was born in Hong Kong into an intact family. She has one older brother who is still in residence in Hong Kong. Mai's mother says that Mai's arrival, while unplanned, was welcomed. There were no complications during gestation and no developmental delays. She did not attend public schools, but instead went through the private English-speaking schools in Hong Kong. She performed well in school, usually placing in the top 5% of her class. As a child, she remembers feeling inadequate because no matter what grades she made in school, her mother would say, "Mai, if you think this is good enough, you are wrong. This time you did not get the top grade in your class." When, with much effort, she placed at the top of her class, her mother would say, "Mai, if you think this is good enough, you are wrong. Even though you got the number 1 spot this time, you will not get it the next time." Her mother said variations of the same message to Mai about many other things, like Mai's attempts to clean her room or choose her clothing. Mai's internal rumination to these pronouncements from her mother was one of befuddlement; how was she ever going to figure out what was "good enough"? Mai had thought that she had discerned her mother's criteria for being good enough every time she achieved some recognition or performed some task. Yet she was met with her mother saying, "You are wrong."

To her mother's great disappointment, and confirmation of Mai's assessment of herself as someone who is not able to figure out the correct answers to the college entrance exams, Mai was not awarded a seat at The University of Hong Kong, the only university that her mother deemed acceptable for her children in Hong Kong. Mai applied to universities in the United Kingdom and in the United States. She was admitted to the University of California, Los Angeles (UCLA). At age 17, Mai migrated to the United States to attend UCLA. In college, she discovered her love of language, majored in English, and studied Japanese, Chinese, and English. After graduation, Mai did not want to return to Hong Kong, and she studied for a teacher's certificate so she could teach language in the United States.

Education. Mai has a bachelor of arts and a teaching certificate.

Work. Mai had no work experience either in Hong Kong or as a foreign student during her undergraduate school years. After graduation, because of her multilanguage skills, she landed a job with the Chinese Consulate General in Los Angeles as a receptionist. Since that first position, Mai has acquired a certificate in interpretation and translation. She continues to work at the Chinese Consulate General in Los Angeles, and she also works as an interpreter for Chinese, Japanese, and English clients. In addition, she works as a part-time instructor at a community college teaching Chinese. At various times when she finds a book of sufficient interest, she translates Chinese novels to English.

Legal. Mai has no history of legal difficulties.

Medical. Mai has no significant reported medical problems.

Psychiatric. Mai reported a history of general anxiety. She acquired a diagnosis of bipolar disorder and completed a course of antidepressants approximately 5 years ago. She has had only one major depressive episode prior to this year, with no reported manic or hypomanic episodes. She reported success in managing her depressive moods with antidepressant medication.

Current Functioning (Mental Status)
The following is an assessment of Mai's current physical and mental status.

Physical. Mai presents as a petite Asian female of slender build. She wears her hair cut short in a bob. She is well groomed, wearing no make-up, and casually dressed in a blouse and slacks. Her only anomalous appearance is the white lace handkerchief she continuously handles. She has no reported weight loss or gain. She does report a disturbance in vegetative state, with excessive drowsiness and fatigue, and says she has slept up to 14 hours a day on some days in the last 2 weeks.

Orientation. Mai is oriented to time, place, and person.

Cognition. Mai's speech is coherent, and her reasoning is sound. She maintains appropriate eye contact throughout the sessions. There are no reported symptoms of thought disorder, hallucinations, or delusions. There is no reported disturbance in memory.

Harm to self or others. Mai reports she does not feel suicidal, although she has had suicidal ideations in the past. She reports no bouts of rage and has never experienced inclinations to physically harm others.

Mood. Mai reports feeling anxious most of the time for most of the day. Additionally, she reports depressed mood most of the time, while simultaneously experiencing irritability and loss of interest in activities that she previously enjoyed.

Case Formulation
Mai has always believed that she is not as good or as smart as her brother. The defining shame to her family was her inability to get into The University of Hong Kong. When she had to move out of Hong Kong in order to attend a university her mother deemed adequate, it was the confirming stroke that sealed her notion of a self that is "a simpleton." She was not smart enough to consistently get top marks in school, not smart enough to get into a university in Hong Kong, not good enough to attract a rich handsome Hong Kong man, and not even smart enough to do a good deed for an ailing older woman without being swindled out of $10,000.

Every time Mai was faced with another situation of feeling not good enough or not smart enough, she thought of the look on her mother's face and the shame she brought to the family name in Hong Kong. The latest confirmation of this notion of a self that is a simpleton was having to tell her family that she would not be making a trip home anytime soon because she had been swindled out of $10,000. When faced with yet more undeniable evidence of her simpleton status, Mai shrank away from the reality of losing $10,000 by looking away, by welcoming the sloth and torpor, and by sleeping.

Treatment Intervention
The approach used was to discern the five aggregates and the five aggregates subject to clinging. Mai reported that the start of her current cycle of depression was her contact with the former student. Upon exploration, it was determined that the critical moment where she recalled something was not right was when she was looking at a bank receipt on her computer. The receipt in question was sent to her WhatsApp by this former student. It was the snapshot of a "receipt of deposit" from his bank in China. She remembered thinking that something was not right about the receipt of deposit because it did not look like others she had seen from Chinese banks. That moment of hesitancy was followed by the thought that she was most likely wrong in her reading of the bank note, so she decided not to embarrass herself by questioning this former student about the receipt.

Analysis of this moment in treatment took the form of first discussing what was not right about that receipt of deposit. Mai said that it was not directly from the bank; rather, it was from this student's email address. Then she remembered thinking, "Maybe the bank emailed him the receipt of deposit." On inquiry into whether there were any other thoughts between Mai looking at the receipt of deposit and concluding that the bank had given the student the receipt, instead of communicating directly with her bank, she said,

> Oh, but he is such a nice man. He was so handsome, always had a smile for me, and got along with the other students in class so well. So, I thought my wondering about the receipt must have been my mistake. Besides, I kept on picturing his elderly mother in pain waiting for the money from her son so she could go to the hospital.

Further exploration of Mai's statement took three different directions: The first discussion focused on Mai's assessment of the student ("he is such a nice man"), the second focused on her self-blame ("it must have been my mistake"), and the third focused on her wish to help.

First, Mai held a stereotypical belief equivalent to "handsome friendly men are all good." For her, there is a halo effect surrounding the combination of handsome and male. This halo effect is commonly presented in mass media and is pervasive in U.S. society. This social message was the obvious source of Mai's stereotype about handsome males. Nonetheless, this halo effect interfered with her ability to accurately evaluate the character of the former student.

Second, inquiry into Mai's self-blame ("it must have been my mistake") started with her moment of doubt about the validity of the receipt from the bank. On recall, she noticed that the receipt was a deposit into his account in China, not into her bank account. But it was confusing since they both had accounts at the same Chinese bank. She also noticed that everything was in English instead of a mix of Chinese and some English. She thought the bank must have printed off a special receipt because he was a U.S. citizen and obviously needed the receipt in English. This line of reasoning gave her justification for dismissing her doubts. Additionally, Mai holds a notion of herself as someone who is always wrong. She heard echoes of her mother saying that she has bad judgment of situations; that if she thought something, it must be wrong. She could hear her mother saying, "Mai, if you think this is good enough, you are wrong." Combining her justifications and memories of her mother saying she is wrong, Mai concluded that her doubts about the receipt must be wrong, again.

Third, Mai reported having the mental image of a suffering older mother in need of medical care. She thought that it would be wrong if she ignored the pain of an older woman. She liked to believe that she was a caring person, so she should help with the money so this older person could receive medical care.

These three areas of inquiry were focused on the moment of sense contact. As time went on, Mai proliferated on variations of the notion of a self that was wrong, again—like going down a well-traveled road. That wrongness notion ballooned into Mai berating herself for being such a simpleton, repeatedly reaffirming her established notion of a self who is a simpleton doomed to be wrong as she goes through life. She despaired of ever getting things right so she could maybe one day have a marriage and a happy life. Not wanting to consider her fate in life, Mai slept as a way to escape the reality of this simpleton self.

Dialogue with the psychotherapist focused on the arena where Mai acted on compassion and generosity, with a genuine wish to be of assistance to an older mother in need of medical care. The psychotherapist raised the alternative notion of a self that is caring and compassionate. Since she had experienced this at the moment of looking at the receipt of deposit on her computer, she could not dispute this alternative notion of a self. Much time was spent in the treatment sessions debating these two notions and finally amending a notion of a self that was compassionate to a fault. It was noted that a common consequence of being compassionate is being blind to the acts of people who are motivated by greed. To safeguard against such bias, Mai thought that she would limit herself to giving no more than $1,000 USD to any one person, regardless of how compelling their story, like the one from her former student with an older mother needing medical care. While relieved, Mai reported a measure of puzzlement about her firmly held notion of self being a simpleton.

The end-of-treatment diagnosis is unipolar depressive episode, in remission.

Annotated Transcript

The following simulated transcription of a process note is a composite based on many such cases from clinical practice over the years. There may be apparent resemblances to any one individual, because the situation depicted in this vignette is relatively common. However, careful consideration of the transcript content regarding any aspect of a case related to any one individual has been made. The names are manufactured and do not refer to any one actual person.

The client starts the session, without giving further context, being visibly agitated, talking about a phone call she had while walking to the psychotherapist's office. It appeared that the phone call was about the family planning for a New Year's dinner at a restaurant with a seating limit. The client and her cousin had the task of planning the New Year's gathering.

	Simulated transcript	Analysis of psychotherapist intervention
CLIENT:	I almost got into a fight over the phone with my cousin just now. . . . My cousin called me and asked me like, "What's wrong?" I said, "Nothing's wrong." I just got a little bit annoyed by her call. I'm not sure why. I was annoyed at the start to get really impatient with my cousin and I said, "I'm out right now and away, because I need to pick up something that you asked for [for] the family dinner." I think I got a little bit impatient at the start. Not yelling, but I was not in a good mood talking to her. She's like, "Fine. We'll talk tonight." I'm like my mom that I don't really have a good temper. I snap off easily. I'm trying to find ways to calm it down. It's really difficult.	• Mental proliferation

(continues)

	Simulated transcript	Analysis of psychotherapist intervention

THERAPIST:	What made you irritated, and why were you irritated?	• Inquiry into mental culture and conditions:
		  – perception/mental formation
		  – trigger point/sense contact

CLIENT:	I don't like being rushed. I felt that when she made the phone call, I think two things annoyed me. First thing was she intervened because her mother, my aunt, asked her, "What does your cousin mean by double-checking?" She kept asking me these questions.	
THERAPIST:	Your cousin was intervening into what? Then somehow now we are talking about your temper, your temperament?	• Tracking and paraphrasing topic of reflection of feeling and the perception of temperament
CLIENT:	Yeah. I know it's annoying when people are rushing you, but I felt like maybe I was a little bit overreacted. My bad temper came out. I could have told her in a more calming way. Then I was like thinking, "Should I have been nicer to her when I was [talking] over the phone?" At that time, I just couldn't control my temper.	Activating notion of self, *bhavāsava*: I don't have a good temper Clinging onto notion of self; I = temper: I don't have a good temper
THERAPIST:	It seems to me that when I put myself in your position, I probably would have responded the same way but maybe not the subjective feeling of ill temper. It does seem your question of, "Why are you talking to me? Why isn't your mom talking to me?" is reasonable; but what I hear is that you think you had an ill temper.	• Suggests alternative perception • Confirming with paraphrasing • Separating condition and context from notion of self, *bhavāsava*
CLIENT:	I think I was more annoyed by my ill temper then. I got caught by . . . I think it was the rage inside me that I couldn't hold on anymore. I just need to let it out.	
THERAPIST:	I get the impression; I'm checking it out, that every day your family pushes you a little, push you a little. Then every now and then you burst out. Then they say, "Well, you have a temper."	Paraphrasing; confirming client perception

	Simulated transcript	Analysis of psychotherapist intervention
CLIENT:	I'm pretty sure I have a temper no matter what. I'm just saying I know I have a temper. I'm not sure if it's because of being pushed and that's how my temper came out. I just know I have a temper because my temper is very similar to my mom's. We kind of have the same temper.	Clinging onto notion of self; self = ill temper, by using selective data to support the conclusion
THERAPIST:	In what way were you overreacting?	Assessing mind, body, and speech
CLIENT:	My bad temper came out. I could have told her in a more calming way like. . . .	Clinging onto the perception of a tempered person
THERAPIST:	Are you saying your tone of voice?	Redirecting attention to the body
CLIENT:	Yeah, my tone of voice to her was not very nice. [laughs]	Noticing bodily sensation of using a nice voice
THERAPIST:	It's not that particular topic; it's your ill temper. When things happen, it seems like you're overreacting. In that situation or in those kinds of situations I go, "OK. Are you the one with the ill temper or are you the one that just got caught?"	Raising awareness of the activation of perception Challenging perception
CLIENT:	I got caught. . . . I think I was more annoyed by my ill temper then.	Clinging onto perception
THERAPIST:	You self-label yourself as someone with a temper? Here's an analogy. You're in school. You're a little kid at school and then there's a bunch of people who are bullies. Every day they come to push you. One day you just had enough so you punch them back. Then those kids cry and cry and say, "You punched him." Then you get in trouble for punching. In that situation, who's really to blame? The kid who was bullying and always pushing you or the kid that one day reacted and punched?	Raising client's awareness on her clinging to set notion of self = bad temper Challenging perception by metaphor
CLIENT:	The logical thinking is both are wrong. In my opinion, I think the kid who started it first.	

(continues)

	Simulated transcript	Analysis of psychotherapist intervention
THERAPIST:	"Which one is this?" Are you the bully or are you the kid who has been bullied and then you punched back, because it's hard to tell in the phone call with your cousin?	Applying metaphor to the critical incident to challenge perception
CLIENT:	When I was a kid, I got bullied a lot. I think in primary school. In secondary school, same. Girls have their own groups and I find it hard to fit in. This has always been my trouble since I was a kid finding it hard to fit in a circle.	Memory of past experience entering to formulation perception/saññā
THERAPIST:	You're the kid who gets bullied?	Paraphrasing
CLIENT:	Yeah.	Confirmation of appropriate application of metaphor
THERAPIST:	Everybody has their own experience in childhood. The thing is that, right now, you're not a child anymore so you're not reliving that situation. I'm using it as an analogy. It sounds to me like the experience with the phone call is that your cousin is the bully, and you are the kid that keeps on being pushed. Every now and then, you will burst out, like push back. Then the comment is, "Oh, you have the temper." That's what it sounds like to me. When I ask about the possibility of similarities of a bully situation, you say, "No, no, no. I really do have a temper." OK, you have a temper. Why do you have this temper? Is it because somebody comes and just pokes at you all the time, or are you just born ill-tempered?	Redirecting to formation of future *kamma* Challenging the clinging onto perception using the bullied kid example
CLIENT:	No. I'll only get bad temper when— I don't know—things happen not . . . I won't say not to my expectation or when I'm being annoyed. Normally, I cannot find any suggestions. I get annoyed when perhaps I plan out things, and then people switch at [the] last minute. I get a little bit upset about that but not to the point I yell or I . . .	Resist alternative perception and cling onto original perception—adoption of a self-view

	Simulated transcript	Analysis of psychotherapist intervention
THERAPIST:	You were concerned about your ill temper with your cousin just before you came. You didn't yell?	Review critical incident to see things as it is
CLIENT:	I didn't yell.	
THERAPIST:	I'm describing the situation and your subjective experience of ill temper. You said, "No, no, no. That's not true. I am just ill-tempered."	Using critical incident data to examine perception
CLIENT:	I'm trying to understand if you're right or not. It's hard to look [at] myself from a distance and then what you explained to me. I'm like, "Am I what you said?" I really don't know because I'm being too close to me. It's hard to get a distance and get a subjective observation of [who] I am.	Dissonance and confusion from starting to detach and/or alter self-view
THERAPIST:	It almost is a split mind. There is a lived subjective experience. I'm angry, right? Then there's almost like you're a fly on the wall watching this show and going, "Is it reasonable for that person to be angry?"	Teaching meta-cognition Pointing out mindfulness of mind in a tailor-made manner at the moment Suggest a detached view of the critical incident
CLIENT:	When I look back now after the phone call . . . It was like after lunch and after the walk to here and then being the fly looking back at the situation that happened an hour ago, I was like, "Maybe I didn't have to be that bad-mannered."	Tried to use a detached view but quickly cling back to perception, and then mental formation to judge herself as a "ill-tempered person"
THERAPIST:	Well, I would say that you didn't have to have the tone of voice and the irritation, but saying, "This is inappropriate for you to be calling. Your mom has the concern. Have her call me." If you could've just said the same thing without the subjective experience of the irritation, would that have been OK?	Exploring other possible choices to test the perception
CLIENT:	That might have happened OK. That might have happened OK if she just told me directly, "Oh, I called because . . ." since she asked me what you meant by double-checking, then I can just explain to her directly of what I just . . .	Attributing incident to single external condition

(continues)

	Simulated transcript	Analysis of psychotherapist intervention
THERAPIST:	Could you have said yes?	Exploring other possible choices to test the perception
CLIENT:	I would've. Then I would have asked her [cousin] why couldn't she [aunt] ask me directly.	
THERAPIST:	Right. In retrospect, you could have done that. You would've been calm. It seems like you don't do that. You don't figure out what's irritating you and then make comment[s] about what's irritating you. You act on the irritation.	Analyzing client's feeling, perception, and mental formation Pointing out how she acts on feelings
CLIENT:	It's true. I didn't let her know that I was annoyed by her.	
THERAPIST:	Do you know how to analyze what you're irritated at?	Introducing idea of aggregates and basis to feeling based on mental formations
CLIENT:	I don't think so. I try to analyze, but I might have gone the wrong way.	
THERAPIST:	When you first talked about this situation with your cousin, I don't think . . . I didn't hear . . . In your description of the situation, I went, "Oh, I would not have liked that." The difference is that I wouldn't have waited until I got irritated then burst out, but I'm someone who can analyze.	Raising awareness of the impact of feeling; normalizing the difficulty Introducing the benefit of knowing aggregate of feeling (*vedanā*)
CLIENT:	It's just that when I'm being irritated, I think I'm too irritated to step back and look at "OK, what's really irritating me?" [N]ot what's going on right now but what [is] the core of the problem that's irritating me. I'm not sure if I put it the right way.	Noticing feeling and how she acted on feeling at the moment
THERAPIST:	Well, if I'm now thinking back about other situations we have talked about, what's in common in all of them is a statement about either implied or pretty blatantly saying you're at fault.	Pointing out the common trigger across critical incidents

	Simulated transcript	Analysis of psychotherapist intervention
CLIENT:	I don't think it's fair. That's why I was irritated. (At this point, client's tone of voice, body posture, and voice volume changed.)	Noticing a thought against perception Insight into the internal conditions for her feeling and the formulation of perception/*saññā*
THERAPIST:	Right, but I don't hear the, "That's not fair," coming into your mind. I just hear your experience of your irritation. There must be a one millisecond of going, "It's not fair." Then you launch into your irritation.	Explaining the mechanism of mind and pointing out possible missed thought
CLIENT:	It's probably true. I never really thought about that's not fair until. . . . Even when I was telling you about the other situations, it never came to my mind it's not fair. I just felt that, "Oh, come on, man. I'm just helping here. Why are you . . .?"	Reflecting on the thought process
THERAPIST:	"Why are you blaming me, or why are you pushing me, or why are you hassling me," right? If you answer the question, "Why is she doing that?" Your answer, as you just told me, is that "it's not fair for you to do that."	Paraphrasing and reframing, reflecting client's thought to challenge perception
CLIENT:	Yeah.	
THERAPIST:	What would you do differently if, for some reason, you were able to catch the, "This is not fair," before you launch into the irritation? What would you do?	Exploring other possible choices to test the perception Conduct (*sīla*), directing to more skillful action Giving more than one alternative perception reduces the rigidity of self-view
CLIENT:	I would just say, "This is not fair." [laughs]	
THERAPIST:	You would've been calm?	Emphasize reframe self-view of "ill temper" Reinforce "right speech" with the absence of harshness in her tone of voice

(continues)

Simulated transcript	Analysis of psychotherapist intervention
CLIENT: Yeah. I probably would say like, "This is not fair. Why can't she just call me instead of you? I feel like I'm being pushed right now or being rushed. I'm not at home working for you on the family because I'm shopping for you."	Visualizing actions based on an alternative perception Practice speech that is not harsh
THERAPIST: If you did do that, what would your own judgment toward yourself be?	Encouraging client to explore the experience of an alternative perception
CLIENT: I don't have a temper. I'm thinking logically.	Experimental the new perception
THERAPIST: Watching the river of your thoughts go by, if you watch closely enough, you'll see the "This is not fair" go by. Normally, most of us don't watch that closely. It goes by, and we just see the big pieces.	Teaching meditation to help client learn to note all the thoughts
CLIENT: Yeah, it will be like on a boat with a big chunk or a couple of boxes floating away in [the] sea, waving by.	
THERAPIST: Yeah, but you don't see the little thing that triggers it.	Teaching nature of mind
CLIENT: No. It doesn't have the words saying like, "This is not fair," going by. No, I didn't see that.	
THERAPIST: Because the "This is not fair" is a really tiny piece that's underneath the water.	Teaching nature of mind
CLIENT: It's true.	
THERAPIST: That is the nature of a lot of what we end up getting caught up with. Those little things go by so fast under the surface water. That's actually why we start having people meditate five minutes a day to practice watching the thoughts go by. The more you're able to do that, the more you'll catch those little thoughts of, "That's not fair." Now that you can hear that, now that you've said it, my guess is that it'll be easier to catch that thought the next time it happens.	Explaining how meditation will help Teaching her to apply meditation skills

	Simulated transcript	Analysis of psychotherapist intervention
CLIENT:	Interesting. I never thought of it this way. It would be easier. It would be nicer to not have to burst out so many times. It's not good for the health.	

CONCLUSION

As discussed in Chapter 1, this book aims to translate Buddhist fundamentals into the lexicon of a theory for psychotherapy. In keeping with the idea expressed by Wampold (2019) that "a theory of psychotherapy ought to be simple enough for the average therapist to understand but comprehensive enough to account for a wide range of eventualities" (pp. 1–2), we use the simplicity of the three marks of existence—impermanence (aniccā), not-self (anattā), and suffering or unsatisfactoriness (dukkha)—as the basics for Buddhist psychotherapy. Treatment interventions by a psychotherapist are as varied as those given by Buddha Gotama to questions posed by individuals from various walks of life.

In Kisā Gotami's story, the Buddha used the homework of finding a mustard seed to teach her the universality of death and impermanence/aniccā. The intervention had the aim of demonstrating the universality of impermanence/aniccā. In the situation with MeiFeng, we used the concept of conditions that underlie the structure of impermanence/aniccā to examine the many facets necessary for the arising of the moment when she punched the wall. In the situation with Mai, we sought the stimuli (rūpa) that initiated the sense contact for the problematic behavior of being swindled out of $10,000, bypassing her notion of a self that she is not smart. In the last transcript, we examine the detailed probing for the stimuli and each of the five aggregates.

Each of the case examples provides a sampling of the possible wide varieties of situations that typically present in psychotherapy. These vignettes indicate that Buddhist psychotherapy can fulfill the second demand for a theory of psychotherapy that it is "comprehensive enough to account for a wide range of eventualities" (Wampold, 2019, pp. 1–2).

AFTERWORD
Summary and Future Directions

Looking back, we provide a brief summary of some key ideas in a Buddhist-based theory of psychotherapy. Looking forward, we provide some possible future directions to explore and utilize the ideas contained in the teachings of the Buddha Gotama. Additionally, in the tradition of the Buddha providing a simile at the end of a topic, we provide a simile for Buddhist psychotherapy.

SUMMARY OF KEY IDEAS FOR A BUDDHIST-BASED THEORY OF PSYCHOTHERAPY

The Buddha Gotama made some observations about the human experience of existence. Some of the Buddha's teachings seem simple—for example, the material element in the form of a body is inexorably linked to the mentality elements of experience. The simplicity of the Buddha's observations belies their vast implications and the nuances in their application to the human experience of existence. For the purpose of psychotherapy, we select for inclusion only those items that are useful in the provision of psychotherapy.

https://doi.org/10.1037/0000453-020
Buddhist Psychotherapy: Connecting Early Buddhism to Mindfulness and Western Psychotherapy, by L. Tien, D. M. Kawahara, and V. Dhammadinna

The selection is restricted and the discussion is narrow so as to meaning-fully speak to psychotherapists in the process of providing psychotherapy treatment. The following is an abbreviated summary of those items most applicable to psychotherapy:

- Humans exist within the limitations of a body that has six sense bases through which information about noumena, the sense object, is received and perceived.

- The human experience of phenomena that arise in consciousness depends on the multiplicity of occurrences, both internally and externally, in the past as well as the present. Phenomena in consciousness are dependently arising (*paṭiccasamuppāda*).

- Consciousness in an ordinary individual with an untrained mind tends to be self-referencing with unarticulated assumption of permanence and unchanging unitary self, both of which are inaccurate. An accurate description of reality is dependent arising (paṭiccasamuppāda), which conditions impermanence (*aniccā*).

- The mind, through the lens of a notion of the self, misconstrues the confluence of events in the flow of consciousness to be a permanent unchanging self (*attā*), which will inevitably result in suffering (*dukkha*). The reverse, the deconstruction of the notion of a solid self-entity to its component parts of the five aggregates subject to clinging, or not-self (*anattā*), results in the end of suffering.

- The method to enable the mind to discern the misconstruction is the development of concentration. Insight (*vipassanā*) meditation is one method in the development of concentration. In session, the psychotherapist functions as mindfulness (*sati*) would in meditation, thus facilitating the discernment of the mind's misconstruction. The aim of the psychotherapeutic treatment is to reframe the client's situation in the framework of the five aggregates subject to clinging.

- Elimination of suffering is the central mission of Buddhism as well as the goal of psychotherapy.

POSSIBLE FUTURE DIRECTIONS

In the arena of mental health treatment, the field has seen the direct application of Buddhist ideas in mindfulness-based stress reduction (MBSR) and dialectical behavior therapy (DBT). These are documented efficacious intervention programs used in mental health treatment. Both Jon Kabat-Zinn (1984) and Marsha Linehan (2017) reported that they translated some of the contemplative aspects of Buddhism in the development of MBSR and DBT, respectively. However, their use of Buddhism is only a very small portion of the Buddhist practice. The Buddhist-based theory for psychotherapy provided in this book gives researchers and practitioners access to a much broader Buddhist base for future work. To facilitate this future work, next we provide one example for each category of research, practice, training, and advocacy. Creative minds will inevitably undertake much more than what we can imagine at this point.

Research on Theory and Efficacy Outcomes of Intervention Programs

Mental health researchers often leave their philosophical and cultural assumptions unexamined. However, a wealth of opportunity unfolds when we start grappling with philosophical assumptions from a culture that is vastly different from Western culture. For example, in the functioning of the five aggregates, the Buddha posited that hedonic feeling tone (*vedanā*) accompanies every single sense contact and that it is the link between the material (i.e., the body) and the mental aspects of experience. Researchers looking into this hypothesis might develop an operational definition of vedanā and test the validity of this claim.

Practice and Development of Intervention Programs

For treatment interventions, exploration could be made for use of other approaches to meditation. There are two main suttas in the *Nikāya* that provide instruction for meditation: These are the Satipaṭṭhāna Sutta (*Majjhima Nikāya* [MN], 1995, 10: Foundation of Mindfulness) and the Ānāpanasati Sutta (MN, 1995, 118: Mindfulness of Breath). The Satipaṭṭhāna Sutta is the basis for the development of MBSR and, by extension, mindfulness-based cognitive therapy. Other intervention programs could easily be developed using the instruction in the Ānāpanasati Sutta. The direction given in the Ānāpanasati Sutta lends itself effortlessly to the management of chronic pain.

Education and Training

Meditation courses are currently included in many graduate training programs. It is also not unusual for students in practicum and internship placements to be called upon to lead meditation treatment groups. Mindfulness-based intervention techniques are often integrated into graduate-level courses. Meditation and mindfulness are taught at the level of technique without a theoretical foundation. Without a theoretical foundation, it is almost impossible to knowledgeably alter interventions to suit the particulars of a client's personality or situation. To enable the utilization of mindfulness in more sophisticated ways, the technique needs to be linked to a theory. Courses that offer such a theoretical foundation can be developed using this book as a starting point. We encourage usage of this book as a starting point to a more advanced examination of the philosophical and theoretical discussions that underly both Western culture–based intervention programs (i.e., psychoanalytic) and future Buddhism-based intervention approaches.

Advocacy

As noted previously, Kabat-Zinn (1984) mentioned that MBSR was based on Buddhist insight meditation, but he then proceeded to divorce MBSR from Buddhism. Likewise, Linehan's writings in the 1980s (Linehan, 1987a, 1987b) gave no hint to DBT's basis in Buddhism. It was not until much later when DBT had been well established as an efficacious intervention approach that Linehan started to discuss how she translated the contemplative practice used in Zen Buddhism into DBT. In her later discussion of DBT, Linehan (2017) explained the 1:1 transfer of Zen meditation to treatment features of DBT.

The avoidance of exposing MBSR and DBT's bases in Buddhist practice and worldview reflects the ethnocentric nature of the mental health field. Catering to this ethnocentric stance detracts from the honor of the field. The approaches taken in the teaching of mindfulness and the widescale use of mindfulness techniques in handling problems ranging from personal stress to corporate leadership evidence the practice of cultural appropriation. The approaches in teaching mindfulness meditation in our graduate programs evidence the field's participation in cultural imperialism. We, as a profession, are called to do better, to move away from cultural superiority and show humility by freely acknowledging practices borrowed from other cultures and philosophical traditions.

Looking to the future, the Buddhist worldview and the Buddhist-based theory for psychotherapy posited in this book provide a vast array of ideas for possible future directions. The Buddha Gotama's Third Noble Truth promises that there is a way out of our experience of dukkha. Translating the methods given in the Fourth Noble Truth and the Eightfold Path from the lexicon of Buddhism of more than 2,500 years ago to the present-day lexicon of psychology and other mental health fields, we are bound to fulfill the Buddha's promise that there are ways out of the experience of dukkha.

SIMILE FOR A BUDDHIST-BASED THEORY OF PSYCHOTHERAPY

Finally, following in the Buddha's tradition of providing a simile after discussion of ideas, we offer a simile for a Buddhist-based theory of psychotherapy. Buddhism aims to understand the totality of reality as it is lived. This conscious reality of a lived experience can be likened to an endless theater improvisation workshop. Reality is the constant flow of words. The words are made up of the letters of the alphabet, which numbers to 26 for the English language. These 26 letters of the English alphabet are the foundation upon which all the words are constructed. The lived experience for those people who are participating in the improvisational skit is the meaning that is attributed to the words and the images of the situations conjured by these words. Each participant in the improvisational skit has some measure of influence in the development and the unfolding of the storyline in the skit, but none of them have complete control over the evolution of the storyline.

Participation in improvisational skits is entertaining and filled with moments of merriment for the exact reason why realization of the three marks of existence would render our experience of existence joyful and satisfactory instead of painful. Because we know that none of the skit's story is personal (not-self) and that the skit is short lived and will end (impermanence), we allow ourselves to enjoy it. In contrast, in our day-to-day lived experience of existence, we fail to recognize that our experience is not personal and that it is temporary. We misperceive our participation as agency and our experience as objective reality. There is a consistent pattern in the misperception:

> perceiving permanence in the impermanent,
> perceiving pleasure in what is suffering,
> perceiving a self in what is non-self,
> and perceiving attractiveness in what is unattractive. (Vipallāsa Sutta [AN 4.49];
>   Bhikkhu Bodhi, Trans.)

The misperceptions contribute to dukkha. When a participant realizes the difference between the mere flow of external stimuli versus the images conjured in their mind, then it is possible to step away from the dukkha. Otherwise, suffering born out of the misconceptions continues for participants in this improvisational skit called life.

PARTING THOUGHT FROM THE BUDDHA GOTAMA TO A BUDDHIST-BASED THEORY OF PSYCHOTHERAPY

Psychology can follow the directive given by the Buddha regarding the use the five aggregates subject to clinging to arrive at the realization of (a) dependent arising (paṭiccasamuppāda), (b) not-self (anattā), and (c) suffering or unsatisfactoriness (dukkha). Ultimately, keep in mind what the Buddha said to his disciples:

> Bhikkhus, when you know the Dhamma [the teachings of the Buddha] to be similar to a raft, you should abandon even the teachings. (Alagaddūpama Sutta; MN, 1995, 22: Simile of the Raft)

In other words, what the Buddha taught, including the material in this book, is likened to a raft. That raft has one purpose, which is to take one on a voyage. In this case, the client's voyage of psychotherapy, including the use of Buddhist psychotherapy, is for the purpose of reducing suffering. The raft has served its purpose once the voyage is done, and thus should be left behind. The client is then encouraged to continue on their journey of life, unburdened by the raft used on that journey. When the client's presenting complaint is resolved, there is no need for them to remain in therapy. Some clients may want to spend additional time in the comfort of having been supported through their struggles by the psychotherapist, but it is best to encourage clients to move on to live their life, having been unburdened by their previous suffering. If they find themselves astray on their journey, they can always return to the raft to regain their moorings.

Glossary of Pali Terms

Abhidhamma theory of the doctrine, the doctrine classified, the doctrine pure and simple (without any admixture of literary grace or of personalities, or of anecdotes, or of arguments ad personam); name of the Third Piṭaka, the third group of the canonical books

akusalā unwholesome

akusalā-mūlaṁ three unwholesome roots

anattā not-self

aniccā impermanence, transitory

arahant an enlightened person

āsava a befuddling, gaslighting force that exerts a subtle but ever-present persistent influence on the mind as the mind navigates the interactions that are the experience of existence; also defined as taint, influx, flow, inflow, outflow, cankers, influence, effluence, defilements, corruptions, mental intoxicants, biases, depravity, misery

ātāpīn ardent, diligent

attā self

avijjāsava ignorance; misconstrue phenomena for noumena

āyatana six internal sense bases and six external sense objects

ayoniso manasikāra unwise attention

bhavāsava escape from fear of annihilation through belief in something everlasting; denial of aniccā (impermanence)

brahmā-vihāras divine abodes

buddha a person who has attained enlightenment

cetanā thinking as active thought, intention, purpose, and/or will

cetasika in the Abhidhamma, collectively the mental properties and factors at work with consciousness

chanda desire

citta mind; hearts and minds; in Abhidhamma, the totality of conscious acts

dhamma laws, teachings; the teachings of the Buddha Gotama

dosa anger, ill will, hatred

dukkha suffering or unsatisfactoriness; unpleasant, painful, causing misery

dukkha-dukkha suffering linked to an embodied existence; physical and emotional pain from the body

kamacchanda sensual desire

kāmāsava influence of the material senses on the mind; merge of self with rūpa (form)

kamma cause and effect of the doing of deeds

karuṇā compassion

kāya body

khandhā aggregates

kusalā skillful, wholesome

lobha greed, covetousness

manasikāra attention

mano mind organ

mettā loving-kindness

moha dullness of mind, delusion

mudita sympathetic joy

nāma part of the accompanying compounded or coordinated condition in *nāmarūpa* for the arising of consciousness

nāmarūpa mentality-materiality

nibbāna a state of total liberation from life's suffering

nikāya collection, class, group, assemblage, or volume; *Sutta Piṭaka* is, by tradition, arranged into five different collections, and each collection is called a *Nikāya*

pañcakkhandhā five aggregates

pañcupādānakkhandhā five aggregates subject to clinging; notion of a self

paññā wisdom

paṭiccasamuppāda dependent arising

phassa contact; first lived moment of an experience

piṭaka baskets

rūpa materiality, form; the material things of the universe

samādhi concentration, meditation, mental development

sampajāna fully aware and clearly knowing

saññā perception, recognition, naming, labeling; the process of labeling a sense object

sankhāra mental formations, mental fabrications, mental proliferations, volitional formations; the stories we tell ourselves about the sense object, which contain the content of the story as well as the emotions associated with the story; the "world of phenomena"

sankhāra-dukkha suffering inflicted from one's own mental formations, mental fabrications, and mental proliferations

sati mindfulness

sīla ethical conduct, behavior

sukha agreeable, pleasant, blessed; well-being, happiness, ease; ideal, success; comfortably, in happiness. Opposite of dukkha

sutta a thread of ideas; refers to the remembered dialogues, teachings, and instructions from the Buddha witnessed and heard by the monks

Sutta Piṭaka collection of the remembered dialogues, teachings, and instruction of the Buddha Gotama

taṇhā craving, hunger for, excitement, the fever of unsatisfied longing

thīna-middha sloth and torpor

uddhacca-kukkucca restlessness and remorse

upādāna clinging, attachment

upekkhā equanimity

vedanā hedonic feeling tone; how humans know a sense object

vicikicchā doubt

Vinaya code of ethics, monastic discipline, rule, rules of morality or of canon law

Vinaya Piṭaka the large collection of rules which grew up in the monastic life and habits of the bhikkhus

vineyya abhijjhādomanassa having put away covetousness and grief as well as free from desires and discontent

viññāna consciousness; when used in reference to sense consciousness, the bare knowing of an object at the point of sense contact, prior to labeling being associated with the stimuli

vipariṇāma-dukkha suffering due to situational change

vipassanā insight

vyāpāda ill will

yoniso manasikāra wise attention

References

Adittapariyaya Sutta: The fire sermon (N. Thera, Trans.). (2010). Access to Insight. https://www.accesstoinsight.org/tipitaka/sn/sn35/sn35.028.nymo.html (Original work published 1981)

American Psychological Association. (n.d.). *APA dictionary of psychology*. Retrieved from https://dictionary.apa.org/

Anālayo, B. (2004). *Satipaṭṭhāna: The direct path to realization*. Windhorse Publications.

Anālayo, B. (2018). *Satipaṭṭhāna meditation: A practice guide*. Windhorse Publications.

Bapat, P. V. (1971). *200 years of Buddhism*. Publication Division, Ministry of Information and Broadcasting, Government of India.

Bodhi, B. (2005). *In the Buddha's words: An anthology of discourses from the Pāli Canon*. Wisdom Publications.

Bodhi, B. (2007). *The all-embracing net of views: The Brahmajāla Sutta and its commentaries*. Buddhist Publication Society.

Bodhi, B. (2013). *A comprehensive manual of Abhidhamma: The Abhidhammattha Sangha of Ācarina Anuruddha*. Buddhist Publication Society Pariyatti Editions.

Bodhi, B. (2016). *The Noble Eightfold Path: Way to the end of suffering*. Buddhist Publication Society Pariyatti Editions.

Bolton, D., & Gillett, G. (2019). *The biopsychosocial model of health and disease: New philosophical and scientific developments*. Springer Nature. https://doi.org/10.1007/978-3-030-11899-0

Britton, W. B., Shahar, B., Szepsenwol, O., & Jacobs, W. J. (2012, June). Mindfulness-based cognitive therapy improves emotional reactivity to social stress: Results from a randomized controlled trial. *Behavior Therapy, 43*(2), 365–380. https://doi.org/10.1016/j.beth.2011.08.006

Bronfenbrenner, U., & Ceci, S. J. (1994). Nature–nurture reconceptualized in developmental perspective: A bioecological model. *Psychological Review, 101*(4), 568–586. https://doi.org/10.1037/0033-295X.101.4.568

Bronfenbrenner, U., & Evans, G. W. (2000). Developmental science in the 1st century: Emerging questions, theoretical models, research designs and empirical findings. *Social Development, 9*(1), 115–125. https://doi.org/10.1111/1467-9507.00114

Bronfenbrenner, U., & Morris, P. A. (2006). The bioecological model of human development. In R. M. Lerner (Ed.), *Handbook of child psychology: Vol. 1. Theoretical models of human development* (6th ed., pp. 793–828). John Wiley & Sons, Inc.

Buddhaghosa, B. (2010). *Visuddhimagga: The path of purification.* Buddhist Publication Society Pariyatti Editions. (Original work published 1956)

Cambridge University Press & Assessment. (n.d.). *Cambridge dictionary.* https://dictionary.cambridge.org/us/

The connected discourses of the Buddha: A translation of the Saṃyutta Nikāya (B. Bodhi, Trans.). (2000). Wisdom Publications.

Copeland, B. (2024, June 14). 11 traditional wedding vows to exchange during your ceremony. *Martha Stewart Weddings.* https://www.marthastewart.com/7888175/traditional-wedding-vows

Davids, R. (1980). *Psalms of the early Buddhists: I. Psalms of the sisters.* Pali Text Society. (Original work published 1909)

Davidson, R. J., & Kaszniak, A. W. (2015). Conceptual and methodological issues in research on mindfulness and meditation. *American Psychologist, 70*(7), 581–592. https://doi.org/10.1037/a0039512

Dhammacakkapavattana Sutta: Rolling forth the wheel of dhamma (B. Sujato, Trans.). (2018). SuttaCentral. https://suttacentral.net/sn56.11/en/sujato?lang=en&layout=plain&reference=none&notes=asterisk&highlight=false&script=latin

Dhammapada: Maggavagga: The path (A. Buddharakkhita, Trans.). (1996). Access to Insight. https://www.accesstoinsight.org/tipitaka/kn/dhp/dhp.20.budd.html

Eeles, J., & Walker, D. M. (2022). Mindfulness as taught in dialectical behaviour therapy: A scoping review. *Clinical Psychology & Psychotherapy, 29*(6), 1843–1853. https://doi.org/10.1002/cpp.2764

Gabel, S. G. (2023). *A human rights-based approach to justice in social work practice.* Oxford University Press.

Gendolla, G. T. (2015). Introduction: Grounding self-regulation in the brain and body. In G. Gendolla, M. Topps, & S. Koole (Eds.), *Handbook of biobehavioral approaches to self-regulation* (pp. 1–6). Springer. https://doi.org/10.1007/978-1-4939-1236-0_1

Goldberg, S. B., Tucker, R. P., Greene, P. A., Davidson, R. J., Wampold, B. E., Kearney, D. J., & Simpson, T. L. (2018). Mindfulness-based interventions for psychiatric disorders: A systematic review and meta-analysis. *Clinical Psychology Review, 59*, 52–60. https://doi.org/10.1016/j.cpr.2017.10.011

Harris, C. (1998). Whiteness as property. In D. R. Roediger (Ed.), *Black on White: Black writers on what it means to be White* (pp. 103–118). Schocken Books.

Kabat-Zinn, J. (1984). An outpatient program in behavior medicine for chronic pain patients based on the practice of mindfulness meditation: Theoretical considerations and preliminary results. *General Hospital Psychiatry, 4*(1), 33–47.

Kalupahana, D. J. (1992). *A history of Buddhist philosophy: Continuities and discontinuities.* Motilal Banarsidass Publishers. https://doi.org/10.1515/9780824844530

Karunadasa, Y. (2015a). *Early Buddhist teachings: The middle position in theory and practice* (Vol. 2013, 2015). Center of Buddhist Studies, The University of Hong Kong.

Karunadasa, Y. (2015b). *The Theravāda Abhidhamma: Its inquiry into the nature of conditioned reality* (Vol. 2010). Buddhist Publication Society.

Kriakous, S. A., Elliott, K. A., Lamers, C., & Owen, R. (2021). The effectiveness of mindfulness-based stress reduction on the psychological functioning of health-care professionals: A systematic review. *Mindfulness, 12*(1), 1–28. https://doi.org/10.1007/s12671-020-01500-9

Lang, C. (2021, February 18). Hate crimes against Asian Americans are on the rise: Many say more policing isn't the answer. *Time.* https://time.com/5938482/asian-american-attacks/

Linardon, J., Messer, M., Goldberg, S. B., & Fuller-Tyszkiewicz, M. (2024). The efficacy of mindfulness apps on symptoms of depression and anxiety: An updated meta-analysis of randomized controlled trials. *Clinical Psychology Review, 107,* 102370. https://doi.org/10.1016/j.cpr.2023.102370

Linehan, M. (2017). *The core components of DBT.* YouTube. https://www.youtube.com/watch?v=bULL3sSc_-I

Linehan, M. M. (1987a). Dialectical behavioral therapy: A cognitive behavioral approach to parasuicide. *Journal of Personality Disorders, 1*(4), 328–333. https://doi.org/10.1521/pedi.1987.1.4.328

Linehan, M. M. (1987b). Dialectical behavior therapy for borderline personality disorder: Theory and method. *Bulletin of the Menninger Clinic, 51*(3), 261–276.

The long discourses of the Buddha: A translation of the Dīgha Nikāya (M. Walshe, Trans.). (1995). Wisdom Publications. (Original work published 1987)

Mahāsatipaṭṭhāna Sutta: The long discourse about the ways of attending to mindfulness (B. Ānandajoti, Trans.). (2011). Prepared by B. Sujato. SuttaCentral. https://suttacentral.net/dn22/en/anandajoti?lang=en&reference=none&highlight=false

Merriam-Webster. (n.d.). *Merriam-Webster dictionary.* https://www.merriam-webster.com

Middle Discourses: A lucid translation of the Majjhima Nikāya (B. Sujato, Trans.). (2018). SuttaCentral. https://suttacentral.net/edition/mn/en/sujato?lang=en

The middle length discourses of the Buddha: A new translation of the Majjhima Nikāya (B. I. Ñāṇamoli, Trans. & B. Bodhi, Ed., Trans.). (1995). Wisdom Publications.

Milindapañha: Paññattipañha Sutta: The chariot simile (T. W. Rhys Davids, Trans.). (1890). Prepared by B. Sujato. SuttaCentral. https://suttacentral.net/mil3.1.1/en/tw_rhysdavids?lang=en&reference=none&highlight=false

Morgan, K. W. (1956). *The path of the Buddha*. The Ronald Press Company.

Nagara Sutta: The fortress (B. Thanissaro, Trans.). (2013). Access to Insight. https://www.accesstoinsight.org/tipitaka/an/an07/an07.063.than.html (Original work published 2004)

Ñāṇamoli, B. (2015). *The life of the Buddha according to the Pali Canon*. Buddhist Publication Society.

National Institute of Mental Health. (n.d.). *Depression*. https://www.nimh.nih.gov/health/topics/depression

The numerical discourses of the Buddha: A translation of the Aṅguttara Nikāya (B. Bodhi, Trans.). (2012). Wisdom Publications.

Pali Text Society. (n.d.). *The Pali Text Society's Pali–English dictionary*. https://dsal.uchicago.edu/dictionaries/pali/

Pande, G. C. (2015). *Studies in the origins of Buddhism* (3rd reprint of 4th ed.). Motilal Banarsidass.

Pesala, B. (2001). *The debate of King Milinda: An abridgement of the Milinda Panha* (3rd ed.). Motilal Banarsidass.

Priyadarshana, W. (2016). *Fall 2016 lectures*. Buddha-Dhamma Centre of Hong Kong. https://buddhadharma.co

Querstret, D., Morison, L., Dickinson, S., Cropley, M., & John, M. (2020). Mindfulness-based stress reduction and mindfulness-based cognitive therapy for psychological health and well-being in nonclinical samples: A systematic review and meta-analysis. *Internal Journal of Stress Management*, *27*(4), 394–411. https://doi.org/10.1037/str0000165

Reat, N. R. (1994). *Buddhism: A history*. Asian Humanities Press.

Sabbasava Sutta: Discourse on all āsavas (Burma Pitaka Association, Trans.). (2010). Access to Insight. https://www.accesstoinsight.org/tipitaka/mn/mn.002.bpit.html

Shults, B. (2013). Brahmanical terminology and the straight way in the Tevijja Sutta. *Journal of the Oxford Centre of Buddhist Studies*, *4*, 105–133.

Sīlānanda, V. S. (2012). *Handbook of Abhidhamms studies* (Vol. I). Selangor Buddhist Vipassana Meditation Society.

Thera Nyanaponika. (1999). *The root of good and evil*. Inward Path.

Thera Nyanaponika. (2013). *The five mental hindrances and their conquest: Selected texts from the Pali canon and the commentaries*. Access to Insight. https://www.accesstoinsight.org/lib/authors/nyanaponika/wheel026.html#intro

Thorndike, E. L. (1911). *Animal intelligence: Experimental studies*. Macmillan Press. https://doi.org/10.5962/bhl.title.55072

U.S. Census Bureau. (2021, April 22). *Number, timing and duration of marriages and divorces*. https://www.census.gov/newsroom/press-releases/2021/marriages-and-divorces.html

U.S. Census Bureau. (2024). *About the topic of race.* https://www.census.gov/topics/population/race/about.html

U.S. Federal Bureau of Investigation. (2020). *2020 FBI hate crimes statistics.* https://www.justice.gov/crs/highlights/2020-hate-crimes-statistics

Wampold, B. E. (2019). *The basics of psychotherapy: An introduction to theory and practice* (2nd ed.). American Psychological Association. https://doi.org/10.1037/0000117-000

Warder, A. K. (2015). *Indian Buddhism* (Vols. 1970, 1980, 2000). Motilal Banarsidass Publishers.

Index

experience of existence and, 65, 71
influence of, on mind, 289–290
internality vs. externality and, 44
rūpa and, 62–65
sensual desire and pleasure-seeking
related to, 158–159
and three unwholesome roots of
craving, 188
Ayoniso manasikāra, 293–294, 349

B

Balance, in pursuit of sensual pleasure,
299
Befuddlement, 169–171, 288
Beginnings, 47, 51
Being attached to unloved, 137–139
Being Devoured (Khajjanīya Sutta, SN 22),
62, 63
Being separated from loved, 137–139
Beldangi Bhutanese refugee camp, vii–viii
Bhadraka Sutta (With Bhadraka, SN 42), 88
Bhavāsava, 289–291, 296, 300–305, 349
Biopsychosocial model, 198–199
Bipolar disorder, 98
Birth, suffering due to. *See* Suffering due
to birth, aging, and death
Blame, 23, 162–164, 179, 332
Bodhi, Bhikkhu, 52, 242, 247, 263, 288
Body. *See also Kāyā; Rūpa*
appropriation and identification with,
150
conduct of. *See* Right action
contemplating, 5, 118, 121–124, 140,
242, 254, 256–260
contemplating health of mind and, 264
contemplating repulsiveness of,
270–271
influence of, on mind, 270
listening to, 270
sense base of, 279
Body dysmorphia, 114, 258, 294
Body posture(s)
contemplating, 121, 123
for sitting meditation, 119
Bojjhaṅgasaṃyutta Sutta (Connected
Discourses on the Factors of
Enlightenment, Fire, SN 46),
171, 172
Boon companion, sympathetic joy for,
231–232
The Bottomless Abyss (Patala Sutta,
SN 36), 314, 317

Brahmā, 57, 58
Brahmajāla Sutta (The All-Embracing Net,
DN 1), 27
Brahmāsahavyatāya. See Divine abodes
Brahmā-vihāras, 224, 225, 234, 349. *See
also* Divine abodes
The Brahmins of Sālā (Sāleyyaka Sutta,
MN 41), 17, 216–218, 220–224, 233
Breath
attempting to control, 269–270
contemplating, 57, 120–123, 169, 245,
256–257, 272, 274
critiquing, 272
direct contact with, 255–256
full awareness and clear knowing of,
248
keeping in mind, during daily activities,
249–250
locating, 77
selecting, as object of contemplation for
client, 248–249
Bronfenbrenner's ecological systems
theory, 49, 149, 198–199
Buddha, 12, 306, 349
Buddhaghosa, Bhadantácariya, 69, 72–73,
167, 172, 225–229, 231–232,
271–272
Buddha Gotama (Siddhartha Gotama
Shakyamuni). *See also specific suttas*
analysis of experience of existence by,
213
authenticity of sayings attributed to, 19
Buddhist religion vs. practices of, 37
and early Buddhist texts, 13–15
as founder of Buddhism, 4
implications of teachings of, 343
interventions from, 17
life of, 11–12
meditation techniques described by,
117
presentation of six internal sense bases
by, 63–64
psychotherapeutic efficacy of sayings
from, 19
social science framework for Noble
Search of, 26–27
Buddhism. *See also specific topics*
Abhidhammas and sects of, 15–16
acknowledging ties between
mindfulness interventions and, 346
attitude for approaching teachings of,
19–24
Buddha Gotama's practices and, 37

consequences and, 236–237
defined, 215, 350
and equanimity, 232
failure to believe in, 289
focusing in-session treatment on
    dependent arising and, 315–316, 319
misconceptions about correlation with,
    234–236
reframing client suffering within
    worldview of, 314, 318
rejecting principles of, 223
and responsibility for actions, 236
Kant, Immanuel, 105
Karaniya Metta Sutta (Loving-Kindness,
    Sn 1), 225–226
Karuṇā, 224, 225, 229–231, 350
Karunadasa, Y., 58, 135–136, 199–200,
    263, 288–289
Kāyā
contemplating, 5, 118, 121–124, 140,
    242, 254, 256–260
contemplating repulsiveness of, 270–271
defined, 350
Kesamutti Sutta (With the Kālāmas of
    Kesamutta, AN 3), 19–21, 23, 24,
    177, 181, 189, 191
Kesaputtiya Sutta (Kesaputtiya, AN 3),
    162, 180
Khajjanīya Sutta (Being Devoured, SN 22),
    62, 63
Khandhā, 36, 55–70. *See also*
    Pañcakkhandh
in assessment stage, 202–207
and cause of *dukkha*, 104
in chariot/car simile for self, 90–91
and conceptual framework for a person,
    56–61
consciousness/*viññāṇa*, 69
contemplating, 254, 275–278
craving/*taṇhā* as animator of, 88–90
defined, 62, 350
differentiating five aggregates subject to
    clinging from, 146–147
focusing in-session treatment on
    workings of, 315, 318
form/*rūpa*, 62–65
hedonic feeling tone/*vedanā*, 65–67
hindrances as hiding, 153, 154
identifying with, 303–304
labeling, 278
meditation to see through hindrances
    to, 157

mental formations/*saṅkhāra*, 67–68
perception/*saññā*, 67
reframing client suffering within
    worldview of, 314, 318
Khandhā Sutta (Aggregates, SN 22), 65,
    67–68, 71, 87–88, 99, 303
Khuddaka Nikāya
Dhammapada, 6–7, 14, 28, 43, 55,
    92, 103, 115, 122, 129, 144, 166,
    176–177, 185, 195, 319
Itivuttaka, 14
Khuddakapatha, 14
subdivisions of, 14
Sutta Nipata, 14, 225–226
Theragatha, 14
Therigatha, 14
Udana, 14
Killing, 217–218
Kindness, 219
Kukkucca, 172
Kusalā, 23, 189, 214, 350

L

Labeling process, 78–82, 205–206.
    See also Saññā
Lamentation, 128, 130–133
Last occurrence of presenting problem,
    momentary analysis of, 50, 197–198
Laws of Behavior in General, 6, 26,
    28, 43
Laziness, 168, 170, 175–177
Lethargy, 168
Lineage of teaching, 21
Linehan, Marsha, 345, 346
Livelihood, right, 30, 31, 216
Lobha
alternative mind states to. *See* Divine
    abodes
characteristics of, 208
chasing feelings due to, 74–75
defined, 74, 189, 350
functions of, 208–209
identifying, in assessment stage,
    208–209
manifestations of, 209
as misconduct of the mind, 223
as motivator to action, 76, 91
as type of desire, 89, 186
types of, 208
as unwholesome root of craving, 187,
    188, 207

Logical reasoning, 22
Long Discourses of the Buddha (Dīgha Nikāya), 14
Loss
  bhavāsava in reaction to, 291
  hindrance of sensual desire and, 161
  job, 47, 105, 106, 129–130
  and separation from the loved, 139
Love, desire for, 165
Loved one, being separated from, 137–139
Loving-kindness, 224–231. *See also Mettā*
Loving-Kindness (Karaniya Metta Sutta, Sn 1), 225–226
Low self-esteem, 179
A Lump of Foam (Phenapiṇḍūpama Sutta, SN 22), 153–154
Lust, 142, 143, 228, 265
Lying, by commission and omission, 220

M

Madhupindika Sutta (The Honeyball, MN 18), 74, 78, 79, 91, 199–202, 206, 207
Mahādukkhakkhandha Sutta (The Greater Discourse on the Mass of Suffering, MN 13), 296–299
Mahākassapa, 13
Mahākoṭṭhita, Venerable, 57
Mahāsatipaṭṭhāna Sutta (The Greater Discourse of the Foundation of Mindfulness, DN 22), 107, 117, 137, 138, 143, 146, 283
Mahātaṇhāsankhaya Sutta (The Greater Discourse on the Destruction of Craving, MN 38), 69
Mahayana Buddhism, 15–16
Majjhima Nikāya (Middle-Length Discourses of the Buddha), 14
  Alagaddūpama Sutta (Simile of the Snake, MN 22), 12, 18, 96–99, 146, 148, 150, 182, 186, 276, 277, 348
  Ambalaṭṭhikāhulovadā Sutta (Advice to Rāhula at Ambalaṭṭhikā, MN 61), 233–234
  Anāpanasati Sutta (Mindfulness of Breath, MN 118), 345
  Ariyapariyesanā Sutta (The Noble Search, MN 26), 26
  Chachakka Sutta (The Six Sets of Six, MN 148), 62

Cūḷavedalla Sutta (The Shorter Series of Questions and Answers, MN 44), 97–98
Madhupindika Sutta (The Honeyball, MN 18), 74, 78, 79, 91, 199–202, 206, 207
Mahādukkhakkhandha Sutta (The Greater Discourse on the Mass of Suffering, MN 13), 296–299
Mahātaṇhāsankhaya Sutta (The Greater Discourse on the Destruction of Craving, MN 38), 69
Potaliya Sutta (With Potaliya the Householder, MN 54), 37
Sabbāsava Sutta (Discourse on All the Taints, MN 2), 17, 108, 287–316
Saccavibhanga Sutta (The Exposition of the Truths, MN 141), 29, 31, 107, 112, 113, 128, 129, 133, 138, 146
Sāleyyaka Sutta (The Brahmins of Sālā, MN 41), 17, 216–218, 220–224, 233
Satipaṭṭhāna Sutta (The Foundations of Mindfulness, MN 10), 5, 17, 38, 57, 108, 113, 117–125, 131, 133, 140–142, 144, 151, 153, 161, 162, 241–243, 246–248, 250–254, 256, 258–264, 266, 267, 269–272, 274, 275, 277–279, 282–284, 345
Vatthāpnma Sutta (The Simile of the Cloth, MN 7), 210, 211
Malicious speech, 220–221
Manasikāra, 350
  for arising of consciousness, 72–73
  directing, to sense object, 257
  at first lived moment of experience, 200
  to identify sense object, 201
  in meditation, 120
  as type of consciousness, 60, 61
  viññāna and, 69
  wise vs. unwise, 293–294
Mano
  defined, 293, 350
  and mind as sense base, 65
  as type of consciousness, 60, 61
Marks of existence. *See* Three marks of existence
Marriage, impermanence of, 92–93
Material elements, contemplating, 121, 123
Material goods, desire for, 298–299
Materialism, 58

Materiality
  balance of mentality and. See
    Mentality-materiality
  concept of. See Rūpa
  hindrance based on. See Sensual desire
MBSR. See Mindfulness-based stress
    reduction
Meditation by clients, 269. See also Insight
    meditation; Mindfulness meditation;
    Silent meditation
  to address dukkha-dukkha, 121–124
  to address hindrances, 155, 157, 167,
    269, 272–274
  to address saṅkhāra-dukkha, 140–141
  to address vipariṇāma-dukkha, 131–132
  to ameliorate dukkha, 108
  contemplating body in, 121–124,
    256–258
  contemplating five aggregates subject to
    clinging in, 278
  contemplating hedonic feeling tone in,
    75, 131–132, 261
  contemplating hindrances in, 267–269
  contemplating mind in, 140–141, 264
  contemplating six sense bases in, 282
  to counter identification with or
    appropriation of body, 121–124
  to detect constructed notion of self,
    151–157
  to develop mindfulness, 116–121
  duration of, 256
  guided, 243, 244
  harmful effects of, 116, 124, 243
  impermanence in, 51
  to notice sense contact, 116
  noticing what one is paying attention to
    during, 272
  in psychotherapy, 124
  restlessness and remorse in, 274
  Satipaṭṭhān Sutta on, 241–243
  sitting, 118–121
  spontaneous generalization from,
    249–250, 284
  tasks for sati during, 246
  training in, 345
  training mind with, 77, 115, 117, 123,
    241
Meditation journal, 257, 258
Meditation practice of mental health
    practitioners
  to develop mindfulness, 116
  embodied knowledge from, 38, 52, 255

as model for psychotherapist in role of
    sati, 243
  objects for contemplation in, 285
  observing hindrances in, 157
Memory encoding, 79
Mental formations. See also Saṅkhāra
  in assessment stage, 206–207
  coordinated function of, 82–84
  creation of, 82–83
  distinguishing sense contact and sense
    objects from, 257
  in five aggregates, 67–68
  offering alternative constructs to
    change, 315
  stance of meta-cognition toward, 251
  suffering due to. See Suffering due to
    mental formations
Mentality
  ethical conduct through, 222–232
  hindrances based on. See Doubt; Ill will;
    Restlessness and remorse; Sloth and
    torpor
Mentality-materiality. See also Nāmarūpa
  in concept of a person, 56–59, 61
  simplicity of, 343
Mental proliferations, 82–84. See also
    Saṅkhāra
Mental qualities, for undertaking
    mindfulness, 246–251
Mental representations. See Saṅkhāra
Mental taints. See Āsavas
Meta-cognition, 141–143, 251, 305
Mettā, 224–231, 350
Middha, 167
Middle-Length Discourses of the Buddha.
    See Majjhima Nikāya
Milinda, King, 90, 99
Milindapañha, 56, 90, 99, 277
Mind. See also Cetasika; Citta
  Buddha Gotama on, 6
  Buddhist categorization of, 263
  contemplating, 140–141, 242, 264
  influence six sense bases and six sense
    objects on, 289–290
  kamma and effect of deeds on, 215
  noticing change in, 122
  observing, 151
  sense base of, 279
  training the, 77, 115, 117, 123, 233–234,
    241
  travel to past and future by, 173–174
  untrained, 115

About the Authors

Liang Tien, PsyD, PhD, is a retired professor from the California School of Professional Psychology PsyD of Clinical Psychology Program, Alliant International University, Hong Kong. Since retirement, she has obtained a PhD in Buddhist studies from the University of Kelaniya, Sri Lanka, and is a cofounder of the Illumination of Mindfulness Institute at Alliant International University. She is a longtime meditator. As a licensed clinical psychologist, her independent practice focuses on individuals with ancestry from Asian Buddhist-based countries and women with histories of abuse. Her research interest has been in ethics and immigrant acculturation.

Debra M. Kawahara, PhD, is the associate dean of academic affairs and a distinguished professor at the California School of Professional Psychology, Alliant International University. She is the American Psychological Association (APA) 2025 President. As a licensed clinical psychologist, her independent practice focuses on psychotherapy with individuals, couples, and families, as well as consulting to, and conducting trainings for, organizations. Dr. Kawahara has published widely as a multicultural feminist scholar and has presented at national and international venues. Her work centers on intersectionality, Buddhist psychotherapy, Asian American mental health, women's issues, leadership, and the application of multicultural, feminist, and social justice principles in practice. Further, she served as editor-in-chief of *Women & Therapy* from 2018 to 2024. Dr. Kawahara is a fellow of the APA and the Asian American Psychological Association. In recognition of her work, several awards have been bestowed on Dr. Kawahara, including an APA Presidential Citation, the Shining Star Award at the National Multicultural Conference and Summit, the APA Society for the Psychological Study of Culture, Ethnicity and Race (APA Division 45) Distinguished Career

Contributions for Service Award, and the Pioneer Award from the Psychology of Asian Pacific American Women section within the Society for the Psychology of Women (APA Division 35).

Venerable Dhammadinna, BS, began meditating at the age of 22 in 1980 at the Insight Meditation Society. After completing a bachelor of science degree at the University of Massachusetts in 1983, she took robes in a small Burmese forest monastery in the Santa Cruz Mountains. Her preceptor was Taungpulu Sayadaw, an ascetic monk who introduced her to insight and calm abiding meditations. In 1984, she was able to return to Massachusetts for a 9-month retreat under the guidance of Ven. U Pandita Sayadaw, one of the outstanding Burmese meditation teachers of the 20th century. Toward the end of that retreat, she was taught by Dipama Barua. Dipama was a Bengali woman, renowned for the profundity of her wisdom and loving-kindness.

In 1985, Ven. Dhammadinna left for Asia, studying again with U Pandita Sayadaw. In the course of time, she shifted to Thailand and lived and taught under the direction of Ajahn Buddhadasa, who was a forest monk, meditator, and scholar. In 2000, she met His Holiness the Dalai Lama and moved to Dharamsala, India, to study and practice Mahayana Buddhism with him. After 20 years of living abroad, she returned to the United States, settling in Seattle, Washington, where she is a resident teacher at the Bodhiheart Sangha Buddhist Meditation Center.